The Phantom Church in Rome

*How neo-Modernists corrupted the Church to establish
Antichrist's kingdom*

T. Stanfill Benns

*(All emphases within quotes in this work are the
author's unless specified otherwise.)*

BookLocker

Published by BookLocker.com, Inc., St. Petersburg, Florida.

BookLocker.com, Inc.
2018

First Edition

Definition of *phantom*

Webster's Seventh Collegiate Dictionary, 1941
1a. *Obs*...Illusion **b**. a delusion ...**3**. Something in appearance
but not in reality

Merriam-Webster online
1a. Something apparent to sense but with no substantial existence
1c. — An object of continual dread or abhorrence
https://www.merriam-webster.com/dictionary/phantom

Synonyms, Roget's Thesauras, 1942
Shadow, fancy, fantasy

*"The man that giveth heed to lying visions is like to him that catcheth at a
shadow, and followeth after the wind." — Ecclesisasticus 34: 2*

The author explicitly disavows anything whatsoever stated in this work which might unintentionally be opposed to the doctrines of the One, Holy, Catholic, Apostolic and Roman Church. This work in its entirety is humbly submitted to the future Roman Pontiff, canonically elected. The author swears to abide by his judgment concerning all that is written here should Our Lord in His wisdom and mercy see fit to provide us with one.

Dedicated to Christ the King and to the Immaculate Conception, Mary Most Holy, Patroness of America and vanquisher of all heresies

Acknowledgements

In compiling this work, I owe a debt of gratitude to the Blessed Trinity, Our Lady of Sorrows, St. Anthony of Padua, "Hammer of Heretics," St. Anthony Claret, missionary to Latin America, St. Francis de Sales, St. Thomas Aquinas, St. Therese of Lisieux, Pope St. Pius X and all those saints in heaven who have patiently listened to and answered my many prayers. I also give special thanks for the teachings of Pope Paul IV, Pope Pius IX and Pope Pius XII, and most especially for the works of Monsignor Joseph Clifford Fenton, who defended these teachings and made them clear. It is no coincidence that Monsignor Fenton died on the anniversary of Pope Pius XII's consecration of the Russian peoples to Our Lady's Immaculate Heart. He has been an amazing teacher and an unfailing inspiration. Last but by no means least, a good number of the fine points in this work were brought to my attention by family members and the Catholics reading my website, who practice their faith at home. A special thanks also goes out to Irene and Bill K., Devonia M. and John C., for their generous financial contributions. Thank you, Irene and Devonia, for painstakingly proofing this work. I also owe a debt of gratitude to Lauri B., who formatted and edited the original version of this manuscript and to the staff at BookLocker, who braved my formatting inexpertise with kindness and patience. Lauri's unflagging support and courage to offer constructive criticism has resulted in a much more readable and orderly work. My heartfelt gratitude also to the designer of the book's cover, who despite my strenuous objections insists on remaining anonymous. Great patience in producing the final product and attention to fine detail is mirrored in the result. May God rain down His many graces on them all for the courage to live their convictions, their longsuffering, and their love of the Catholic faith. Without the help of all those mentioned here — and especially without the support of my husband Larry — I could never have completed this work.

Table of Contents

PREFACE

This book is a compilation of a lifetime of study that began in the 1980s and continues to the present. Had it been written four years ago, the proofs presented would still have been just as compelling, but the evidence for the case would have remained largely circumstantial. Thanks to the issuance of a monumental work by David Wemhoff, published in 2015, the landscape has changed dramatically. The evidence has arrived, and it is mind-blowing. In fact it is reflected in the headlines today, as the liberal media continues to pump out even more propaganda, just as they have done for over 100 years. If Catholics and God-fearing men of good will only knew the role the media — not to mention the American government — has played in manipulating the news and destroying the Church, they would be hard-pressed to believe it. And even if they managed to believe it, they still would not be able to draw from it the enormous theological consequences that have cascaded relentlessly around us through the past five decades of our existence. It is the purpose of this book to draw out these consequences and demonstrate how we have arrived at where we are today and where we go from here.

Wemhoff's work, *John Courtney Murray, Time/Life, and the American Proposition: How the C.I.A.'s Doctrinal Warfare Program Changed the Catholic Church* is the itemized documentation, taken largely from declassified material, of just how the American government set out to infiltrate, subvert and subjugate the Catholic Church — and other more orthodox Christian churches — using religion as a means of building empire under the guise of combating Communism. As Wemhoff explains, it was an intense psychological campaign harnessing the print and broadcast media — employing government officials, professors, priests, ministers and American business leaders — to make it appear that the Church had abandoned Her condemnation of Americanism as a heresy. It involved active infiltration and subversion. This out-and-out warfare was declared in order to coerce Catholics worldwide into embracing the Americanist conception of religious liberty. This was accomplished in large part long before Vatican 2 convened; in fact, it was this very protracted campaign that paved the way for the modernization of the Church, largely carried out by its own clergy and liberal members of the educated laity.

Those living in the 1940s-50s had to know there was an ideological war going on, even if they were only the sort of Catholics who seldom did any more than attend Mass on Sunday. It was in the air, and publications from that time period clearly reflect this. But as it turns out, they cannot be blamed entirely for not being able to pin it down, or effectively resist it. When an intelligence agency sets out to deliberately wage psychological warfare on an entire segment of the population, it successfully distorts reality and actually reprograms brains., Edward Hunter, a C.I.A. propaganda operator who worked undercover as a journalist, wrote in his 1956 work:

> The highly educated person who bends medical discoveries to the practice of mind attack is incalculably more evil than any savage using potions, trances, and incantations…The word brain-changing became obscured as brainwashing and began to embrace all the available pressures that could be utilized to bend a man's will and change his attitudes fundamentally. Brain-changing specifically refers to the complete job in all its wickedness. Cardinal Mindszenty underwent a brain-changing. That was how his vigorous mind was bent. A man's memory can be physically eliminated, if at all possible, only at the price of permanent damage to the brain. In such a brain-changing, drugs have to be used to destroy the natural alertness and strong character of the individual, and hypnotism must be employed, too, to help in breaking down resistance. Information obtained through the most persistent inquiry by every possible channel reveals that drugs and hypnotism were used on the cardinal. [1]

And techniques today have been further perfected to anticipate all possibilities and eventualities and to better bind captives to the particular mindset at play.

Hunter spoke at length with servicemen and others who were victims of brainwashing; individuals who, following their release, clung to the beliefs they had imbibed while prisoners of the Communists. He became convinced that at some deep level, all who had experienced "brain-changing" had the tentative idea they were deluded and even could be brought to this conclusion through intensive debriefing. "If truth can linger in the mind in spite of the strongest hallucinations, and the evidence I have accumulated indicates it can, the reason is clear why the Reds cannot be sure of even their completest victories, their Mindszentys. They never capture their minds completely!" And this remark is very revealing. The primary difference between those who were the initial lab rats for brain-changing then and those who experienced it years later is this: *Hunter and others noticed that Americans were far more susceptible to these tactics, for some reason, than others, and this cannot have improved with the passage of time.* Those wishing to use these tactics always look for the weakest, most vulnerable links — the elderly, the young, the disoriented, the uneducated, the grieving, and those emotionally or mentally unstable, for whatever reason. We read everywhere that prior to the false Vatican 2 council, Catholics in general were not well instructed in their faith and tended to lay undue emphasis on external religion. They certainly never possessed the level of faith and spiritual formation of a Cardinal Mindszenty. And so it is not surprising that they became sitting ducks for those wishing to finish the destruction of the juridical Church once and for all.

Despite the fact that Mindszenty was entirely broken by his captors and his brain thoroughly changed or "washed" — even to the extent that he appeared to deny his faith and concede to all Communist demands — Pope Pius XII neither condemned nor deserted him for these forced concessions. Pope Pius XII's example concerning Cardinal Mindszenty should indicate the mind of the Church in this matter. His behavior in Mindszenty's case should prompt us to be more open-minded in dealing with those who have experienced what modern experts adjudge to be even worse and more seductive torments than Mindszenty himself experienced. It is interesting that one of the last constitutions Pope Pius XII wrote contained a section on brain-changing and its evils. In *Ad Apostolorum Principis*, (June 29, 1958) he taught:

> 17. There should also be noted those courses of instruction by which pupils are forced to imbibe and embrace…false doctrine. Priests, religious men and women, ecclesiastical students, and faithful of all ages are forced to attend these courses. An almost endless series of lectures and discussions, lasting for weeks and months, so weaken and benumb the strength of mind and will *that by a kind of psychic coercion an assent is extracted which contains almost no human element, an assent which is not freely asked for as should be the case.*

> 18. In addition to these there are the methods by which minds are upset — by every device, in private and in public, by traps, deceits, grave fear, by so-called forced confessions, by custody in a place where citizens are forcibly 'reeducated,' and those 'Peoples' Courts' to which even venerable bishops are ignominiously dragged for trial.

> 19. Against methods of acting such as these, which violate the principal rights of the human person and trample on the sacred liberty of the sons of God, all Christians from every part of the world, indeed all men of good sense cannot refrain from raising their voices with Us in real horror and from uttering a protest deploring the deranged conscience of their fellow men.

> 20. And since these crimes are being committed *under the guise of patriotism*, We consider it Our duty to remind everyone once again of the Church's teaching on this subject. [2]

Sadly, the doctrinal warfare conducted by the C.I.A. against Catholics and conservative non-Catholics alike continues even following Vatican 2, but in subtler forms. It is waged today by the successors of those infiltrators implanted during the 1950s-60s, to corral those who weren't complying with the norms set down at the false Vatican 2 council. These individuals, both those belonging to the church of Rome and those known as Traditionalists, believe themselves to be Catholics. They follow some of the teachings and traditions of the Church prior to Vatican 2, but they are as much the victims of brain-changing as those living in the 1940s-50s. The intelligence sector in that time employed scholars and other experts to twist and manipulate Catholic doctrine. They presented this warped version as authoritative teaching in order to compel acceptance of it and obedience to it. The Catholics of this time naturally passed on their adherence to this manipulated Church doctrine to their unwitting children.

Wemhoff explains in his work how these change agents insisted on misinterpreting the papal teachings to fit their own skewed view of Christ's message. Even though American theological giants such as Monsignor Joseph C. Fenton and Reverend Francis Connell of Catholic University of America fame vigorously refuted their assertions, others with greater power and all the money needed were assisting the enemy from the other side. These two men's valiant defense of magisterial teaching serves today as the illuminating beacon guiding true Catholics out of their brain-changed darkness. And just because Fenton and Connell lost the battle, this doesn't mean Catholics won't win the war.

The cunning and devious method employed to approach those wishing to remain Catholic has not been appreciated nor properly understood. Using a strategy which Hunter describes in *Brainwashing*, the C.I.A. provided Traditionalists with a straw man on which to project their rightful suspicions they had been toyed with and duped. Working with the Jesuits, the C.I.A. allowed the "Jewish menace" to be used as the perfect scapegoat on which Traditionalists could project all their anger and frustrations. This served the dual purpose of demonizing Traditionalists as an unhealthy and anti-Semitic sect, while distracting them from the real source of the problem. Books were even written to this purpose and circulated by those Jesuits presumably placed in the service of the C.I.A. Traditionalists who did not blame the Jews, or at least not primarily, blamed the Communists or secret societies. While this blame was not misplaced, those wishing to remain Catholic failed to comprehend the entire scope of what had actually occurred. Nor was it possible to fully understand what had happened until only recently.

It is the author's hope that what is written in this work will resonate with all sincere Catholics everywhere, despite the mental torture to which they have been subjected; that this book will help finally and completely dislodge any residual cognitive dissonance in order to liberate that "truth [which] can linger in the mind in spite of the strongest hallucinations." After all, this cognitive dissonance is in all likelihood the result of that operation of error spoken of by St. Paul:

> And then that wicked one shall be revealed...Whose coming is according to the working of Satan, in all power, and signs, and lying wonders, and in all seduction of iniquity to them that perish: because they receive not the love of the truth that they might be saved. *Therefore God shall send them the operation of error, to believe a lie.* That all may be judged, who have not believed the truth, but have consented to iniquity. [3]

This passage is a chilling and accurate description of exactly what took place. The C.I.A. agents were operatives engaging in an actual *operation.* God Himself sent that operation to see if the faithful would believe the lie of Americanism; and they did.

True Catholics then — if they love the truth — will seek the meaning of what they have been calling themselves all these years. A description can be found in the *Catholic Encyclopedia* (1911) under "Tradition," [4] where Catholics will learn that to live up to the name, they must accept *all* the truths contained in the continual magisterium. This, Holy Scripture avers in this same book of St. Paul, is the only remedy for escaping the operation of error, as the apostle teaches in verse 14: "Therefore, brethren, stand *firm;* and hold the *traditions* which you have learned, whether by word, or by our epistle." And those traditions, the *Catholic Encyclopedia* article explains, are the teachings of Our Lord as conveyed by the popes from St. Peter to Pope Pius XII.

A word here to our non-Catholic brethren: all Catholics have ever wanted is to be re-united with those who, they believe, truly love Christ but have been seduced by the very people described in this work. Non-Catholics too, although by different means, have been targeted with perverted doctrines and coerced into believing a false interpretation of Scripture. This in addition to being misled by the ecumenists who worked with the Americanist forces to implement doctrinal warfare. A Protestant author writing in the 1980s was one of the many authors who alerted this writer to the true nature of what has now come to pass, and some of the prognostications in her work have proven to be truly prophetic.

Authors Flo Conway and Jim Siegelman remarkably describe the very phenomenon we are witnessing across America today — the subjection of Americans to endless streams of what amounts to propaganda, "pouring out a constant flow of information to the American public, designed to stimulate the consumers guilts, fears, weaknesses, insecurities and fantasies" — and then reward each individual in immediate physical and emotional terms for succumbing to them. This simple ploy is carried out on Americans literally hundreds of times each day, stunning them with a barrage of false promises, distorted values and jumbled personal priorities, then urging them to give into every whim and impulse. This propaganda campaign is accompanied by

> a cultural confusion of new goals, shifting values and collapsing traditions...It could be that in subtle ways, these stresses and techniques which shape our modern lives have started every American down the sloping catastrophe curve of snapping and information disease. Television may be our country's primary contributor to snapping in everyday life...

And this state of affairs was described before cell phones, computers and social media! Still, Conway and Siegelman note that

Even under conditions of impaired awareness, delusion and domination, there is always the possibility they will snap out of it. After years have passed, these robots may still regain their freedom of thought, their responses as individuals may be restored, and the skeleton of their personalities may drop back into place. [5]

At least for some, then, it may not be too late; there may yet be hope. St. Paul reminds us that "snapping back" is essential to salvation: "It is now the hour for us to arise from sleep. For now our salvation is nearer than when we believed…Cast off the works of darkness, and put on the armour of light" (Rom. 13: 11, 12).

T. Stanfill Benns
Easter Sunday, 2017

Preface Endnotes

[1] Edward Hunter, *Brainwashing: The Story of Men Who Defied It,* Farrar, Strauss and Cudahy, New York, N.Y., 1956
[2] http://www.papalencyclicals.net/pius12/p12apost.htm
[3] Douay-Rheims edition of Holy Scripture, 2 Thess. 2:8, 9-11
[4] http://www.newadvent.org/cathen/15006b.htm
[5] Flo Conway and Jim Siegelman, *Snapping: America's Epidemic of Sudden Personality Change*, Dell Publishing Co., New York, N.Y., 1978

INTRODUCTION

THE MOST DIABOLICAL DECISION ON EARTH

The hijacking of the Roman Catholic Church

"He that readeth, let him understand." (Matt. 24:15)

In 1948, a high-profile member of the U.S. hierarchy predicted the imminent collapse of the Catholic Church. Despite his superb oratory skills, those predictions obviously were lost in the pandemonium that followed the death of Pope Pius XII in 1958. Incredibly, in the span of only one decade, this popular archbishop would cast aside his prognostications to become a part of the bogus replacement for the Church he described so accurately, and in such lurid terms.

> [Satan] will set up a counterchurch which will be the ape of the [Catholic] Church ... It will have all the notes and characteristics of the Church, but in reverse and emptied of its divine content. We are living in the days of the Apocalypse, the last days of our era. The two great forces – the Mystical Body of Christ and the Mystical Body of the anti-Christ – are beginning to draw battle lines for the catastrophic contest.

> The 'false prophet' will have a religion without a cross. A religion without a world to come. A religion to destroy religions...or a politics which is a religion, one that renders unto Caesar even the things that are God's...There will be a counterfeit 'Church.' Christ's Church, the Catholic Church, will be One; and the false 'prophet' will create the other.

The false 'Church' will be worldly, ecumenical, and global. It will be a loose federation of 'churches' and religions, forming some type of global association. A world parliament of 'churches.' It will be emptied of all Divine content; *it will be the mystical body of the Antichrist.* The Mystical Body on Earth today will have its Judas Iscariot, and he will be the false 'prophet.' Satan will recruit him from our bishops.

The Antichrist will not be so called; otherwise he would have no followers. He will not wear red tights, nor vomit sulphur, nor carry a trident nor wave an arrowed tail as Mephistopheles in Faust. *This masquerade has helped the devil convince men that he does not exist.* When no man recognizes, the more power he exercises. God has defined Himself as "I Am Who I Am," and the Devil as "I am who I am not.

In the midst of all his seeming love for humanity, and his glib talk of freedom and equality, he will have one great secret, which he will tell to no one. He will not believe in God. Because his religion will be brotherhood without the fatherhood of God, he will deceive even the elect. He will set up a counterchurch... a mystical body of the Antichrist that will in all externals resemble the Mystical Body of Christ. [1]

Archbishop Fulton Sheen only echoes Reverend E. Sylvester Berry, who wrote: "Satan will imitate the Church of Christ to deceive mankind; he will set up a church of Satan in opposition to the Church of Christ." [2] As Sheen also notes, Catholics of the 20th century will join the counterchurch because it claims to be infallible "when its visible head speaks ex cathedra...in matters of economics and politics." [3] Ironically, Sheen's description of the counterchurch was first found in the writings of the Freemason Limouisin, who had written over 50 years earlier: "Freemasonry is a Church: it is the counter-Church, counter-Catholicism. It is the other church — the church of heresy, of free thought. The Catholic Church is the archetype church, the first church, church of dogmatism and orthodoxy." [4]

Sheen's inexplicable adherence to the very church he foretold, following the death of Pope Pius XII, only crystallized the sum total of Catholic teaching regarding Antichrist's deceits and his ability to master the art of doublespeak. The truly diabolical nature of those who would later embrace this counterchurch lay hidden until the very end. Once Pius XII died, Sheen effectively helped implement the very evils he foretold, successfully placing stumbling blocks of immense proportions along the path of those who would later try to prove his scenario had come to pass.

Presenting the case

There is nothing more demeaning or more effectively dismissive, in the literary world, than the styling of an historical account of an event as a baseless conspiracy theory or a hack job pulled off by those lacking credentials and sufficient evidence. That is why it is so intellectually dishonest to pretend that a considerable body of theological evidence concerning the anticipated destruction of the Roman Catholic Church and the coming of Antichrist does not exist. The diligent researcher can easily disprove this, but doing so takes time and dedication, which few seem willing to devote to matters of faith. To venture the opinion today that the *true* Church of Christ has long since disappeared is tantamount to inviting an on-the-spot excommunication or taunts for being a conspiracy theorist, at best. Some might even suggest a strait jacket and a padded cell.

But a careful look at what the Heads of the Church themselves have to say about what to expect and when — and the authority with which Christ Himself invested them to say it — tells a straightforward tale and leaves no wiggle room from a doctrinal standpoint. Nor does it need to be anything but an anthology of authoritative writings by the hierarchy and Church-approved theologians, taking it out of the realm of any conspiracy or hypothetical meanderings. For those who genuinely value both history and theology, this is far more credible — especially from a theological standpoint — than the mere opinion of present-day laypeople or the purported possessors of the Roman See and their modern-day appointees.

Of course, those denigrating conspiracy theorists forget the term conspiracy has legal connotations. In legal terms it is defined as, "An agreement between two or more persons to engage jointly in an unlawful or criminal act, or an act that is innocent in itself but becomes unlawful when done by the combination of actors; a secret plan or agreement to carry out an illegal or harmful act, especially with a political motivation (plot)...The act of making such plans in secret." [5] This is the very definition of what is described in the preface of this work. Certainly, in the political and governmental sphere there are many combinations of such incidents that were never proven and prosecuted. It is actually, however, *a matter of faith* for Catholics to believe in certain "conspiracy theories" and failure to so believe costs them Church membership. Furthermore, Catholics owe a firm and irrevocable assent to infallible papal teaching, even if it issues only from the Pope's ordinary magisterium, (i.e., his teaching delivered worldwide to all the bishops, to be passed on to the faithful).

The $64,000 question is this: since the Catholic Church has always and everywhere maintained and demonstrated that Her teachings are irreformable and incapable of adaptation to modern ideas and moral standards, how does one account for the evident changes in doctrine and discipline articulated at the Vatican 2 council (1962-65)? Can it really be said that the teachings and standards proposed as Catholic teaching by the "church" in Rome since Vatican 2 are the same as those held prior? Or, since the reign of Angelo Roncalli (John 23, omitting the Roman numerals to distinguish him from the others as a non-pope), has the church in Rome, once synonymous with unchangeable teaching, violated the ideals it professed and held for nearly 20 centuries?

Catholics cannot believe the latter, so they must cite the reply of St. Thomas More to his Anglican interrogators prior to his death:

> For I doubt not, but of the learned and virtuous men now
> alive — I do not speak only of this Realm, but of all

Christendom — there are ten to one of my mind in this matter; but if I should take notice of those learned Doctors and virtuous Fathers that are already dead, many of whom are Saints in Heaven, I am sure there are far more, who all the while they lived thought in this Cause as I do now. And therefore, my Lord, I do not think myself bound to conform my Conscience to the Counsel of one Kingdom, against the general Consent of all Christendom. [6]

It is precisely the general consent of all 20 centuries of Christendom that those calling themselves Catholics today are being asked to discount — and demonstrating that is the purpose of this present work.

Since Jorge Bergoglio's election as "Pope Francis," murmurings that he is not a true pope have been making the rounds. Remarkably, similar murmurings have circulated for many decades, beginning with the election of Angelo Roncalli as "Pope John XXIII." Those asking questions about the validity and liceity of these men are categorized as kooks and their objections discredited out of hand, and this by some members of the same generation of college graduates and "erudite scholars" who have demonstrated publicly, on camera, how little they know about *American* history, far less world or Church history. Never mind that a total of 31 antipopes have previously reigned in the Church, with no guarantee this phenomenon could not occur again. In fact, the Church actually teaches that there will be an unprecedented time when the Church will suffer the pretensions of a papal usurper. Saints, popes, theologians, holy people — all have spoken of it, and their testimony is compelling. This doctrine is reflected in Church law and the teachings of ecumenical councils concerning the content of Divine revelation, but most importantly it issues from infallible decrees of the Roman Pontiffs, the significance of which cannot be underestimated. Even faithful Catholics who believe themselves well versed in Church teaching are unlikely to appreciate the full extent of the binding power of such decrees.

Culture shock

Consider the psychological impact alone the changes in the Church had on the faithful.   Over a brief period of time, everything about the Church that Catholics had come to know, love and cherish disappeared into thin air. The churches were rearranged and the altars obscured by new, modern altars facing the people. Gregorian chant was gone; *Latin* was gone. Already some of the older and more conservative priests and nuns had either retired or left their orders. Catholics became trapped in the inescapable maze of Vatican 2 with no guides to help them. Those who welcomed the ecumenical changes to the Church which began in the 1950s worked feverishly to advance the Church's modernization or *aggiornamento*; the rest simply dropped out and many, in the 1960s, unfortunately, "turned on." Foolishly some began "looking" for the Church they lost and found it in "Traditional" mass chapels (men calling themselves priests who set up chapels independent of the Holy See, forbidden by the Church). But this was only another blind alley. Figuring out what happened was like peeling successive layers of paint and wallpaper off the walls of a very old home. Just when you think you've peeled off the final layer, another one appears.

Traditionalists tended to bounce from one "Trad" sect to the other, in search of what they had lost. They often found each Traditional "priest" or leader was worse than the first, and in a different way. The amount of research and study it took in order to determine that these men were the wolves in sheep's clothing and false christs about whom Our Lord had warned in the Gospels was staggering. This bizarre odyssey sometimes entailed cult involvement. At the very least it consisted in the manipulation of information by these clerics and self-proclaimed lay leaders to suit the mindset of their particular Traditional sect and justify their own position among other warring sects. Not surprisingly, these leaders' techniques involved the suppression of that very information necessary to make educated decisions regarding the faith. The toll it took on families and personal relationships was heartbreaking; the guilt felt at having been so mistaken for so long, crippling. Perhaps the dropouts had it right after all, (sans the turned-on part). By the time Catholics realized what had taken place, it was too late to turn back, too late to prevent the damage to themselves and others. In the end, they chose their own pathways and walked on alone, sometimes not even in the company of loved ones. They bowed their heads and accepted their fate, knowing they were destined to share in Christ's own suffering and Passion, still being reenacted in the Passion of His Church.

Imagine the trauma that (orthodox) Catholics endure when hateful invective is aimed against the organization to which they believe that they belong, but which in fact is not that organization at all. The sexual abuse horrors in the Novus Ordo church, [7] the money scandals, abominable perversions of the liturgy, the departure from dogma, all the lies flung at the Church, revived and refined from the past — everything has been employed to make her a laughingstock, defame Her in the eyes of the world and ultimately destroy Her. But that "church" is not in reality the Catholic Church, but only the empty shell, Her external trappings and grandeur, which yet represents Her glorious past. These knives have been thrust to the hilt in the Mystical Body of Christ, over and over again. And those at least trying to be true members of that Body are penetrated by these instruments of torture as well. The all-too-acute agony of the situation is the knowledge of the faithful that they cannot properly defend the Church they love because so few believe what has happened to Her could be true. They are faceless bodies with hands raised in supplication to Heaven, deprived of any voice.

The Church that disappeared

It is astounding that in less than a century, the carefully guarded and transmitted teachings of nearly 2,000 years could so completely disappear that no one today would accept or believe them as the integral body of truths that Christ imparted to His Church. An enemy has done this. That enemy, the creator of all political and historical revisionist propaganda — all public opinion now prevailing today — has succeeded in convincing the last few generations that the Catholic Church was the primary historical source of religious tyranny, political machinations, underhanded financial dealings, slavery, anti-feminism, sexual perversion, even covert Satanism. What was once revered as sound moral teachings and faithfulness to the Gospels has long been cast aside as foolishness unsuited to the times, even out and out fanaticism. All that is left of the Church is Her external rites, manipulated by so-called Traditionalists who can only simulate what once was the sacrificial reality.

There is an explanation for all this, but no one wishes to consider it. It would raise the possibility that just as easily as the transformation came in less than a century, the world could return to what existed before. The old moral code would prevail once again and the Church would be unhindered in her activities. All would be open to the truth, and true conversions would be possible. This the powers that be today would prevent at all costs. Most would readily die defending their freedom to sin rather than live to lead a life serving God who created them and His Divine Son who redeemed them. That such evil would exist in the world was foretold in Holy Scripture. That this particular time is described in those verses is something the enemy has gone to great lengths to conceal. Many calling themselves Catholic clergy know full well we live in what is described as the latter days or end times, yet they want none of the deprivations and call to sacrifice that go with it. They have allowed themselves to be convinced that they live at the bare beginning of these times, not the end of them; and they have succeeded in convincing their followers of the same. But for that "success" they have paid a great price.

These leaders have committed a grievous sin against the Holy Ghost by rejecting the known truth, a truth that can easily be demonstrated and proven. Only objective truth can set them free, but first it will make those accepting it miserable, as one sage observed. And it is that very misery they wish most of all to avoid. No one wants to champion an unpopular cause. The misery of being set apart, of being different — of being mocked and derided, jeered at and shunned; the naked terror of being alone — it is these fears which keep them huddled together with their followers, clinging to the make-believe shreds of a security blanket that doesn't even exist. All these years they believed that the primary purpose for the

Church's existence was all about them and their needs, not the preservation, whole and entire, of the sacred truths Christ entrusted to His Church; and they cannot look like fools in the eyes of their followers now and run it back. Those truths are essential to salvation, and once they are fully demonstrated and understood, the true nature of the Church — who She really is and has always been and how it has been made to appear that She could ever change — will become abundantly clear.

While those who quietly mouth the possibility that Francis in Rome is not a true pope may believe they are entertaining a novel idea, Catholics today have good reason to question not only Francis' validity as pope, but also the validity of all popes since the death of Pope Pius XII. The reason is simple: Catholic truth never changes; yet beginning years before the reign of Angelo Roncalli as John 23 in 1958, many things changed in the Church. From the earliest ages of Catholicity, novelty has been recognized as a sure sign of departure from Catholic faith. And novelty, which abounded a full decade and more before the advent of the false Vatican 2 Council (V2) — convened by John 23 October 11, 1962 and closed by his successor, Giovanni Battista Montini ("Pope" Paul 6) in December of 1965 — was only concluded at that council. But more importantly, those currently in positions of authority in Rome and even those who pretend to reject that authority do not employ the methods sanctioned by the Church to demonstrate the truth of what they are doing. In fact, they generally ignore these methods, which in itself is a rejection of Church teaching condemned by several popes, resulting in the loss of Church membership. Christ Himself designated the popes as the teachers of His divine message. Theologians, priests, and even bishops are authorized to teach only if they are in communion with a validly and canonically elected pope. This has been the constant teaching of the Church since Her inception. For nearly 60 years the Church has existed in an acephalic or leaderless state, not non-existent as some might assume, but merely comatose, so to speak. For Christ, Her true Head (the brain or intellect of the Mystical Body, with the Holy Ghost as Her soul, since She cannot be brain-dead or soulless), keeps Her alive, and at some juncture He will see either that She is restored to health or He will return as Eternal Judge. While most may be oblivious to the Church's current predicament, it is very real. The fact that it would be met with such disbelief and scorn is the very proof that it does indeed exist.

Here, perhaps, is the place where the players in this tragedy should be introduced.

False sects and the appearance of truth

Those remaining with the new church in Rome following the death of Pope Pius XII will be called here Novus Ordo (NO) catholics but are not really Catholics as the Church of all time has always understood the word. They range on the belief scale from ultra-liberal to conservative. They attend the "new mass" introduced in 1969 by Paul 6, attenuated somewhat by "Pope" Benedict XVI. They receive the new rites of the sacraments also approved by Paul 6 in 1968. They also accept the heretical idea of religious liberty as taught by the suspected Modernist John Courtney Murray, and a host of other heresies and errors propagated at the false Vatican 2 council. Most people today consider these NO catholics to belong to the established Church of all time, but this is not the case. It is important that non-Catholics, especially, understand that just because Rome retains the name Catholic, and their followers call themselves Catholics, that doesn't mean they are what they say they are. The same applies to those presenting below as "traditional" Catholics, that is, as heirs to all the Catholic Church once was, for they do not correspond to the meaning of the word Catholic, either.

Since the conclusion of Vatican 2 in 1965, but especially following the abrogation of the Latin Mass in 1969, "Traditional" Catholics came into existence. These individuals exited the church in Rome sometime after the completion of the council in 1965 or the introduction of the *Novus Ordo Missae* or "New Mass" (NOM) in 1969. Some Traditionalists believe that the present leader of the church in Rome is a true pope but is not to be obeyed wherever he departs from the faith. Sedevacantists believe that the Church has been without a true pope since the death of either Pius XII or John 23. There are many sects within the Traditionalist fold. All claim to be Catholic but none can prove their Catholicity, and their "clerics" cannot prove any claim to apostolicity. [8]

One particular traditionalist-like sect was established in the 1940s within the Church itself, although its co-founder was not formally excommunicated until the 1950s. This is the St. Benedict Center legitimately founded by Catherine Goddard in Boston in 1940 to instruct college students. In 1942, the Jesuit Leonard Feeney became a lecturer at the center. Feeney was excommunicated for his crusade on the doctrine "outside the Church no salvation." Pope Pius XII warned him many times he was wrong in his teaching on this subject and tried to reconcile him to the Church's true teaching, but Feeney would not budge. At one point, he even called Pope Pius XII a heretic. Following Feeney's excommunication, St. Benedict's Center also broke with Rome. This group today is reconciled with the Novus Ordo church but some Traditionalists (and even some calling themselves stay-at-home Catholics) still hold Feeney's teachings as Catholic, claiming his excommunication was only a "disciplinary" matter.

There also are lay "conclavists" who have elected various "popes" throughout the world, an act condemned as heretical by the Church. [9] For want of proper form and subject matter, none of these groups are Catholic. Some claim the successor to Pope Pius XII was Cardinal Giuseppe Siri, now deceased, and that his successor is now pope somewhere in Europe. There are no proofs accepted as such by Catholic standards that his election ever occurred, and abundant proof that Siri was loyal to the Novus Ordo church until his death. As will be demonstrated below, very few of those cardinals casting votes in the 1958 election were even Catholic, and therefore could not have validly elected anyone. They had long before fallen away without the faithful even realizing it.

Finally, there is the vast sea of non-Catholics who identify themselves as Christians, some of whom are validly baptized and, according to Church teaching, are actually subject to Church teaching and laws. The majority of this population is what the Church would describe as invincibly ignorant (a prejudice against Catholicism unable to be overcome) and indeed, it is believed many of them are in good faith. Since Vatican 2, many denominations believe the Church has come more to their way of thinking and is not the intolerant organization that once sought to convert them to "Romish ways." Their ministers are often accepted as equals by some NO officials and after all, they were invited to be consultants during Vatican 2. Therefore, they now count these "Catholics" as Christians in the full sense. Other denominations, however, are not as forgiving. They yet believe the Church, as She existed throughout history and up to the present, is the Antichrist, the Scarlet Whore of Revelations. This is often accompanied by the teaching that Rome is behind the creation of a New World Order, which is certainly true of the anti-Church now reigning in Rome but is entirely untrue of the Church as She existed prior to the death of Pope Pius XII.

While the primary purpose of this book is to demonstrate how the Catholic Church was infiltrated and destroyed from within by sinister forces and how Her continual teaching was perverted, the infiltration was not limited to the Catholic Church. It was simply accommodated to Protestant beliefs, targeting mainly biblical teaching and interpretation. In addition, Wemhoff's book relates that it was actually a Presbyterian minister and missionary, John Mackay, who on the Protestant side worked with fellow Presbyterian minister Robert Speer and YMCA founder John Mott to advance religious liberty as the concept was understood and promoted by Murray. Mackay was a huge proponent of ecumenism and evangelism. He was also active in the Federal Council of Churches, forerunner of the World Council of Churches. The influence of these men within the Protestant church helped those working to destroy the Catholic Church accomplish their desired end. And yet not all Protestants agreed at the time with their ideology. Nevertheless, the biblical view of non-Catholics was successfully skewed and their basic understanding of Scripture perverted, regardless of which denomination they were affiliated with.

Phenomenalism and Modernism
The philosophy underlying the belief systems of both Traditionalists and the Novus Ordo can be classified as

Phenomenalism. Phenomenalism (Gr., phainomenon, from *phainesthai*, to appear) literally means any system of thought that has to do with appearances. It is the theory that knowledge is limited to phenomena including (a) physical phenomena or the totality of objects of actual and possible perception and (b) mental phenomena, the totality of objects of introspection. Phenomenalism assumes two forms according as it (a) denies reality behind the phenomena (Renouvier, Shadworth, Hodgson), or (b) expressly affirms the reality of things-in-themselves but denies their knowability (Kant, Comte, Spencer). [10] They accept the shadow, not its substance; the appearance of truth, not truth itself. For according to Reverend A.C. Cotter, "Error is impossible unless it has the *appearance* of being true." [11] Pope St. Pius X condemns this Modernist teaching as follows: "Human reason is entirely restricted to phenomena, namely things that appear, and that appearance by which they appear..." [12]

Phenomenalism is actually condemned by Christ Himself in Holy Scripture, where He warns: "Judge not according to the appearance, but judge just judgment"[13] And in St. Matthew, "For by the *fruit* the tree is known" [14] and such fruit means what a man reaps through his works or actions. According to the *Catholic Encyclopedia* (1911), this heresy is related to errors regarding the attainment of certitude and to pragmatism, which teaches that an *unproved* hypothesis or hypothetical cause, if it explains the facts observed, fulfills the same purpose and serves the same ends as a *true cause* or established law; truth perpetually evolves, (evolutionism). Phenomenalism is also associated with dialectical materialism, the foundational philosophical system of Communism.

> Marxism, as we have seen, believes that the mind acquires an imperfect and obscure knowledge of reality by the very fact that it receives a sense-image. It bases this contention on its belief that there is no difference between the accidents or phenomena of a thing and its nature. It is sufficient to point out here that Marxism's identification of the phenomena and the nature of a thing is an error common to many materialistic philosophies. [15]

Because Traditionalists and others falsely perceive reality, they are unable to arrive at truth. Instead, needs and impulses dictate their actions and fuel their experience. Pope St. Pius X condemned this error as Modernism:

> For them the Sacraments are the resultant of a double need, for...everything in their system is explained by impulses or necessities...The first need is that of giving some manifestation to religion; the second is that of propagating it, which could not be done without some sensible forms and consecrating acts, and these are called Sacraments... The Sacraments are mere symbols and signs, though not devoid of a certain efficacy...What the phrases are to the ideas, the Sacraments are to the religious sentiment — that and nothing more.

> Modernists claim to arrive at knowing by experiencing a "kind of intuition of the heart which puts man in immediate contact with the very reality of God... [But] *everything that leads the heart captive proves a hindrance instead of a help to the discovery of the truth...*The vast majority of mankind hold and always will hold firmly that sentiment and experience alone, when not enlightened and guided by reason, do not lead to the knowledge of God." [16]

Reverend A.C. Cotter S.J. teaches that "Truth is conformity of the mind to reality...Reality means...that which exists, did exist, will exist." [17] As St. Thomas Aquinas expounds, man must be able to express what is in his mind in words and then convert knowing and believing to action ("thought, word and deed"). This is true reality. But Traditionalists perceive God and His Church only in terms of what satisfies their insatiable needs and makes them feel good, not the obedience owed to God and His vicar on earth. "If you love Me, keep my commandments" has no meaning for them. All they know is that they have rights to the Church's spiritual goods, and they believe that God loves them so much that He would never deprive them of these goods. It doesn't matter that the Church teaches otherwise on this subject, or that others have been deprived of Mass and

Sacraments for decades and still kept their faith. These facts do not apply to Traditionalists, even though among those who have been deprived of Mass and Sacraments are today's "stay-at-home" or catacomb Catholics, who follow only the popes up to and including Pius XII, say their prayers at home, study and defend their faith and perform good works, as they are able.

Separating these purported Catholics into several distinct groups effectively destroys any pretension to the necessary mark of unity required for the Catholic Church's existence, for unity is achieved only when the faithful and hierarchy are in communion with a true and canonically elected pope.

But who would ever believe the once most renowned religious body in the world could be the victim of a hostile takeover right under everyone's noses, and with few objections whatsoever from Catholics? It is an imposture so outrageous that even to contemplate the possibility seems to qualify one for inclusion in the lunatic fringe. Yet what if such an imposture had been predicted in Holy Scripture for the end times? And what if it had been perpetrated in such a way that results, as Sheen indicates above, in the very surreal experience that Catholics have been enduring for decades? "And he did great signs...and he seduced them that dwell on the earth by the signs." [18] St. Paul describes these signs as "lying wonders." [19] That great Doctor of the Church, St. Francis de Sales taught: "The miracles of Antichrist will be *simply an illusion*... [They will be] unnatural and will not endure." [20] What greater lie or illusion than to pretend to be something one is not *and could never be*, without being detected or called out? To pose as the world's most prestigious religious leader, head of the ancient and venerable Roman Catholic Church, while violating its most sacred principles and being accepted universally as the genuine article?!

False prophets and wolves in sheep's clothing

How did this happen? The entire collapse of the Church cannot be explained alone by the implementation of doctrinal warfare. Already in the late 1800s, false teachers had penetrated the Church and began disseminating error in Catholic schools during the

Modernist infestation. So a certain number of Catholics received a false education in the faith without even realizing it. Others chose not to educate themselves or to learn only the basics concerning the faith. In short, Catholics had grown lax, worldly and careless. Pope St. Pius X was able to halt this cancer (Modernism) for a time in the first decade of the 20th century, but it resurged again in the 1920s. The ill-educated, the willfully uneducated and the semi-educated who came of age in the 1940s-50s were not equipped to repulse the predations of government-funded change agents, who began actively lobbying for doctrinal change by subverting the clergy. These poor rubes didn't have anything close to the background needed to unravel the sophisticated arguments of the Modernists.

Had they engaged in Catholic Action, as the popes commanded them to do, they might have had a fighting chance. But as will be explained below, already they had been effectively sidelined. Like the Apostles in the Garden of Gethsemane, Catholics were asleep when the enemy arrived. It would never have occurred to them to question a papal election. Their perception of the Church's attribute of indefectibility would not allow them to countenance treachery within the Church itself, even though the early history of the papacy is replete with examples of turmoil in seating the pope and keeping him in office, including kidnapping and even death. The only thing they knew about the popes and the possibility they could err as pope and lead the Church astray came from Protestants calling the Church the Antichrist, and this they understandably dismissed out of hand. If anything, it made them less likely than ever to even allow such a thought to cross their minds.

Books have been written portraying the Church as the Scarlet Whore of Rome [21] and the popes as perpetual Antichrists persecuting down through the ages. Many of these authors also have linked today's church in Rome with the New World Order; and if they would limit their theory to the past nearly six decades and abandon their verifiably unsubstantiated claim (according to both Protestant and Catholic Scripture scholars) of a perpetual Antichrist persecuting, they would definitely be onto something. For in so doing they would discover a wealth of comparisons and proofs that would solidly establish their case and perhaps prepare the way for a true understanding of the evil times we experience today. Unbeknownst to Catholics today, the Protestant teaching on a papal Antichrist was a perversion of a long-held tradition in the Church. Following papal teaching, certain saints and theologians identify the Man of Sin as a false pope reigning as a true pope. Catholic theologians as recently as the 1800s also interpret St. Paul's "he who withholdeth" [22] as the pope and the papacy itself.

Some Catholics despise the Roman church as the whore of Babylon along with many Protestants, yet with this distinction: that this whore is NOT the authentic Catholic Church of antiquity. For how could she be the true Church and be drunk with the blood of saints and martyrs? [23] On her forehead is inscribed the word "mystery," [24] which the angel explains as the beast "that was and is not" [25] — pagan Rome reborn. The true Catholic Church was dispersed among the nations decades ago following Vatican 2, as foretold in Holy Scripture. For the remnant is commanded to separate themselves from the Babylonish whore [26] (St. Paul refers to pagan Rome as Babylon), lest they partake of her sins and receive her plagues. This command was issued to the universal Church, meaning it would apply to faithful in all parts of the world who would potentially heed it. Catholics also must remember that Christ warned the faithful that when the Shepherd (Himself and by analogy His Vicar) was struck, the flock would be dispersed. [27]

Ecumenism: the visible Church's death gasp

Ecumenism was deliberately fostered and manufactured by those secretly waging doctrinal warfare around the world, but especially in America, following World War II. It is interesting to note that John Foster Dulles, leader of the Federal Council of Churches in the 1940s and chairman of a commission headed by ecumenical proponent John Mackay, was the brother of Allen Dulles, future head of the C.I.A. Avery Dulles, the son of John Foster Dulles and nephew of Allen Dulles, later worked his way up through the clerical ranks of the Novus Ordo church to become a "cardinal."

The president of the Federal Council of Churches was a Methodist Bishop, Bromley Oxnam, who by all reports was fiercely anti-Catholic. When the ecumenical movement matured in the 1960s, it spelled the end for both Catholicism and any remaining "Christian" orthodoxy. The Church of previous ages may have been perceived as oppressive and unyielding, Her Latin liturgy condemned as mummery and papal infallibility billed only as an attempt to enforce the dictates of a man with pretensions to Godhead. Yet Catholics are well aware that even non-Catholics respected the Church; the Pope's assistance in worldly matters was tolerated, even welcomed in some cases, despite these widespread prejudices. Prior to Pope Pius XII's death in 1958, they definitely did not enter as the all-embracing, doctrinally bereft pop heroes as today's "popes" have done.

Pope Pius XI described what happened to papal authority as "moral, juridical and social Modernism…an (outward) profession of loyalty to Catholic social doctrine plus a disregard for the encyclicals as though they were 'out of date'." [28] Indifferentism thinly disguised as ecumenism, deliberately foisted on society by deceptive means, has failed to bring non-Catholics into the fold as promised; one flock under one shepherd. Instead it has unleashed a moral and spiritual calamity that will soon culminate in the inevitable punishment of those who, while passing as the elect, have savaged Christ's eternal plan for all mankind. True freedom comes not from being able to believe and to act as one wishes, but in knowing which beliefs and behaviors will please God and obtain salvation. Christ instructs in His mention of the abomination of desolation in Matt. 24:15, "He that readeth, let him understand." Because Christ granted St. Peter and his successors the charism of infallibility in matters of faith and morals, this means the Church alone can impart that understanding: She alone possesses the unchangeable truth that releases man from the bondage of sin and error and sets him free to pursue eternal happiness. Even if none other than Catholics ever believe this, no one has the right to force them to believe otherwise. And if Catholics claim that right only to be psychologically manipulated to deny or doubt the very beliefs they are bound to hold in order to remain

Catholic, then "freedom of religion" is exposed for the lie that it truly is.

In order to be able to undersand the Church's true teachings throughout the ages, the following chapters are dedicated to helping those who have been so confused all these years discern what constitutes Catholic truth, and what they must believe in order to enjoy happiness in heaven with the Blessed Trinity and the Church Triumphant.

Introduction Endnotes

[1] Fulton J. Sheen, *Communism and the Conscience of the West,* (Indianapolis: Bobbs-Merrill Company, 1948), 24-25.
[2] Fr. E. Sylvester Berry, D.D., *The Church of Christ,* (St. Louis, Mo. and London: B. Herder Book Co., 1927), 119.
[3] Sheen, *Communism and the Conscience of the West*, 24-25.
[4] First edition of the Masonic review *L'Acacia,* 1902
[5] *Free Dictionary* online, http://www.thefreedictionary.com/conspiracy.
[6] From *The Trial of Sir Thomas More,* May 7, 1535 in *A Complete Collection of State Trials and Proceeding Upon Impeachments for High Treason, etc.* (London, 1719), http://law2.umkc.edu/faculty/projects/ftrials/more/moretrialreport.html.
[7] Please see the book information posted at www.betrayedcatholics.com on the articles page under *Phantom Church* references. ***The majority of the incidents that have occurred with minors over the past 65 years were the result of deliberate infiltration of the Church by Her enemies, with the intent to degrade Her in the eyes of the world and ruin any chances the next generation would remain Catholic.*** Pope St. Pius V's constitution *Horrendum illud scelus* is still in effect, save for the conclusion he arrives at regarding the intent of secular governments to put priests perverting young boys to death. Randy Engel's work, *The Rite of Sodomy,* explains that the Church has fought this plague for centuries and regularly turned over clerics guilty of sex crimes to the authorities for the death sentence even before the issuance of Pope St. Pius V's constitution. The efforts made to eradicate sexual abuse in seminaries and religious insititutes was not generally made public, in order that the faithful not be scandalized. So

it is unfair to intimate that in the past this problem has existed, but the Church has ignored it.

[8] However, it should be noted that those men claiming to be Traditional priests, while not priests of the Catholic Church, are indeed ministers of a *non-Catholic* religion. No one here is disputing their ministry as such. What is denied categorically here is their claim to possess the apostolicity guaranteed the priests and bishops of the *Catholic* faith. For these men were never ordained or consecrated according to the infallible precepts of that faith, i.e., in accordance with Canon Law and Catholic dogma. See http://www.betrayedcatholics.com/free-content/reference-links/7-recent-articles/binding-power-of-papacy-voids-traditionalist-acts/.

[9] Henry Denzinger, *The Sources of Catholic Dogma*, 30th Edition, (Powers Lake, N.D.: Marian House, 1957 (DZ 960, 967.)

[10] Dagobert Runes, *Dictionary of Philosophy,* (New York: Littlefield, Adams and Co., 1942)

[11] Rev. A.C. Cotter, *ABC of Scholastic Philosophy* (Weston, Mass.: Weston College Press, 1949), 282. (Emph. Cotter's.)

[12] "Pascendi Domenici Gregis," (Sept. 8, 1907) in Denzinger, *The Sources of Catholic Dogma*, (DZ 2072.)

[13] Douay-Rheims version of Holy Scripture, John 7:24.

[14] Douay-Rheims version of Holy Scripture, Matt. 12: 33; commentary compiled by Rev. George Leo Haydock, reprint 1859, (Monrovia Calif.: Catholic Treasures, 1991).

[15] Charles J. McFadden, O.S.A., Ph.D. *The Philosophy of Communism*; (New York, Cincinnati, Chicago: Benziger Brothers, printers to the Holy See, 1939), 194.

[16] "Pascendi Domenici Gregis," (Sept. 8, 1907) in Denzinger, *The Sources of Catholic Dogma.* (DZ 2081, 2089.)

[17] Cotter, *ABC of Scholastic Philosophy,* 269.

[18] Douay-Rheims version of Holy Scripture, Apoc. 13: 13-14.

[19] Ibid., 2 Thess. 2: 9.

[20] Rev. Henry Ryder, *The Catholic Controversy,* (New York: Burnes and Oates, Catholic Publication Society, 1886), 183.

[21] Douay-Rheims version of Holy Scripture, Apoc. 17: 3-6.

[22] Ibid., 2 Thess. 2: 6-9.

[23] Ibid., Apoc. 17:6.

[24] Ibid., Apoc. 17:7.

[25] Ibid., Apoc. 17:8.

---

[26] Ibid., Apoc. 18: 4.

[27] Ibid., Matt. 26: 30.

[28] "On Reconstructing the Social Order," para. 46 (May 15, 1931) in *The Church and the Reconstruction of the Modern World, The Social Encyclicals of Pius XI, Quadregessimo Anno,* (Garden City, N.Y.: Image Books, Doubleday and Co., 1957), 234.

PART ONE: THE OPERATION OF ERROR AND CATHOLIC TRUTH

Chapter I — The City of God
The Church as a Divine Society headed by the Roman Pontiff

A. The Church established by Christ

In his classic work *City of God,* St. Augustine of Hippo described two cities, one the City of God, and the other the City of this World (or of the Devil, who is lord of this world). Just as there was the clash of the two camps in Heaven when St. Michael dispatched Lucifer to Hell, this same battle continues on earth. In his foreword to St. Augustine's *City of God*, Etienne Gilson addresses the subject of organizing a universal society, a topic popular even in his day. He writes:

> Our contemporaries aspire after a complete unity of all peoples: one world. They are right. The universal society…they are endeavoring to organize aims at being a political and temporal society. In this regard, they again are right. Perhaps their most serious mistake is in imagining…a universal and purely natural society of men is possible without a universal religious society, which would unite men in the acceptance of the same supernatural truth and in the love of the same supernatural good…The desire of the worldwide unity which fills the heart of man will, in all likelihood, never die…[But] the only force capable of preserving a thing is the force which created it. It is completely useless to pursue a Christian end except by Christian means. If we really want one world, we must first have one Church, and the only Church that is one is the Catholic Church…One world is impossible without

one God and one Church. In this truth lies the ever-timely
message conveyed to man by St. Augustine. [1]

If the Devil were to construct a one-world society, he would first
need to preclude any possibility that the City of God would be the
religion governing that world. In order to assure this, he would need
to wipe all memory of that city from the face of the earth and model
something as similar as possible in its place to serve as the necessary
religion. It would need to amalgamate all aspects of each religion
rolled into one, representing all religions ever practiced by any
society. This is the democratic model of true religious equality
enforced by world governments today, a model all true Catholics
must reject as heresy (religious indifferentism). The Catholic Church
is the only true religion; it has no equal because truth is one. This has
been the perpetual bone of contention between the City of God and
the Devil's city, and the City of God gives no quarter. So the City of
God had to be cleverly undermined and attenuated, its dogmas
obscured, its authority and dignity destroyed. It had to be made
acceptable to all people to appear to embrace the religious traditions
of all societies across the world unconditionally rather than on the
condition of conversion. The worship of God had to be reduced to
the worship of that "Divine spark" present in all men — secular
humanism — and then God's city would become the city of men
alone, and God a mere anachronism. The head of that society would
appear to be a pope. But in embracing such heresies that head would,
in reality, be Antichrist.

Every society must have a head; this is true even in the animal
world. As Catholics know, the Head of the Catholic Church is Christ
Himself; but the Vicars of His Church on earth, acting in His stead,
are the Roman Pontiffs: "He that heareth you, heareth Me." [2] If it
seems to some that the Catholic Church has assigned a sort of deity
to the popes, it is only in the sense that Christ has invested them with
His own power concerning matters of faith and morals. In those
things, which initially came from His own mouth, Christ could not
help but guarantee his Vicars the privilege of infallibility. No pope
could ever teach heresy as pope, *ex cathedra*, (i.e., in any official

document intended for the entire Church). This teaching was guaranteed as issuing from Divine faith at the (only) Vatican Council, for Christ promised the gates of Hell would never prevail against His Church. That ecumenical council taught how Catholics are actually required to view their Church and why they believe the Roman Pontiffs' teachings must be followed to the letter. This is best explained below by Reverend W. Wilmers, S.J., an advisor to the Vatican Council:

> The very nature of religion requires that its members form a society. For where one and the same end is pursued, there is one of the conditions requisite for a society. The existence of one common object naturally awakens the desire to secure it by united effort and common means. The multitude will therefore, if there exist no common bond of authority, create such, however imperfect it may be; and thus a religious society naturally will spring up. *The Church has been founded directly by Christ; it is beyond all doubt that [it] is the work of Christ Himself.* He is the sole author of the Christian religion…also the immediate founder of the Church. He directly instituted that authority which is the soul, or principle, of life, that binds together in one body all those who profess His religion. It is easily shown that it was Christ Himself, not His followers or even His Apostles, who created that external bond of authority which was intended to unite all the Church's members…[For] Christ declared His intention of founding a Church, and that by institution of a living authority, when he said to Simon Peter: "Thou art Peter, and upon this rock I will build my Church and the gates of hell shall not prevail against it. [3]

Now if Christ intends personally to build His Church, it is not to be the work of men but a truly divine society. He promised to bind and loose in Heaven whatever Peter and His successors bound and loosed upon earth. He fulfilled the promise to establish Peter as the sole head of the Church following his Resurrection, when He commissioned him to "Feed my lambs; feed my sheep." [4]

So since this Church is founded directly by Christ, who lent His own authority to Peter, guaranteeing it would never fail, in obeying Peter true Catholics are only obeying Christ who speaks through His vicar: "He that heareth you, heareth Me." [5]

B. Where do we find the Deposit of Faith?
St. Francis de Sales teaches:

> The Christian Faith is grounded on the Word of God. This is what places it in the sovereign degree of certainty, as having the warrant of that eternal and infallible truth... *Faith which rests on anything else is not Christian*...The Word of God, the formal rule of...faith, is either in Scripture or Tradition. The Church, the rule of application, expresses Herself, by a general belief of all Christians...by a consent of her pastors and doctors; in a general council; [and by] Her head minister...And these are four explaining and applying rules of our faith; the Church as a whole [continual magisterium], the General Council, the consent of the Fathers, the Pope. [6]

Lest St. Francis de Sales' teaching be misconstrued as placing other authorities above the pope, he states in another section of his work: "For it is usual that the head should speak for the whole body, and what the head says is considered to be said by all the rest." [7] Catholics must follow the long-accepted order known to students of sacred theology as the *loci theologici*, compiled by Reverend Melchior Cano O.P., which serves as the foundation for the scholastic method, consisting of:

> i. Holy Scripture, contained in the canonical books;
> ii. The oral Traditions of Christ and the Apostles, rightly called oracles of the living voice;
> iii. The Catholic Church, (the continual extraordinary and ordinary magisterium);
> iv. The General Councils specifically, but also the regional councils;

v. The Roman Church, called by divine privilege Apostolic (the Holy See and the Sacred Congregations)

vi. The authority of the ancient Fathers;

vii. The authority of *scholastic* theologians, to whom the *teachers of Canon Law* are joined;

viii. Natural reason, contained in all the naturally acquired sciences;

ix. The authority of philosophers following the natural light of human reason and the masters of the civil law;

x. The authority of human history *written by trustworthy authors* or expressed in serious, national tradition. [8]

The Vatican Council thus teaches:

This supernatural revelation, according to the faith of the universal Church, as declared by the holy synod of Trent, is contained 'in the written books and in the unwritten traditions which have been received from the apostles from the mouth of Christ Himself; or through the inspiration of the Holy Ghost, have been handed down to us by the apostles themselves, and have thus come to us,' (DZ 783)...The books of the Old and New Testament...have God as their author, and as such have been handed down to the Church Herself...*In matters of faith and morals pertaining to the instruction of Christian Doctrine, that must be considered as the true sense of Sacred Scripture which Holy Mother Church has held and holds...No one is permitted to interpret Sacred Scripture itself contrary to this sense, or even contrary to the unanimous opinions of the Fathers.* [9]

As Monsignor Joseph C. Fenton (whose orthodoxy was personally commended by Pope Pius XII) noted:

Every dogmatic definition is the statement of a truth given to the Church before the death of the last Apostle. The expressed acceptance of the body of truth within which the defined doctrine belongs constitutes the profession of faith necessary for membership in the true Church of Jesus Christ. [10]

Reverend Peter Finlay, S.J., professor of Catholic theology at the National University of Ireland, writes:

> *Every truth set forward distinctly in Holy Scripture, every article of the Catholic Creeds, every solemn dogmatic definition of a Pope or of a General Council is included in the Deposit...*The Church not only defines infallibly the Articles of Faith, She determines infallibly the meaning of the Sacred texts in which an article is enshrined...She is infallible in Her judgments and teachings on matters so intimately connected with [Divine Faith] that they must stand or fall, be accepted or rejected, together...We cannot doubt or deny, or even withhold assent, from any doctrine which it is certain God reveals to us; and it is of Divine and Catholic Faith that the Church is infallible when She teaches that any given Doctrine is contained in the Divine Deposit. We must believe, and we are prepared to believe firmly all Divinely revealed truth; *and the teaching of the Church makes clearly and infallibly certain for us what has been divinely revealed.* [11]

C. Divine Faith

During a series of lectures on Divine Faith later gathered into a book and presented at the National University of Ireland, Reverend Peter Finlay, S.J. describes the Divine Faith Christ entrusted to St. Peter and the Apostles. He explains its nature and expounds on its necessity as preceding all other grades of belief. And he makes it clear that without Divine Faith and all its prerequisites, one cannot claim to be a Catholic possessing membership in Christ's Church.

Reverend Finlay writes:

> In treating of 'The Church of Christ, its Foundation and Constitution' [a book written by Reverend Finlay], we have had occasion repeatedly to make mention of...the Deposit of Faith, which the Church has been divinely commissioned to teach and preserve...And this whole body of revelation is spoken of as a 'Deposit' because it is entrusted to the Church's keeping; 'of faith' because its

whole content, all the truths contained in it, are to be accepted and believed by the members of the Church... Divine faith is an intellectual...and unhesitating...assent to revealed truths on the ground that God Himself has revealed them; and acceptance and an assertion of their truth on the grounds that God Himself declares them to be true...The Council of the Vatican...in the Dogmatic Constitution on Catholic Faith declares: 'This faith is a supernatural virtue by which we, with the aid and inspiration of God, believe that the things revealed by Him are true, not because the intrinsic truth of the revealed things has been perceived by the natural light of reason, *but because of the authority of God revealing them* — of God, who can neither deceive nor be deceived.' And, in the corresponding Canon: 'If anyone shall say that Divine Faith is not to be distinguished from natural knowledge of God and morals, and therefore Divine Faith does not require that revealed truth shall be believed because of the authority of God revealing it: Let him be anathema.'...And the teaching of the Vatican is the perpetual tradition of the Church... [12]

Next Reverend Finlay provides several Scripture quotes which prove Christ Himself demanded such belief in His revelation; that the Apostles did not preach in their own names, but in Christ's.

Even in the Old Testament, the message of the Prophet is generally authenticated by the declaration: 'Thus saith the Lord'... Christ Himself, in His discourse with Nicodemus, after reproaching the Pharisee with his slowness to believe continues: 'Amen, Amen, I say to thee: that we speak what we know and testify what we have seen, and you receive not our testimony.' (Douay-Rheims Bible, John 3:2). And St. John writes of the Faith in Christ the Son of God: 'If we receive the testimony of men the testimony of God is greater...He that believeth in the Son of God hath the testimony of God in Himself...He that believeth not in the Son maketh God a liar,' (John 5:9)...And St. Paul reminds the Thessalonians: 'that, when you had received of us the word of the message of God, you received it not as the word of men, but as it is in truth, the word of God, who also worketh in you that believe' (Thess. 2:13).

Indeed the whole preaching of the Apostles, throughout the Acts and their Epistles, assumes what St. John and St. Paul expressly state in the passages I have just quoted: for the Apostles deliver their message as one entrusted to them; they do not recommend it for acceptance by human arguments; they do not ask it should be believed because of any authority they themselves possess; *they present it as a message from God which God Himself attests*, and which is to be submitted to and received, because He attests it...Hence in the early Church and at all times since, the argument of Christian apologists and teachers: *'You believe men; how much more ought you to believe God Himself?'* (Heb. Ch. 11) ...We hold then on these grounds that the immediate motive or reason of our assent, in an act of Divine Faith, is and must be the Divine testimony. We Catholics do not and cannot believe in divinely revealed truths because we have received or discovered rational demonstration of them.

We do not and cannot believe in them [primarily] because the Church teaches and guarantees them to us," (although only by the Church's approval of the canonical books of Scripture and Her interpretation of these books, or the interpretation of scriptural scholars which She approves, can we be certain of what Christ actually said. The Church alone is the authentic interpreter of Scripture and Tradition — Ed.). "We do not and cannot believe in them because the whole community accepts them, and the clergy preach them, and parents and friends believe, and have ever taught us to believe, in them. No one of these reasons, not all of them combined, will enable us to make an act of Divine Faith — of that Faith which Our Lord has said: 'He that believeth and is baptized the same shall be saved; he that believeth not shall be condemned,' (Mark 16:16). The motive of such an act of Faith must be the testimony not of human reason, not even of the Catholic Church, still less of the Catholic community, of priest, of parents or of friends; it must be the testimony of God Himself," made known to us by the Catholic Church. [13]

What is not Divine Faith

Reverend Finlay then explains that those who accept the teachings of Popes and Councils, confess the infallibility of the pope, profess the Presence of Christ in the Eucharist, or recite the Apostles Creed must always rest their belief on Divine authority.

> Do they really formulate their assent — even if it be in their own minds — in such a way as this: 'I believe these truths because God, the infallible Truth has revealed them to me? '...Are the faithful, then, of whom we speak conscious to themselves; do they know and feel, in the very act of assent, that their reason for believing is that God has revealed to them the truths which they believe? If not, they may indeed elicit an act of ecclesiastical faith, if the motive of their belief be the authority of the Church; of human faith, if their motive be the authority of their priest, their parents, or their friends; but it cannot be Divine Faith, of which the essential motive, Divine authority, is wanting to them. [14]

All the catechisms, prayer books, religious instructions and liturgical services set forth the proper formula for eliciting this act of Divine Faith, Reverend Finlay states. And yet how many fail to meditate upon and fully comprehend even the words found in the Act of Faith, and therefore fail to realize that their motive for belief cannot rest on some mechanical formula or on other motives, but only on the testimony and activities of Our Lord Himself? For St. Cyprian wrote:

> Most of the bishops...set over the Lord's churches throughout the world, hold to the method of evangelical truth and of the Lord's tradition, and depart not by any human and novel institution, *from that which Christ our master both taught and did*." Likewise the Asiatic bishops,

commenting on the approbation of the canonical books of Scripture, stated that: "As, *on this principle of what Christ had done and taught,* the writings of which we are speaking were admitted as sacred and divine... [15]

As Reverend Finlay notes:

> The importance of the subject [believing on Divine faith alone] is so vital, and the danger of believing for human reasons so present, that religious teachers should unceasingly direct attention to the question, and we ourselves should keep it habitually in mind...Our clergy, in their instructions, insist so frequently that the doctrines that they preach are the doctrines of the Church, we appeal so commonly to the decisions of the Church, and our Catholic people are so accustomed to look with reverence on the authority of the Church, that great care should be taken to place the motive of Divine Faith firmly before them. [16]

Why is the necessity of excluding all human reasons for belief so very important? Because, as the Athanasian Creed states: "This is the Catholic Faith, which unless a man believe faithfully and firmly, he cannot be saved." Blessed Pope Innocent XI condemned the proposition that "Faith, improperly so-called, based on the testimony of creatures or some other similar motive, is sufficient for justification (DZ 1173)." As Reverend Finlay points out, it is not enough that when the Church defines some truth, we give *implicit* assent to the fact Christ first taught it to the world. Such assent must be *explicit*, else we credit the creature and not the Creator. Such assent also must be unhesitating, for as Pope Pius IX taught in *Qui Pluribus*:

> Who is ignorant or can be ignorant that we must believe unhesitatingly when God speaks to us, and that nothing is more in accord with reason itself than to assent and hold fast to those things which it is certain have been revealed to us by God, who can neither deceive nor be deceived?

Why is it so difficult for man to understand this when he accepts natural truths so readily? All know that one and one are two; that water is H_2O on the chemical scale, that dark clouds nearly always bring rain. Who would question these things? Why then do men question their own God and Savior, Jesus Christ?

D. Development of doctrine and human intelligence

As Reverend Finlay states in his conclusions, there is one rule of faith and one only; that one was given to us by St. Vincent Lerins, who wrote in his *Commonitorium* that we must believe: "What has been believed everywhere, always and by all...universality, antiquity and general consent. [17] Here Reverend Finlay explains how the development of Faith applies to this rule:

> Whenever revealed doctrines were called in question, or heretical opinions were set up against them, and the Church judged fitting to decide and examine such controversies, Her method has been ever to consult tradition; what is the testimony of the Scriptures? What was the mind and teaching of the Church in earlier times?...[Not] in the determining of doctrines, nor in Her explanation of them, has the Church ever had recourse to private revelation, or human reasonings, or any special inspiration; but solely to the revelation that was made by Christ and His Holy Spirit to the Apostles, and which was preserved and handed on by the Bishops, the Divinely appointed guardians and teachers of the Deposit of Faith...We have the same body of doctrines set out for us [as the first Christians]; *we have the advantages of [almost 20] centuries of Christian thought and meditation on them. Is it any wonder we should have a better understanding of the contents of the Divine Deposit than the Christians of the early centuries?...* Revelation, dogma, in its most developed state is the same revelation which was preached by the Apostles to the first Christians; which was taught and explained by the early Fathers; which was studied and discussed by the schoolmen and the apologists; which was believed in every age by the simple Faithful; but which is now better

understood, more clearly distinguished into its own component parts, more evidently opposed to the errors which it condemns. [18]

For the Vatican Council solemnly proclaimed: "The doctrine of Faith, which God has revealed, has not been given over *to be perfected by human intelligence,* as though it were a philosophical theory." [19] And again, Pope Pius IX condemned the following proposition in his *Syllabus*: "Divine Revelation is imperfect, and is consequently subject to continuous and indefinite progress, corresponding to the progress of human reason." [20] Pope St. Pius X condemned these heresies further in his *Syllabus* against the Modernists. So how can it be that so many have taken it upon themselves to falsify Divine faith, to distort its meaning, to present it according to their own reasonings and the reasoning of (liberal) theologians, despite the clear teachings of Christ proposed for belief by His Church? The answer is that, regardless of all their protestations to the contrary, there are many today who do not possess Divine faith, although there are exceptions to this general rule. It is for those exceptions that this work has been written, and for all who can yet recognize and embrace the truth.

We can read all the books on the faith that we choose, through all the ages, and these facts will not change. The Popes were *always* members of the hierarchy, and the "exceptions" (only a few) to this statement were accidental, owing to tumultuous times or to premature death. In times such as the Arian persecution, the Reformation, the Revolution in France, the unrest in Russia in the early 1900s, and the Communist persecution, Catholics were never allowed, despite the rigors of persecution, to approach schismatics or priests not possessing jurisdiction, except in danger of death. (For then there was a Roman Pontiff who could supply such jurisdiction). This is reflected in numerous replies from the Holy Office on this matter, in the lives of the saints and martyrs, and in Catholic history books. Where does Christ or the Church approve the reception of the Sacraments when sacrilege could result? Where is it taught that apostolic succession can exist without the ability to sanctify (Holy Orders)?

And likewise, the three attributes and the four marks also are contained in the Deposit of Faith: authority, infallibility, indefectibility. The Baltimore Catechism #3 teaches the Church must have both the four marks and the three attributes to exist, but without the three attributes she cannot have the four marks. [21] *The Vatican Council defined that the attributes and marks are matters of Divine Faith contained in Holy Scripture. They also are found in the Creed.* We must believe they exist and will exist until the end of time with an unhesitating assent. But we cannot believe this on the one hand, assenting to Divine Faith, and on the other hand deny another tenet of Divine Faith. These attributes and marks cannot exist in a "Church" not possessing unity (achievable only under one head, the pope) or apostolic succession, as Reverend Kinkead indicates in his catechetical discussion on the attributes. Pope Pius IX taught in 1864 that if even *one mark* of the Church was lacking, She could not exist at all. [22] Refusing to admit that these marks are lacking in the manner in which Christ intended them to exist is not invincible ignorance but a most insidious brand of self-deceit and ultimately a denial of faith. Unity based on such deceit may be the same sort of solidarity claimed among the various non-Catholic sects, including the sect now occupying Rome, but it is not and cannot be Catholic unity. When Reverend G. H. Guyot defines unity, he cites the Baltimore Catechism question on this subject as follows:

> The Catholic Church is one because all her members, according to the will of Christ, profess the same faith, have the same Sacrifice and Sacraments, and are united under the one and same visible head, the Pope. [23]

And here should be added what Pope Pius XII infallibly factored into this equation for Church membership in his encyclical *Mystici Corporis Christi*: they also must follow all the same laws.

Therefore, if those calling themselves Catholics are not united (and this is obvious), if some have no Sacrifice and only the necessary Sacraments and others all seven (but illicit and invalid ones), if only some obey Church laws, and if there is no Pope to whom they all are united, *then there is no unity and hence no Church, which contradicts Divine Faith.* Those who say that despite the lack of Apostolic Succession (and Traditional priests admit they do not possess jurisdiction) the Church DOES exist because it cannot *not* exist, else the promises of Christ have failed, have it entirely backwards. They fail to understand the true meaning of faith or what is necessary to it. If you come into my store and insist you absolutely must have an item which the government forbids me to sell to you, and state that the law which forbids me to sell it is wrong, I will tell you that it is not the law that is wrong but your wants that are wrong. For as Holy Scripture tells us, *all* authority is from God. Those wishing to remain truly Catholic are where they are at this point in time entirely because God wills them to be here. If Catholics truly knew what Divine Faith really entailed, if they were better versed in Holy Scripture, Tradition, and the content of the Divine Deposit, they would know this. And they also would know what God expects them to do. All is contained in the Deposit of Faith.

E. The reality of Divine Faith

We return once more to Reverend Finlay, who describes Scriptural instances of what Faith, the only true reality, really means. He cites St. Paul, who points out striking examples of belief resting only on Divine Faith in his Epistle to the Hebrews:

> Through faith...we understand that the world was framed by the word of God...By faith Abel offered God a sacrifice exceeding that of Cain...By faith Noe framed the Ark for the saving of his house...By faith Abraham, when he was tried, offered Isaac...By Faith Moses left Egypt, not fearing the anger of the king...Gideon, Barac, Samson, Jepthe, David, Samuel, and the prophets, who by Faith conquered kingdoms, wrought justice, obtained promises, stopped the mouths of lions, quenched the violence of fire, escaped the edge of the sword, recovered strength from weakness, became valiant in battle, put to flight foreign armies...And

others had trials of mockeries and stripes, bonds and prisons; They were stoned, they were cut asunder, they were put to death by the sword, they wandered about in sheepskins, in goatskins, begging in want, distressed, afflicted, of whom the world was not worthy, wandering in deserts, in mountains, in dens, and in caves of the earth. [24]

Does this description in any way resemble what Traditionalists — never exiled, never imprisoned, never beaten, never hunted down, never martyred, enjoying most of the comforts of modern life, complete with "Mass and Sacraments" — have suffered for *their* Faith?! The only ones who could possibly qualify in our times are those behind the Iron Curtain, who seem to have all but disappeared from sight. St. Paul defined Faith as "the substance of things to be hoped for, the evidence of things that appear not." [25] The one thing Christ was most insistent upon — the perpetual existence of a visible head for the Church's very existence — Traditionalists can easily accept as "unseen." They have been exiled to the desert as the Israelites of old, and whether God Himself miraculously sends them manna or not, they will have it! Clearly this is not Divine Faith. Traditionalists have no problem demanding their *rights*, but they are unwilling to make the sacrifices that fidelity to Divine Faith commands.

As Reverend Patrick Madgett wrote: "*The complete and ultimate rule of faith is the living voice of the living Church, ...sometimes referred to as active Tradition,* i.e., the teaching and handing on to successive generations, by authoritative teachers, of all Christ's doctrine." [26] Traditionalists, by their very name, should know this and reflect it, but do not. And from *The Catholic Encyclopedia*: "The organ of tradition...must be an official organ, a *magisterium*, or teaching authority." [27] "Traditionalists" are all about the Sacraments and external rituals, which can only legitimately proceed from those in communion with a true Pope. They take their name instead from the heresy of Traditionalism, described in the same *Catholic Encyclopedia* article "Tradition" just cited. That heresy relies on the false belief that they are endowed with an unfailing Catholic "instinct" preserving them from error. Instinct or intuition relies on the *emotions* to dictate to the intellect what one will believe. Certainty must be arrived at by an *intellectual* process that confirms the truths of faith handed down from Christ to His Apostles as the only standard for belief.

Before examining Monsignor Fenton's explanation of this false reasoning process, it is necessary to return for a moment to Reverend Finlay's treatment of divine faith. He says, "I believe most firmly that there are three persons in Thy One Divine Nature...but I have only a probability, not a certainty...," (Lecture V, p. 81), and without certainty there can be no belief.

Again, Reverend Finlay tells us:

> "An act of deliberate doubt or disbelief is a grievous insult to the majesty of God. It cannot, therefore, but be a sin; for what do we understand by sin unless a deliberate rejection of a Divine claim, a deliberate insult offered to the Divine Majesty?... And we are to bear in mind that the infinite dignity of God gives a special heinousness to unbelief, which sets it in a category by itself.[28]

Traditionalists may not have had the guidance of a visible Church, but they had Her testimony, Her *Tradition*. They had the tools they needed to study the matter thoroughly and question those who claimed to be able to interpret and present the truths of faith. Reverend Finlay writes:

> It is clear that faith in a very few simple truths, in two or three of those contained in the Apostles Creed, will not be insufficient [to constitute Divine Faith]. This is indeed one ground of our earnest hope that many without the visible communion of the Church, whose faith is incomplete and mutilated, may yet see God in Heaven. If they are honest in the errors which they hold, they may still believe with Divine Faith these few fundamental Truths...And this, too, is the ground of our certainty that the faith of our Catholic people, however imperfectly they may seem to be instructed, is far more than what is absolutely necessary... No full and detailed preparation for reception into the

Christian body was possible in Apostolic times as is commonly judged necessary in the case of converts to the Church in our day and amongst ourselves. Nor is it always possible, even now, in missions to the heathen.

When we read of St. Francis Xavier baptizing hundreds, sometimes thousands, in India or Japan, after a single sermon, we know that he can have preached to them only a few, and those most fundamental doctrines, of the Faith. Of course converts in the early Church, as converts, and indeed all Christians, at all times, were bound to perfect their knowledge as opportunity offered... God intends His whole revelation to mankind to be known and believed; He never speaks to us idly and without purpose. All the truths which He reveals must have an important bearing on our lives; else an all-wise God would never have revealed them to us. Hence the serious obligation to seek out and hold firmly the chief doctrines of revelation, those more particularly which are set before us in the teachings of the Church, in Her creed, in Her solemn definitions and in the voice of Her Episcopate. [29]

Unless we believe God and not men, we cannot claim to possess Divine Faith or expect to be saved. When St. Paul tried to reason with the Jews in Thessalonica "out of the Scriptures," they set the city in an uproar and Paul had to flee; all because they would not investigate or inquire. When Paul then went to the Bereans, "they received the word with all eagerness, daily searching the Scriptures, whether those things were so. And many indeed of them believed."[30] Truly these Bereans earned the blessing imparted by Christ to St. Thomas: "Blessed are they that have *not* seen, but have believed." [31] It is time for those who believe themselves Catholic to likewise search the Scriptures, true Tradition and the Church's definition of what Christ revealed to His Church.

As Monsignor Joseph C. Fenton quoted above says, we find these truths in "every dogmatic definition, [which] is the statement of a truth given to the Church before the death of the last Apostle." The express acceptance of the body of truth within which the defined doctrine belongs constitutes the profession of faith necessary for membership in the true Church of Jesus Christ. In other words, these definitions are expressions of Divine and Catholic Faith, which demand our firm and irrevocable assent if we wish to retain membership in the Catholic Church. Without that assent, we can never be Catholic.

Monsignor Fenton held degrees in Sacred Theology and Canon Law from the University of Montreal and then pursued his doctoral studies at the Angelicum in Rome. He taught at several seminaries before becoming a professor of dogmatic theology at the Catholic University of America (CUA), where he taught for 25 years. He also was the editor of the CUA's *American Ecclesiastical Review*, contributing some 189 articles to the periodical. In addition, he wrote for several other Catholic publications and published several theological works. In 1954, he received the papal medal *Pro Ecclesia et Pontifice* and later served as one of Pope Pius XII's papal chamberlains. (A chamberlain is an honor bestowed by the Holy See on those who have so distinguished themselves in things Catholic, the Holy See deigns to pay tribute to them in a very public way.) According to one source, the good monsignor attacked the liberal reforms within the Church from the pulpit until his death in 1969. [32]

Monsignor Fenton will be quoted frequently throughout this work as one of the most knowledgeable theologians of his day, whose faithfulness to the Holy See was recognized and rewarded. His erudite defense of the Church's doctrine on religious liberty, and dogged combat against the Americanist C.I.A operative John Courtney Murray, reveals his love of the faith and intolerance of error. In this work he was assisted by his longtime mentor Father Francis J. Connell, CSsR., and Monsignor (Dr.) George Shea. And while some may object to his almost exclusive use as an expert in this work, [33] it should be remembered that as a scholastic, Fenton seldom relies on his own "take" on things, but rather demonstrates the pros and cons among scholastics writing throughout the centuries. As Reverend A. C. Cotter writes, "Sometimes formal certitude is had from the testimony of one witness; [if he] knows the truth, error on his part is excluded...and lying is excluded...The case becomes stronger, of course when the witness is officially appointed as such…" And so was Monsignor Fenton appointed by the Church to give witness to Her truth. He elaborates on what Reverend Finlay says above as follows:

> Now the body of Catholic doctrine is that deposit of truth which the Church finds in Sacred Scripture and in divine apostolic tradition, and which, by its solemn judgment or in its ordinary and universal teaching activity, it presents as having been revealed by God to be believed by all men with the assent of Divine faith. Since the Catholic Church has been divinely commissioned and empowered to teach God's revealed message infallibly and *adequately* to all men, it is evident that, at any time during the course of the Church's long history, the body of Catholic dogma has always been and will even be objectively identical with the original deposit of revelation as the Church originally received it from the apostles themselves. What the Church sets forth as God's revealed teaching is always exactly and substantially what the apostles told the Church to hold and teach as the divine message.
>
> Just as obviously, however, the form and language in which that teaching is expressed has developed over the course of the centuries. The doctrine the Church teaches is exactly the same as the doctrine the apostles gave the Church, but a great many of the words and the forms in which the Church asserts this body of truth are and manifestly must be quite distinct from those employed by the apostles themselves. The Church would not be an adequate and effective infallible teaching agency otherwise. Teaching necessarily involves a process of setting forth a body of truth, in the language and in the terms of the mentality of those who are to learn this truth. It implies *labor* in the direction of clarity and accuracy. It demands *effort* to prevent ambiguity and misunderstanding, and to answer the questions which occur to particular sets of learners. Unless the teacher of any body of doctrine is

able to answer queries about the content of his message, his efforts are valueless…

There is an observable modern tendency to understress or even to deny the fact that the original divine deposit of revealed truth communicated to the Church by the Apostles was and is a body of *intellectual* teaching. We are sometimes solicited to imagine that the original deposit did not consist in a set of explicitly revealed propositions at all, but rather in the Godhead or in the Person of Christ. In other words, we are told to believe that what the Apostles delivered to the Church at the beginning was a thing which could be described, *rather than a definite teaching about that reality*…If the deposit of revelation given to the Church by the Apostles had consisted in Our Lord Himself to the exclusion of a body of teaching, then obviously the subsequent dogmatic statements of the Church would be merely expressions of its experience of Christ.

Another aspect of this same highly objectionable tendency in modern writing manifests itself in a denial of the fact that the implicit content of the original deposit of revelation can be ascertained by way of theological reasoning. Not infrequently in these times we encounter a hint or statement to the effect that the choice of a new dogmatic formulae and the content of new dogmatic definitions has resulted from some sort of religious instinct [a false "Catholic sense"] within the Church, or even from the indwelling of the Holy Ghost within this society [outside the direction of the Roman Pontiff], to the exclusion of any properly logical evidence that the more recent propositions have been really though implicitly contained in the original apostolic deposit from the very beginning. The men who follow this trend are not slow to stigmatize the methods of their opponents as "theologistic" or intellectualistic.

The truth of the matter is, however, that the Church does not make dogmatic pronouncements apart from logically satisfactory evidence that the truth it asserts as divinely revealed actually forms a part of that body of revealed teaching which it received from the apostles and which it is commissioned and empowered infallibly to teach until the end of time. It remains perfectly true that the evidence upon which the Church acts may well be something which has escaped the notice of a good number of its own theologians and even of the best among its theologians. Such a case occurred when the dogma of Our Lady's Immaculate Conception was defined by Pope Pius IX. Nevertheless, the evidence was in existence and was examined by the Holy Father before he issued his definition. [34]

Monsignor Fenton here is explaining and synthesizing the 1869 teaching of the Vatican Council, Pope Pius IX's *Syllabus of Errors* and Pope St. Pius X's teaching on Modernism. Anyone who reads this excerpt carefully gains an all-inclusive idea of what Catholics are to believe and the popular (Modernist) errors of the day that they must avoid. Regardless of what non-Catholics might think about the Church, they cannot disagree that Catholics have an inalienable and inherent right to know and believe everything the Church teaches, exactly as She has always taught it. Nor can they impose on Catholics the secular belief that because so few today accept the Church for what She was and has always been, this somehow is an indication the Church has failed or was in error, based on the principles of modern democracy. For Pope Pius IX condemned this teaching in his *Syllabus of Errors* as follows: "Authority is nothing more than numbers and the sum of material strengths."

So what should the reader come away with from this chapter?

- The Church is a divine, not a human institution, founded by Christ.
- The Church's true head is Christ. His unchangeable truths, taught while on earth, are only preserved, safeguarded and their true interpretation proclaimed by the men he left on earth as His Vicars.

- These men rule in His stead, possessing His own authority.
- These unchangeable truths are called the Deposit of Faith, and the transmission of this Deposit ended with the death of the last Apostle.
- These teachings issue from Sacred Scripture and Divine Apostolic Tradition.
- *Every truth set forward distinctly in Holy Scripture, every article of the Catholic Creeds, and every solemn dogmatic definition of a Pope or of a General Council is included in the Deposit.*
- This Divine Deposit is a definitive body of intellectual teaching, not the apostolic *experience* of Christ's divinity.
- Christ promised St. Peter, and his successors, immunity from error when teaching the entire Church concerning matters of faith, morals (and discipline).

Having reviewed these explanations of how the Church is constituted will provide readers with a foundation for the next two sections on papal authority and scholasticism.[35]

Chapter I Endnotes

[1] St. Augustine of Hippo, *City of God*, Image Books, Doubleday and Co., Garden City, N.Y., 1958, 13, 34

[2] Douay-Rheims edition of Holy Scripture, Luke 10:16

[3] Rev. W. Wilmers, S. J., *Handbook of the Christian Religion*, Benziger Bros., New York, N.Y., Cincinnati, Ohio, Chicago, Ill., 1891, 70

[4] Douay-Rheims edition of Holy Scripture, John 26: 15, 17

[5] Ibid., Luke 10:16

[6] St. Francis de Sales, *The Catholic Controversy*, Burnes and Oates, Catholic Publication Society, New York, N.Y., 1886, 83-85

[7] Ibid., 295

[8] Msgr. Joseph C. Fenton, *The Concept of Sacred Theology,* Bruce Publishing Co., Milwaukee, Wis., 1941, 82-83

[9] Henry Denzinger, *The Sources of Catholic Dogma*, 30th Edition, Marian House, Powers Lake, N.D., 1957, The Vatican Council, Dogmatic Constitution Concerning the Catholic Faith, DZ 1787-1788

[10] Msgr. J.C. Fenton, *The American Ecclesiastical Review*, "The Necessity for the Definition of Papal Infallibility..." The Catholic University of America Press, Washington, D.C., December 1946

[11] Rev. Peter Finlay, S. J. *Divine Faith*, Longmans, Green and Co., New York, N.Y., 1917, Lecture III, 51

[12] Ibid., Lecture I

[13] Ibid., Lecture II, 23-26

[14] Ibid., Lecture II, 26-27

[15] Compiled by Rev. Berington and Rt. Rev. T.J. Capel, *The Faith of Catholics*, Fr. Pustet and Co., New York, N.Y. and Cincinnati, Ohio, 1885, 325, 402

[16] Rev. Peter Finlay, S. J. *Divine Faith*, Longmans, Green and Co., New York, N.Y., 1917, Lecture II, 27

[17] St. Vincent Lerins, *Commonitorium*, Tradibooks edition, p. 20

[18] Rev. Peter Finlay, S. J. *Divine Faith*, Longmans, Green and Co., New York, N.Y., 1917, Lecture XIII, p. 225-26; 230

[19] Henry Denzinger, *The Sources of Catholic Dogma*, 30th Edition, Marian House, Powers Lake, N.D., 1957, DZ 1705

[20] Ibid., DZ 1800

[21] Rev. Thomas Kinkead, Baltimore Catechism #3, Benziger Bros., New York, N.Y., Cincinnati, Ohio, Chicago, Ill., 1885; reprinted by TAN Books, Rockford, Illinois, 1974, Q. 520-522

[22] Henry Denzinger, *The Sources of Catholic Dogma*, 30th Edition, Marian House, Powers Lake, N.D., 1957, DZ 1686

[23] Rev. G. H. Guyot C.M., S.T.L., S.S. crB defines unity in his *Scriptural References for the Baltimore Catechism,* Joseph Wagner Inc., New York, N.Y., 1946, #156

[24] Rev. Peter Finlay, S. J. *Divine Faith*, Longmans, Green and Co., New York, N.Y., 1917, Lecture II, p. 24: additional quotes taken from Heb. 11: 32-38

[25] Douay-Rheims edition of Holy Scripture, Hebrews 11:1

[26] Rev. Patrick Madgett, *Christian Origins*, Vol. II, Xavier University, Cincinnati, Ohio, 1943, 184

[27] See Tradition, www.newadvent.org

[28] Rev. Peter Finlay, S. J. *Divine Faith*, Longmans, Green and Co., New York, N.Y.,1917, Lecture VII, 123

[29] Ibid., Lecture XI, p. 185

[30] Douay-Rheims edition of Holy Scripture, Acts 17: 11-12

[31] Ibid., John 20:28

[32] Patrick Carey, *Biographical Dictionary of Christian Theologians*, Westport, Conn., Greenwood Press, 2000

[33] It should be noted here that in no way can the use of Msgr. Fenton's works as a primary source for this work be considered as one-sided or detrimental to what is presented here. In his work *Logic* (1940, Fordham University Press), Rev. Joseph Walsh observes: "There is an old maxim: the student should be a persistent student of one book and the teacher the discriminating master of many. In reading books, the standing and reliability of the author should be considered, and discrimination used in reading the book," (p.113). Certainly there can be no doubt in the standing and reliability of Msgr. Fenton or his works. This author considers herself a perpetual student of the "one book" that represents the bulk of all the articles and books written by Msgr. Fenton. None today can consider themselves teachers or masters; we are allowed only to proceed from the approved works that existed prior to the death of Pope Pius XII, as well as those teachers and masters Msgr. Fenton personally endorsed and cited in his works.

[34] Msgr. Joseph Clifford Fenton, *The American Ecclesiastical Review*, The Catholic University of America Press, Washington, D.C., "The Necessity for the Definition of Papal Infallibility...", Dec. 1946

Chapter II —Papal Authority, a Summary
The Popes rule in Christ's stead; they constitute His living voice

A. The Church can never change

The doctrine of faith God revealed...has been entrusted as a divine deposit to the spouse of Christ to be faithfully guarded and infallibly interpreted. Hence, also, that understanding of Her sacred dogmas must be perpetually retained which Holy Mother Church has once declared; and there must never be recession from that meaning under the specious name of a deeper understanding...Let it be solely in its own genus, namely on the same dogma, with the same sense and the same understanding. [1]

The doctrines of faith are transmitted from the Apostles through the orthodox Fathers, always in the same sense and interpretation, even to us; and so I reject the heretical invention of the evolution of dogmas, passing from one meaning to another, different from that which the Church first had. [2]

Those genuine and clear [truths] which flow from the very pure fountains of the Scriptures cannot be disturbed by any arguments of misty subtlety. For this same norm of apostolic doctrine endures in the successors of him upon whom the Lord imposed the care of the whole sheepfold...
Let whoever, as the Apostle proclaimed, attempts to disseminate something other than what we have received be anathema [Gal. 1:8]. [3]

- No one forces anyone to become a Catholic or remain a Catholic.
- But as with any society or organization, those who join must agree to abide by the rules, attend liturgical celebrations (when available), meetings/functions and support the

organization. And the Catholic Church is not just any civic organization — Christ Himself founded it.

- Christ left a certain body of written and oral teachings with His Apostles to be preserved and safeguarded. He set a head over His Church beginning with St. Peter, (authority). He guaranteed St. Peter His own power, granting him the privilege of freedom from error in preserving, presenting and interpreting these teachings (infallibility). He promised St. Peter would have perpetual successors in his See possessing that same power, "*meant* to be exercised until the end of time." [4]
- Therefore, the doctrines asserted in pontifical definitions are not new teachings God has revealed to the Church, but "an unerring statement of matter conveyed in that same divine message which was complete with the death of the last Apostle." [5]
- We refer to Christ's teachings as revealed truth or Divine revelation, found in Scripture and Tradition. The Protestants refuse to acknowledge Tradition as a valid source of revelation, but the Chosen People carefully preserved and abided by their traditions as coming from God long before Christ was born.
- Christ is the Head of the Catholic Church. The popes constitute the Church's *visible* head on earth; they act in Christ's stead. The bishops, successors of the Apostles, receive their powers from Christ but can exercise them only under the direction and with the express permission of the Roman Pontiff. (See the encyclicals *Mystici Corporis Christi* and *Ad Sinarum Gentum*.)
- The pope can define matters of his own accord and does not need the consent of the bishops, far less the faithful (condemned as the Gallicanist heresy).
- The Pope exercises his infallibility whenever he speaks *ex cathedra* (from the chair):
  - in his capacity as ruler and teacher of the entire Church,
  - using his supreme apostolic authority,

-     to define a matter of faith and morals,
-     by issuing a certain and definitive judgment
-     and willing that this judgment be accepted as such by the universal Church. [6]

• Canon Law teaches:

By the Divine and Catholic faith must be believed all those truths which are contained in the Word of God as written or handed down to us, and which are, either by solemn pronouncement or by the ordinary and universal teaching of the Church, proposed for belief as divinely revealed truths. The solemn judgment in this matter is reserved to an Ecumenical Council and the Roman Pontiff speaking ex cathedra (that is, in his capacity of supreme teaching authority). No religious teaching is to be understood as dogmatically declared and defined unless such declaration or definition has clearly been made. [7]

• The Roman Pontiff utilizes all the resources of Sacred Theology and seeks the consultation of his advisors before arriving at his decisions, but is not, strictly speaking, required to do so.
• In exercising his infallibility, the Holy Father can either define a doctrine concerning faith or morals positively to be believed by all the faithful, or condemn certain teachings as heretical, which all the faithful must accept as condemned and avoid.
• Decisions concerning certain disciplinary matters also are to be considered binding papal decrees.

The pastors and faithful…are bound by the duty of hierarchical subordination and true obedience, not only in things which pertain to faith and morals *but also in those which pertain to the discipline and government of the Church*…If anyone says that the Roman Pontiff has only the office of inspection or direction, but not the full and supreme power of jurisdiction over the universal Church, not only in things which pertain to faith and morals *but also in those which pertain to the discipline and government of the Church*...let him be anathema. [8]

- *Ex cathedra* pronouncements can be solemn pronouncements, such as the definitions of the Immaculate Conception and the Assumption, or the canonization of saints, or they can be weighty documents issued by the pope as mentioned above; all are binding on the faithful. [9]
- Since the publication of *Humani Generis* by Pope Pius XII in August 1950, it is without doubt the pope can deliver definitive statements using his supreme apostolic authority even in his ordinary magisterium, i.e., encyclicals and simple allocutions. This was first affirmed by the Vatican Council, where it states:

By Divine and Catholic faith *all* those things must be believed which are contained in the written word of God and in tradition, and those things which are proposed by the Church, either in a solemn pronouncement or in Her ordinary and universal teaching power, to be believed as divinely revealed. [10]

Monsignor J. C. Fenton comments:

Documents...promptly entered into the *Acta* of the Holy Father are thus indirectly sent, as normative documents, to the entire world...Those allocutions and other papal instructions, which, although primarily directed to some individual or group of individuals, are then printed in the *Acta Apostolica Sedis* as directives valid for all of the Church Militant. We must not lose sight of the fact that, in the encyclical *Humani Generis*, the Holy Father made it clear that any doctrinal decision printed in the pontifical Acta must be accepted as normative by all theologians. This would apply to all decisions made in the course of the Sovereign Pontiff's ordinary magisterium. [11]

- Pope St. Pius X established the *Acta Apostolica Sedis* (AAS) in 1908 as a monthly publication (constitution *Promulgandi*; see Canon 9 of the 1917 Code of Canon Law, Revs. Woywod-Smith). This is confirmed by Henry Cardinal Manning, writing as an Archbishop:
  We have been told lately, by those who desire to hinder the definition of this doctrine by secular opposition rather than theological reason, that there are some twenty opinions as to the conditions required to authenticate an utterance of the Pontiff *ex cathedra*. I will therefore venture to affirm that no other conditions are required than this: *That the doctrinal acts be published by the Pontiff, as Universal Teacher, with the intention of requiring the assent of the Church.* [12]

Manning calls to witness Cardinal Franzelin as well on this definition of *ex cathedra*. These definitions are confirmed in *Humani Generis* by Pope Pius XII:

> But if the Supreme Pontiffs, in their acts, after due consideration, express an opinion on a hitherto controversial matter, it is clear to all that this matter, according to the mind and will of the same Pontiffs, cannot any longer be considered a question of free discussion among the theologians. [13]

- Pope Pius XII further wrote the following in *Humani Generis*, contradicting those who maintain there have been only 12 documents or fewer of *ex cathedra* pronouncements in the history of the Church:

> But if the Church does exercise this function of teaching as She often has through the centuries, either in the ordinary or the extraordinary way, it is clear how false is a procedure which would attempt to explain what is clear by means of what is obscure.

Some theologians, even after the issuance of *Humani Generis*, yet held that there are infallible statements issued by the Holy Father which cannot be classified as binding. Other theologians, including Monsignor Fenton, believe that there is no infallible hence binding teaching by the Roman Pontiffs that is not an *ex cathedra* pronouncement.

- According to Monsignor Fenton and other theologians, it doesn't really matter. If what the pope teaches is an infallible definition, it must be accepted with a firm and irrevocable assent. If what he teaches is only certain, it must be accepted with a firm but conditional mental consent. For as Fenton notes:

   Actually, there is no such thing as a teaching issued by the Holy Father in his capacity as the teacher and spiritual ruler of all followers of Jesus Christ which is other than authoritative. Our Lord did not teach in any way other than authoritatively, nor does his Vicar on earth when teaching in the name and by the authority of his Master. Every doctrine proposed by the Holy Father to the entire Church militant, is by that very fact, imposed upon all the faithful for their firm and sincere acceptance. [14]

- Here Monsignor Fenton quotes Pope Pius IX in *Tuas Libentur* (1863), where he defines:

   Catholic scholars must take cognizance of dogmas proposed by the *ordinary magisterium* as well as those defined 'by explicit decrees of the ecumenical councils or of the Roman Pontiff and of his See.' Furthermore, it calls attention to the fact that those scholars are bound in conscience to accept and to reverence the doctrinal decisions proposed by the Pontifical Congregations as well as those 'held by the common and constant consent of Catholics as theological truths and as conclusions which are so certain that, although opinions opposed to these points of doctrine cannot be characterized as heretical, they still deserve another theological censure.' [15]

- It is important to fully understand and internalize what Reverend Patrick Madgett teaches:

In analyzing the solemn teaching of the Church, we find that the Church exercises the fullness of Her infallible teaching authority to demand an irrevocable assent to matters which are not explicitly revealed, and apparently not even implicitly revealed. These definitions and decisions... of Ecclesiastical Faith are so intimately connected with faith that one could not deny them without implicitly denying some article of faith. They are to be believed...on the word of the Church, God's infallible teacher. [16]

See also the 1911 Catholic Encyclopedia article on infallibility under the subhead "Scope and Object of Infallibility." [17]

- *This same Catholic Encyclopedia* article also states:

Catholic theologians are agreed in recognizing the general principle that has just been stated, but it cannot be said that they are equally unanimous in regard to the concrete applications of this principle, [concerning those matters intimately connected to faith]. Yet it is generally held, and may be said to be theologically certain, (a) that what are technically described as 'theological conclusions,' i.e. inferences deduced from two premises, one of which is revealed and the other verified by reason, fall under the scope of the Church's infallible authority. (b) *It is also generally held, and rightly, that questions of dogmatic fact, in regard to which definite certainty is required for the safe custody and interpretation of revealed truth, may be determined infallibly by the Church. Such questions, for example, would be: whether a certain pope is legitimate,* or a certain council ecumenical, or whether objective heresy or error is taught in a certain book or other published document. [18]

Ordinarily, Monsignor Fenton writes, it is the teachings set forth by the Roman Rota as well as the Roman Congregations and the Pontifical Biblical Commission, approved by the Roman Pontiff, which command a sincere internal assent that is only conditional.

- Monsignor Fenton notes that *Tuas Libentur* speaks only of *dogmatic* definitions, taking "no cognizance whatsoever of any teaching emanating from the Sovereign Pontiff himself which could be designated as other than infallibly true." Fenton quotes also Pope Leo XIII in *Immortale Dei* (November 1885), detailing the duties of Catholics, as follows: "It is necessary to hold whatever the Roman Pontiffs have taught or are going to teach as accepted with firm assent and to profess these things openly whenever the occasion requires it," (DZ 1880). "It is necessary for all to stand by the Apostolic See and judge as it has judged." [19]

- Monsignor Fenton comments further that the faithful must accept *even the Holy Father's opinions about certain things as actual certainties*, because Pope Leo XIII has told them to do so. So basically, as any sincere Catholic knows, whatever the pope teaches must be taken as at least certain and beyond any doubt. Fenton assures the faithful that he speaks to them "in a way that they are able to understand," so they will know when something is only morally certain and when it is "definitive and morally irrevocable."

- While all theologians, Monsignor Fenton included, admit that not every doctrinal decision must be accepted as *ex cathedra*, the fact nevertheless remains that the pope's unqualified decisions on matters previously the subject of legitimate debate among theologians must be met with a firm, not conditional, acceptance by the faithful. This is true whether such a decision is made *directly* (addressed specifically to the entire Church), or *indirectly* (addressed to a certain group in way of an address or allocution, but printed in the *Acta*

Apostolica Sedis, which is published for the faithful of the entire world).

- *The Catholic Encyclopedia* article 'Discipline' states:

  It is the unanimous opinion of the theologians that discipline enjoys a negative, indirect infallibility, i.e., the Church can prescribe nothing that would be contrary to the natural or Divine law, nor prohibit anything that the natural or Divine law would exact. [20]

This is because nearly all of what we find in Canon Law is taken from the ecumenical councils and pontifical documents. "The Supreme Pontiff is *the chief, the ordinary and the undying source of canon law, both general and particular.*" [21]

- In *Humani Generis*, Pope Pius XII explained that no one may presume to replace with conjectural notions "the things composed through common effort by Catholic teachers over the course of the centuries...[by] men endowed with no common talent and holiness, working under the vigilant supervision of the holy magisterium." [22]
- The unanimous opinion of the Fathers on Holy Scripture also is considered a rule of faith. [23] Monsignor Fenton says it is considered identical to the interpretation of the Church itself. [24]
- In the matter of papal and other documents used as evidence, Canon Law comes into play. We find the following canons under the section of the Code entitled, "Title X: Of Proofs, Ch. V., documentary proof" in the section of Canon Law regarding trials and ecclesiastical courts. [25] (Some of the introductory canons of the Code also are cited here as a foundation for what follows.)

1. The pope and his successors hold the primacy of jurisdiction and are the supreme legislators in the Church. [26]

2. The pope, his successors, the Commission for the Authentic Interpretation of the Code, and the Sacred Congregations alone can authentically interpret Canon Law. [27]

3. Those decisions concerning the law entered into the *Acta Apostolica Sedis* are considered authentic (Canon 9; *Humani Generis*). They are binding in conscience and are to be held with at least a firm assent (Canon 9; also Monsignor J. C. Fenton, Reverend Billot, Reverend Connell, and others, as will be demonstrated below).

4. Canon 1812 §1 tells us that acts issuing from the Roman Pontiff and the Roman Curia during the exercise of their office are public documents accepted as proof in ecclesiastical courts. Canon 1816 states these public (papal) documents "prove the facts asserted." No further proof is required and the judge is forced to pronounce in favor of the party producing the document.

5. *"Proof to the contrary is not admitted against Letters of the Roman Pontiff bearing his signature."* [28] Documents entered into the *Acta Apostolic Sedis* do not need to be submitted in the original or be an authenticated copy (Canon 1819).

6. "In doubt about the validity of a positive law, the law is presumed to be valid for the sake of the common good and to preserve the certain right of authority." [29]

7. Any true doubt of law is referred to Canon 18, which requires those maintaining the doubt to consult the text and context of the words of the law. If they remain doubtful, then parallel passages of the Code, the end and circumstances of the law, and the mind of the lawgiver are to be consulted.

B. Integral truth or no truth

Progressivism vs. Integralism

The situation prior to the death of Pope Pius XII has often been described as a Machiavellian battle waged by two opposing "forces" in the Church — liberal progressivism (the new theology) and "restorationist" integralism (a return to the pre-1959 Church). In reality, the conflict was between heresy and orthodoxy, as explained by Pope St. Pius X in his condemnation of the Modernists, *Pascendi Dominici Gregis*, (DZ 2071, et al). There he exposes the Modernist conception of an "evolution" of the Church occurring through the interplay of Tradition as a conserving force and another force, tending to progress. According to them, it is Tradition which holds together the Church, *and religious authority which must protect Tradition.* [30] The Modernists believed the laity must advocate for progress as their consciences dictate and a compromise must be reached with authority (shades of Lefebvrism, as we shall see below).

It is common today to find authors attempting to depict widespread apostasy during the 20th century as a mere, albeit "diabolic," watering down of doctrine. When these authors describe change in terms of a struggle between progressive and conservative forces, they imply their acceptance, either knowingly or unknowingly, of the same erroneous notion underlying the Communist worldview: dialectical materialism, which understands change to occur through a process by which a "synthesis" is achieved between "thesis" and "antithesis," with each successive "synthesis," in turn, becoming the next "thesis" in an endless progression or evolution.

As it happens, Modernists in the 1940s and 1950s (who believed in the necessity of change through this dialectical process) routinely applied the label "integralist" to anyone who did not accept the tenets of liberal democracy. The term was also applied to orthodox theologians who reacted against the novelties proposed by the new theologians, who complacently accepted the orthodox reaction as part of the necessary process of doctrinal "evolution." Eventually, with the Cinderella-story "success" of the new theologians at the false Vatican 2 council, the term "integralism" came to be associated with an aberration of the religious "right" that is just as dangerous to orthodox Christianity as Modernism itself.

It is interesting to note that in this doctrinal warfare, both sides had to be managed and properly channeled in order to demonize "integralism" later. After Vatican 2, integralism found its supposed outlet in "Traditionalism," but the adherence to dogmas essential to the true meaning of the word was missing in Traditional practice. At best, Traditionalism evinces a selective adherence to some dogmas only, at the expense of minimizing or ignoring others. Furthermore, the desire of Traditionalist laity and their vagrant clergy for the Sacraments in the context of the Latin Tridentine is just fine with the Modernists. After all, Traditionalists operate outside of authority and in contradiction of its established norms, and therefore pose no threat. In the end, all will be reunited and allowed to follow their own preferences.

Contrary to what some Traditionalists believe today (as a direct result of doctrinal warfare inroads), integralism is actually a *deterrent* to modernism, not an equally dangerous aberration of the religious "right." Monsignor Joseph C. Fenton explains:

> [The Catholic unfamiliar with modernism] might possibly come to the dangerously false conclusion that modernism and integralism, as we know them, are two contrary false doctrines, one, as it were to the left, and the other to the right, of genuine Catholic teaching. Nothing, of course, could be farther from the truth. Modernism, in the technical language of Catholic doctrine, is the name applied to the definite series of errors condemned in the decree Lamentabili Sane Exitu, the encyclical Pascendi Dominici Gregis, and in the motu proprio Sacra Antistitum. Pope Pius X spoke of Modernism as the 'conglomeration of all heresies.' Integralism, on the other hand, is essentially the teaching or the attitude of those who worked for the presentation of an integral Catholicism, of Catholic dogma set forth accurately and in its entirety. Most frequently the name of integralism was applied to the doctrine and the

viewpoint of those Catholic writers who entered into controversy against the modernists during the first decade of the present century. Understood in this fashion, integralism was nothing else than the contradiction of heretical modernism. It was thus basically only the exposition of Catholic truth. [31]

In a later article on integralism, Monsignor Fenton reviews Reverend Yves Congar's comments concerning Catholic integralists in his book *The Church*. According to Fenton, Congar describes integralists as those who "proceed from an attitude of the right," which stresses "the determination of things by way of authority...It is instinctively for what is done and defined, and what has only to be imposed and received." Fenton comments:

> The religious proposition of the integralists is also represented as characterized by a rigidity of doctrine. All that this expression would seem to mean is a resistance to any teaching which the integralist regards as involving a change in Catholic doctrine. Certainly there can be little to stigmatize in this attitude. And just as certainly the designation of the activity of the integralists under these terms makes it difficult to see how Fr. Congar can believe that theirs is not a primarily doctrinal position. [32]

And here Fenton reminds Congar that it was these very integralists who fought the Modernists in Pope St. Pius X's time.

True and false Integralism

As many are only beginning to understand, the Church is a body in need of a true Head. The systematic dismembering of that Body can be attributed to the *nouvelle theologiens* (new theologians) in the Church, authors of the interpretive theory regarding jurisdiction. Modernists in disguise, liberalized Catholics embraced these men as the means of bringing doctrine into sync with "the times." But as Pope St. Pius X taught: "I sincerely hold that the doctrine of faith was handed down to us from the apostles through the orthodox

Fathers *always in the same sense and interpretation, even to us; and so I entirely reject the heretical invention of the evolution of dogmas, passing from one meaning to another, different from that which the Church first had...* " [33]

The history of this subject carries us back to the pontificate of Pope St. Pius X and his condemnation of the Modernists. At that time, a society was set up under which Modernists would be actively pursued and called out, in order to purge the Church of this heresy. It was called the *Sodalitum Pianum*, and its operations were highly controversial. In his *The Life of Pope Benedict XV*, Walter H. Peters explains how the activities of the *Sodalitum* became a matter of concern and why.

Peters alleges that the *Sodalitum* operated under code names and often in secrecy. (This charge was never proven, as he later notes.) Its manner of gathering evidence was not always fair to the accused, being taken out of context or not taken from a truly representative sample of writings. Peters cites claims made at the time that some of these writings were even falsified or invented in an unholy zeal to hunt these Modernists down. They were unfairly circulated then without qualification and the authors whose works were condemned were thus falsely maligned. At the same time, other ecclesiastics and theologians were defending Pope St. Pius X's teachings in *Lamentabili* and *Pascendi*, "an exposition of Catholic truth [expressed] in the framework of a very conservative orthodoxy. In itself this was most laudable. They called themselves 'integral Catholics' or 'Catholic integralists.'" However, their political views, Peters says, quoting Monsignor Fenton, "were unfortunate [and] the men who supported them brought a certain amount of discredit upon their doctrinal attitudes, [causing] the name of integralism to be stretched to cover fields quite distinct from that it originally served to designate." [34] In France it became *Action Francaise*, later condemned by Pope Pius XI.

The problem with the false integralism engaged in by these men was that a) routine practices were passed off as tradition, b) Catholic thought was impeded and legitimate opinions impugned, and c) those promoting this false integralism refused to separate pure doctrine from those commentaries written in bygone ages which imposed upon this doctrine conformity with the thought of a past epoch. Regarding (a), custom and tradition are not to be confused: A practice can become routine for a time only to be later reformed and prohibited by a future Roman Pontiff. Such was the case regarding laypersons carrying communion to the sick in the early ages and nominating candidates for bishop, to mention only a few. Concerning (b), those engaging in theological discussions about matters not yet defined by the Roman Pontiff were characterized as disobedient or even lacking in faith. And in (c), the doctrines were not rightly separated from their past applications to be applied to new situations. This is reminiscent of people who insist, for example, that all must follow the laws of the Church and not teach because only the hierarchy may do so. True, when legitimate authority exists to rule the Church. But Pope Pius XII has empowered Catholics to teach and preach in the absence of the hierarchy, [35] because, as scholasticism teaches, a law that is impossible of observance, whose purpose no longer can be fulfilled, ceases to exist.

Enter onto the scene Pope Benedict XV, who surveyed the matter and decided that measures must be taken to rein in the *Sodalitum* and prevent those who might be mistaken (but were otherwise loyal Catholics) from being treated unfairly. His encyclical could be addressed to Traditionalists of all varieties — including certain "stay-at-home Catholics" — for it condemns many "false integralists" still at work today.

> 22. The enemies of God and of the Church are perfectly well aware that any internal quarrel amongst Catholics is a real victory for them. Hence it is their usual practice when they see Catholics strongly united, to endeavor by cleverly sowing the seeds of discord, to break up that union. And would that the result had not frequently justified their hopes, to the great detriment of the interests of religion! Hence, therefore, whenever legitimate authority has once given a clear command, let no one transgress that command, because it does not happen to commend itself to him...Again, let no private individual, whether in books or

in the press, or in public speeches, take upon himself the position of an authoritative teacher in the Church. All know to whom the teaching authority of the Church has been given by God: he, then, possesses a perfect right to speak as he wishes and when he thinks it opportune. The duty of others is to hearken to him reverently when he speaks and to carry out what he says.

23. As regards matters in which without harm to faith or discipline — in the absence of any authoritative intervention of the Apostolic See — there is room for divergent opinions, it is clearly the right of everyone to express and defend his own opinion. But in such discussions no expressions should be used which might constitute serious breaches of charity; let each one freely defend his own opinion, but let it be done with due moderation, so that no one should consider himself entitled to affix on those who merely do not agree with his ideas the stigma of disloyalty to faith or to discipline.

24. It is, moreover, Our will that Catholics should abstain from certain appellations which have recently been brought into use to distinguish one group of Catholics from another. They are to be avoided not only as "profane novelties of words," out of harmony with both truth and justice, but also because they give rise to great trouble and confusion among Catholics. Such is the nature of Catholicism that it does not admit of more or less, but must be held as a whole or as a whole rejected, (Athanasian Creed)... There is no need of adding any qualifying terms to the profession of Catholicism: it is quite enough for each one to proclaim 'Christian is my name and Catholic my surname,' only let him endeavour to be in reality what he calls himself.

25. Besides, the Church demands from those who have devoted themselves to furthering her interests, something very different from the dwelling upon profitless questions; she demands that they should devote the whole of their energy to preserve the faith intact and unsullied by any

breath of error, and follow most closely him whom Christ has appointed to be the guardian and interpreter of the truth. [36]

Finally, a December 20, 1949 instruction on ecumenism issued by the Holy Office summarizes the Church's true teaching on integralism for Catholics as follows:

> Therefore, the *whole* and *entire* Catholic doctrine is to be presented and explained: by no means is it permitted to pass over in silence or to veil in ambiguous terms the Catholic truth regarding the nature and way of justification, the constitution of the Church, the primacy of jurisdiction of the Roman Pontiff, and the only true union by the return of the dissidents to the one, true Church of Christ." [37]

It is precisely the constitution of the Church and primacy of the Roman Pontiff that Traditionalists unbelievably misinterpret and ignore. They just as surely practice ecumenism as the false church in Rome practices it, no matter how loudly they may condemn this heresy.

"New theologians" and the jurisdiction controversy
A prime example of this practice by the new theologians of adapting dogma to suit "the times" or the "needs of the people" is seen in Reverend Francis Miaskiewicz's Canon Law thesis below, where he goes into the problems surrounding the interpretive and ignorance theories and explains why they were not tenable, even then. He refutes the canonist Reverend James Kelly for his erroneous views on common error or the "interpretative theory" as regards supplied jurisdiction. Kelly himself cites the Jesuit canonists Wernz-Vidal as sharing his opinion (although Miaskiewicz says Wernz-Vidal do not share Kelly's opinion), and the canon law commentary written by these two Jesuits is favored by a good number of Traditionalists. Miaskiewicz writes:

Once there was a *public fact* that could lead others into error, [some theologians teach] common error is *already* present ... [This] reflects an attempt on their part to close a gap in logic without the aid of a logical connecting link," (pg. 139). *"If any and all jurisdictional activity is to be considered as valid because of the verification of common ignorance, what jurisdictional act could ever be considered as invalid?* (p. 155). The difficulties of the interpretive theory are difficulties resulting from *an attempt to break away from a traditionally accepted doctrine.* They are difficulties which border closer and closer upon pure absurdity according as the individual authors venture to reduce common error to greater and greater insignificance. And it must be said that for such veering away from the traditional concept no limit can properly be set, precisely because it seems that *the interpretive school has substituted its PERSONAL FEELING of how they would want the law to be interpreted* for the ordinary legal and objective norms which the law maintains must be followed... [38]

As will be duly noted below, it is precisely the ignorance of Traditionalists that these Modernists fed upon so eagerly, and nothing is more indicative of the Modernist mindset than their reliance on *funny internal feelings* versus clear facts and traditional Church teaching as the basis for their own opinions and conclusions.

C. What if one denies an infallible truth of faith?

A denial of such a truth would constitute heresy. Reverend Adolphe Tanquerey, whose works were used as seminary texts internationally for decades, teaches:

Apostates, heretics and schismatics incur, on the ordinary conditions of full guilt, knowledge, etc., an excommunication specially reserved to the Holy See...All theologians teach that *publicly known heretics,* that those *who belong to a heterodox sect through public profession, or those who refuse the infallible teaching of the authority of the Church*, are excluded from the body of the Church, *even if their heresy is only material heresy.* [39]

As Monsignor Fenton notes regarding the works of Tanquerey:

> "If the theses taught by Tanquerey were opposed to those of 'the most authentic Catholic tradition of all ages,' then thousands of priests, educated during the first part of the twentieth century were being led into error by the men whom Our Lord had constituted as the guardians of His revealed message. [40]

In this Fenton only reiterates the words of Pope Pius XII in *Humani Generis*:

> The things that have been composed through the common effort of Catholic teachers over the centuries are certainly not based on [a] weak foundation. These things are based on principles and notions deduced from a true knowledge of created things. [41]

Quoted below is a good definition of heresy from Reverend Michael Muller's work: *The Catholic Dogma:*

> Now, to show plainly and understand well his grave errors, we must state clearly the point in question. This point is: — 'Out[side] of the Roman Catholic Church there is no salvation.' Heretics are out of the Roman Catholic Church; therefore, if they die as heretics, they are lost forever.

> Here the question arises — Who is a heretic?

> The word "heretic" is derived from the Greek and means to choose or adhere to a certain thing. Hence a baptized person, professing Christianity, and choosing for himself what to believe and what not to believe as he pleases, in obstinate opposition to any particular truth which he knows is taught by the Catholic Church as a truth revealed by God, is a heretic.

To make a person guilty of the sin of heresy, three things are required:

- He must be baptized and profess Christianity. This distinguishes him from a Jew and idolater;

- *He must refuse to believe a truth revealed by God, and taught by the Church as so revealed;*

- He must obstinately adhere to error, preferring his own private judgment in matters of faith and morals to the infallible teaching of the Catholic Church. Hence it follows that the following persons are guilty of the sin of heresy:

  1. All those baptized persons who profess Christianity and obstinately reject a truth revealed by God and taught by the Church as so revealed;

  2. Those who embrace an opinion contrary to faith, maintain it obstinately, and refuse to submit to the authority of the Catholic Church;

  3. Those who willfully doubt the truth of an article of faith, for, by such a willful doubt, they actually question God's knowledge and truth, and to do this is to be guilty of heresy;

  4. Those who know the Catholic Church to be the only true Church, but do not embrace her faith;
  5. *Those who could know the Church, if they would candidly search, but who, through indifference and other culpable motives, neglect to do so and*

6. Those Anglicans who know the true Church, but do not become Roman Catholics, thinking that they approach very near the Catholic Church, because their prayers and ceremonies are like many prayers and ceremonies of the Catholic Church, and because their creed is the Apostles' Creed. These are heretics in principle, for *the real character of rank heresy, says St. Thomas Aquinas, consists in want of submission to the divine teaching authority in the Head of the Church.*

Heresy, therefore, is a corruption of the true faith. This corruption, says St. Thomas Aquinas, takes place either by altering truths which constitute the principal articles of faith, or by denying obstinately those which result therefrom. But, as the error of a geometrician does not affect the principles of geometry, so is the error of a person which does not affect the fundamental truths of faith, no real heresy.

Should a person have embraced an opinion which is contrary to faith, without knowing that it is opposed to faith, he is, in this case, no heretic, if he is disposed to renounce his error as soon as he comes to know the truth. *But it is false to say that only those truths are of faith which have been defined by the Church, and that therefore he only is a heretic who denies a defined truth,*" (end of Reverend Muller's quote). [42]

Note that Reverend Muller emphasizes corruption of the faith as the cause of man's loss of eternal salvation. He also teaches those who do not search to discover the truth and especially those who fail to recognize the Roman Pontiff and submit to him are guilty of "rank" heresy. Reverends McHugh and Callan comment further on what St. Thomas Aquinas teaches, explaining in the Preface to their work that the teachings they present are "based on the principles, teachings and method of St. Thomas Aquinas, while supplementing that great Doctor of the Church from the best modern authorities." In brief, they state:

1. Heresy is defined as "an error manifestly opposed to faith and assented to obstinately by one who had sincerely embraced the faith of Christ, (meaning only catechumens and the baptized, who after baptism have retained the name of Christian – Canon 1325 §2)," (#826, 827).

2. Heresy is particularly opposed to divine and Catholic faith (#826b). Divine and Catholic faith is belief in a revealed truth that has been proposed as such by the Church *either solemnly or ordinarily*, including dogmas contained in the Creeds *and definitions of the Popes and Councils*, (#755b).

3. By "opposed to faith" means any judgment which, according to the logical rules of opposition between propositions, *is irreconcilable with the truth of a formula of dogma or a censure for heresy*. Example: The Council of Trent teaches that, "All sins committed after Baptism can be forgiven in the Sacrament of Penance." It would be heretical, therefore, to hold that no sins committed after Baptism can be pardoned in the Sacrament of Penance, or that some sins cannot be absolved, #826c).

4. One who declares *in public addresses or articles* that he agrees with Modernism, *or who joins openly an heretical sect*...is a public heretic, (#828c).

5. Heresy is not formal unless one pertinaciously rejects the truth, knowing his error and consenting to it. *But for formal heresy it is not required that a person give his consent out of malice, or that he continue in obstinate rejection for a long time*, or that he refuses to heed admonitions given him. *Pertinacity here means true consent to recognized error, and this can...be given in an instant and does not presuppose an admonition disregarded*," (#829b).

6. Circumstances that aggravate the sin include: *its external and manifest nature, manifestation to a large number of people joined with apostasy and adhesion to an heretical sect, denying several articles or defined truths at the same time,* (#832b&c).
7. Faith…must be firm assent, excluding doubt, (#840). Real, voluntary but *especially positive doubt, deliberately entertained with full knowledge, also constitutes heresy,* (nos. 841-45). [43]Agreeing with Reverend Muller, Monsignor J. C. Fenton explains:

The statement stigmatized as heretical need not necessarily have been the contradiction to a formula previously defined in the solemn magisterium of the Church. *It suffices that the teaching denied in the condemned proposition should have been that which was proposed as divinely revealed in the ordinary magisterium.* [44]

Also, the Very Reverend H. A. Ayrinhac, S.S, D.D., D.C.L., observed:

Schism is formally assimilated now to heresy and apostasy in every respect," (Canon 2314). "Apostates, heretics and schismatics incur, on the ordinary conditions of full guilt, knowledge, etc.., an excommunication specially reserved to the Holy See… [45]

Under Canon 1325, Catholics are bound to expose and refute even the *appearance* of heresy or cooperate in heresy itself. To deny that the laity is obligated to do this is a denial of the Church's teaching that Canon Law is negatively infallible, for the laws of the Church could never order Catholics to perform an act contrary to the Catholic Faith.

Those accusing laypersons of heresy, especially today, when all must be done in a lay capacity, should be very careful in approaching this task (privately at the outset), even if what they believe to be heresy is publicly stated. Those who consider themselves members of the Mystical Body must first obey Canon Law to claim such membership according to Pope Pius XII in *Mystici Corporis*. For the

Church has always taught that Canon Law is indirectly infallible, issuing as it does from the teachings of popes and councils.

The Canon Laws [46] regarding the judging of heresy teach:

1) The Church does not favor hasty and rash use of extremely severe penalties and censures (Canon 2214).

2) "In penalties, the milder interpretation is to be applied"

3) The immutability of the offense depends on the evil will of the delinquent…All causes which increase, diminish or destroy the evil will or culpability automatically increase, diminish or destroy the immutability of the offense (Canon 2199).

4) In the application of penalties, attention must be paid to the subject matter and gravity of a law, *age, knowledge, education, sex, state of life and mental condition of the person [allegedly committing the offense], the purpose intended…and whether the delinquent repented of his misdeed* (Canon 2218).

5) *No penalty can be inflicted unless it is proved that the offense has been committed* (Canon 2233), and it is not a matter in the cases presenting today of "inflicting" penalties, but rather in noting that such penalties have automatically (*ipso facto*) been incurred. This is usually accomplished by citing the teaching contradicted and the alleged delinquent's contradiction of that teaching, side by side. (See the example given in no. 3 above, under the quotations from Revs. McHugh and Callan.)

How many does it take to make an offense *public* when one is speaking of a small community? In their commentary on Canon 2197, canonists Reverends Woywod-Smith state: "It is maintained by many canonists that *at least six persons* in a small town or community must know of [an] offense before it can be called public." Canon 2197, no. 1 states: "An offense is public if it has already been divulged...or if...*its divulgation may and must be prudently considered possible.*" Therefore, even in small private groups, online or any individuals gathering together for study or prayer, heresy can become public rather quickly. Those who study the faith must be careful to understand it from the best pre-1959 approved sources and be willing to correct themselves immediately if it can be demonstrated they have erred in any matter regarding faith or morals. Otherwise, they fall under censure for at least material heresy.

D. Father Frederick Faber on heresy
The beloved author Reverend Frederick Faber outlines the mindset the truly devout Catholic should possess concerning heresy:

> If we hated sin as we ought to hate it, purely, keenly, manfully, we should do more penance, we should inflict more self-punishment, we should sorrow for our sins more abidingly. *Then, again, the crowning disloyalty to God is heresy.* It is the sin of sins, the very loathsomest of things which God looks down upon in this malignant world. Yet how little do we understand of its excessive hatefulness! It is the polluting of God's truth, which is the worst of all impurities.
>
> Yet how light we make of it! We look at it, and are calm. We touch it and do not shudder. We mix with it, and have no fear. We see it touch holy things, and we have no sense of sacrilege. We breathe its odor, and show no signs of detestation or disgust. Some of us affect its friendship; *and some even extenuate its guilt. We do not love God enough to be angry for His glory. We do not love men enough to be charitably truthful for their souls.*
>
> *Having lost the touch, the taste, the sight, and all the senses of heavenly-mindedness, we can dwell amidst this odious plague, in imperturbable tranquility, reconciled to its foulness, not without some boastful professions of liberal admiration, perhaps even with a solicitous show of tolerant sympathies.*

Why are we so far below the old saints, and even the modern apostles of these latter times, in the abundance of our conversations? *Because we have not the antique sternness?* We want the old Church-spirit, the old ecclesiastical genius. *Our charity is untruthful, because it is not severe; and it is unpersuasive, because it is untruthful.*

We lack devotion to truth as truth, as God's truth. Our zeal for souls is puny, because we have no zeal for God's honor. *We act as if God were complimented by conversions, instead of trembling souls rescued by a stretch of mercy.*

We tell men half the truth, the half that best suits our own pusillanimity and their conceit; and then we wonder that so few are converted, and that of those few so many apostatize.

We are so weak as to be surprised that our half-truth has not succeeded so well as God's whole truth. *Where there is no hatred of heresy, there is no holiness.* [47]

A man, who might be an apostle, *becomes a fester in the Church* for the want of this righteous indignation. (Father Faber, *The Precious Blood*, all emphases added).

Conclusion

The truths taught by the Catholic Church are never-changing and sacred; they emanate from the teachings of Christ Himself. As Monsignor Fenton observed above,

Actually, there is no such thing as a teaching issued by the Holy Father in his capacity as the teacher and spiritual ruler of all followers of Jesus Christ which is other than authoritative. Our Lord did not teach in any way other than authoritatively, nor does his Vicar on earth when teaching in the name and by the authority of his Master. Every doctrine proposed by the Holy Father to the entire Church militant, is by that very fact, imposed upon all the faithful for their firm and sincere acceptance.

Papal documents and conciliar decrees comprise most of Canon Law. Therefore these laws also are binding on the faithful and obedience to them is necessary for Church membership.

Papal teaching and the teachings of the ecumenical councils is not to be taken in piecemeal fashion but as an undivided and integral whole. Pope Pius XII proclaimed Catholic truth is to be taught "whole and entire." The *nouvelle theolgiens* pretended there could be alternative ways to perceive the truth and this destroys all unity. As Henry Cardinal Manning wrote:

Truth goes before unity. Where unity is divided, truth cannot be. Unity before truth is deception. Unity without truth is indifference or unbelief. Truth before unity is the law, principle and safeguard of unity. [48]

To sum up the preceding sections:
- Those who do not follow the teachings of the Roman Pontiffs, even if expressed only as opinions or certainties, are not true Catholics.
- Those who refuse to obey the infallible teachings of the Roman Pontiffs, even if such a teaching is not classified as a divine truth, commit heresy and lose their membership in the Church.
- The denial of papal authority is "the rankest of all heresies," as all must be subject to the Roman Pontiff in order to attain salvation, (DZ 469).
- This is true because the Pope represents Christ on earth when defining matters of faith and morals, meaning that the denial of papal authority is tantamount to denying Christ.
- If those who refer to themselves as Catholic refuse to obey these infallible decrees, they cease to be Catholic.

To better understand the subject of heresy and answer any remaining questions, please visit www.betrayedcatholics.com, under the "Free Content" section regarding heresy. Also see the articles on material heresy in the "Recent Articles" section, same page. Later in this work, readers will see how Catholics exiting the church in Rome following the changes imposed by the false Vatican 2 council denied a positive definition promulgated for belief by the (only) Vatican Council and a legitimate pontiff. Also later in this work, readers will learn how those who remained with the church in Rome following the election of John 23 embraced the heresies of ecumenism, Freemasonry and Communism, all formally condemned by the Roman Pontiffs as heretical on numerous occasions. But first, in the following two chapters, the infallibility of disciplinary decrees will be demonstrated, a truth effectively eclipsed both by the Novus Ordo (NO) Church and especially by Traditionalists. The false representation of disciplinary decrees as non-binding by these two groups has been used to water down and even eliminate doctrinal teaching in order to destroy the authority of the continual magisterium.

Chapter II Endnotes

[1] Henry Denzinger, *The Sources of Catholic Dogma*, 30th Edition, Marian House, Powers Lake, N. D., 1957, The Vatican Council, DZ 1800

[2] Ibid., DZ 2145

[3] Ibid., Pope St. Simplicius, Jan. 10, 476, DZ 160

[4] Msgr. Joseph C. Fenton, *The Concept of Sacred Theology*, Bruce Publishing Co., Milwaukee, Wis., 1941, 118

[5] Ibid., 116

[6] Henry Denzinger, *The Sources of Catholic Dogma*, 30th Edition, Marian House, Powers Lake, N. D., 1957, Vatican Council, DZ 1839

[7] Revs. Stanislaus Woywod and Callistus Smith, *A Practical Commentary on the Code of Canon Law*, Joseph F. Wagner, Inc., New York and London, 1957, Can. 1323

[8] Henry Denzinger, *The Sources of Catholic Dogma*, 30th Edition, Marian House, Powers Lake, N. D., 1957, The Vatican Council, DZ 1827, 1831. Because there has been so much confusion on this teaching, it will be addressed separately in the next chapter

[9] Pope Pius XII, *Humani Generis*, Aug. 12, 1950, N.C.W.C translation, Daughters of St. Paul

[10] Henry Denzinger, *The Sources of Catholic Dogma*, 30th Edition, Marian House, Powers Lake, N. D., 1957, DZ 1792

[11] Msgr. Joseph C. Fenton, *American Ecclesiastical Review,* The Catholic University of America Press, Washington, D.C., "Infallibility in the Encyclicals," March 1953

[12] Archbishop Henry Edward Manning, *The Ecumenical Councils and the Infallibility of the Roman Pontiff, A Pastoral Letter to the Clergy*, Longmans and Green, London, 1869, 61

[13] Henry Denzinger, *The Sources of Catholic Dogma*, 30th Edition, Marian House, Powers Lake, N. D., 1957, DZ 2313

[14] Msgr. Joseph C. Fenton, *American Ecclesiastical Review*, The Catholic University of America Press, Washington, D.C., "Infallibility in the Encyclicals," Pt. II, May 1953

[15] (Ibid.; Pius IX quotes from DZ 1683).

[16] Rev. Patrick Madgett, *Christian Origins*, Vol. II, Xavier University, Cincinnati, Ohio, 1943, 190

[17] Article on infallibility under the subhead "Scope and Object of Infallibility," http://www.newadvent.org/cathen/07790a.htm

[18] Ibid.

[19] Msgr. Joseph C. Fenton, *American Ecclesiastical Review,* The Catholic University of America Press, Washington, D.C., "Infallibility in the Encyclicals," March 1953

[20] http://www.newadvent.org/cathen/05030a.htm

[21] Rev. Amleto Cicognani, *Canon Law*, Dolphin Press, Philadelphia, Penn., 1935, 70

[22] Pope Pius XII, *Humani Generis*, Aug. 12, 1950, N.C.W.C translation, Daughters of St. Paul, para. 17

[23] Henry Denzinger, *The Sources of Catholic Dogma*, 30th Edition, Marian House, Powers Lake, N. D., 1957, Council of Trent, DZ 786

[24] Msgr. Joseph C. Fenton, *The Concept of Sacred Theology,* Bruce Publishing Co., Milwaukee, Wis., 1941, 135

[25] All canons referred to in this section quoted from Revs. Stanislaus Woywod and Callistus Smith, *A Practical Commentary on the Code of Canon Law*, Joseph F. Wagner, Inc., New York, N.Y. and London, 1957
[26] Henry Denzinger, *The Sources of Catholic Dogma*, 30th Edition, Marian House, Powers Lake, N. D., 1957, The Vatican Council, DZ 1823, 1831
[27] Rev. Amleto Cicognani, *Canon Law*, Dolphin Press, Philadelphia, 1935, Can. 17
[28] Ibid., 626, ft. note
[29] Taught by St. Alphonsus Liguori as quoted by Revs. McHugh and Callan; quote from Rev. Bernard Wuellner, *Principles of Scholastic Theology*, Loyola University Press, Chicago, 1956, no. 67, 20
[30] Rev. J. B. Lemius, O.M.I, *A Catechism of Modernism* (St. Pius X's *Pascendi Dominici Gregis* in question form, originally published in 1908), reprinted by TAN Books, Rockford Ill., 1981, *75*
[31] Rev. Joseph C. Fenton, *The American Ecclesiastical Review,* The Catholic University of America Press, Washington, D.C., "Two Currents in Contemporary Catholic Thought," 1948 article reprinted by The Catholic Archives
[32] Rev. Joseph C. Fenton, *The American Ecclesiastical Review*, The Catholic University of America Press, Washington, D.C., "Integralism and Reform," February 1952
[33] Henry Denzinger, *The Sources of Catholic Dogma*, 30th Edition, Marian House, Powers Lake, N. D., 1957, oath against Modernism, DZ 2145
[34] Walter H. Peters, *The Life of Pope Benedict XV*, Bruce Publishing Co., Milwaukee, Wis., 1959, 48
[35] "The Mission of the Catholic Woman," Sept. 29, 1957, Summer Edition, *The Pope Speaks Magazine*, Joseph Sprug editor, Washington, D.C: "The initiative of the lay apostolate is perfectly justified *even without a prior explicit 'mission' from the hierarchy*...Personal initiative plays a great part in protecting the faith and Catholic life, especially in countries were contact with the hierarchy are difficult or practically impossible. *In such circumstances, the Christians upon whom this task falls must, with God's grace, assume all their responsibilities*...Even so, nothing can be undertaken against the explicit or implicit will of the Church, or contrary in any way to the rules of faith or morals, or ecclesiastical discipline."
[36] *Ad Beatissimi Apostolorum*, Nov. 1, 1914, http://w2.vatican.va/content/benedict-xv/en/encyclicals/documents/hf_ben-xv_enc_01111914_ad-beatissimi-apostolorum.html

[37] *Canon Law Digest*, Vol. III, T. Lincoln Bouscaren, S. J., LL.B., S.T.D., Bruce Publishing Co., Milwaukee, Wis., 1954, 536-542, emphasis is in the original; AAS 42-142

[38] Rev. Francis Miaskiewicz, *Supplied Jurisdiction According to Canon 209*, Catholic University of America, Washington, D.C., 1940, 142-143

[39] Rev. Adolphe Tanquerey, *Manual of Dogmatic Theology*, translated by Rt. Rev. Msgr. John J. Byrnes, Desclee Co., New York, N.Y., Tournai, Paris, Rome, 1959, Vol. I, 160

[40] Rev. Joseph C. Fenton, *The American Ecclesiastical Review*, The Catholic University of America Press, Washington, D.C., "The Teaching of the Theological Manuals," April 1963

[41] See footnote 20, this section

[42] Rev. Michael Muller, C.S.S.R., *The Catholic Dogma: Extra Ecclesiam Nullus Omnino Salvatur*, Benziger Brothers, New York, N.Y., (Printers to the Holy Apostolic See),1888, 33-34.

[43] Revs. John A McHugh and Charles J. Callan, *Moral Theology, A Complete Course*, Joseph Wagner, New York, N. Y., 1930, Vol. 1

[44] Msgr. Joseph C. Fenton, *The Concept of Sacred Theology*, Bruce Publishing Co., Milwaukee, Wis., 1941, 120-121

[45] Very Rev. H. A. Ayrinhac, S.S, D.D., D.C.L., *Penal Legislation in the New Code of Canon Law*, (Benziger Bros., New York, N.Y., 1920, 192-93, no. 200-201

[46] All canons referred to in this section quoted from Revs. Stanislaus Woywod and Callistus Smith, *A Practical Commentary on the Code of Canon Law*, Joseph F. Wagner, Inc., New York and London, 1957

[47] Fr. Frederick William Faber, D.D., *The Precious Blood*, 22nd American Edition, John Murphy Company, Baltimore Md. and New York, N.Y., 352-353

[48] Henry Cardinal Manning, *The True Story of the Vatican Council*, American Council on Economics and Society, Fraser, MI, 1996 (reprint of 1870 original), 183.

Chapter III — The Popes Speak on Discipline
Papal disciplinary decrees are often infallible

A. Decrees up to the Vatican Council

Remembering what has been presented above, that the popes also can be infallible in matters of discipline, it is now time to examine the proofs from the popes themselves on this subject. Anytime the popes deal with matters involving heresy, apostasy or schism — and denial of the pope's authority to discipline and command is a heresy, which foments schism — then their decisions on such matters fall under the scope of infallibility, as explained in Chapter II. Here we are not just speaking of the *indirect infallibility* papal laws enjoy when retained and reiterated in the Code of Canon Law, but rather those laws that clearly are infallible for their condemnation of some heresy, apostasy or schism.

Pope Pius VI, *Charitas* (On the constitutional bishops illegitimately created in France):

> 10. For the right of ordaining bishops belongs only to the Apostolic See, as the Council of Trent declares; it cannot be assumed by any bishop or metropolitan without obliging Us to declare schismatic both those who ordain and those who are ordained, *thus invalidating their future actions.*
>
> 24. "We therefore severely forbid the said Expilly and the other wickedly elected and illicitly consecrated men, under this punishment of suspension, to assume episcopal jurisdiction or any other authority for the guidance of souls since they have never received it. They must not grant dimissorial letters for ordinations. Nor must they appoint, depute, or confirm pastors, vicars, missionaries, helpers, functionaries, ministers, or others, whatever their title, for the care of souls and the administration of the Sacraments *under pretext of any necessity whatsoever... For We declare and proclaim publicly that all their dimissorial letters and deputations or confirmations, past and future,*

*as well as all their rash proceedings and their
consequences, are utterly void and without force...*"
26. We *command* those who have been or are to be elected,
to behave in no way as archbishops, bishops, parish priests,
or vicars nor to call themselves by the name of any
cathedral or parochial church, nor to assume any
jurisdiction, authority, or faculty for the care of souls *under
the penalty of suspension and invalidity.* [1]

Pope Gregory XVI, *Mirari Vos*:

It would be beyond any doubt blameworthy and entirely
contrary to the respect with which the laws of the Church
should be received by a senseless aberration to find fault
with the regulation of morals, and the laws of the Church
and her ministers; or *to speak of this discipline* as opposed
to certain principles of the natural law, or to present it as
defective, imperfect, and subject to civil authority.[2]

And from the same Pope in *Quo Graviora*:

Are they not trying, moreover, to make of the Church
something human; are they not openly diminishing her
infallible authority and the divine power which guides her,
in holding that her *present discipline* is subject to decay, to
weakness, and to other failures of the same nature, and in
imagining that it contains many elements which are not
only useless but even prejudicial to the well-being of the
Catholic religion? [3]

The Vatican Council:

The pastors and faithful...are bound by the duty of
hierarchical subordination and true obedience, not only in
things which pertain to faith and morals *but also in those
which pertain to the discipline and government of the
Church*...If anyone says that the Roman Pontiff has only
the office of inspection or direction, but not the full and
supreme power of jurisdiction over the universal Church,

not only in things which pertain to faith and morals *but also in those which pertain to the discipline and government of the Church...* let him be anathema. [4]

B. Decrees by Pope Pius IX

Following the Vatican Council, we hear these absolutely definitive words from Pope Pius IX in *Quartus Supra* (1873):

> But the neo-schismatics say that it was not a case of doctrine *but of discipline*, so the name and prerogatives of Catholics cannot be denied to those who object. Our Constitution *Reversurus*, published on July 12, 1867, answers this objection. We do not doubt that you know well how vain and worthless this evasion is. *For the Catholic Church has always regarded as schismatic those who obstinately oppose the lawful prelates of the Church and in particular, the chief shepherd of all. Schismatics avoid carrying out their orders* and even deny their very rank. Since the Armenian faction of Constantinople is like this, *they are schismatics even if they had not yet been condemned as such by Apostolic authority.* For the Church consists of the people in union with the priest, and the flock following its shepherd. Consequently, the bishop is in the Church and the Church in the bishop, and whoever is not with the bishop is not in the Church. Furthermore, as Our predecessor Pius VI warned in his Apostolic letter condemning the civil constitution of the clergy in France, *discipline is often so closely related to doctrine and has such a great influence on its preservation and its purity, that the sacred councils have not hesitated to cut off from the Church by their anathema those who have infringed its discipline.*

> But the neo-schismatics have gone further, since 'every schism fabricates a heresy for itself to justify its withdrawal from the Church.' Indeed, they have even accused this Apostolic See as well, *as if We had exceeded the limits of Our power in commanding that certain points of discipline were to be observed...* Nor can the Eastern

Churches preserve communion and unity of faith with Us without being subject to the Apostolic power in matters of discipline. *Now such teaching is not only heretical after the definitions and declarations of the Ecumenical Council of the Vatican on the nature and reasons for the primacy of the Sovereign Pontiff, but it has always been considered to be such and has been abhorred by the Catholic Church.* It is for this reason that the bishops of the Ecumenical Council of Chalcedon openly declared the supreme authority of the Apostolic See in their proceedings; then they humbly requested Our predecessor, St. Leo, to sanction and confirm their decrees, even those which concerned discipline. [5]

Pope Pius IX, *Quae in Patriarchatu* (1876):

In fact, Venerable Brothers and beloved Sons, it is a question of recognizing the power (of this See), even over your churches, not merely in what pertains to faith, but also in what concerns discipline. *He who would deny this is a heretic*; he who recognizes this and obstinately refuses to obey is worthy of anathema." [6]

It is for this reason that Henry Cardinal Manning stated:

The Pope, speaking *ex cathedra*, is infallible; this definition, by retrospective action, makes all Pontifical acts infallible, such as the Bull *Unam Sanctam*, the Bull *Unigenitus*, the Bull *Auctorum Fidei*, [which] were held to be infallible as fully before the Vatican Council as now...*The doctrine of the Church does not determine the doctrine of the Primacy, but the doctrine of the Primacy does precisely determine the doctrine of the Church.* [7]

This only repeats Pope Pius IX's teaching in *Quartus Supra*. And to the list of bulls provided by Cardinal Manning could be added also Pope Pius IX's own *Syllabus of Errors*, so many times dismissed as disciplinary and non-infallible.

One cannot underestimate the importance of what Pope Pius IX says above. For he warns those who avoid carrying out the orders of the Roman Pontiffs, and these orders are not a few, that they become heretics and schismatics by so doing, per the teachings of the Vatican Council. This pertains to disciplinary decrees as well as those decrees on matters of faith and morals. This is the very legislator of the Vatican Council who infallibly promoted these teachings. No one can contest his teaching on this matter, and yet sadly this does not stop many from doing so.

Etsi Multa (on the Old Catholics)

In *Quartus Supra*, Pope Pius IX clearly states that even without a formal declaration, the Armenians resisting the authority of the papal see were considered schismatics. Likewise, all who "*avoid carrying out their orders*" (those of the Roman Pontiffs) are reckoned as schismatics. A similar declaration in *Etsi Multa* on the Old Catholics proves that the judgment expressed in *Quartus Supra* is not just a "one-off" for a particular situation, but an application of general disciplinary consequences of resisting papal authority:

> 24. But these…heretical sects…*have wished to create a hierarchy also for themselves*…They have chosen and set up *a pseudo-bishop*, a certain notorious apostate from the Catholic faith, Joseph Humbert Reinkens…For his consecration they have had refuge to those very Jansenists of Utrecht, whom they themselves, before they separated from the Church, considered as heretics and schismatics, as do all other Catholics. However, [Reinkens] dares to say that he is a bishop…and is proposed to all his subjects as a lawful bishop. But as even the rudiments of Catholic faith declare, *no one can be considered a bishop who is not linked in communion of faith and love with Peter, upon whom is built the Church of Christ; who does not adhere to the supreme Pastor to whom the sheep of Christ are committed to be pastured; and who is not bound to the confirmer of fraternity which is in the world.* And indeed 'the Lord spoke to Peter; to one person therefore, so that

He might found unity from one'…He never gave, except through him, what He did not deny to the others.' *Hence it is from this Apostolic See, where blessed Peter 'lives and presides and grants the truth of faith to those seeking it,' that the rights of venerable communion flow to all…*
25. Therefore the holy martyr Cyprian, writing about schism, denied to the pseudo-bishop Novatian even the title of Christian, on the grounds that he was cut off and separated from the Church of Christ. 'Whoever he is,' he says, 'and whatever sort he is, he is not a Christian who is not in the Church of Christ.' … Since by Christ one Church was founded divided into many members throughout the world, so likewise one episcopate, diffused in the harmonious multiplicity of many bishops. Subsequent to the teaching of God and the conjoined unity of the Catholic Church, *he attempts to build a human church. Therefore, he who does not retain unity of spirit nor communion of peace and thus separates himself from the bond of the Church and the college of the priesthood cannot have the power nor the honor of a bishop because he kept not the unity or the peace of the episcopacy.*

Excommunication
26. …Therefore following the custom and example of Our Predecessors and of holy legislation, by the power granted to Us from heaven, *We declare the election of the said Joseph Humbert Reinkens, performed against the sanctions of the holy canons to be illicit, null, and void. We furthermore declare his consecration sacrilegious.* Therefore, by the authority of Almighty God, We excommunicate and hold as anathema Joseph Humbert himself and all those who attempted to choose him, and who aided in his sacrilegious consecration. *We additionally excommunicate whoever has adhered to them and belonging to their party has furnished help, favor, aid, or consent.* We declare, proclaim, and *command* that they are separated from the communion of the Church. *They are to be considered among those with whom all faithful Christians are forbidden by the Apostle to associate and*

have social exchange to such an extent that, as he plainly states, they may not even be greeted. [8] (This is the equivalent of excommunication as a *vitandus* heretic.)

Graves Ac Diurturnae

In this March 23, 1875 letter to Swiss bishops Pope Pius IX again addresses the same Old Catholics, who have taken up residence in Switzerland:

Deceit a characteristic of schism

2. They repeatedly state openly that they do not in the least reject the Catholic Church and its visible head but rather that they are zealous for the purity of Catholic doctrine declaring that they are the heirs of the ancient faith and the only true Catholics. But in fact, they refuse to acknowledge all the divine prerogatives of the vicar of Christ on earth and do not submit to His supreme magisterium...that sect should be considered as schismatics and separated from communion with the Church.

4. The faithful...should totally shun their religious celebrations, their buildings, and their chairs of pestilence which they have with impunity established to transmit the sacred teachings. They should shun their writings and all contact with them. They should not have any dealings or meetings with usurping priests and apostates from the faith who dare to exercise the duties of an ecclesiastical minister without possessing a legitimate mission or any jurisdiction. They should avoid them as strangers and thieves who come only to steal, slay, and destroy.

Obedience to lawful authority

7. Dearly beloved faithful children who live in Switzerland...*We urge you with the greatest enthusiasm to give support strongly and constantly to your legitimate shepherds who have received a legitimate mission from this Apostolic See.* [9]

C. Modern popes on discipline

In the decrees of Pope Pius IX, we see the pontiff elaborating upon and interpreting the infallible teachings of the Vatican Council. This more than demonstrates that no one can possibly question disciplinary decrees issued by the Roman Pontiff on the grounds that such decrees are not authoritative and do not bind. How could it be otherwise, when they merely apply infallible general principles to particular historical situations (one regarding the Armenian situation in 1873 and two addressing the Old Catholics, spawned by heretics rejecting the Vatican Council decisions, just as the French Church rejected the condemnation of Gallicanism and the Jansenists under Pope Pius VI). In several different encyclicals and constitutions, he defends the pope's infallibility in disciplinary matters, teaching in *Quartus Supra* (1873):

> Nor can the Eastern Churches preserve communion and unity of faith with Us without being subject to the Apostolic power in matters of discipline... Teaching of this kind is heretical, and not just since the definition of the power and nature of the papal primacy was determined by the ecumenical Vatican Council: the Catholic Church has always considered it such and abhorred it. Furthermore, as Our predecessor Pius VI warned in his Apostolic letter condemning the civil constitution of the clergy in France (Charitas), discipline is often so closely related to doctrine and has such a great influence on its preservation and its purity, that the sacred councils have not hesitated to cut off from the Church by their anathema those who have infringed its discipline.

And again, Pope Pius IX writes in *Quae in Patriarchatu* (1876):

> In fact, Venerable Brothers and beloved Sons, it is a question of recognizing the
> power (of this See), even over your churches, not merely in what pertains to faith, but also in what concerns discipline. He who would deny this is a heretic;

he who recognizes this and obstinately refuses to obey is worthy of anathema.

Pope St. Pius X was once again forced to address this error in *Pascendi Dominici Gregis,* against the Modernists. He states that the intent of these heretics was to reform all aspects of the Church, but especially *"its disciplinary and dogmatic parts"* [10] (Notice that the two are mentioned as joined together, on a par, by this pope. It was not a coincidence that the vigilance councils founded by Pope St. Pius X to combat Modernism, before their abolition by Pope Benedict XV, helped finger one Angelo Roncalli, later to become John 23, as a suspected Modernist.

Pope Pius XII, *Ad Apostolorum Principis* (1958):
> We are aware that those who belittle obedience in order to justify themselves with regard to those functions which they have unrighteously assumed defend their position by recalling a usage which prevailed in ages past. Yet everyone sees that all ecclesiastical discipline is overthrown if it is in any way lawful for one to restore arrangements which are no longer valid because the supreme authority of the Church long ago decreed otherwise. In no sense do they excuse their way of acting by appealing to another custom, and they indisputably prove that they follow this line deliberately in order to escape from the discipline which now prevails and which they ought to be obeying...The faithful are bound by the duty of hierarchical subordination and true obedience not only in matters which pertain to faith and morals, but also in those which concern the discipline and government of the Church. [11]

The Catholic Encyclopedia article "Discipline" explains the separation between the disciplinary act itself and its source:

> From the disciplinary infallibility of the Church, correctly understood as an indirect consequence of her doctrinal infallibility, it follows that she cannot be rightly accused of

introducing into her discipline anything opposed to the Divine law; the most remarkable instance of this being the suppression of the chalice in the Communion of the laity. This has often been violently attacked as contrary to the Gospel. Concerning it the Council of Constance (1415) declared (Sess. XIII): 'The claim that it is sacrilegious or illicit to observe this custom or law [Communion under one kind] must be regarded as erroneous, and those who obstinately affirm it must be cast aside as heretics.' [12]

So those rejecting disciplinary decrees not specifically dealing with heresy *per se* as non-infallible are condemned (at least in the case above) as heretics! This is *not* because what they are denying (the suppression of the chalice) is heretical in and of itself, but because *it is heresy* to accuse the Church of introducing into her discipline anything contrary to faith: *that* is the distinction made in the above paragraph. The opinion, generally admitted by theologians, that the Church is infallible in her approbation of religious orders, must be interpreted in the same sense — it means that in her regulation of a manner of life destined to provide for the practice of the evangelical counsels, she cannot come into conflict with these counsels as received from Christ together with the rest of the Gospel revelation. *What this tells us is that while the disciplinary decree itself may not be positively infallible, but only indirectly so, to refuse to recognize it is to deny the authority of the magisterium which ultimately has promulgated it.*

The decrees cited above, especially those promulgated by Pope Pius IX, only strengthen the teaching of the Vatican Council concerning disciplinary matters. Do these papal decrees condemn any errors opposed to Divine faith? They most certainly do, since all these errors contradict the truth that Christ imparted supreme power and jurisdiction to St. Peter and his successors, a truth solemnly defined by the Church as revealed by the Vatican Council. Canon 1325 states that Catholics commit heresy whenever they implicitly or explicitly, by their "silence, subterfuge or manner of acting," deny a truth "proposed for belief by the divine and Catholic faith." By their manner of acting, Traditionalists today contradict the teaching of the

Vatican Council, for they function and have functioned for decades *as* the Catholic Church, claiming to possess all four of Her marks. And yet their church does not obey papal teaching in matters of divine faith. But most importantly, it is operating outside the jurisdiction of the Roman Pontiff and is therefore lacking a true head... This is forbidden by Pope Pius XII's constitution *Vacantis Apostolicae Sedis,* [13] where Pius XII exercises his supreme authority in stating that nothing can be done during an interregnum, even by the cardinals, which would usurp the jurisdiction of the Roman Pontiff (see Ch. V, D). Whatever acts are done in defiance of all his warnings are null and void, the Pope teaches.

D. Who qualify as *vitandus*?

Clearly, in *Etsi Multa* above, Pope Pius IX characterizes any who would receive episcopal consecration at the hands of schismatics without a papal mandate (papal permission for bishops to consecrate) as *vitandus. Vitandus* is the most severe form of excommunication; those who incur it cannot be associated with and are barred from administering the Sacraments except in danger of death. Canon 2258 states no one is to be considered a *vitandus* unless the Holy See publicly excommunicates the individual *by name* and orders him/her to be avoided. So while no one is saying that those operating without a papal mandate have all been excommunicated by name as *vitandus*, since no pope exists to pronounce this excommunication, they are to be avoided for other reasons that make all their ministrations of no effect.

Therefore, they are only *equivalent* to *vitandus*, using the rules of Canon Law concerning similar cases, and only the judgment of a true pope can determine their status. Catholics should avoid them not because they have been declared by Pope Pius IX as *vitandus, but because he has defined that they are not bishops*, simply because they are not in communion with the Holy See. So such men, who even if they *were* validly ordained priests by a true bishop in communion with the Church, could not exercise their orders. This is true because the bishop ordaining them did not possess — and could not possess, without being in communion with the Roman Pontiff —

the jurisdiction necessary to call them as priests to the ministry and train them, far less validly ordain them. (See Ch. XI, C below.)

The hue and cry of Traditionalist "clerics" has ever been that they are obligated by virtue of their "ordination" to provide the sacraments, in order to "save souls." Not only is this contrary to the teachings of Pope St. Pius X, but Canon Law teaches that even if validly ordained, only *legitimate* pastors are obligated to administer sacraments, and then only to those faithful who *legitimately* request them (Canon 467). The laity has the right to receive the Sacraments from *legitimate* pastors but only "according to the rules of ecclesiastical discipline" (Canon 682). "*It is forbidden to administer the Sacraments to heretics or schismatics, even though they err in good faith,* unless they have first renounced their errors and been reconciled with the Church" (Canon 731). Nor in making these requests do Catholics even realize they are inviting these men to commit grave mortal sin, in which they cooperate. During an interregnum, the hierarchy are forbidden to posit acts contrary to papal law or usurp the power of the papacy by presuming permission to consecrate, establishing churches and seminaries, and in essence carrying on as though the pope need not even exist (see *Vacantis Apostolicae Sedis* link in endnotes, no. 13).

What does Father Thomas Kinkead tell American Catholics about lawful pastors in the catechism used in Catholic schools in the 1940s and 1950s, before the decline of the Church? In Question 115 of his *An Explanation of the Baltimore Catechism*, no. 4, Father Kinkead writes:

> Q. What is the Church? A. The Church is the congregation of all those who profess the faith of Christ, partake of the same sacraments, *and are governed by their lawful pastors under one visible head.*

Those who are not legitimate pastors have *no right* to govern the faithful. The Baltimore Council's approved Catechism no. 3 for adults, also written by Father Kinkead, tells us in the answer to Question 494 that lawful pastors are "those in the Church who have been appointed by *lawful authority* and who have therefore a right to rule us." [14] Note that this says nothing of the supposedly "validly" consecrated bishops who have created these priests; it mentions only *lawful* authority. *Lawful* bishops, papal teaching proves, are only those consecrated with papal mandate following their appointment by the pope. For as Reverend Thomas Cox taught, "Even if valid orders exist, where jurisdiction is lacking there is no real apostolicity. *Schism, as well as heresy, destroys apostolic succession.*" [15]

In his manual written for religious congregations and Catholic institutions of higher learning, seminary professor Reverend John Joseph McVey wrote in 1926:

> Q. 60: Who after the pope are lawful pastors of the Church?
> A. The bishops who have been canonically instituted, i.e., who have received from the Sovereign Pontiff a diocese to govern.
>
> Q. 73: Why is it not sufficient to be a bishop or priest in order to be a lawful pastor?
> A. Because a bishop must also be sent into a diocese by the Pope, and a priest must be sent into a parish by the bishop. In other words, a pastor must have not only the power of order, but also *the power of jurisdiction*, (emphasis by McVey).
>
> Q. 77: How is the power of jurisdiction communicated?
> A. Priests receive their jurisdiction from the bishop of the diocese; bishops receive theirs from the pope; and the Pope holds jurisdiction from Jesus Christ. A bishop who did not receive his spiritual powers from the Pope and a pastor who did not receive his from a lawful bishop, would be *an intruder or schismatic*" (emphasis, McVey). [16]

So not only are Traditionalist "priests" and "bishops" illicitly ordained and consecrated, without a true pope they possess no jurisdiction whatsoever. And, as the *Catholic Encyclopedia* articles "Apostolic Succession" and "Apostolicity" teach, no apostolic succession exists unless priests and bishops possess both orders *and* jurisdiction.

Pope Pius XII, by special precept, solidified Church teaching on this topic by declaring those who dare violate Canon 147 excommunicated *specialissimi modo* (in a special manner; absolution from the censure able to be removed only by the pope). In pronouncing this excommunication on behalf of the pope, the Sacred Congregation quotes DZ 967 to the effect that if anyone, including those who "assume office on their own authority, are all to be regarded not as ministers of Christ, but as thieves and robbers who have entered not by the door." Traditionalists say they do not claim to occupy any offices, but this will not save them. For the actual anathema states only that these men "come from a different source" and, as Trent explains, "by their own temerity [they] take these offices upon themselves." This excommunication is found mentioned in Reverends Woywod and Smith's commentary under Canon 2394.

In the *Canon Law Digest*, we find the following comment: "Excommunication *as vitandus* is inflicted for accepting office from lay authority." [17] This is exactly the penalty prescribed by Pope Pius VI in *Charitas* and Pope Pius IX against the Old Catholic "bishop" Reinken in *Etsi Multa*; and both these papal pronouncements are listed above as the old laws governing Canon 147. Are all laity following or aiding Traditionalists priests and bishops with donations and other assistance considered the equivalent of *vitandus?* Since they have been the victims of fraud, disinformation and actual brainwashing, they are probably laboring under censure (but not as *vitandus*), if for nothing else, *for failing to accept Pope Pius IX's pronouncement against the faithful on this and Pope Pius XII's determination of such priests as vitandus.* Those who presume to present and act as clerics, however, are certainly candidates for this title. Canon 2218 excuses (especially lay) offenders in certain cases where the person *has tried to repent and repair the damage*, having been caught in circumstances beyond his/her control and understanding. How many Traditionalists have left their sects to publicly condemn these sects and then make reparation? For unless they have done this, Canon Law says they cannot be readmitted to the Church (Canon 731).

In *Quartus Supra*, Pope Pius IX clearly states that even without a formal declaration, the Armenians resisting the authority of the papal see were considered schismatics. Likewise, all who "*avoid carrying out their orders*" (those of the Roman Pontiffs) are reckoned as schismatics. Even *tolerati* are not permitted to receive the Sacraments. According to the well-respected canonist, the Very Reverend H. A. Ayrinhac:

> Active participation in a divine office ought not to be permitted *to a vitandus, nor to a toleratus* after a condemnatory or declaratory sentence has been pronounced against him *or when his censure is publicly known*... Notoriety dispenses from declaratory sentence in the case of a *latae sententiae* sentence [and this is taken from Pope Paul IV's bull *Cum ex Apostolatus Officio*, defining heresy, apostasy and schism in the case of the hierarchy- Ed.]...To enforce even censures or irregularities in the external forum, notoriety of the guilt is required for a declaratory sentence. [18]

Those who take heresy seriously will realize that committing *communicatio in sacris* brings with it the vindicative penalty of infamy of law (an irregularity), which bars clergy and laity alike from functioning in any capacity whatsoever until the Roman Pontiff lifts the penalty.

Reverends Woywod and Smith explain the effects of infamy of law under Canon 2294 §1 [19]:

> A person who has incurred infamy of law is not only irregular, as declared by Canon 984 n. 5, but in addition, he is incapacitated from obtaining ecclesiastical benefices, pensions, offices and dignities, from performing legal ecclesiastical acts, from discharging any ecclesiastical right or duty, and must be restrained from the exercise of sacred functions of the ministry.

The authors continue under this same Canon:

> The person who has incurred...an infamy of law...cannot validly obtain ecclesiastical benefices, pensions, offices and dignities, nor can he validly exercise the rights connected with the same, nor perform a valid, legal ecclesiastical act. (According to Canon 2295: "Infamy of law ceases only on dispensation granted by the Apostolic See.")

Canon 2314 §1, 3 declares that those guilty of heresy, apostasy or schism also incur infamy *ipso facto*. When imposed in the form of a penalty attached to law, this sentence takes place immediately. In essence, this vindicative penalty is even more restrictive than *vitandus* excommunication, which would at least allow the *vitandus* to validly confer absolution and Extreme Unction (Canon 2261 § 3). This, however, is not possible today — for in allowing the *vitandus* to absolve, Canon Law was assuming the Pope would supply jurisdiction for this act; and today we have no true pope.

Conclusion

The teaching of the popes cited in this chapter further strengthens what was said in Chapter II. Not only what the continual magisterium teaches concerning faith and morals is to be held as infallible, but also those things regarding discipline, especially when the pontiffs are defining what is to be held as heresy and schism by the faithful. Only those who possess *lawful* authority are to be obeyed, and clearly this does not include those who have gone outside the channels of papal approval to obtain ordination and consecration, or to lay claim to an office to which they were not officially assigned by lawful authority. In fact, those who do such things are to be avoided by the faithful; and if the faithful associate with them in any way or appear to support them, then they too are considered heretics and/or schismatics.

Chapter III Endnotes

[1] http://www.papalencyclicals.net/Pius06/p6charit.htm
[2] http://www.papalencyclicals.net/Greg16/g16mirar.htm
[3] (http://www.papalencyclicals.net/Leo12/l12quogr.htm
[4] Henry Denzinger, *The Sources of Catholic Dogma*, 30th Edition, Marian House, Powers Lake, N. D., 1957, The Vatican Council, DZ 1827, 1831
[5] Pope Pius IX, *Quartus Supra*, http://www.papalencyclicals.net/Pius09/p9quartu.htm
[6] Pope Pius IX, *Quae in Patriarchatu September 1, 1876, to the clergy and faithful of the Chaldean Rite.* http://www.papalencyclicals.net/Pius09/p9quaein.htm
[7] Henry Cardinal Manning, *The Vatican Decrees in Their Bearing on Civil Allegiance*, The Catholic Publication Society, New York, N.Y., 1875, 20-21; 30-31
[8] http://www.papalencyclicals.net/Pius09/p9etsimu.htm
[9] http://www.papalencyclicals.net/Pius09/p9graves.htm
[10] http://w2.vatican.va/content/pius-x/en/encyclicals/documents/hf_p-x_enc_19070908_pascendi-dominici-gregis.html).
[11] (http://www.papalencyclicals.net/Pius12/P12APOST.HTM
[12] www.newadvent.org
[13] http://www.betrayedcatholics.com/free-content/reference-links/1-what-constitutes-the-papacy/apostolic-constitution-vacantis-apostolicae-sedis/
[14] Fr. Thomas Kinkead, *An Explanation of the Baltimore Catechism*, no. 4, 1921 reprint By TAN Books and Publishers, Rockford, Ill., 1978
[15] Rev. Thomas Cox, *Pillar and Ground of Truth*, 1900 (available through Amazon)
[16] Rev. John Joseph McVey, *Manual of Christian Doctrine*, Philadelphia, Penn., 1926,
[17] *Canon Law Digest*, Vol. III, T. Lincoln Bouscaren, S. J., S.T.D., L.L.B, Bruce Publishing Co., Milwaukee, Wis., 1954, under Can. 147
[18] Very Rev. H. A. Ayrinhac, S.S, D.D., D.C.L., *Penal Legislation in the New Code of Canon Law*, Benziger Bros., New York, N.Y., Cincinnati, Ohio, Chicago, Ill., 1920, pgs. 73, 75, 122; no. 58, 60, 115c
[19] All canons referred to in this section quoted from Revs. Stanislaus Woywod and Callistus Smith, *A Practical Commentary on the Code of Canon Law*, Joseph F. Wagner, Inc., New York and London, 1957

Chapter IV — The Perversion of Papal Disciplinary Decrees

Using canonical discipline to tear down doctrine

Owing to the inroads made by Gallicanism and Modernism, many Traditionalists attempt to escape the censures attached to disciplinary teachings, including censures a) issued by the Council of Trent for men acting in the place of clerics at the behest of or by the appointment of the people, minus any canonical mission; b) against bishops who fail to obtain the papal mandate for episcopal consecration; c) against those who attempt to usurp papal jurisdiction or transgress Canon Law during an interregnum, in violation of Pope Pius XII's *Vacantis Apostolicae Sedis*; and d) against those who question the Holy See's condemnation of the teachings of Reverend Leonard Feeney, as well as Pope Pius XII's excommunication of Father Feeney as detailed in the Holy Office's letter to Richard James Cardinal Cushing of Boston. Even if Pope Pius XII's excommunication of Father Feeney was for disciplinary reasons, it was an infallible act, officially entered into the *Acta Apostolica Sedis* (AAS, February 16, 1953 Volume XXXXV, p.100).

As will be seen below, those in the Novus Ordo believed that most disciplinary decrees were not infallible and as such did not require an irrevocable assent. This included bulls such as Pope Paul IV's *Cum ex Apostolatus Officio* and other documents disciplinary in nature. Soon Traditionalists believed the same. They conveniently forget that when Angelo Roncalli began his destruction of the Church, a revision of the Code of Canon Law was promised from the time he called the Council, even though it was not realized until Karol Wojtyla's (John Paul 2's) reign. C. Leroux writes:

> John XXIII's [Angelo Roncalli's] only preoccupation, apart from the opening of the Council, had been 'the adaptation of Canon Law to the needs of our times.' [He] announced (it), right at the beginning…the reform of Canon Law, that 'iron collar.' That loose-tongued Cardinal Tardini artlessly admitted, 'From now on, one can say that the principal goal

of the Council will be more particularly ecclesiastical jurisdiction, the renovation of the Code of Canon Law which might be altered, and then the whole gamut of the customs of Catholic life.'...*If one does not wish to subject oneself to divine institutions, the simplest answer is to transform the law...*In promising to modify [Canon Law] 'very shortly,' he reassured Canon Lawyers who might have raised objections in front of the upheavals which were going to affect not only the interior government of the Church and her doctrines, *but Her relations with Her implacable enemies such as the Jews and Freemasons.* [1]

A. A Modernist omits 'discipline' from an infallible pronouncement

Leroux also reports that in a 1961 communique concerning the coming Council, Franz Cardinal Koenig listed as one of the topics to be addressed "a reform of Canon Law, of the Index, and of penitential practices." Roncalli let it be assumed that all these things would be "set right" by the alteration of Canon Law. Montini relates that among the "innovations" to be expected following the Council was the reform of Canon Law. "The Pope himself already announced them when, in connection with the opening of the Council, he declared his intention of submitting to a general revision the entire code of canon law that Pope Benedict XV promulgated in 1917." [2] That revision would not occur until 1983, five years after the usurper John Paul 2's election. But essentially Traditionalists have gutted the law on their own authority. All are laboring under a grave misconception concerning the Church's true teaching on the subject of discipline. This topic has been shamefully confused even further by a misprint (?) in the 1957 edition of Henry Denzinger's *The Sources of Catholic Dogma*. In the Introduction to this edition, the 30th translator Roy Deffarari credits none other than Charles (Karl) Rahner, S. J., as responsible for "the 28th, 29th and 30th editions." This may well account for any discrepancies in these editions of Denzinger's work. The problem concerns an omission in a condemnation of various heresies under Pope Nicholas I by the Roman Council in 860 and 863 A.D. There Denzinger's printed:

> If anyone condemns dogmas, mandates, interdicts, sanctions or decrees, promulgated by the one presiding in the Apostolic See, for the Catholic Faith, for the correction of the faithful, for the emendation of criminals, either by an interdict of threatening or future ills, let him be anathema. [3]

Writing in 1875, Henry Cardinal Manning gives this rendition of the council's condemnation of that same error:

> Si quis dogmata, mandata, interdicta, sanctiones vel decreta, pro Catholica fide, *pro ecclesiastica disciplina*, pro correctione fidelium, pro emendatione scleratorum, vel interdictione imminentium vel futurorum malorum, a Sedis Apostolica Praeside salubriter promulgata contempserit,: Anathema sit." This is clearly an infallible proclamation, since to it is attached an anathema. [4]

Notice the italicized words above, clearly translated as "for ecclesiastical discipline," are omitted from Denzinger's translation. Nor can it be argued that a Pope and an ecumenical council erred, or that such teaching was later amended without denying the infallible teaching of the Church. In *Auctorum Fidei* Pope Pius VI condemned the following proposition (maintained by the Jansenists) as at least erroneous, dangerous and injurious to the Church, among other things: "In every article, that which pertains to faith and to the essence of religion must be distinguished from that which is proper to discipline." [5] Pope Pius VI taught: "As if the Church, which is ruled by the Spirit of God, could have established discipline which is not only useless and burdensome for Christian liberty but which is dangerous and harmful." [5]

Under Canon 2317, those clerics who teach condemned propositions are "barred from the ministry of preaching the Word of God and of hearing sacramental confessions, and from every other office of teaching, without prejudice to other penalties which the sentence of condemnation of the doctrine may perhaps have decreed." One of the sources for this Canon listed in Pietro Cardinal Gasparri's *Fontes* is none other than Pope Paul IV's *Cum ex*

Apostolatus Officio. And once the Vatican Council was held, Cardinal Manning teaches, *Auctorem Fidei* could formally be considered an infallible decree.

B. Professor Carlos Disandro on Church discipline

Dr. Carlos A. Disandro, a sedevacantist, was a professor at the University of La Plata prior to the collapse of the Peron government in Argentina. He also was a teacher at the Catholic University of Valparaiso. His 1979 work *Doctrinal Precisions* sheds much light even today on the current situation and how little things really have changed. But most importantly, his writings point out that the misunderstanding of the relationship between doctrine and discipline, begun at "Vatican 2" has continued to plague remnant Catholicism to this day. It had deepened the rift between the various Traditional sects even in Disandro's time to such an extent that discipline already was reduced to a matter of inexpert opinion in which everyone having access to a Canon Law book qualified as a "canonist," able to interpret the law or even to declare it to have ceased to apply. As a result, those laws issuing from the doctrinal authority of the Church were lost in the canonical shuffle, as Disandro ably points out in his *Doctrinal Precisions*. Disandro wrote that it is impossible that a bull for perpetuity such as *Cum ex Apostolatus Officio* or *Quo Primum* could "be abrogated and secondly, that a disciplinary code would be able to nullify as positive legislation of the Church a question which refers to the very heart of doctrine." He continues:

> Discipline thus would acquire primacy over doctrine, and there would be completed also, in a manner surreptitious but effective, one of the great longings of progressivism: to include all dispute, ancient and modern in the context of a disciplinary law. It is logical that the change in this would be able to bring about a change in doctrine, skillfully veiled by the operation of a subtle theological and semantic transference. Therefore, if even worship turns out to be a disciplinary matter (a certainty for Progressives), it does not seem that Paul VI would be unable to dictate, reform, annul, or confirm his Novus Ordo contrary to Tradition, *in*

> *the name of discipline.* Therefore, for the historicist, Judaeo-Christian mentality of progressivism, all the abolitions, immersions, and subtle changes took place in the proving ground of discipline, with the changes in Doctrine, as in an evolutionary process, transferring over and following consecutively. [Ed. note: In other words, change the discipline and the doctrine will change automatically.] In the Church, the *chain of Doctrine with discipline* follows the course of inviolable faith — of the Paradosis (Greek word for tradition, or handing down) of the Apostles — through whose care, vigilance and utterance the Pontificate exists...*It is the Montinian system of using the canonical discipline in order to tear down doctrines and Tradition*, a thing which is important because it uncovers the null character of such decisions and substitutions. [6]

Here we see described the very blueprint used by the V2 usurpers to destroy the Traditions of the Church, primarily the liturgy. But we also see that in order to arrive at the destruction of Tradition, authority — both doctrinal and disciplinary — must be attacked first. The weak link was discipline; none of the liberals and Modernist sympathizers wished to be the recipients of excommunications or warnings. Once their C.I.A. plants were in the Vatican, they simply failed to exercise this power to arrest liturgical renewal and ecumenism. The rest disintegrated of its own accord. This is the process Disandro observed and described. His critics were the SSPX, who openly and insistently have declared Pope Paul IV's *Cum ex Apostolatus Officio* a disciplinary decree, hence not infallible, and also have ignored the requirement for papal mandate in creating their clerics and jurisdiction in operating their chapels. That this was, from the beginning, a necessary part of the Traditionalist plan to keep its many fractured but related sects afloat was recognized by Disandro even at this early date.

Quoting a biographer of Pope St. Pius X, Disandro explains in his work how the codification of Canon Law was one of the first works Pius X embarked upon following his election.

"On March 19, 1904, he published the Motu Proprio, *Arduum Sane Munus*, establishing the group charged with the task of codification: a commission of cardinals presided over by the Pope himself. The opinions, editings and reworkings reached their definitive conclusions between the years 1912-14. When this global project was completed, copies were sent to all the bishops, to make the last pertinent modifications. In 1914 the war came, and Pius X died. Benedict XV completed and concluded the project. The Code was promulgated on May 27, 1917, with the Constitution *Providentissima Mater Ecclesiae*, in which Benedict XV renders pointed homage to his predecessor and makes very opportune reflections about the legislation of the Church, following the spirit of Pius X. And later, by the Motu Proprio *Cum Iuris Canonici*, Sept. 15, 1917, he instituted a commission of cardinals to authentically interpret the canons of the Code." Here he recognized again the fundamental authorship of Pius X, whose doctrine is, in reality, *the foundation of this discipline.*

It is no coincidence that the condemnations of the Modernists issued by Pope St. Pius X explained so well the contempt of the Modernists for Tradition, discipline and authority. For it was Pope St. Pius X himself who assisted the cardinals in maintaining the disciplinary traditions of the Church in codifying the sacred canons, an act that should convince one and all of the truly binding nature of the Code. As Disandro points out,

[In the Code] we find the Profession of the Catholic Faith, which is in substance a reiteration of the anti-Modernist oath. (ED. NOTE: This Profession is found in Cardinal Gasparri's Latin edition immediately preceding Canon 1.) The Bull of Paul IV is precisely on the level of the Profession of Faith, a level complementary and identical regardless of the passage of the centuries, because it also treats of the immutable apostolic tradition. Therefore, to affirm that the Code, in any of its chapters, canons, clauses, (explicitly or implicitly) considered the Bull to be abolished, would be to affirm that these very textual instances of the Code itself would be able to abolish some point of the profession of faith, which is the porch, that is the condition, for all the rest.

As will be explained in a later chapter, Disandro's conclusions were eventually confirmed following his death. For *Cum ex Apostolatus Officio* was not only the source for Canon 188 no. 4, but was retained as a source in the Code for numerous other canons, mainly those defining heresy. This qualifies the Bull for retention in the Code under Canon 6 no. 6.

C. V2 called *Quo Primum* a disciplinary decree

All know that this bull written by Pope St. Pius V forever preserved the Roman liturgy (Latin Mass) as the form of worship to be followed absolutely in the Church. By calling it a disciplinary decree and dismissing disciplinary decrees as non-binding, not only can the enemies of the Church dismiss the Mass and justify the institution of the Novus Ordo Missae; they can also dismiss other "disciplinary" works as nonbinding that help Catholics understand what has happened to the Church.

Quo Primum, infallible by virtue of the Vatican Council declaration, reads:

> These men consulted the works of ancient and approved authors concerning the same sacred rites; and thus they have *restored the Missal itself to the original form and rite of the holy Fathers."* [Note "restored," not rewritten and reorganized, as done with the Novus Ordo Missae] When this work has been gone over numerous times and further emended, after serious study and reflection, We commanded that the finished product be printed and published as soon as possible, so that all might enjoy the fruits of this labor; and thus, priests would know which prayers to use and which rites and ceremonies they were required to observe from now on in the celebration of Masses. *In virtue of Our Apostolic authority, We grant and concede in perpetuity that, for the chanting or reading of*

*the Mass in any church whatsoever, this Missal is hereafter to be followed absolutely...*Nor are superiors, administrators, canons, chaplains, and other secular priests, or religious, of whatever title designated, obliged to celebrate the Mass otherwise than as enjoined by Us. *We likewise declare and ordain that no one whosoever is forced or coerced to alter this Missal, and that this present document cannot be revoked or modified, but remain always valid and retains its full force notwithstanding the previous constitutions and decrees of the Holy See.* [7]

- If anyone doubted *Quo Primum* was an infallible Bull, that doubt is resolved. And neither should doubt exist concerning any other disciplinary decrees issued by the Roman Pontiff or the General Councils the Pontiffs have approved. In *Quartus Supra* (see above), Pope Pius IX clearly states that even without a formal declaration, the Armenians resisting the authority of the papal see were considered schismatics. Likewise, all who *"avoid carrying out their orders"* (those of the Roman Pontiffs) are reckoned as schismatics. This would include any who ignore:

- the decrees of the Roman Pontiffs who excommunicated them for not observing their condemnations or obeying the teachings found in their decrees;

- papal mandates for episcopal consecration, necessary for obtaining the actual office of bishop and the jurisdiction that accompanies it;

- the teachings of the Council of Trent and other papal teachings concerning jurisdiction;

- excommunications for heresy and schism for ministering to the faithful when no supplied jurisdiction can be granted because there is no pope to supply;

- the commands of the Roman Pontiffs issued to the laity to engage in Catholic Action and

- those teachings found in *Quartus Supra* concerning the inability of the laity to participate in the election of bishops and other clerics:

> Concerning the exclusion of the laity from the election of bishops, a clear distinction must be made, *lest a doctrine at variance with the Catholic faith result*. This distinction is between the right to elect bishops and the ability to give testimony as to their life and morals. The former claim must be credited to the wrong notions of Luther and Calvin, who even asserted that it was a matter of divine law that the bishops should be elected by the people; *as everybody realizes, such false teaching has been and is still rejected by the Catholic Church. For no power of electing bishops or other ministers of religion has ever been given to the people by either divine or ecclesiastical law.* [8]

Not only do certain Conclavists reserve the right for laymen to "elect" a pope as the bishop of Rome "in exile," but Traditionalist bishops elected by fellow "clerics" — who have been *ipso facto* excommunicated for schism and/or heresy and who, in previous times would have been reduced to the lay state, (if indeed they were ever clerics to begin with) — are, in effect, "elected" only by laymen as well (Canon 188 no. 4, also *Cum ex Apostolatus Officio*). As Pope Pius IX teaches, such actions are "at variance with the Catholic faith" and are "rejected by the Catholic Church."

And so it can be seen that the destruction of discipline and undermining of disciplinary decrees was planned long before the council, and its erosion carefully attended to at the parish, diocesan and even higher levels in the Vatican itself. Occasionally one finds objections by champions like Monsignor Joseph C. Fenton, who repeatedly warned against the dangerous trends prevailing in the Church for well over a decade prior to Pope Pius XII's death. But already Monsignor Fenton was becoming a voice crying in the wilderness, and in the early 1960s he would be forced to resign his position at the Catholic University of America owing to ill health.

Conclusion

Many Protestants believe that Catholics can never think for themselves but must obey the pope even in the most absurd details concerning day-to-day life. And Catholics, in failing to intellectualize their faith, did nothing to convince them otherwise. As Monsignor Fenton explains above, the Church expects us to exercise the intellect in order to understand our faith and to decide on moral problems. We are obligated to study our faith, even as adults, and this is especially true when the Church is under attack as She is today. The popes exercised their infallible authority in pointing out to us exactly what system of philosophy must be used in exercising the intellect. Over the centuries, she created laws that always allow us to know what we are required to do and how we are to conduct ourselves. This method and these rules will be presented next.

Chapter IV Endnotes

[1] C. Leroux, *The Son of Perdition*, Calais, France, 1982, translated by Dolores Rose Morris, 5, 20
[2] Giovanni Battista "Cardinal" Montini, *The Church*, Helicon, Baltimore, Md. and Dublin, Ireland, 1964, 178
[3] Henry Denzinger, *The Sources of Catholic Dogma*, 30th Edition, Marian House, Powers Lake, N. D., 1957, DZ 326
[4] Henry Cardinal Manning, *The Vatican Decrees in Their Bearing on Civil Allegiance*, The Catholic Publication Society, New York, N.Y., 1875, 19
[5] Henry Denzinger, *The Sources of Catholic Dogma*, 30th Edition, Marian House, Powers Lake, N. D., 1957, DZ 1578
[6] Dr. Carlos Disandro, *Paulo IV and Benedicto XV, Precisiones Doctrinales*, Instituto De Cultura Classica "San Antanasio," Cordoba, Argentina, 1979; translated anonymously in 1989; see www.betrayedCatholics.com, Archives and other articles, 6. Canon Law, Dr. Disandro's "Precisions"

[7] Pope St. Pius V, *Quo Primum*,
http://www.papalencyclicals.net/Pius05/p5quopri.htm
[8] Pope Pius IX, *Quartus Supra*,
http://www.papalencyclicals.net/Pius09/p9quartu.htm

Chapter V — The Scholastic Method
St. Thomas Aquinas' philosophic method
binding on Catholics

A. What is Scholasticism?

Reverend A. C. Cotter, S.J., tells us that St. Justin and Origen founded scholastic theology in the second and third centuries. St. Augustine later defined the system as the process whereby those who have already accepted Christian revelation on faith use human reason to *understand* the truths of faith. The early system was based on the writings of Plato, but when better translations of Aristotle were obtained, it was discovered that his philosophy was superior to Plato's, so Aristotle's works were used as the basis for the Scholastic system. The Scholastic method relies on theology for its philosophical conclusions. There are five steps to the Scholastic method, Cotter relates, those being:

1. To state clearly and without ambiguity the precise point at issue without ambiguity or equivocation;
2. To define clearly the terms which enter into the dispute and to divide off their various meanings;
3. To prove the solution adopted and show its position within the system;
4. To answer real or possible objections and
5. To draw, if possible, further conclusions. [1]

Cotter notes that "Scholasticism strives everywhere for brevity and precision." Questions are divided and subdivided, the problem is viewed from every angle, and each problem is solved definitively before moving on to the next question. But the method is not the soul of the system, he cautions. "Its soul, the driving power, was St. Augustine's principle: *the defense and systemization of the deposit of faith.*" [2]

Scholasticism is the only method of philosophy prescribed by the Church. Logicians equate it with reality. We have experienced its absence, because when the Faith is cast aside, *unreality* is all that is left. What is reality? Something that actually exists as a thing, state or quality; true to life or to fact; not fictitious or imaginary (*Webster's Collegiate Dictionary*, 7th edition). Webster's defines reality as "fact" and then defines fact as "a deed, especially a criminal deed; anything true to be used as a basis for argument," which in turn brings up the question of the definition of truth. Attwater's *A Catholic Dictionary* defines reality as "That which has or can have existence. Actual reality is that which exists; possible reality is that which can exist. Reality is distinct from mental being...which is in, or is wholly dependent on, the mind..." [3] Reverend Michael Mahony, S. J., writes:

> Logic lays down the rules of right reasoning and treats of the means given us by the Author of nature to acquire the knowledge of truth...Minor logic...has to do directly and primarily with the correctness of our thought operations and secondarily and indirectly with...the truth of our mental operations. Major logic...has primarily to do with the latter aspect, the truth, and indirectly and secondarily with their correctness...The laws the mind must follow, Scholasticism admits...are *in* the mind but not *of* the mind. They are engendered in the mind by objective reality [and] put us therefore in touch with reality. [4]

Pope Pius XII, speaking of the scholastic system and its connection to reality, teaches:

> This philosophy acknowledged and accepted by the Church, safeguards the genuine validity of human knowledge...the mind's ability to attain certain and unchangeable truth...*Whatever new truth the human mind is able to find cannot be opposed to truth already acquired*, since God, the Highest Truth, has created and guides the human intellect, not that it may daily oppose new truths to rightly established ones, but rather that, *having eliminated errors which may have crept in, it may build truth upon truth in the same order and structure that exist in reality, the source of truth.* [5]

Reverend A. D. Sertillanges, O.P., has this to say about knowledge and reality:

> In the last analysis, God is our only Master, He who speaks within us, and from Him along with us all instruction comes to us; strictly speaking, thought is incommunicable from man to man.... The source of knowledge is not in books, it is in reality, and in our thought. Books are signposts; the road is older and no one can make the journey to truth for us. It is not what a writer says that is of importance to us; the important thing is what it *is.* Our mind has the task not of repeating but of comprehending, — that is we must 'take with us,' *cum+prehendere*; we must vitally assimilate what we read, and we must finally think for ourselves.... We must recreate for our own use the sum total of knowledge. [6]

So basically, God speaks to us through our conscience, when rightly formed, and uses human reason to assimilate and apply these truths of Faith.

Reverend William Turner, S.T.D., describes Scholasticism as:

> The theology and philosophy which flourished in the Christian schools of Europe during the...ninth to fifteenth [centuries], and which, after the fifteenth century, continued to influence the theological and philosophical thought in Catholic circles down to our own times. [Yet] the extent of that influence has varied. At the beginning of the nineteenth century, there was not much evidence of the Scholastic method in the teaching of philosophy in the Catholic Schools of Europe... Cartesianism and the spiritual Eclecticism of Cousin predominated in the colleges... The reaction against Fideism and Traditionalism brought Scholasticism once more to the front. [7]

What are Fideism and Traditionalism? *The Catholic Encyclopedia* states that Fideism teaches that there is no need of intellectual assent based on objective evidence, observing that: "Denying intellectual knowledge, [fideism] ruins faith itself." [8] Father Turner defines Traditionalism as: "A philosophico-religious system, which depreciates human reason and establishes the tradition of mankind, which is bound up with language, as the criterion of truth and certainty." [9] Continuing his explanation of Scholasticism, Turner notes:

> Modernists are opposed [to]...the *intellectual formalism* of the Scholastics. As in the case of Fideism and Traditionalism, so in the Modernist system: *the starting point is the denial of the adequacy of the intellect to solve the highest problems of human thought.* Reason, it is maintained, cannot explain God, human destiny, moral duty, legal right and social institutions because these things antedate reason as facts. [10]

According to the Modernists, reason cannot explain man, his emotions and impulse, or nature either, Turner explains. He continues:

> Because Scholasticism on these questions is made the object of attack on the part of the Modernists, and precisely because of its affirmation of the powers of reason, it is offered by ecclesiastical authority as a remedy against Modernism...But the intellectualism for which it stands is not the intellectualism which its opponents ascribe to it. [11]

That some Scholastics indulged in "frivolous and futile...discussion of the higher things of faith," made egotistical assumptions, and neglected to consult the outside sources of positive knowledge cannot be denied, Turner admits. But he also states, "No system is to be judged by the extremists who abuse its method...Modernists ought to know that between [these abuses] and the same empirical intellectualism of St. Thomas there is a vast difference." [12]

Between the opposite poles of rationality and mysticism, St. Thomas Aquinas "strives to hold a middle course between the two," Turner says. Thomistic intellectualism consists in:

> the ability of reason to attain a knowledge of natural truth of the higher order and to elucidate — not to prove as a comprehend — the Mysteries of Faith.... *Here intuitive perception, the mystic contemplation of higher truths...the affective aspect or feeling is subordinated to dialectical discussion, logical definition, systematic reasoning, clear, cold, calm intellect.* [13]

Turner concludes with a quote from Townsend's *The Great Schoolmen*, pointing out that in any area of study, in all departments of knowledge, the analysis of facts, natures and qualities must be reduced to a system. Given such facts, their arrangement and analysis leading to theories and conclusions is inevitable.

> If a logical method be allowed in relation to scientific facts or philosophical principles, it cannot with fairness or reason be denied in relation to religion; and if it be of advantage with respect to the former, it cannot be of disadvantage in regard to the latter. The problem is, as has been said, a problem of method. [14]

If reason is not to be relied upon, what is its substitute? Affections, sentiment, totality of life,

> ...all have their proper place in the struggle of the soul towards a realization of spiritual truth. That place, however, is a secondary one. None of these faculties or functions can, of itself, systemize, analyze, defend or prove.... Sometimes [these very things] function against the cogency of proof by entrenching a prejudice. [15]

And sometimes they place obstacles in the way of arriving at unity and symmetry of the proof by idealizing it or by striving too much or too little to assimilate it. The Church has excellent reasons for preferring and prescribing Scholasticism as Her own philosophy, and even if Her children cannot understand why, they still must obey. For the popes acting in Christ's stead are the ones who command them.

B. The popes command adherence to scholastic method

Pope Leo XIII, *Aeterni Patris* (August 4, 1879):

> And, indeed, the knowledge and use of so salutary a science, which flows from the fertilizing founts of the sacred writings, the sovereign Pontiffs, the holy Fathers and the councils, must always be of the greatest assistance to the Church, whether with the view of really and soundly understanding and interpreting the Scriptures, or more safely and to better purpose reading and explaining the Fathers, or for exposing and refuting the various errors and heresies; and in these late days, when those dangerous times described by the Apostle are already upon us, when the blasphemers, the proud, and the seducers go from bad to worse, erring themselves and causing others to err, there is surely a very great need of confirming the dogmas of Catholic faith and confuting heresies.
>
> Our predecessors in the Roman pontificate have celebrated the wisdom of Thomas Aquinas by exceptional tributes of praise and the most ample testimonials. Clement VI in the bull *In Ordine*; Nicholas V in his brief to the friars of the Order of Preachers, 1451; Benedict XIII in the bull *Pretiosus*, and others bear witness that the universal Church borrows lustre from his admirable teaching; while St. Pius V declares in the bull *Mirabilis* that heresies, confounded and convicted by the same teaching, were dissipated, and the whole world daily freed from fatal errors; others, such as Clement XII in the bull *Verbo Dei*, affirm that most fruitful blessings have spread abroad from his writings over the whole Church, and that he is worthy of the honor which is bestowed on the greatest Doctors of the Church, on Gregory and Ambrose, Augustine and

Jerome; while others have not hesitated to propose St. Thomas for the exemplar and master of the universities and great centers of learning whom they may follow with unfaltering feet. On which point the words of Blessed Urban V to the University of Toulouse are worthy of recall: 'It is our will, which We hereby enjoin upon you, that ye follow the teaching of Blessed Thomas as the true and Catholic doctrine and that ye labor with all your force to profit by the same.'

Innocent XII, followed the example of Urban in the case of the University of Louvain, in the letter in the form of a brief addressed to that university on February 6, 1694, and Benedict XIV in the letter in the form of a brief addressed on August 26, 1752, to the Dionysian College in Granada; while to these judgments of great Pontiffs on Thomas Aquinas comes the crowning testimony of Innocent VI: 'His teaching above that of others, the canonical writings alone excepted, enjoys such a precision of language, an order of matters, a truth of conclusions, that those who hold to it are never found swerving from the path of truth, and he who dare assail it will always be suspected of error.' ...The ecumenical councils, also, where blossoms the flower of all earthly wisdom, have always been careful to hold Thomas Aquinas in singular honor. In the Councils of Lyons, Vienna, Florence, and the Vatican one might almost say that Thomas took part and presided over the deliberations and decrees of the Fathers, contending against the errors of the Greeks, of heretics and rationalists, with invincible force and with the happiest results. But the chief and special glory of Thomas, one which he has shared with none of the Catholic Doctors, is that the Fathers of Trent made it part of the order of conclave to lay upon the altar, together with sacred Scripture and the decrees of the supreme Pontiffs, the Summa of Thomas Aquinas, whence to seek counsel, reason, and inspiration. [16]

Pope Leo XIII, *Depuis Le Jour* (September 8, 1889):

It is by the empty subtleties of false philosophy *'per philosophiam et inanem fallaciam'* that the minds of the faithful are most frequently led astray and the purity of the faith corrupted among men... and the events of the last twenty years have furnished bitter confirmation of the[se] reflections and apprehensions...If one notes the critical condition of the times in which we live and ponders on the state of affairs in public and private life he will have no difficulty in seeing that the cause of the evils which oppress us, as well as those which menace, lies in the fact that erroneous opinions on all subjects, human and divine, have gradually percolated from philosophical schools through all ranks of society, and have come to be accepted by a large number of minds...Theology is the science of the things of faith. It is nourished, Pope Sixtus V tells us, at those ever-willing springs — the Holy Scriptures, the decisions of the Popes, the decrees of the Councils.

Called positive and speculative or scholastic, according to the method followed in studying it, theology does not confine itself to proposing the truths which are to be believed; it scrutinizes their inmost depths, shows their relations with human reason, and, aided by the resources which true philosophy supplies, explains, develops and adapts them accurately to all the needs of the defense and propagation of the faith. Like Beseleel, to whom the Lord gave His spirit of wisdom, intelligence and knowledge, when intrusting him with the mission of building His temple, the theologian 'cuts the precious stones' of divine dogma, assorts them skillfully, and, by the setting he gives them, brings out their brilliancy, charm and beauty.

Rightly, then, does the same Sixtus V call theology (and here he is referring especially to scholastic theology) a gift from heaven, and ask that it be maintained in the schools and cultivated with great ardor, as being abundant in fruitfulness for the Church. Is it necessary to add that the book par excellence in which students may with most profit study scholastic theology is the *Summa Theologica* of St. Thomas Aquinas? It is our wish, therefore, that professors be sure to explain to all their pupils its method, as well as the principal articles relating to Catholic faith. (end of Pope Leo XIII quotes). [17]

Pope St. Pius X, *Pascendi Dominici Gregis* (September 8, 1907):

42. Against scholastic philosophy and theology they use the weapons of ridicule and contempt. Whether it is ignorance or fear, or both, that inspires this conduct in them, certain it is that the passion for novelty is always united in them with hatred of scholasticism, and there is no surer sign that a man is tending to Modernism than when he begins to show his dislike for the scholastic method.

45. In the first place, with regard to studies, We will and ordain that scholastic philosophy be made the basis of the sacred sciences. It goes without saying that if anything is met with among the scholastic doctors which may be regarded as an excess of subtlety, or which is altogether destitute of probability, We have no desire whatever to propose it for the imitation of present generations (Leo XIII. Enc. *Aeterni Patris*). And let it be clearly understood above all things that the scholastic philosophy We prescribe is that which the Angelic Doctor has bequeathed to us, and We, therefore, declare that all the ordinances of Our Predecessor on this subject continue fully in force, and, as far as may be necessary, We do decree anew, and confirm, and ordain that they be by all strictly observed. In seminaries where they may have been neglected let the Bishops impose them and require their observance, and let this apply also to the Superiors of religious institutions. Further let Professors remember that they cannot set St. Thomas aside, especially in metaphysical questions, without grave detriment. [18]

Pope Benedict XV, papal brief (February 5, 1919):

The manifold honours paid by the Holy See to St. Thomas Aquinas exclude forever any doubt from the mind of

Catholics with regard to his being raised up by God as the Master of Doctrine to be followed by the Church through all ages.[19]

Pope Pius XI, *Studiorem Ducem* (June 29, 1943):

10. After this slight sketch of the great virtues of Thomas, it is easy to understand the pre-eminence of his doctrine and the marvelous authority it enjoys in the Church. Our Predecessors, indeed, have always unanimously extolled it. Even during the lifetime of the saint, Alexander IV had no hesitation in addressing him in these terms: 'To Our beloved son, Thomas Aquinas, distinguished alike for nobility of blood and integrity of character, who has acquired by the grace of God the treasure of divine and human learning.' After his death, again, John XXII seemed to consecrate both his virtues and his doctrine when, addressing the Cardinals, he uttered in full Consistory the memorable sentence: 'He alone enlightened the Church more than all other doctors; a man can derive more profit in a year from his books than from pondering all his life the teaching of others.'[20]

Pope Pius XII, *Humani Generis* (August 12, 1950):

31. If one considers all this well, he will easily see why the Church demands that future priests be instructed in philosophy 'according to the method, doctrine, and principles of the Angelic Doctor,' since, as we well know from the experience of centuries, the method of Aquinas is singularly preeminent both of teaching students and for bringing truth to light; his doctrine is in harmony with Divine Revelation, and is most effective both for safeguarding the foundation of the faith and for reaping, safely and usefully, the fruits of sound progress. [21]

C. The Scholastic method and the necessity of certitude
What is certitude? As Reverend A. C. Cotter explains:

> Certitude (conviction) is unhesitating, firm assent (or
> dissent) without fear of error... [There are] various types
> of certitude...We may understand a truth *more fully* and
> completely as we grow up, or a truth may come home to us
> on a special occasion...But that does not change the truth
> in itself, nor does it make our former cognition of it
> false...An individual...may lose his certitude and drift
> back or be forced back to doubt. [22]

Cotter goes on to explain that certain types of certitude
(subjective, practical, respective) can be true while they last, since
they are based primarily on the human reasoning and judgment
process. But only an infallible motive "can exclude the very
possibility of error...Only that judgment is necessarily true which
cannot err. Now *only an infallible motive excludes the very
possibility of error*; every other motive, no matter how alluring or
appealing, leaves the door open for error." [23]

Concerning the causes of error, Cotter writes:

> Card. Newman says: "Inaccuracy is the besetting sin of all,
> of both young and old, learned and unlearned. We don't
> know what we are talking about." This slovenly habit
> appears in the use of sentences, arguments, single words.
> Do we examine each of our statements as to its exact
> meaning? Do we see in what sense it is true and in what
> sense it might be false?... Or rather do we not prefer wide
> and vague half-truths, arbitrary and ambiguous definitions?
> More particularly, when arguing pro and con about
> anything, do we make sure of the precise point to be
> proved and of the soundness of the proof itself? Are we
> courageous enough...to abandon them if they contain a
> flaw?
>
> By far the most fruitful source of error is our careless use
> of *words*, or rather the *vague notions* we have of the
> meaning of words. How many people will talk on
> education, religion, progress, child labor, economics,
> dogma, evolution — without having first made absolutely
> sure (a) of the various meanings of the terms or (b) of the

exact meaning which they attach to them in the present discussion." [24]

This positive source of error was discussed at length in the online article *"The Mistranslation of ONE WORD Changed the Church Forever."* [25] The article explored the malicious mischief caused by the disingenuous mistranslation of *one word* — whether that word can be found in the Consecration of the wine during the Novus Ordo falsification of the true Mass or a papal act of the ordinary magisterium. Truly Catholic authors are obliged to help their readers better understand and express ideas and beliefs clearly; to lay out facts understandably and in their proper order. Writing and research, when taken seriously, is a discipline and as such cannot consist of making blanket statements on one's own authority and without referring to a set context of beliefs against which they may be measured. Understanding this context is essential to arriving at objective truth; and while many believe they have grasped it, closer examination shows, as Cotter explains above, how far they really are from understanding it at all. Thus the importance of predicating all with definitions, as shall be seen below.

Definition comprises an entire chapter in Cotter's work, showing it is truly something necessary to scholastic thought and application. There are two kinds of definition: nominal and real. Nominal definitions "are used chiefly at the beginning of a disputation, to indicate what is the subject under dispute." Nominal definitions can be demonstrated by distinguishing between the various meanings of an ambiguous term, giving synonyms or words better known, providing the etymology of a word, listing all the things it signifies, or appealing to what people usually mean when they use the word. "If a word has only one *definite meaning,* this is to be adhered to," Cotter notes.

> The most commonly accepted terms should be employed in their most commonly accepted meanings...Never employ a word to which you cannot apply a precise and *clearly defined meaning.* Where any doubt concerning a word

exists, define carefully. This is not pedantry, but a sign of education. [26]

Until the real definition is distinguished by debate, Cotter says, both definitions may be admitted in the beginning. Nominal definitions taken from Scholastic theology itself are of a higher order than other definitions, since scholasticism has been defined specifically by the ordinary magisterium as the only basis for determining reality and arriving at the truth.

Cotter then distinguishes between subjective and formal certitude.

> Purely *subjective* certitude is an assent or dissent which is indeed firm, *but really should not be firm*, as when our ancestors believed that the earth was flat... Purely subjective [certitude] does not rest on anything objective... Prejudice or stubbornness is the usual reason for purely subjective certitude. *Practical* certitude is an assent (or dissent) which is firm merely for practical reasons, viz. because otherwise life would be impossible. Thus, we are practically certain the cook will not poison the soup. *Respective* certitude is an assent (or dissent) based on [motives] which are sufficient for certain minds, but not for all. Thus, the child is convinced when his mother says no. *Formal* certitude is a firm assent (or dissent) which is necessarily true and known to be true. [It] is often called 'objective' because it corresponds with objective reality and because it rests on objective grounds... Though every certitude is firm and unhesitating, yet neither purely subjective, nor practical nor respective certitude can be called *necessarily* true. [27]

Formal certitude informs us that in reality the earth was *not* flat, the cook *could* poison the soup, and mother *could* be wrong in saying no. Even those since Vatican 2 who have written on certitude have not made these distinctions as they ought and therefore themselves mistook and caused others to mistake subjective, practical and respective certitude for formal certitude. They then proceeded to make decisions on extremely serious matters based on this misapprehension, when Pope Pius XII states that the more serious the decision to be made, the higher the degree of *formal* certitude needs to be.

Speaking primarily of marriage cases in 1942, Pope Pius XII instructs judges to *"not be satisfied with a low degree of certitude, especially in cases of great importance."* Judgment should be reserved until that *"grade of certitude is attained which corresponds to the requirements of law and the importance of the case."* [28] This document is a statement issuing from the ordinary magisterium, and *Humani Generis* states all binding documents can be found in the *Acta Apostolica Sedis* (AAS).

The importance of the case determines how it must be handled and the degree of certitude necessary to properly judge it. Here we must remember that a judge deals with witnesses and proofs — evidence — that is not as compelling, nor convincing, as that evidence that can be produced from unimpeachable sources when dealing mainly with matters of dogma. A judge may not come across an irrefutable papal document (Canons 1812, 1816, 1819) that is unable to be questioned in ecclesiastical court, but many such documents may be produced in the course of a strictly theological presentation. The primary consideration should be: how important is the necessity of the papacy to the Church, the necessity of the priesthood and episcopacy, of the availability of Mass and Sacraments? It is clear these questions are all of the utmost importance, and in fact all these things must exist for the (juridical) Church itself to exist.

There is one answer and one answer only to this conundrum, and it is central to the premise of this work: the disappearance of the juridical Church, a premise identified as heretical by the ancient Fathers and the magisterium of the Church itself, could *only* occur briefly (in God's time, not ours) during the reign of Antichrist and his system. This is why *Cum ex Apostolatus Officio* and Pope Pius XII's *Vacantis Apostolicae Sedis* are so important to our understanding of the situation today. The inevitable conclusions at which Catholics must arrive after reading these two documents leave them with only one option if they are to remain Catholic: the faithful are living in the time period analogous to that of Christ's three days in the tomb prior to His Resurrection. This is the only conclusion at which we can arrive without the fear of heresy, and from which we can, if all things are taken into consideration, achieve formal certitude.

Degrees of certitude

A summary of Reverend Cotter's principles on formal certitude is presented below.

There are three degrees of formal certitude: metaphysical, physical, and moral, with metaphysical being the highest and moral the lowest. Metaphysical or absolute certitude is a firm assent based on an absolutely infallible motive. (The infallibility spoken of here, however, is only of the type found in natural truths, such as mathematics, physics, etc.). Physical certitude is a firm assent based on the known laws of science. Moral certitude is a firm assent based on infallible moral motives, although the perversity of man could render such a judgment false, (parents generally love their children as a rule, but this is not always true).

Both direct and reflex certitude are formal, direct certitude being knowledge of something from research and reflection; reflex certitude being the acceptance of some truth as pertaining to oneself on the reliable authority of others.

> Direct certitude, too, is formal certitude, nor does it differ essentially from reflex certitude...In reflex certitude we know *explicitly* and distinctly that our motive is infallible; in direct certitude we only know it *implicitly* and distinctly. [29]

Certitude may be either mathematical (conforming to the laws and truths of mathematics) or non-mathematical, necessary or free. Necessary means certitude based on a motive which makes all doubt impossible. Free is simply another term for moral certitude, which does not exclude prudent doubt.

> Formal certitude is a firm assent (or dissent) based on motives which are in themselves infallible and are known to be infallible... Now only an infallible motive excludes the very possibility of error... Therefore, only an infallible motive is a sufficient guarantee for the (logical) truth of a judgment... A guide is not called infallible because there is no special reason for doubting his knowledge or because it is highly improbable he will lead us astray... We call a *motive or reason for judging infallible only when it cannot lead us into error.* [30]

The belief that this time period is that of Antichrist's reign and the appearance of the abomination of desolation is based on infallible teaching found in *Vacantis Apostolicae Sedis, Cum ex Apostolatus Officio* and the teachings of other reliable authorities on the latter days. It is not heretical only because it is the one biblical exception to the general rule regarding the constitution of the Church, as will be explained in detail below. We find in *Mystici Corporis* that the Church is the Mystical Body of Christ. That Body has not ceased to exist because Christ still heads His Church and has promised to be with us unto the consummation. The proofs presented in this work should help most achieve at least reflex certitude. And the reasons why so many today believe they can avoid forming certitude will be explained next.

Traditionalists and false certitude

A one-sentence heading in the 1911 *Catholic Encyclopedia* defines Traditionalism as: "A philosophical system which makes tradition the supreme criterion and rule of certitude." [31] The French priest Félicité Robert de Lammenais proposed this system, condemned by the Church as false doctrine. He insisted on the necessity of human tradition, which should hand down the elements of an initial revelation by God. According to Lammenais,

> We can only be sure of what all men agree upon — not precisely because they all agree on it, but because this agreement is due to divine revelation vouchsafed to our

first parents in paradise and handed on from generation to generation. [32]

Traditionalism basically taught that it is *faith* that produces reason, and man cannot know with any certainty basic truths of the natural, moral and religious order. While universal assent can be a powerful motive for belief in certain cases, the *Catholic Encyclopedia* notes that "it can never be the supreme criterion and rule of truth." Even if all true Catholics supported Traditionalist thought today without reservation, which they do not, it still would not mean that Traditional "Catholicism" is necessarily true simply because they supported it. If the certitude causing them to support such beliefs is less than formal, and we know that it is, it is not "necessarily true." The human tradition they refer to, even if it remotely originates from God, cannot be used as any real measure of the truth.

As Reverend Cotter notes: "Though every certitude is firm and unhesitating, yet neither purely subjective, nor practical nor respective certitude can be called *necessarily* true." [33] Certain types of certitude (subjective, practical, respective) can be true while they last, since they are based primarily on the reasoning and judgment process of humans. The assent given by Traditionalists is an assent based on human tradition, which is indeed firm, yet inadequate as a motive of divine faith. Their certitude about the situation after Vatican 2 may have been true while it lasted but was long ago disproven. Theology has been made a complex science when in all reality it should not be anything of the sort. Where understanding may fail, obedience to the continual magisterium fills in any perceived gap. To believe otherwise is to circumvent the Church and the authority of the papacy as established by Jesus Christ. Unlike the mother of the child used as an example of respective certitude above, or certitude based on the say-so of a lesser authority, the popes speaking in their ordinary magisterium, as they have on so many subjects, is not just *any* guide, but instead is an infallible guide, which must be obeyed if one is to remain Catholic. The papacy is a continual and living entity and must be taken as a whole, even during this interminable interregnum, not parceled off as one pleases. The continual magisterium is the repository of integral truth coming directly from the Holy Ghost — it is as indivisible as the Trinity Itself.

D. Fallacies in scholastic argument

Before ending this chapter, it is necessary to demonstrate just how scholasticism affects the actual reasoning process, to better understand how Catholics became so confused in the 1960s. Logic is a science that supplies us with the rules for constructing valid arguments and detecting false arguments according to the Thomistic method of philosophy. Since St. Thomas based his system on that of Aristotle, it is important to note Aristotle's second fallacy, listed by Reverend Joseph B. Walsh, S.J., under "Fallacies of Diction" in his work *Logic*: "(2) *Amphibology*: employing a sentence or phrase whose structure makes its meaning ambiguous."

Catholics are quite familiar with ambiguity primarily because the "papal" documents proceeding from Rome since the reign of John 23 are littered with such statements. Given the papal endorsements of Scholasticism listed in Section B above, true Roman Pontiffs would scarcely violate the very unambiguous system they praise so consistently by making statements the faithful could interpret either one way or the other.

It must be remembered that St. Thomas himself separated philosophical questions from those teachings of faith.

> Besides philosophical science built up by reason, there should be a sacred science learned through revelation...Hence theology included in sacred doctrine differs in kind from that theology which is part of philosophy. [34]

St. Thomas teaches further:

> Other sciences are called the handmaidens of this one...because other sciences derive their certitude from the natural light of human reason, which can err; whereas this

derives its certitude from the light of the divine knowledge, which cannot be misled. [35]

Therefore the fallacy of amphibology, being a fallacy of logic, can only apply to philosophy—not to sacred theology. And yet, one encounters one ambiguous statement after another, not only in the documents issued by the usurpers, but also in Traditionalist arguments as well. The Church's adoption of Thomism, which embraces Aristotelian rules and methods, renders these amphibological statements and arguments invalid. For they are grounded in another system of philosophy, not Thomism; and Thomism is the only system which the popes have approved.

Here are the most common false arguments treated by theologians prior to the death of Pope Pius XII, along with a modern-day example of each:

- *Ignoratio Elenchi*: *Missing the point, arguing beside the point, evading the issue, proving the wrong conclusion.* An example of this would be Traditionalists insisting that they possess the four marks of the Church when the popes teach that the Church with its four marks cannot exist without a pope. Traditionalists completely ignore the fact that there is no certainly identifiable pope.
- *Appeal to the populace by arousing passions and prejudices.* A prime example of this is the book *The Plot Against the Church,* written in the 1960s and distributed at Vatican 2 by Traditionalists. They use anti-Semitic claims condemned by the Church Herself to try and raise animosity against the Jews as the sole cause of the changes in the Church.

- *Appeal to the venerated positions of those holding the same opinions.* A favorite trick of Traditionalists and Novus Ordo clergy is to set their bishops and priests up as lawful authorities without ever proving that they possess the necessary Orders *or* jurisdiction. Then they claim that their followers must obey them based on this false authority. Or they champion some theologian or group of theologians holding opinions contrary to the teachings of the continual magisterium.

- *An appeal to the ignorance of the hearers, tricking them by statements they are unable to test.* This is a widespread problem. Few Catholics exiting the Church in Rome were educated in the first place concerning the truths of faith, and even fewer today are knowledgeable about their faith.

- *Argumentation* ad miseracordium, *or an appeal for sympathy.* Traditionalists falsely believe they *must* receive the Sacraments because they so need the graces. They do not realize graces also can come from other sources, and even more abundantly. Traditionalist clergy and lay leaders often ask how anyone could believe God would be so cruel as to deprive them of their Mass and Sacraments, appealing to the *pathos* of their followers. They seem to forget that the Jews lost their sacrifice and that Holy Scripture prophesies the Continual Sacrifice will cease in the end times.

- *Argumentation* ad hominem, *including personal attack, abusive language, ridicule of an adversary, charges of inconsistency.* According to Father Walsh, those who descend to ridicule and personal attacks most always lack any substantive proofs with which to refute their opponent; they try and discredit the person since they cannot destroy the argument.

- *Argumentation* ad balculum, *or appeal to physical force by threats.* This happens more often than most would think. Bullying is an age-old art.

- Petitio principii *or begging the question and all its variants: Assuming as true that which has yet to be proved.*

Traditionalists and others argue the question of jurisdiction when they have failed even to prove that their "priests" were validly ordained. Without certainly valid orders there can *be* no jurisdiction. This fact is found in the *Catholic Encyclopedia* under apostolicity, apostolic mission.

• *False analogy: When an argument is drawn from another subject which only in appearance resembles the subject in question.* Comparing the Western Schism, during which there actually was a true pope reigning (even if no one could agree on who he was) with the situation today, when we have no ascertainable pope.

• *Fallacy of accident and fallacies regarding special cases: What is true generally is not true in every case because "circumstances alter cases." And what is true in a certain restricted case is not true generally.* [36] Traditionalists are fond of explaining how bishops in previous times were consecrated without papal mandate during interregnums, pretending they can use this occurrence as a precedent. These were special cases, and as Pope Pius XII points out in *Ad Apostolorum Principis*:

> We are aware that those who belittle obedience in order to justify themselves with regard to those functions which they have unrighteously assumed defend their position by *recalling a usage which prevailed in ages past....Yet everyone sees that all ecclesiastical discipline is overthrown if it is in any way lawful for one to restore arrangements which are no longer valid because the supreme authority of the Church long ago decreed otherwise.* [37]

In addition to these false arguments, errors in inductive reasoning are also widespread. According to Reverend Michael Mahony, S. J., errors of false induction include: a) seeing what we wish to see, b) not seeing what we do not wish to see, and c) false interpretation. [38] Nothing describes the majority of those calling themselves Catholics today better than Father Mahoney's description of false induction. They do *not* want anyone to confuse them with facts or spoil their long-treasured beliefs about something by presenting the truth. They prefer to let the collective consciences of bygone ages, as presented to them by their "leaders," do their thinking, not realizing that by so doing they are deliberately stifling the function of their souls. For as St. Thomas Aquinas says, "It is not *the intellect* that understands, but the soul *through* the intellect." [39] The *Catholic Encyclopedia* article "Soul" defines the soul as "the ultimate internal principle by which we think, feel, and will, and by which our bodies are animated. The term 'mind' usually denotes this principle...." [40] The article "Intellect" has this to say:

> The faculty of conscience is in fact merely the practical intellect, or the intellect passing judgment on the moral quality of actions. *The intellect is essentially the faculty of truth and falsity*, and in its judicial acts it at the same time affirms the union of subject and predicate and the agreement between its own representation *and the objective reality.* [41]

In other words, those who will not engage the intellect in sorting out what has happened to the Church by using the scholastic method not only deny that they are able to perform this action using the abilities with which God invested them, but they also deliberately refuse to realize the full potential of their God-given souls, implicitly denying the existence of this potential. It is interesting to note that Father Turner (cited in Section A above) describes this very tendency in his treatment of Modernist opposition to Scholasticism:

> Modernists are opposed [to]...the *intellectual formalism* of the Scholastics. As in the case of Fideism and Traditionalism, so in the Modernist system: *the starting point is the denial of the adequacy of the intellect to solve the highest problems of human thought.* Because

> Scholasticism on these questions is made the object of attack on the part of the Modernists, *and precisely because of its affirmation of the powers of reason*, it is offered by ecclesiastical authority as a remedy against Modernism. [42]

Those who believe they are Catholics yet think in this fashion deny the very foundation of scholasticism — "the adequacy of the intellect to solve the highest problems of human thought"— and embrace Fideism, Traditionalism and Modernism. They condemn as guilty of "intellectual pride" Catholic writers who dare to demonstrate and apply the integral teachings of faith from the popes, councils, and approved theologians in agreement with them, because they adduce that such teachings yet bind Catholics. They will reason only so far, as long as it does not make them subject to the ridicule of their fellows or disrupt their false humility. And there they come to a screeching halt.

But if they do not follow St. Thomas' system in reasoning out the implications of their faith, they cannot be Catholic because they fail to obey the Roman Pontiffs' clear teaching that only this system of philosophy may be used. If they deny the full potential of the soul, they cannot be Catholic because teachings on the soul are essential truths of Catholicism. These errors have been condemned by the popes and councils, whose teachings and decisions were formulated according to scholastic principles. Catholics must obey these teachings if they wish to obtain salvation. Theologians like Monsignor Fenton and others show us how it was done, and how they used scholastic method, which can be adapted to solve the problems Catholics face today. But most importantly, they emphasize the need to understand and respect the teachings of the continual magisterium, papal authority exercised throughout the ages.

E. Canon Law and Scholasticism

Scholastic method is very much tied in to Canon Law. While Canon Law is beyond the scope of this work to fully explain, let it be said that every society must have its own system of laws to function, and the Church is no exception to this general rule. Pope Leo XIII describes Canon Law as "the science of the laws and jurisprudence of the Church." He writes:

> This science is connected by very close and logical ties with that of Theology, which it applies practically to all that concerns the government of the Church, the dispensation of holy things, the rights and duties of her ministers, the use of temporal goods which she needs for the accomplishment of her mission. Without a knowledge of Canon Law...theology is imperfect, incomplete, like a man with only one arm. Ignorance of Canon Law has favored the birth and diffusion of numerous errors about the rights of the Roman Pontiffs and of Bishops, and about the powers which the Church derives from her own Constitution — powers whose exercise she adapts to circumstances. [43]

A definition to better aid lay understanding should be included here.

> From the earliest times, the determinations of the Church received the name of Canons, that is, directory rules in matters of faith and conduct... A tendency afterwards appeared to restrict the term Canon to matters of discipline, and to give the name of Dogma to decisions bearing on faith. But the Council of Trent confirmed the ancient use of the word, calling its determinations 'canons,' whether they bore on points of belief or were directed to the reformation of discipline. *Canon Law is the assemblage of rules or laws relating to faith, morals and discipline*, prescribed or propounded by ecclesiastical authority... 'Or laws' [means] *binding laws*, liable to be enforced by penalties; 'propounded' [means] *some of these rules belong to the natural or Divine law*, and as such are not originally proposed by the Church but are proposed and explained by Her. [44]

The constitutions and decrees of the Holy Pontiffs are most especially embodied in Canon Law, according to the *Catholic Encyclopedia*:

> The ultimate source of Canon Law is God, whose will is manifested either by the very nature of things (natural Divine law) or by Revelation (positive Divine law) .... To attain its sublime end, the Church, endowed by its Founder with legislative power, makes laws in conformity with natural and Divine law. The sources or authors of this positive ecclesiastical law are essentially the episcopate and its head, the pope, the successors of the Apostolic College and its divinely appointed head, St. Peter. They are, properly speaking, the active sources of Canon Law. Their activity is exercised in its most solemn form by the ecumenical councils... (These) councils, especially...Trent, hold an exceptional place in ecclesiastical law... The sovereign pontiff is the most fruitful source of Canon Law... From the earliest ages the letters of the Roman Pontiffs constitute, with the canons of the Councils, the principal element of Canon Law; ...they are everywhere relied upon and collected, and the ancient canonical compilations contain a large number of these precious decretals. [45]

So to know the will of God, and the mind of the Church as it has been consistently expressed throughout the ages, Catholics need only look to Canon Law. And they need not fear that by following such laws today they may somehow be in error.

Reverend Nicolas Neuberger, in his commentary on Canon 6 (written as a thesis to receive his doctorate in Canon Law), cites the Church's laws concerning discipline as *negatively infallible*, meaning that they cannot work to the harm of souls or the destruction of the divine principle of perpetuity and infallibility on which the Church is built. *The Catholic Encyclopedia* article "Discipline" states:

> It is the unanimous opinion of the theologians that discipline enjoys a negative, indirect infallibility, i.e., the

Church can prescribe nothing that would be contrary to the natural or Divine law, nor prohibit anything that the natural or Divine law would exact. [46]

Pope Pius IX declared the unanimous opinion of theologians to be infallible, and hence anything determined by them unanimously must be firmly believed (DZ 1683). Furthermore, Pope Pius IX teaches in his encyclical *Quartus Supra*:

Discipline is often so closely united to dogma, it has such an influence on its preservation and on its purity, that the sacred Councils have not hesitated in many cases to pronounce anathemas against those guilty of disciplinary violations and separated them from communion with the Church. [47]

Leo XIII states in his encyclical *Sapientiae Christianae*:

In setting how far the limits of obedience extend, let no one imagine that the authority of the sacred pastors, and above all of the Roman Pontiff, need be obeyed only insofar as it is concerned with dogma, the obstinate denial of which entails the guilt of heresy. [...] Christian men must be willing to be ruled and governed by the authority and direction of... (in the first place) the Apostolic See. [...] When the Church speaks, even when She does not speak with all the weight of Her infallible utterance, She does so invariably to give us safe guidance... A Catholic is practically secure in listening to the voice of those whom God has set to rule the Church. [48]

So there can be no doubt concerning the continual magisterium's mind in this matter. It has been the constant teaching of the Church that unless the method of St. Thomas is used, there can be no guarantee of doctrinal integrity. And yet the laws of popes and councils now codified as Canon Law governing the use of that method must have their place as well. In ages past, when the popes could easily intervene and silence the contesting parties or decide the issue, theologians were allowed to contend on various theological topics until such a determination was made. Today the safer course must be taken because there is no pontiff, so past papal decisions must be followed to the letter. Where method is concerned, Catholics must abide by those well known for their expertise in the scholastic system. One of these experts is Bernard Wuellner, S.J., who wrote a work summarizing the principles of scholastic philosophy. "Masters of philosophy know these principles well," Wuellner writes in his Preface. "They are ...the household truths of their tradition," [49] much as rules of law are for jurists and proverbs are for the layperson. Numbers 3, 4, 7, and 8 below are taken from his work; the others are from Moral Theology, Canon Law and the teachings of Pope Pius XII.

1. "If no serious reasons can be found to prove or directly disprove that *a certain law has ceased or been abrogated,* the principle to be followed is: 'In doubt, decide for that which has the presumption.' *In this case the presumption is for the continuance of the law, since it was certainly made, and there is no probability for its non-continuance."* [50]
2. "Public documents prove the facts that are directly and principally asserted." [51]
3. "No proof is required for... (1) notorious facts, (2) facts presumed by law, and (3) facts asserted by one contending party and admitted by the other." [52]
4. A proof based on experience is a proof of facts [if a witness has been proven credible] and so must be supported by concrete instances in experience.
5. Every judgment must be based on evidence.
6. In doubt, facts cannot be presumed, but must be demonstrated. [53]
7. Against a presumption *juris et de jure* no proofs are admitted except the evident truth. [54]
8. There is no argument against the evidence.
9. No argument or conclusion contrary to the evident facts is valid.
10. No *inference* contrary to the evident facts is true; conjectural opinions are dangerous. [55]

In *Mirari Vos* and *Quo Graviora,* Pope Gregory XVI decries the false teaching that Church discipline "is subject to decay, to weakness, and to other failures of the same nature, and in imagining that it contains many elements which are not only useless but even prejudicial to the well-being of the Catholic religion..." Here he only echoes his predecessor Pope Pius VI in *Auctorem Fidei.* Pope Pius XII would later restate his teaching as follows:

> The good of the Church demands that we take all possible care that the stability of Canon Law be not endangered by the uncertain opinions and conjectures of private parties regarding the true sense of the canons, and that interpretations which rest on subtleties and cavils against the clear will of the legislator do not result in undue indulgence toward violators of the law, a thing which disrupts the nerve of ecclesiastical discipline . [56]

All these papal teachings on discipline should be considered carefully, for a great many of those who consider themselves Catholics today either ignore the law, do not hesitate to attenuate it, or even go so far as to say the entire Code is nothing but doubtful laws in this present crisis. For man to presume that Church law is something he can dismiss, alter, authoritatively interpret outside the rules laid down by Canon Law itself, or disobey on the grounds they have ceased to bind is tantamount to assuming the role of Christ's Vicar, endowed with infallibility, and usurping Christ's own role as Head of His Church. Especially during an interregnum (and it will be proven below that one definitely has existed since 1958), Pope Pius XII teaches that not even the cardinals, if any valid cardinals existed, could so contravene Church law during a vacancy of the Holy See. As Pope Leo XIII taught in his encyclical *Depuis Le Jour* (cited above), *"the powers which the Church derives from her own Constitution* [are] *powers whose exercise she adapts to circumstances."* An example of this adaptation is found in Pope Pius XII's infallible *Vacantis Apostolicae Sedis* on papal elections, specifying that even any *attempt* to violate these laws results in nullification and voidance of the act.

1. While the Apostolic Seat is vacant, *let the Sacred College of Cardinals have no power or jurisdiction at all in those things which pertain to the Pope while he was alive...*but let everything be held, reserved for the future Pope. And thus we decree that whatever power or jurisdiction pertaining to the Roman Pontiff, while he is alive (unless in as far as it is expressly permitted in this, Our Constitution) the meeting of Cardinals itself may have taken for exercising, *is null and void.*

2. *"Likewise we order that the Sacred College of Cardinals is not able to dispose of the laws of the Apostolic Seat and the Roman Church in any manner it wishes, nor may it attempt to detract wheresoever from the laws of the same, either directly or indirectly through a species of connivance, or through dissimulation of crimes perpetrated against the same laws, either after the death of the Pontiff or in time of vacancy*, [however] it may seem to be attempted. Indeed, we will that it ought to guard and defend against the same contention of all men.

3. *"Laws given by the Roman Pontiffs are in no way able to be corrected or changed through the meeting of the cardinals of the Roman Church [the See] being vacant*; nor is anything able to be taken away or added, nor is there able to be made any dispensation in any manner concerning the laws themselves or some part of them. This is very evident from pontifical Constitutions [on]...the election of the Roman Pontiff. *But if anything contrary to this prescript occurs or is by chance attempted, we declare it* by Our Supreme authority *to be null and void.* [57]

These laws and infallible teachings in sections C and D demonstrate that Catholics' first major error, when they saw that the Church had been hijacked, was the acceptance of the alternative reality offered by the NO church and Traditionalism's various sects. Had they understood the canon laws applying to the laity and to the hierarchy in service of the laity more clearly, and had they realized that their thinking had gone awry without the use of scholastic method, much of the confusion and misunderstanding of those times could have been avoided. That they were deliberately misled as explained in the Preface and in Section A is a fact. That instead of becoming part of the solution they chose to stay in the problem — even after sufficient evidence was provided to prove they were falsifying the Catholic faith — is also a fact. The Church teaches that one can claim innocence regarding a truth of faith as long as one does not reject that truth when it is presented to him/her, but instead concedes the error and accepts the truth. If this is not the case, the person not relinquishing the error is considered guilty of at least material heresy and is outside the Church. This is not to say that a person is guilty of sin until a hearing can be held on the matter. But the Church does teach that until the proper authorities make a decision, such a person is technically outside the Church, (Canon 2200).

Conclusion

It is perfectly correct to say that the scholastic method is the only method the Church recognizes as true regarding the study and application of philosophy and the presentation of dogmatic theology. Use any other method and there is no guarantee that what one is presenting is the Catholic idea of truth, (although certain exceptions to this rule are made for the sake of theological argument and exposition). Certitude is the most valuable aspect of scholasticism. The difference between Catholics and their non-Catholic brethren is that most non-Catholics deny that it is possible to develop sufficient certitude through scholastic reasoning to exclude all doubt. This was the error of Lammenais, condemned by the Church. And yet countless stay-at-home Catholics torment themselves that they may be on the wrong path and cannot know the truth even after arriving at certitude, because many of them believe it is somehow prideful to be so certain of something that it excludes all doubt. Yet this method does not rely solely on human reasoning; such certainty cannot be obtained unless Catholics achieve formal certitude by relying not on themselves, but on the teachings of the Church. It is a false pride, and a denial of truths of faith, that would refuse to believe in the reliability of certitude. Essentially those believers who question it are saying they cannot trust the dogmatic truths of faith as taught by the Church.

The Modernists were the most vociferous opponents of the scholastics. The next chapter chronicles the attempts of this enemy to destroy all authority — especially the authority of the continual magisterium and scholastic teaching — and replace it with their own infernal system.

Chapter V Endnotes

[1] Rev. A. C. Cotter, S. J., *The ABC of Scholastic Philosophy*, Weston College Press, Weston, Mass., 1949, 21-22
[2] Ibid., 23
[3] Donald Attwater, *A Catholic Dictionary*, McMillan Company, New York, N.Y., 1941
[4] Rev. Michael Mahony S. J., *Essentials of Formal Logic*, Frank Meany Co., New York, N.Y., 1918, 2, 8-9
[5] *Humani Generis*: http://w2.vatican.va/content/pius-xii/en/encyclicals/documents/hf_p-xii_enc_12081950_humani-generis.html
[6] Rev. A. D. Sertillanges, O.P., *The Intellectual Life*, Newman Press, Westminster, Md., 1956, 122-23
[7] Rev. William Turner, Catholic University of America, *Ecclesiastical Review*, Vol. Xl. 1909, Dolphin Press, 123
[8] See Fideism, Traditionalism at www.newadvent.org
[9] Pietro Parente, Antonio Piolanti, Salvatore Garofalo, *The Dictionary of Dogmatic Theology*, Bruce Publishing Company, Milwaukee, Wis., 1951
[10] Rev. William Turner, Catholic University of America, *Ecclesiastical Review*, Vol. Xl. 1909, Dolphin Press, 123
[11] Rev. William Turner, Catholic University of America, *Ecclesiastical Review*, Vol. Xl. 1909, Dolphin Press, 123
[12] Ibid.
[13] Ibid.
[14] Ibid.

[15] Ibid.

[16] http://w2.vatican.va/content/leo-xiii/en/encyclicals/documents/hf_l-xiii_enc_04081879_aeterni-patris.html

[17] http://w2.vatican.va/content/leo-xiii/en/encyclicals/documents/hf_l-xiii_enc_08091899_depuis-le-jour.html

[18] http://w2.vatican.va/content/pius-x/en/encyclicals/documents/hf_p-x_enc_19070908_pascendi-dominici-gregis.html

[19] From a Feb. 5, 1919 papal brief approving the *Catechism of the "Summa Theologica" of Saint Thomas Aquinas For the Use of the Faithful*, R. P. Pegues, O.P., printed originally in 1922 and reprinted by Roman Catholic Books, Harrison New York, N.Y., v-vi

[20] *Studiorem Ducem*, http://www.papalencyclicals.net/Pius11/P11STUDI.HTM

[21] *Humani Generis*: http://w2.vatican.va/content/pius-xii/en/encyclicals/documents/hf_p-xii_enc_12081950_humani-generis.html

[22] Rev. A.C. Cotter, *ABC of Scholastic Philosophy,* Weston College Press, Weston, Mass., 1949, 130-131, 142, 235-236

[23] Ibid.

[24] Ibid., 283

[25] http://www.betrayedcatholics.com/articles/a-catholics-course-of-study/lay-elections-and-false-popes/the-mistranslation-of-one-word-changed-the-church-forever/

[26] Ibid., 103-104

[27] Ibid., 283-284

[28] Rev. T. Lincoln Bouscaren, J.C.L, S.T.D., L.L.B., Canon Law Digest, Vol. II, Bruce Publishing Co., Milwaukee, Wis., 1954, AAS 34-338; Can. 1869

[29] Rev. A.C. Cotter, *ABC of Scholastic Philosophy,* Weston College Press, Weston, Mass., 1949, 250

[30] Ibid., 234-235

[31] Traditionalism, www.newadvent.org

[32] Rev. A.C. Cotter, *ABC of Scholastic Philosophy,* Weston College Press, Weston, Mass., 1949, 246

[33] Ibid., 234

[34] (Summa Pt. I, Q. 1, Art. 1; also Reply Obj. 2).

[35] (Summa Pt. I, Q. 1, Art. 5).

[36] Rev. Joseph Walsh, S. J., (then a professor at Fordham University), from *Logic*, Fordham University Press, New York, N.Y., 1940,102-111

[37] *Ad Apostolorum Principis,* June 29, 1958, http://w2.vatican.va/content/pius-xii/en/encyclicals/documents/hf_p-xii_enc_29061958_ad-apostolorum-principis.html
[38] Rev. Michael Mahony S. J., *Essentials of Formal Logic,* Encyclopedia Press, New York, N.Y., 1918, 86
[39] Quæst. *Disp., De Veritate,* x, 9, ad 3 *Catholic Encyclopedia* under Soul, www.newadvent.org
[40] *Catholic Encyclopedia* under Soul, www.newadvent.org.
[41] *Catholic Encyclopedia* under intellect, www.newadvent.org.
[42] Rev. William Turner, Catholic University of America, *Ecclesiastical Review,* Vol. XI. 1909, Dolphin Press, 123
[43] *Depuis Le Jour,* encyclical on the Education of the Clergy, September, 1899, http://w2.vatican.va/content/leo-xiii/en/encyclicals/documents/hf_l-xiii_enc_08091899_depuis-le-jour.html
[44] *A Cabinet of Catholic Information,* various editors, Duggan Publishing, Buffalo, N.Y., 1903
[45] *Catholic Encyclopedia,* 1911, Volume IX (iii) Canon Law, Rev. Francis J. Schaeffer
[46] Ibid., Volume V (v) see Discipline, www.newadvent.org
[47] Pope Pius IX, *Quartus Supra,* http://www.papalencyclicals.net/Pius09/p9quartu.htm : see also DZ 1673 and 1792
[48] Pope Leo XIII, *Sapientiae Christianae* (1890) §24, http://www.papalencyclicals.net/leo13/l13sapie.htm
[49] Rev. Bernard Wuellner, *Principles of Scholastic Theology,* Loyola University Press, Chicago, 1956, nos. 288-300.
[50] Revs. John A McHugh and Charles J. Callan, *Moral Theology, A Complete Course,* Joseph Wagner, New York, N. Y., 1930, Vol. 1, no. 612 (quoting from St. Alphonsus Liguori.
[51] Canon 1816, 1917 Code of Canon Law
[52] Canon 1747
[53] Pierre Gury, S. J., *Compendium of Moral Theology,* (condensed and adapted for use in American Seminaries by Aloysius Sabetti, S. J. and harmonized with the new Code of Canon Law by Timothy Barrett, S. J.; translated by Paul H. Hallett, St. Thomas Seminary, Denver, Colo.) no date given, 66, no. VI
[54] http://www.newadvent.org/cathen/12403b.htm

[55] Pope Pius XII, *Humani Generis*, http://w2.vatican.va/content/pius-xii/en/encyclicals/documents/hf_p-xii_enc_12081950_humani-generis.html
[56] *Canon Law Digest*, Vol. III, T. Lincoln Bouscaren, S. J., S.T.D., L.L.B, Bruce Publishing Co., Milwaukee, Wis., 1953, decision concerning Can. 2319 § 1,1; Pope Pius XII Motu Proprio 1953
[57] *Vacantis Apostolicae Sedis*, paras. 1-3, Ch. 1; Pope Pius XII, 1945, http://www.betrayedcatholics.com/free-content/reference-links/1-what-constitutes-the-papacy/apostolic-constitution-vacantis-apostolicae-sedis/

Chapter VI — Papal Warnings on the Subversion of the Church
If only the faithful had listened...

A. "Say ye not: a conspiracy..."

Conspiracy theories and actual conspiracies are nothing new; they have existed from the earliest times. The prophet Isaias [1] cautions the Israelites against blaming a conspiracy for their misfortunes. "For thus saith the Lord to me...Say ye not: a conspiracy, for all this people speak is a conspiracy: neither fear ye their fear, nor be afraid, but sanctify the Lord of Hosts Himself." Reverend George Haydock's commentary explains this admonition is made to prevent the Israelites from losing hope and giving in to their enemies. While Catholics may tend to blame Freemasons — and Traditionalists, especially, blame the Jews for destroying the Church — they cannot let themselves off the hook for maintaining silence and falling prey to change agents and Quietistic passivity.

Holy Scripture clearly identifies the attacks of the enemy against God's Chosen People as a conspiracy. Certainly the prophetic books of Scripture, particularly those of Daniel, Ezechiel, and Apocalypse leave little doubt that the plans of the enemy span many centuries and are well choreographed. St. Jude even speaks of "Certain men... secretly entered in" [2] and 2 Peter 1:22 warns of false prophets, lying teachers, and sects of perdition. The popes from the earliest ages accused the various heretical sects of collusion, especially the diverse yet inter-related Masonic sects and other secret societies. Pope Pius IX [3] threatened members of the faithful with Divine vengeance if they cooperated in the schemes of Socialism and Communism, warning, "There will come *from these conspiracies* an increase in miseries and calamities."

Quoting a Masonic publication, the Catholic author Leon de Poncins wrote, "Freemasonry is...a permanent *conspiracy* against political and religious despotism." [4] And from another Masonic source: "[Freemasons are] called to act in the spirit of initiation, that is to say, in a veritable conspiracy of thought and will." [5] So

Masonry refers to *itself* as a conspiracy. Henry Cardinal Manning, in several of his works, also referred to the machinations of various governments against the Church, particularly the German government during *Kulturkampf*, as a conspiracy. De Poncins noted: "Freemasonry...prepares the way for Communism" [6] And Dom Prosper Gueranger predicted in the 1800s:

> "The spiritists, as they are called, in concert with Freemasonry, are preparing the way for the final invasion of the exterior world by infernal bands. *Antichrist, with his usurped power and vain prestige,* will be but the common product of political lodges and of this sect which proposes to bring back, *under a new form,* the ancient mysteries of paganism." [7]

These theologians ably demonstrate how each of these diabolical errors spawns the next. Conservative theologians and laity fighting the liberal influences in this country in the 1800s "believed the Secret Societies to be the distillation, if not the active agent, of all the evils of the centuries." [8]

For Catholics obedient to the teachings of Christ's Vicars who speak in His name, belief in the Masonic conspiracy is not an option but a bounden duty dependent on their very membership in the Church. This is the teaching of the Vatican Council on infallibility. The Council designated four distinguishing marks of infallibility: The Pope must be speaking to all the faithful, as the Universal Pastor, on a matter of faith or morals, and he must somehow indicate that his teaching is to be held as infallible, irreversible. [9] If the faithful refuse to recognize a document bearing these marks as infallible — or if, in the case of Freemasonry, they join a Masonic sect or favor such sects or their teachings, contrary to the laws of the Church — they suffer automatic excommunication, losing their status as Church members. The excommunication pronounced against those who conspire against the Church or any lawful government can be found in Canon 2335.[10] This grave disciplinary measure is a sign that such a condemnation is very serious in nature and is irreversible unless one repents and is absolved; for baptized Catholics who willfully remain outside the Church cannot be saved.

Therefore, those who ridicule Catholic belief in a Masonic conspiracy actually deny true Catholics free exercise of their religion. They also contradict the wise counsels of those Popes esteemed as knowledgeable and credible, even by their enemies, at the time these condemnations were written. Few indeed would dispute the obvious meaning of these words from Pope Leo XIII's *Humanum Genus*:

> Our predecessors, ever vigilant and solicitous for the safety of the Christian people, promptly detected the presence of this dangerous enemy and its designs, as soon as it came out of the darkness in which it had been secretly plotting...Whatever Our Predecessors have decreed in view of opposing the designs and machinations of Freemasonry...We ratify and confirm. Full of confidence in the good will of Christians *We beg and beseech each one of them, for the sake of his eternal salvation,* to consider it a sacred obligation never in the least to deviate from what the Apostolic See has enjoined in this matter. [11]

What is it about Freemasonry that the Church objects to so strenuously? Namely, that from its origin in 1717 according to its own constitutions, it set out to establish a "Universal Church," or as Monsignor Ernest Jouin reported in 1930, from a Masonic publication printed in 1902, "a counter-Church, counter-Catholicism." Pope Pius VII warned that Masonry was conspiring to overthrow the papal see in the early 1800s. Pope Leo XII in *Quo Graviora* taught they were planning "to overthrow the legitimate heads of state and completely destroy the Church." Pope Leo XIII said the same in *Humanum Genus*, writing that Masons wished to destroy completely "the Roman Pontiff's sacred power...which is divinely instituted." He also condemned "Red Masonry," or the Masonic fomentation of revolution contributing to Communism. But according to Monsignor Jouin, it was Pope Benedict XIV who laid out in his constitution *Providas* the reasons that Pope Clement XII condemned the Masonic sect in the beginning. He lists these as: "1) their interfaith activities; 2) their secret; 3) their oath; 4) their opposition to Church and State; 5) the interdiction pronounced against them in several states by the heads of such countries; and 6) their immorality," which Pope Benedict XIV warned would lead decent men to "evil and perversion." [12]

So, there can be no doubt the Masons despised Catholicism and saw it as an obstacle to their dream of a one-world religion. For those who question Masonic persecution of Catholics, the following may be of interest. It is taken from the work *Christianity and American Freemasonry* by William J. Whalen: "A dip into the The New Age [official Masonic publication] itself should convince the most skeptical Mason that the Scottish rite, Southern jurisdiction [especially] is waging a full-scale war on Catholicism, parochial and private schools and any venture of the Christian Church into the area of public morals."

Whalen gives several examples of this persecution in his book, including a quote from a February 1957 article from *The New Age* which states: "One of the foulest and most pernicious of the pressure groups that infests the world of international politics today is the Roman Church hierarchy and its several instrumentalities." [13] In the March issue of the same year, one article styles the Church as "a gigantic force for evil in world politics for 15 centuries." A second article in this same issue accuses the clergy of using "'sophistry, distortion, innuendo, and outright falsehood' to advance their aims." The August issue urges non-Catholics to support a shelter for the rehabilitation of renegade priests "who have been freed 'from the slavery the Roman Church demands.'" All this, Whalen notes, from a publication that "ridicules the idea that Masonry wishes to destroy the Catholic Church," and whose editor claims the magazine "will not tolerate 'any criticism of any religious faith or church' on the back cover of every issue..." [14]

Older examples of this same invective against Catholics can be found in the Masonic Grand Master Albert Pike's handbook *Morals and Dogma,* widely circulated among American members of the Lodge. There Pike writes:

Now from the tomb in which after his murders he rotted, Clement the Fifth howls against the successors of his victims, in the Allocutions of Pio Nono [Pope Pius IX] against the Freemasons. The ghosts of the dead Templars haunt the Vatican and disturb the slumbers of the paralyzed Papacy, which, dreading the dead, shrieks out its excommunications and impotent anathemas against the living. [15]

Other examples are found in the *Alta Vendita* released in the mid-1800s. One section of this work reads:

You wish to cause the last vestige of tyranny and of oppression to disappear? Lay your nets…in the depths of sacristies, seminaries and convents… Bring yourselves as friends around the Apostolic Chair. You will have fished up a revolution in Tiara and Cope, marching with Cross and banner, a Revolution…which [will] put the four quarters of the earth on fire.

And in another place: "Catholicism has no more fear of a well-sharpened stiletto than monarchies have, but these two bases of social order can fall by corruption. Let us then never cease to corrupt." [16] It should be sufficiently clear that Freemasonry set its sights on the Church and State long ago, and its members found their mark.

After having worked long and hard to conspire against the Roman Church in order to portray Her as apparently complicit in all their dealings, the political arm of Freemasonry will destroy even what remains of her external existence, having already gutted Her from within. Some believe the "pope" will move to Jerusalem once Rome is destroyed, there to reign jointly with the Jewish "messiah." Others believe that all vestiges of Rome will be obliterated, and the new reign of Satanism intended all along by Freemasonry will then be ushered in. Master Mason Albert Pike wrote over 150 years ago concerning the approaching world wars:

The Third World War must be fomented by taking advantage of the differences caused by the 'agentur' of the 'Illuminati;' *between the political Zionists and the leaders of the Islamic world. The war must be conducted in such a way that Islam...and the...State of Israel mutually destroy each other.* We shall unleash the nihilists and the atheists and we shall provoke a great social cataclysm which in all its horror will show clearly to all nations the effect of absolute atheism. Then everywhere the people will...exterminate these destroyers of civilization and the multitudes disillusioned with Christianity, whose spirits will be from that moment without direction and leadership and anxious for an ideal, ...*will receive the true light through the manifestation of the pure doctrine of Lucifer, finally out into public view.* A manifestation which will result from a general reactionary movement which will follow the destruction of Christianity and Atheism; both conquered and exterminated at the same time. [17]

The Jews and Muslims, according to Masonic plan, will mutually destroy each other. The nihilists and atheists already are manufacturing strife and civil unrest on a much larger scale than ever before. But what final blow will be dealt the church in Rome, outside its actual physical destruction? The now deceased British Israel "prophet" Herbert Armstrong gave us the following idea of what sort of deception the enemies of the Church might try to foist upon the world:

> The ancient Babylonians migrated west and settled in Italy. Their religion was the Assyrian-Babylonian mystery religion. It is going to come as a breathtaking, awesome, shocking surprise when the world learns that one Simon, the sorcerer of Samaria in the time of the original Apostles, leader of the Babylonian mystery religion having the title of Pater or Peter, meaning Papa, actually appropriated the name of Christ and the Christian principle of grace...and started what today is called Christianity. How astonished the world will be to discover that it is not, and never was,

the outgrowth of the Church of God founded by Jesus Christ and His Apostles...People will be shocked to learn how they have been deceived. [18]

But the meaning of "mystery Babylon" has taken on a new dimension with the discovery of America's direct involvement with the betrayal of the Church. This ties together the fortunes and political destinies of today's Vatican with those of the U.S., possibly making Rome the spiritual and primary intended object of the prophecy but America the secondary and literal object. As St. Jerome once said, in the Apocalypse there are as many meanings as there are words; but the primary meaning and the sense in which it is to be taken first, commentators caution, is the spiritual. Apocalypse Chapters 17 and 18 seem to lay out in great detail the destruction of both Rome and its partner in crime, America, in punishment for creating the false church and deceiving those who believed they were Catholic. Without the help of "democracy" and the direct influence of Freemasonry, neither the "elections" of Angelo Roncalli and Giovanni Battista Montini nor the false Vatican 2 council could ever have taken place. Had Catholics listened to the Roman Pontiffs who began condemning Masonry long ago, they would have seen this coming. Had their bishops ordered pastors to warn them from the pulpits on a regular basis, they could have known what to expect today. But in America, especially, these warnings were played down to pacify the liberal element then making itself felt as a presence among the faithful. However, the papal decrees below offer no excuse for Americans' unquestioning acceptance of tenets contrary to Catholic faith.

B. The Popes condemn Freemasonry

The first papal bull routing the Masons, Pope Clement XII's *In Eminenti*, was published in 1738. This bull pronounced automatic excommunication for all laymen who joined secret societies *or favored them in any way*, an excommunication reserved *speciali modo* (in a special manner) only to the Roman Pontiff, and then only at the point of the offender's death. Clement declared his bull "valid forever," but it was not promulgated or enforced in some countries owing to Gallicanist inroads. (Gallicanism was a heresy that eroded papal authority insofar as it considered the body of bishops together with the faithful equal to or above the power of the pope. This group of primarily French and later English theologians taught that in reality the pope was only a ministerial figurehead and the bishops and laity were "the Church.")

Pope Clement's irrevocable and perpetual excommunication was reaffirmed and reissued by Benedict XIV with his constitution *Providas* in 1751, because previously it had been dismissed and ignored. Pope Pius VI, later exiled from the Vatican, lamented that already Masonry had penetrated into the royal courts, houses of nobility, the universities, and even into "the Lord's sanctuary." Monsignor Jouin, a Catholic historian specializing in things Masonic, notes that the names of the clergy could already be found entered on the rolls of Masonic lodges during the French Revolution. According to Jouin, Pope Pius VII singled out the 18th degree Rose-Croix in 1821when he condemned Masons for "holding in contempt the sacraments of the Church." Jouin comments, "To what does the Pope refer if not to the [Rose-Croix's] odious parody of the Sacrament of the Eucharist?" [19] And if clergy were members of the lodges already in the late 1700s, how could anyone today be surprised they now control the church in Rome?

Pope Leo XII decried the Masonic penetration of public schools and ratified and confirmed forever all previous decrees against Masonry in his encyclical *Quo Graviora* issued in 1825. [20] Impervious to papal decrees, fueled by its Rosseauistic-democratic promises of "liberty, equality and fraternity," Masonry flourished as the Age of Mary dawned in Paris with Our Lady's apparition to St. Catherine Laboure. The world might revel in Masonic degeneracy, but Our Lady would console her children. On May 13, 1846, four months prior to Our Lady's arrival at La Salette, Pope Gregory XVI received a packet containing *The Permanent Instructions of the Alta Vendita* from the hands of one Jacques Cretineau-Joly, a French Catholic journalist and historian. According to Monsignor George Dillon, the "supreme government of all the secret societies of the world," formerly exercised by the Illuminati, passed to the highest lodge of the Italian Carbonari following Illuminati founder Adam Weishaupt's death. [21] The *Permanent Instruction* was the Carbonari's declared blueprint for the years 1820-1846. Two weeks after receiving this declaration of war against the Church, Pope Gregory XVI died. His successor Pope Pius IX, personally warned by La Salette seer Melanie Calvat about the Church's imminent downfall, renewed all his predecessors' anathemas against "all these and many other abuses and errors," and also against any and all secret sects, which by then were multiplying furiously.

In his first encyclical delivered on November 8, 1846, Pope Pius IX especially brought attention to "'those secret societies, which, while working in the dark, are undermining religion, morality and political prosperity,' and condemned the widespread infidelity of the times and the pernicious influence of false teachers." [22] This Pope later petitioned Cretineau-Joly to publish the text of *The Permanent Instructions of the Alta Vendita* in his upcoming work, *The Roman Church and Revolution*, which Joly did. In 1858, Pius IX issued the long-awaited definition of Our Lady's Immaculate Conception, and while the Masonic demons ground their teeth and groaned, they also struck back. Although the Blessed Virgin had instructed Melanie to publish the La Salette secret also in 1858 (just one year before Cretineau-Joly's *The Roman Church and Revolution* was published), it was suppressed and Gallicanist bishops and their sympathizers viciously attacked the apparition.

It was Pope Pius IX who formulated the following concise summary of Masonic activity:

> If one takes into consideration the immense development which these secret societies have attained; the length of time they are persevering in their vigor; their furious aggressiveness; the tenacity with which their members cling to the association, and to the false principles it professes; the persevering mutual cooperation of so many different types of men in the promotion of evil; one can hardly deny that the 'Supreme Architect' of their association (seeing that the cause must be proportionate to

the effect) *can be none other than he who in the sacred writings is styled the Prince of this World; and that Satan himself,* even by his physical cooperation, directs and inspires at least the leaders of these bodies, physically cooperating with them. [23]

Pope Pius IX also condemned Freemasonry in 1846, 1864, 1873 and 1876. In an Allocution given on March 12, 1877, he went so far as to say:

> The work of demolition and general destruction of everything connected with the structure and order of the Church is almost consummated, if not to the extent of the desires and hatred of the persecutors, it is at least so far as concerns the sad heap of ruins they have succeeded, up to this time, in piling up...Piece by piece, little by little, day after day and one after another, they took the means and resources we so much needed for the proper guidance and direction of the Catholic Church. [24]

Those who stood to lose the most from the divulgence of the La Salette secret ruthlessly discredited it for years. Yet what little was known about the secret may have been more instrumental in directing the Church's advance against Masonry than Catholics will ever realize. In writing her (never published) private communication to Pope Pius IX, Melanie used the word 'infallibly,' prompting some historians to speculate that this message inspired Pope Pius IX to call the Vatican Council. The thundering anathemas of the Popes against Freemasonry had been largely ignored on the Gallicanist premise that not all the bishops endorsed the condemnations. Once the Vatican definition made individual papal pronouncements as binding as those confirmed by an ecumenical council, even in matters of science and politics that touched on religion, all doubt was removed. Freemasonry had to be rejected as the avowed enemy of the Church, and true Catholics could not hide behind Gallicanism or any other pretense and remain in the fold of Christ.

As predicted at La Salette, Satan manifested himself in more audacious ways, even in convents and monasteries, shortly after the definition of papal infallibility. In the 1870s, the Rosicrucians established an English branch of their Society open only to 33rd degree Masons. Fabian Socialism also flourished in England, and Marx wrote his Communist Manifesto. Everywhere science triumphed; and if Catholics could not be seduced by even the lowest degrees of Masonry, certainly they became intoxicated with the luxuries and conveniences wrought by (Kabbalistic-Masonic) capitalism and materialism. The Rosicrucians, who had long labored to secretly perfect the true alchemic gold — mechanical inventions, modern medicine, and scientific theory — first introduced the processes of these theories with all their accompanying philosophies. The Industrial Revolution changed the face of modern society with such inventions as the steam engine, cotton gin, motorcar, light bulb and the telephone. Madame Helena Blavatsky founded her Theosophical Society in New York in 1874 and began promoting table rappings, seances, and necromancy (communication with the dead.) The Ouija board became a parlor pastime, the effects of magnetism came to light, and hypnotism entertained the curious at social events and theaters. The volumes *Frankenstein* and *Dracula* were written; werewolf legends gained popularity. And in Africa, but especially in Haiti, secret societies adept in Voodoo were developing what would eventually constitute the basis for modern pharmacology.

Pius IX's successor Pope Leo XIII, delivered the final papal blow against Masonry in his famous encyclical *Humanum Genus*, written in 1884. This encyclical was issued the same year that the pope experienced a frightening vision in which all the forces of evil converged upon the Church, very nearly succeeding in destroying the Catholic faith. This pope understood the enemy well, describing secret societies as "the Manichees of old" and denouncing their goals to revive paganism, destroy Church and State, and seize control for themselves. He renewed once again all the condemnations of his predecessors, who had described Masonry in various documents as "the enemy of all good, ravening wolves, perverts, first-born of the

Devil" and other appropriate epithets. Most importantly, however, both Popes Pius IX and Leo XIII made it unmistakably clear that although the sects all took great pains to appear unrelated, they "are identical to Freemasonry, which is the central point from which they proceed and toward which they converge." [25] Certainly this encompasses a much wider scope today than ever could have been imagined in Pope Leo's time. Leo XIII also requested the publication of *The Permanent Instruction of the Alta Vendita*, personally financing the reprinting of Monsignor Dillon's work. He referred again to Freemasonry in 1890, 1892, and in 1894. In 1902, Leo XIII described Freemasonry as "the permanent personification of the Revolution. It constitutes a sort of society in reverse whose aim is to exercise an occult overlordship upon society as we know it, and whose sole *raison d'etre* consists in waging war against God and His Church." [26]

In condemning Modernism and the Sillonists, Pope St. Pius X struck his particular blow to the Masonic menace then engaged in employing disaffected Catholics to do their publicity work. He also condemned "the ungodly sects" by name in 1906, according to Léon de Poncins, who also noted that Benedict XV had personally commended Monsignor Jouin in 1919 for his studies devoted to the exposition of Freemasonry.

Condemning communism, Pope Pius XI refers to certain (Masonic) groups that appear unrelated to this error: "Under various auspices totally unconnected to Communism, they form societies and found periodicals with the exclusive aim of infiltrating their ideas into spheres which otherwise would not be readily accessible to them." [27] Communism and Socialism both are listed as actual Masonic rites on Lady Queensborough's pyramid. [28] In his above-mentioned work, de Poncins commends both Lady Queensborough and also famed Freemasonry expert Nesta Webster for their adept exposure of the sect.]

During the reign of Pope Pius XII, the Holy Office condemned the secret societies in 1946 and 1949. In the 1949 decision, the Holy Office reiterated what had been stated in 1947: "Since nothing has happened to cause any change in the decisions of the Holy See on this question, the provisions of Canon Law remain in full force for every kind of Masonry whatsoever." In his address to the Seventh Week Pastoral Adaptation Conference on May 23, 1958, Pope Pius XII stated: "The roots of modern apostasy lie in scientific atheism, dialectical materialism, rationalism, Illuminism, laicism *and Freemasonry, which is the mother of them all...*" [29]

Right up until the reign of John 23, then, the Catholic Church consistently condemned this diabolical sect and all its affiliates. Can there be any doubt whatsoever that these decrees of the popes, issued for more than 200 years, bound the faithful absolutely and still bind them even today? And seeing the Church lying in ruins and civil governments failing at every turn, is it not indisputable that what they warned the faithful about has come to pass? This destruction of all order and especially the disappearance of the Church as the champion of Divine truth and civil order would lay the foundation for the reign of Antichrist. And it began in the Vatican itself.

C. "Certain men, secretly entered in..." (Jude 1:4)

In 2015, David A. Wemhoff published his monumental 990-page biography on Jesuit John Courtney Murray, detailing how the Central Intelligence Agency (C.I.A.) waged doctrinal warfare against the Catholic Church. [30] Given the extensive documentation of this process in *John Courtney Murray, Time/Life, and the American Proposition: How the C.I.A.'s Doctrinal Warfare Program Changed the Catholic Church*, the book must be read in its entirety in order to comprehend the full import of this heinous act and the methods used to carry it out. The declassified documents presented in Wemhoff's work demonstrate the completion of the plan to subvert the Church.

Wemhoff is an attorney in South Bend, Indiana and currently serves as the Chair of the International Trade and Customs Law Committee for the FBA International Law Section. As the title suggests, those who read this work will forever change their thinking on the "freedoms" offered to Catholics in this country, and American Catholics will sorrowfully realize the true source of the final demise of their beloved Church. Most Catholics know that high-level Freemasons (and, some believe, certain Jewish factions) helped bring the Church to Her knees. But American intelligence officials? Many Catholics will find this difficult to process, although all these groups interconnect, as Pope Leo XIII explains in *Humanum Genus*. While Wemhoff's book is a masterpiece, he does not support the premise of this work; and therefore, he does not correlate what happened to the Church at the hands of the C.I.A with what was prophesied to happen on the spiritual level. Nor does he relate this program of doctrinal warfare chronologically with what was transpiring in the Vatican. Nevertheless, his work casts even greater doubt on the nature of certain events occurring in the final years of Pope Pius XII's reign than many supposed.

Wemhoff's book describes the C.I.A.'s effort as a classified operation officially beginning in 1953 which included the necessary (coercive) psychological component [31] devised to reshape the thinking of *American Catholics* regarding religious liberty and their belief in Americanism as a heresy. If one studies this heresy it is quickly seen that Pope Leo XIII, in condemning it, was actually addressing the slow slide into indifferentism regarding the Church's pre-eminence as the one true ark of salvation, in stark contrast to so many other Protestant sects. The pope basically forbade any minimalizing of Catholic truth that would tend to place all religions on an equal footing in order to satisfy political unity. This would be placing state over Church, condemned repeatedly by the popes as heretical. But leveling the field was precisely what the C.I.A set out to do. [32]

According to Stephen Good, author of *The CIA*, doctrinal warfare was waged despite the C.I.A.'s own charter signed in 1947, which "forbade intelligence activity by the C.I.A. within the borders of the United States." [33] So the organization wasted no time in betraying its own professed promises to Americans, since only six years later it was busy using its vast spy network, developed during the war years, to subvert the Catholic Church here and abroad. Those outraged over the intelligence agency scandals today forget the C.I.A. was investigated in 1974-75 by a presidential panel and two congressional investigative committees for what some reported as "wrongdoing and misuse of power on a massive scale." [34] Goode continues: *"The Dallas Morning News* believed that the charges of domestic spying by the C.I.A. should send 'shudders of apprehension through all Americans who revere this country's constitutional freedoms.'"[35] While Democrats pushed to reform the agency, Republicans believed weakening the C.I.A. in any way could play into the hands of U.S. enemies. Yet what defense is this now, when it is clear from declassified information that the agency egregiously violated the constitutional rights of millions of American Catholics and more importantly, used brainwashing tactics to accomplish its mission?

Doctrinal warfare also was referred to as "psychological warfare," later described in one of Isaac Asimov's works as "psychopolitics." The military refers to it as "psyops," or:

> Planned operations to convey selected information and indicators to foreign audiences to influence their emotions, motives, objective reasoning, and ultimately [their] behavior...The purpose of psychological operations is to induce behavior favorable to the originator's objectives. [36]

This method was employed recently during the 2016 elections and continues to operate today. American intelligence agencies developed and perfected it during World War II and the Cold War, but the method was actually formulated in the private sector and later expanded on by U.S. intelligence officials. Wemhoff explains how media baron Henry R. Luce, co-founder of *Time/Life* magazine, carefully honed the psyop as a weapon using the written word and, with the help of his associates, embedded it in magazines, newspapers, and other publications throughout the world.

The goal was to change the thinking of the Catholic hierarchy and leadership in order to convince them America was the ideal society and that the Church should endorse its underlying principles. The ready hook used by the C.I.A. to promote doctrinal warfare was Pope Pius XII's understandably morbid fear of Communism: the operatives convinced most of the American hierarchy that without the spread of democracy to the world and the endorsement of democratic principles, the Cold War (Wemhoff calls it World War

III) would end in a Communist win. While the plan was to use the Catholic Church primarily to propagate these views, operatives also worked to infiltrate and convince other conservative religious bodies as well. The goal was to change entirely the Church's view and definition of religious liberty and to prevent the application of any and all religious principles to public policy. The Church had consistently condemned as indifferentism the notion that any non-Catholic religion or all religious teaching in general could be said to suffice for the attainment of eternal salvation. Men can sin and reject Catholicism as the one, true Church; but this absolute freedom of conscience cannot be styled as a "right," for error has no rights. The Church also teaches that democratic governments are wrong in separating Church from state [37] and in promoting even paganism and Satanism as valid religions. Pope Gregory XVI condemned this "liberty of error," calling it "insanity" and teaching that it would open up "the bottomless pit from which John saw the smoke which darkened the sun arise, while scorpions came out of it to afflict the earth," (Apoc. 9: 2-3). [38]

Doctrinal warfare promoting the obliteration of these doctrines in the minds of the faithful was waged on Catholics and others beginning in 1941 (unofficially) and concluding with the closing of the false Vatican 2 council in 1967. In the end, the false council document *Dignitatus humanae* contradicted the constant teaching of the Church by removing any possibility of the existence of a truly Catholic state, which would violate inalienable rights to "freedom of worship." A Catholic state could neither "command or inhibit acts that are religious," meaning the Catholic state could no longer forbid the proselytizing efforts of other religions or teach its own religion as the state religion (due to the new necessity to maintain separation of Church and state). [39] This false teaching denied the right of the Church to exist in the temporal realm, a right that She has always upheld and insisted on exercising anytime Her subjects are under the rule of a Catholic leader. Henry Cardinal Manning best expounds on this topic in his *Temporal Power of the Vicar of Jesus Christ*. As he points out in his first lecture, "The power of the pope, spiritual and temporal, taken in its complex, is an ordinance partly direct and partly indirect, yet in both characters divine." So here Manning is speaking of Divine law, not any law or decree *only* of the popes. Pope Pius IX, furthermore, condemns in his *Syllabus of Errors* the following:

- We must have at least good hope concerning the eternal salvation of all those who in no wise are in the true Church of Christ.

- It belongs to the civil power to define which are the rights of the Church and the limits within which it may exercise these rights.

- The Church does not have the power of defining dogmatically that the religion of the Catholic Church is the only true religion.

- The Church does not have the power of using force, nor does it have any temporal power, direct or indirect.

- The sacred ministers of the Church and the Roman Pontiff should be entirely excluded from all administration and dominion over temporal things.

- It does not belong exclusively to the ecclesiastical power of jurisdiction, by proper and natural right, to direct the teaching of theological matters. [40]

And it was precisely the Syllabus that would become the target and the sticking point for the "council fathers" at Vatican 2. Later Traditionalists, especially members of Marcel Lefebvre's St. Pius X Society, would teach their followers that Pope Pius IX's *Syllabus of Errors* was never intended to be accepted by Catholics as an infallible document, and in this they were simply echoing Novus Ordo teaching. In a 1960 work exposing the continuing dangers of Modernism and Liberalism, Monsignor J.C. Fenton wrote the following:

[The Modernists] were perfectly willing that the Catholic Church should continue to exist as a religious society, as long as it did not insist upon the acceptance of that message which, all during the course of the previous centuries of its existence, it had proposed as a message supernaturally revealed by the Lord and Creator of heaven and earth. They were willing and even anxious to retain their membership in the Catholic Church, as long as they were not obliged to accept on the authority of divine faith such unfashionable dogmas as, for example, the truth that there is truly no salvation outside of the Church... What these men were really working for was the transformation of the Catholic Church into an essentially non-doctrinal religious body. They considered that their era would be willing to accept the Church as a kind of humanitarian institution, vaguely religious, tastefully patriotic, and eminently cultural. And they definitely intended to tailor the Church to fit the needs and the tastes of their own era.[41]

And so it seems the Modernists and the Freemasons reached some kind of accord to allow the Church to exist, stripped of her Traditions and her dogma, as long as it could be assured She would readily accept Americanism. Monsignor Fenton continues:

The liberal Catholic since the time of Montalembert has been well aware of the fact that the basic theses he proposes as acceptable Catholic doctrine have been specifically and vehemently repudiated by the doctrinal authority of the Roman Church. If he is to continue to propose these teachings as a member of the Church, he is obliged by the very force of self-consistency to claim that the declarations of the *magisterium,* which condemned his favorite theses do not at this moment mean objectively what they meant at the time they were issued. And, if such a claim is advanced about the *Mirari vos arbitramur,* there is very little to prevent its being put forward on the subject of the Athanasian Creed. Pope Leo XIII and St. Pius X were well aware of the fact that the advocates of the false Americanism and the teachers and the protectors of the Modernist heresy were employing this same discredited tactic. This common basis of the false doctrinal Americanism and of the Modernist heresy is, like doctrinal indifferentism itself, ultimately a rejection of Catholic dogma as a genuine supernatural message or communication from the living God Himself. [42]

Clearly, liberalism led to Americanism and contributed to Modernism in its mad rush for progress and modernization. As Pope St. Pius X had warned, Modernism was the "synthesis of all heresies," and it was first and foremost dedicated to impugning papal authority. Conservatives today fighting the inroads of sexual perversion into society in general but especially public schools, the erosion of basic rights to freedom of belief, encroaching euthanasia, and the continual plague of abortion and birth control promotion would benefit greatly from the strong and unflagging support of a true pope for their efforts. As it is, they are fighting alone since Francis is such a namby-pamby character, even for a false pope. Protestants have suffered too as a result of the Church's subversion, and honest ones will readily admit it. Trace the increase in acts of anarchy, murder, divorce, social unrest, sexual perversion, sexual assault, gang violence, terrorism, and the abuse of those unable to defend themselves — all have skyrocketed since the rise of the false church in Rome, and the situation is only going to worsen. Protestants need to see that what they attribute as evil to the church in Rome today only dates back to the betrayal by Montini and others, not to the Church's inception or to some other point along the line. Evidence of the Church's deliberate infiltration, coercion, and subsequent subversion might just convince them.

It would be wise for Catholics and Protestants alike today to closely scrutinize the political lay of the land regarding the above statements and to see what stage these traitors have now reached in their goal of world dominion and total eradication of Christianity. It is clear they have made great strides. The Catholic religion was targeted and actual infallible teaching discarded, yet today the Muslims — who immigrated to this country and are not American born — are not hindered in the least in the practice of their (pagan) beliefs. In fact, they are protected and assisted should any sign of prejudice appear. Politicians can pretend all they want that the C.I.A.

would never violate "the sacred trust" between the intelligence community and the American people, as one congressman commented during intelligence leak investigations in early 2017; but this is disingenuous at best. "Conservative" (even Novus Ordo) news commentators can praise the C.I.A. for their "brave actions taken" in the service of the American people, but where was this sacred trust, these brave actions, where Catholics were concerned? Are *they* not American citizens? Isn't it perfectly clear that the disinformation and psychological warfare continues on a daily basis, in order to perpetuate the lie?

So then who is surprised that former C.I.A. Director John Brennan was named as one of three top Obama officials to participate in unmasking members of the Trump campaign? Unmasking consists in identifying those Americans caught in a wiretap who are (usually innocently) speaking with foreign agents being monitored by the American government for one reason or another. The names of these Americans, under federal law, are supposed to remain anonymous where the public is concerned, although they are known (or can be learned) by those doing the wiretapping. Many Americans find it difficult to believe that their own government would brazenly violate the Fourth Amendment rights of American citizens for political reasons, but this is no new deviation from the tactics this organization has engaged in since its inception. If they would not hesitate to subvert the faith of millions, when most Americans believe this country was founded on Christian tenets, why would politics stop them, when the goal was to topple both the Church as well as civil governments? The overall current state of affairs gives the distinct impression that Catholics, as a religious group, had to be neutralized at all costs. That one religion in the celebrated land of religious freedom was so singled out is proof not only that the Masonic conspiracy spoken of by numerous popes was and is a reality, but also that the Catholic Church Herself is all that She ever claimed to be.

But what was the essence of the religious liberty debates, and how did Murray's proposition contradict the teachings of the continual magisterium? Monsignor Fenton details the Church's position below.

Correct Catholic position on religious liberty, rights

In his encyclical *Longinque Oceani* addressed to the American bishops, Pope Leo XIII prophetically identified the problem with society that most specifically plagues America today, and also condemned separation of Church and State.

> Without morality, the State cannot endure — a truth which that illustrious citizen of yours [George Washington] ...perceived and proclaimed. But the best and strongest support of morality is religion. She, by her very nature, guards and defends all the principles on which duties are founded, and setting before us the motives most powerful to influence us, commands us to live virtuously and forbids us to transgress. Now what is the Church other than a legitimate society, founded by the will and ordinance of Jesus Christ, for the preservation of morality and the defense of religion? [...]
>
> [In America], the Church is free to live and act without hindrance. Yet though...this is true, it would be very erroneous to draw the conclusion that in America is to be sought the type of the most desirable status of the Church, or that it would be universally lawful for or expedient for State and Church, to be, as in America, dissevered and divorced. [43]

Here the pope pinpoints the solution to the present evils we witness today. Media "experts" and government officials go on endlessly about what will resolve the many problems America is currently facing, the deep divide between the "right" and "left." They pretend new elections, more regulations, better laws, better leaders, and always more money will provide the ultimate fix for what ails us. They never allude to the fact that without a true return to morality, as Pope Leo XIII stresses above, no effective and meaningful change is possible. And he reminds his readers that only the legitimate heir to Christ's teachings, the Catholic Church, can successfully defend religion and preserve that morality. He warns the American hierarchy, however, that it is dangerous to think exactly what some of them, even then, were thinking — that the status of the Church under American democracy was the "most desirable," or that separation of Church and state is "universally lawful." Yet that is exactly what Murray, Felix Morlion and Professsor Lilly would later succeed in promoting. And it was nothing less than the revival of the original Americanist heresy.

The Church's battle with Americanism began over a century ago when Pope Leo XIII condemned the heresy in *Testem Benevolentiae.* [44] That heresy consisted of the opinions of the Americanists, to be discussed further below. Murray's teaching, which was only a slightly revised version of Americanism, was subtle; it basically fell in line with John 23's *Pacem in Terris* which actually crossed a line by teaching that man has an inherent *right* to follow his conscience in choosing the religion to which he wishes to belong. Because this ambiguous document did not properly distinguish between the different types of rights and obligations affecting Catholics, it deliberately left the door open for the ecumenists to forge ahead with all their overtures to the Protestants, Jews and pagans, while stomping on the rights of Catholic states, at least in principle. But early in the debate, Monsignor Fenton summed up the Church's true position on religious liberty, referring to several articles written by Connell and Shea as well as his own contributions on the topic. Carefully separating out the matter, he wrote:

(1) Every American has the *civil right* to choose his religion. By force of our Constitution, Congress is prevented from "prohibiting the free exercise" of any religion.

(2) Every American, and for that matter, every human being, has the *moral right* to *choose* his religion [for] ...there can be no rightful attachment to a religious body other than by way of free choice. To frustrate such a choice is, according to Catholic teaching, a moral wrong.

(3) Every American has the *civil right* to choose a religion forbidden by God....Civil law makes no attempt to enforce the divine precept...according to Catholic teaching. This is, according to Catholic teaching, perfectly right and proper. The state exists in

order to procure and to protect the common temporal well-being of its citizens. For the achievement of this end, the state commands those actions which are manifestly necessary to its purpose, allows those things which are indifferent to it, and forbids what is manifestly destructive or detrimental to its aim. Thus there are many acts contrary to the natural law and to the divine positive law, as, for example, sins of thought or desire, with which civil law is not concerned.

(4) It is *objectively and morally wrong* for any American, or for that matter, any human being, to disregard or to disobey a command issued by God Himself, when that demand is directed to all men and when it is brought to the attention of mankind with adequate clarity….No man or no group of men would be objectively guilty of moral wrong were they to fail to act in accordance with the divine injunction because it had never come to their attention through no fault of their own. Such persons are in a state of invincible ignorance which renders [their] activity…subjectively blameless. [45]

Monsignor Fenton goes on to note that man has "a moral right to act in conformity with the moral law" and no right, strictly speaking, to violate that law. Man is never free to disregard or disobey a divine precept. As regards the civil law, Reverend Cicognani notes that it is always to be obeyed unless it is contrary to Divine law. [46] According to the principles advanced by Pope Pius XII in *Ci riesce*, "While religious and moral deviation ought always to be hindered whenever possible, because the toleration of that deviation is immoral in itself," nevertheless "under certain circumstances…when there is a question of achieving a higher good or of avoiding a more serious evil, these higher standards render it permissible and sometimes even preferable not to impede an error or evil" which the state might hinder or repress. [47] The Pope notes that this has always been the practice of the Church Herself, and is not to be seen as any sort of concession to modern states or compromise of Catholic teaching. This is evidenced in the Church's concordats with various nations, he comments. This principle, however, is qualified by Pius XII as follows: When those governing a Catholic state are faced with such questions of fact, they must consult the pope in order to resolve them, and this only after an intensive investigation. This statement of Catholic belief is *not* in agreement with Murray's teachings.

Instead, Murray believed that the state need only proceed politically and in practice according to the natural law. St. Thomas Aquinas holds that all rational creatures to some extent know the eternal law, if not in itself then at least in its reflection. "For every knowledge of truth is a kind of reflection and participation of the eternal law, which is the unchangeable truth, as Augustine says (*De Vera Relig.* xxxi). Now all men know the truth to a certain extent, at least as to the common principles of the natural law: and as to the others, they partake of the knowledge of truth, some more, some less; and in this respect are more or less cognizant of the eternal law." *Natural Law* is "the rational creature's participation of the eternal law." The first precept of natural law is that "good is to be done and pursued, and evil is to be avoided.... An action is said to be against the natural law if it is not in keeping with the end intended by nature. The light of reason that enables man to discern what is good and what is evil is an imprint of the divine Light on his soul." [48]

While the natural law is part of the divine positive law, it is an imperfect part. Divine positive law in its perfect fulfillment is the exposition of revealed truths about attaining the desired supernatural end, truths revealed by Jesus Christ and defined by the Roman Pontiffs acting in Christ's stead. Originally Murray recognized the New Law as superseding the Old, but this changed over the course of his teaching on the American Proposition, excluding all necessity for the Church to continue in Her evangelization of the world and establish the reign of Christ as King. As true Catholics know, this is contrary to Catholic teaching. While Pope Pius XII granted Catholics in the U.S. what amounts to a dispensation from public evangelization in certain circumstances, as will be seen below, he never pretended that this was the ideal situation for the Church. Catholic theologians such as Reverend John Ryan, D.D., Monsignor Fenton, Reverend Francis Connell, CSsR, and Dr./Monsignor George Shea defended the Church's right to spread the Catholic faith, defend it, and protect Catholics from the assaults of those teaching false doctrines.

"Various documents indicate that Murray was placed under prior Roman censorship for all his writings for publication" (as of 1954). [49] Secret propositions based on Murray's errors that were to be condemned had been forwarded by Cardinal Ottaviani to Fenton and others. Unfortunately, Pope Pius XII died before the official condemnation of Murray and other liberal theologians, including Jacques Maritain, could be issued. But at the very least, it would seem Murray was considered as suspect of heresy. So even before any official condemnation by the Holy Office, he was excluded from the Church as a member and presumed guilty under Canon 2200 until his innocence was proven or he recanted. Murray's errors as reflected in the propositions included the denial that the Catholic state was the true ideal to be pursued by society, the belief that full-blown religious liberty in a democracy is a valid political principle, the teaching that it is enough that the democratic state generally guarantee the Church full freedom of religion and nothing more, and the implication that Pope Leo XIII's *Immortale Dei* can be interpreted in such a way that it denies God His supreme right to be worshipped. [50]

Wemhoff goes into great detail to prove that although the proclamation from the false council *Dignitatus Humanae* enshrined Murray's teachings, nothing strictly erroneous or heretical is contained in the proclamation. But this is a moot point. Murray was spreading his errors long before the council convened, and his goals already had been achieved. He worked from the old Americanist heresy model; and his aims were the same as Americanists Archbishop John Ireland, James Cardinal Gibbons, and Bishop John J. Keane. And it is not surprising that the reputed Freemason Mariano Cardinal Rampolla worked in concert with these men, especially Keane. One of the errors of this "American Catholicity…was the teaching that the American government 'is the best possible and most suited to our religion' and that the 'Sovereign Pontiff['s] …temporal principality…in this country be waived.'" [51] There is no need to paint Murray here as anything other than a successor to the cause of Americanism, already condemned as a heresy. All the Americanist seeds were sown in the late 1800s, and

Murray simply tended the sprouting plants. Author Thomas McAvoy relates that Americanist proponents then were already discussing the evolution of dogma and the cautious, gradual introduction of changes that would allow the Church to align with democracy. We hear from Keane that even among the pagans, "God has given to all of them some part of the truth." [52] This would later be repeated in John Paul 2's first "encyclical" as follows: "The Fathers of the Church rightly saw in the various religions as it were so many reflections of the one truth, 'seeds of the Word...'" [53]

Most telling of all, however, was Isaac Hecker's remark that Gibbons would make a great pope after Leo XIII, but since he could not be elected, "politics" would need to resolve the problem by introducing a Pope favorable to Americanism. Already these men were looking forward to a "new spirit" in the Church, and talk was made of not separating oneself from the Church but "taking over" the Church. "The ultimate religion, then, will be the synthesis of all religions," one anonymous Americanist wrote; and we know where such language comes from. [54] This is precisely the scenario Bishop Fulton Sheen foretold. Murray was no new and brilliant theorist — he had been sent to complete the execution of the *Alta Vendita:*

> What we must ask for, what we should look for and wait for...is a pope according to our needs. We have the little finger of the successor of Peter engaged in the ploy...This pontiff, like most of his contemporaries, will be more or less imbued with the [revolutionary] Italian and humanitarian principles that we are going to begin to put into circulation. [55]

Perhaps then the plan called for the election of Mariano Cardinal Rampolla to the papacy, a plan which went awry. Murray would later succeed in finding his replacement.

Religious liberty only a means to an end

The dual-purpose aim of the American government was not just to spread democracy throughout the world; it was first to democratize then to destroy the Church Herself. This automatically erased any claim that the Church once had to temporal dominion, a second heresy. This was achieved in 1964 when Paul 6 forever laid aside his tiara, announcing he intended it to symbolize the renouncement of the Church's claim to temporal authority. Intelligence operatives treated Her as any other political enemy the U.S. had ever encountered, sending in agents well-versed in the practice of a more generalized version of coercive or psychic persuasion to reduce the Catholic Church, founded by Christ Himself, to democracy. And what happens today when the American government wishes to plant American-style democracy in a "newly converted" country? They set up elections and monitor them, as done during the Obama administration with Israel, to secure the desired outcome! The papal election held in 1958 was not an ecclesiastical election; it was a *secular* election, with newly converted Americanists poised to elect one of their own as head of the Church. *This was a crucial first step to guaranteeing the "redefinition" of religious liberty and the abandonment of the Church's teaching on Her temporal rights, both realized at Vatican 2.* During an interview Feb. 16, 2018 with former CIA director James Woolsey, Fox News host Laura Ingraham posed this question: "Do we meddle in other people's elections? Woolsey answered: "Only for a very good cause, in the interests of democracy…But it was for the good of the system in order to avoid communists taking over." So setting up Montini, the pro-Communist, as the preferred "pope" was for "a very good cause"? Try again, Woolsey.

Unbeknownst to all but a few, as Monsignor Fenton reports in his *Diaries*, [56] Pope Pius XII was preparing an important encyclical on Church and State at the time of his death. This may explain why he delayed the condemnation of Murray and the other liberals, and it may possibly provide a motive for his demise.

Because the Lateran Treaty had declared the Vatican as its own state in the 1920s, world leaders were free to deal with the head of Vatican State just as they would any other head of state. Once the spiritual aspect of the papacy was compromised and reduced to the level of all other religions, the Church simply became another civil government to be democratically fine-tuned by American operatives.

This attenuation could not have occurred under Pope Pius XII or any of his predecessors or true successors. But of course, the "powers that be" could not have actively promoted the idea of a "modern" pope during the reign of a legitimate pope without raising suspicion. So they appealed instead to the prized sense of autonomy and broadmindedness of Americans, with the help of Montini's favorite collaborators, the C.I.A. — aided by Reverend John Courtney Murray, Reverend Felix Morlion, and Henry Luce.

The Church's teaching on the temporal power is that governments must follow the divine positive law taught by Our Lord. Ideally civil governments, when the leaders of these governments are truly Catholic, are obligated to adopt the Catholic faith as the state religion and to rule from a Catholic legal and moral perspective. Conversion cannot be forced, as Pope Leo XIII and Pope Pius XII taught, but the formation of public policy must proceed based on *Catholic* principles, not just the natural law. In contrast, the liberal theologians promoting Americanism taught that the natural law was to be used as the basis for such policy, and the meaning of the natural law was left open to much obfuscation and misinterpretation. The particular natural law interpretation referred to here can be traced to the teachings of John of Paris, who defined it not only as the 10 Commandments and Jewish law pre-Moses, but the "laws of nations" in existence prior to the coming of Christ. John of Paris also supported the idea of deposing true popes and taught that the College of Cardinals as well as the "whole Church" is superior to a (true) pope, the very error later condemned by the Church as the Gallicanist heresy. [57] This was the beginning of the shift from emphasis on the reign of Christ the King in the political spectrum to the purely political aspect of government existing in the pre-Christian era. This explains why there is always talk today of "Father God" by the Protestants in their prayers, and, in some denominations, little mention of Christ.

Already in the late 1800s, the Americanists were toying with the idea of such an arrangement; but as Robert Cross notes, "Non-Catholics have seldom been able to agree among themselves on the dictates of the natural law..." [58] Basically this appeal to the natural

170

law was used to sidestep belief in Jesus Christ and appeal to the already existing liberal Protestant, "Judaeo-Christian" mentality; to deny, effectively, the Incarnation. Writing in the mid-1950s, author Will Herberg accurately described and detailed in his *Protestant, Catholic, Jew* the amalgamation of these three religions then underway, without referencing the (then unknown) entity responsible for engineering it.

Henry Luce and his close friend John Courtney Murray, S.J., funded by the Rockefellers, worked from America to spread this new "gospel" across the nation and beyond. Jesuit Gustave Weigel and other liberal-minded "Catholic" clergy were only too happy to help. But the real action was in Rome; it fell to Luce's above-mentioned collaborator Reverend Felix Morlion, whose role in this hostile takeover of the Church is recounted below. It is believed his organization somehow began its interface with Luce's in the early 1940s.

The Knights of Malta and public opinion manipulation

Because Morlion's media vehicle to promote Luce's philosophy is entitled *The Apostolate of Public Opinion*, some background on exactly where the public opinion concept originated is necessary. Grand Master Mason Albert Pike explains how useful it is to those in power to mold public opinion, a practice we have seen shamefully exhibited (primarily) by the liberal media over the past several decades. Pike writes:

> Public opinion is an immense force, and its currents are as incomprehensible as those of the atmosphere. Nevertheless, *in free governments it is omnipotent; and the business of the statesman is to find the means to shape, control and direct it.* According as that is done, it is beneficial and conservative or destructive and ruinous. [59]

Pike's openly anti-Catholic work clearly indicates Masonry's intent to secretly shape and control governments before overturning them completely. This plan is elaborated upon at greater length by

Sigmund Freud's nephew, Edward Bernays, in his work *Propaganda.*

> The conscious and intelligent manipulation of the organized habits and opinions of the masses is an important element in democratic society. Those who manipulate this unseen mechanism of society constitute an invisible government which is the true ruling power of our country. We are governed, our minds are molded, our tastes formed, our ideas suggested, largely by men we have never heard of. This is a logical result of the way in which our democratic society is organized. Vast numbers of human beings must cooperate in this manner if they are to live together as a smoothly functioning society.

> Our invisible governors are, in many cases, unaware of the identity of their fellow members in the inner cabinet. They govern us by their qualities of natural leadership, their ability to supply needed ideas and by their key position in the social structure. Whatever attitude one chooses to take toward this condition, it remains a fact that in almost every act of our daily lives, whether in the sphere of politics or business, in our social conduct or our ethical thinking, we are dominated by the relatively small number of persons — a trifling fraction of our hundred and twenty million — who understand the mental processes and social patterns of the masses. It is they who pull the wires which control the public mind, who harness old social forces and contrive new ways to bind and guide the world. [60]

What Catholics would not expect is to see propaganda inserted by an international "Catholic" organization into Catholic publications, in any form; and yet this is precisely what happened, and in the name of Catholic Action no less. The establishment of such an organization was very carefully executed, well supported financially by the C.I.A., and traceable to entities that later became change agents for liturgical and other reforms. At the time this organization was established, Pope Pius XII probably believed it was a worthwhile project. But in his address to the International Convention of the Catholic Press given Feb. 18, 1950, he told Catholic journalists "to always refrain from 'making' public opinion," and instead advised them to "serve it," but only if they do so with "unalterable respect and deep love toward the Divine order; that is to say, to the Church as She exists…here below…in space and time." [61] If anything the pope said or did appeared to deviate from his official teaching on public opinion, entered into the *AAS*, [62] his choices in this matter may have been constrained by others, and "official" statements may even have been made in his name without his knowledge. Only later would he discover the true intent and identity of those working for the destruction of the Church and the nature of their relations with others who cooperated in bringing it about.

Prior to World War II, Morlion was the one who established just such an organization, an international intelligence agency known as The Center of Information Pro Deo (INTERCIP) in Lisbon, Portugal. Morlion's agency was actually the brain child of Goncalves Cardinal Cerejeira, Patriarch of Lisbon, who requested that Morlion operate it to train his staff in the journalism techniques the priest had developed while instructing Catholic Action members in propaganda techniques. Prior to his Pro Deo work, Morlion operated an anti-Communist, anti-Nazi offensive in Belgium, a press service specializing in film subject matter, and opened an additional Catholic Press Center in Belgium. In 1942, William Donovan, head of the Office of Strategic Services (OSS), the wartime forerunner of the Central Intelligence Agency (C.I.A.), brought Morlion to the U.S. from Portugal. In 1944, Pope Pius XII rewarded Donovan with a papal knighthood for service rendered to the Catholic hierarchy during the war. Donovan would later fund Catholic Action projects in America. *Shortly after the Allied victory in Europe, Donovan and Morlion succeeded in establishing Pro Deo in the Vatican itself.* Author Martin A. Lee, writing in a 1983 issue of *Mother Jones,* notes:

When the Allies liberated Rome in 1944, Morlion re-
established his spy network in the Vatican; from there he
helped the OSS obtain confidential reports provided by
apostolic delegates in the Far East, which included
information about strategic bombing targets in Japan. [63]
It was the Knights of Malta aided by Montini and others who
helped Nazi war criminals escape to South America, according to the
same *Mother Jones* article.

In the period following the war, the United States hastened
to capitalize on the apparatus Donovan had established,
particularly in Italy...C.I.A. money was dispensed to many
[Italian] bishops and monsignors, one of whom was the
future Paul VI, and Catholic Action became another
primary recipient of C.I.A. funds...Dr. Joseph Retinger
[who was advocating for the European union]...through Dr.
Luigi Gedda [Pope Pius XII's medical advisor], was able to
conscript the services of the future Pope Paul VI [who
formerly was one of four section leaders of Vatican
intelligence]....Even during the war, Montini had worked
with the American intelligence services, passing
information to and fro between the Vatican and the
OSS...As Archbishop of Milan, he turned over the dossiers
of politically active priests...The rapport between the
C.I.A. and the Vatican became closer in 1963 when John
XXIII died and was succeeded by Paul VI. [64]

This narrative is corroborated by David Wemhoff in Part IV,
Chapter 11 of his work cited above. In it, Wemhoff quotes private
correspondence listing Montini, also his great friend Jacques
Maritain, as avid Pro Deo supporters. Later in Part XIV, Chapter 59,
Wemhoff cites declassified documents in which a C.I.A.
correspondent names Montini as co-founder of Pro Deo and Cardinal
Giuseppe Siri as being appointed in some way to participate in Pro
Deo operations. C.I.A. operatives also claim that Pope Pius XII
(unofficially) endorsed Pro Deo, but his official papal documents do
not reflect Morlion's statements regarding democracy, nor could they
reflect his Americanist viewpoint.

In November 1953, Pope Pius XII was ill and had been for months — some believe he was poisoned. At the time, Montini was his acting pro-secretary. In the early 1950s, the C.I.A. was experimenting with a number of mind-altering drugs for use on targeted subjects, including marijuana, LSD, mescaline, PCP, cocaine, heroin, and other combinations that would later emerge as psychotropic medications. The beginning of Pius XII's illness in 1953 coincided with the year that marked the successful conclusion of doctrinal warfare in earnest according to Wemhoff. Luce gave his first speech on The American Proposition at Pro Deo University on November 29, 1953, before "thousands" of clerical and secular dignitaries. At that time Pope Pius XII's illness was beginning to worsen; and if aware of the speech, he was probably not in any shape to object to it. It is not a far stretch to think that perhaps the first act of the American operatives was to try to eliminate Pius XII as a possible obstacle to their grand plan. Since Montini had easy access to Pius XII, he would have been the most logical person to perform the C.I.A.'s dirty work. But the doer of the deed could have been anyone. And in fact, Pope Pius XII did not die although his doctors expected it. Instead, he was revived, he confided to friends, by a vision of Christ. He would live four more years, and those years would be the occasion of many conflicts with his staff and a hostage mentality (actuality?) that would prevent him from fully functioning as pope in the Vatican.

It was shortly before his illness worsened that Pope Pius XII learned of Montini's true role as a U.S. agent. Ill or not, the pope took action. Following the additional discovery that Montini was actively cooperating with the Communists and that some of the information he had leaked to the Soviets resulted in the assassination of bishops and priests sent secretly into Russia, he confronted Montini. At the insistence of Francis Cardinal Spellman,[65] Pope Pius XII dismissed Montini from the Vatican and assigned him to Milan as archbishop, opting not to grant him the expected red hat that usually went with the appointment. But Montini remained popular among C.I.A. circles, continuing to receive C.I.A. project money. The organization clearly knew that Montini was a fully invested player; and according to Lee's *Mother Jones* article, they later predicted he would be elected "pope."

Although Wemhoff does not specifically address this in his work, Catholics cannot lose sight of the inescapable fact that the real objective here was to place Roncalli and Montini in St. Peter's Chair — not as true popes, but as leaders of a New Order amalgamated church. And while it appeared the C.I.A had been the driving force behind the Vatican takeover, the real movers and shakers, the elite entities to which Wemhoff refers in his book as directing American interests were the true behind-the-scenes operators dictating the outcome. They were double agents of a sort, acting as both intelligence officials in certain cases but also as members of a (secret) society. That society was the Knights of Malta Order of St. John Hospitallers, and its immense influence in American financial affairs continues to this day. Author Penny Lernoux points out the double role of several Knights of Malta members as intelligence officials occupying various positions in successive presidential administrations. [66] One of these was Claire Booth Luce, wife of Henry Luce and a later-in-life convert to Catholicism. She served first as a congresswoman, supporting Sen. Joseph McCarthy's probe into Communist infiltrators in the State Department and elsewhere and later as an ambassador and intelligence committee member. While McCarthy may have been confused concerning the source of the "infiltration," he was correct in suspecting something was definitely up. He also may have been used as a dupe by Luce to distract attention from the doctrinal warfare process itself and focus it on Communism. His last speech to Congress indicates he eventually became aware Freemasonry was the true culprit. In his final communication to Congress before he died of cancer, McCarthy wrote:

> Jonathan Williams recorded in his *Legions of Satan*, 1781, that Cornwallis revealed to Gen. Washington that '...in less than 200 years...the whole nation will be working for divine world government...and they will all be under the invisible all-seeing eye of the Grand Architect of Freemasonry'...American statesmen and military leaders

down through the years [have] given aid *and intelligence* to the enemies of the United States because they did not have knowledge of the invisible subterfuge that stalks this land. My eyes were opened the day my colleague from Ohio handed me *Wagners Freemasonry, an Interpretation.* If every American would read it, they would no longer ask why and how it has happened. [67]

But that it definitely *has* happened — and happened at the hands of Freemasons doubling as U.S. intelligence officials — is beyond dispute.

> Between 1948 and 1950, the then Bishop Montini said to P. Felix A. Morlion, O.P.: 'A generation would not even pass before peace would be made between the two societies (Church and Freemasonry)'....In a private letter of Count Léon de Poncins, an expert on Masonic matters, one reads: 'with Pius X and Pius XII, we, Freemasons, were able to do very little, but with Paul VI, we won.' In his book... *Ecumenism As Seen by a Freemason of Tradition*, Mr. Marsaudon, a leader of Freemasons, wrote on the subject of Montini: 'You can talk about the reality of the Revolution, which advanced from our Masonic lodges, extending beautifully over the Basilica of St. Peter.' Indeed, the "liturgical reform" was provided by the Mason, [Abbe] Roca, in 1883. He had written: 'In an ecumenical council [Vatican 2 – Ed.], the Church will undergo a transformation that will put one in harmony with the state of modern civilization.' [68]

That Morlion, Murray, and Luce were primary change agents in promoting Masonic ideals is evident from what is presented here and from the very men who supported and funded them. Morlion boldly names his funders in his book, and they are none other than the kings of business and finance found on the rolls of the American Knights of Malta. It was no coincidence, then, that Morlion hailed the "business-like spirit of America" to better effect the international redirection of *public opinion* he advocated, based largely on

Americanist principles modeled on the teachings of John Courtney Murray. As will be shown below, Pope Pius XII was suspicious of the make-up of the Knights, even though his friend from papal nuncio days in Germany, Cardinal Spellman, was their supporter and spiritual advisor. Angelo Cardinal Roncalli, the future John 23, also was a patron of the group. It was rumored the Knights were shot through and through with Freemasons; and Pope Pius XII must have received at least partial confirmation of these rumors, although an investigation into the organization by Cardinal Tisserant in 1949-50 seemed to exonerate them. In 1951, Pope Pius XII refused to name a new head (grand master) for the Knights, *a leader whose power is equal to that of a cardinal*. This vacancy persisted until the pope's death. [69] It was following the investigation and later fateful decision to leave the Knights headless that Pius XII's health issues began.

Lee's *Mother Jones* article relates that the Knights of Malta presented a high-ranking C.I.A. operative, James Jesus Angleton, with a prestigious award in 1948.

> Angleton was head of the Rome station of the OSS. Later, on his return to Washington, he ran what was tantamount to the 'Vatican desk' for the C.I.A...During the early years of the Cold War, Angleton organized an elaborate spy network that enabled the C.I.A. to obtain intelligence reports sent to the Vatican by papal nuncios stationed behind the Iron Curtain and in other 'denied' areas. This was, at the time, one of the few means available to the C.I.A. of penetrating the Eastern Bloc.[70]

Lee details how many C.I.A. heads and operatives were also Knights of Malta and the intimate interaction, especially following Pius XII's death, between the agency and Rome. Particularly prominent among the Knights was (Joseph) Peter Grace, Chairman of W. R. Grace and Co., with Grace himself and nine of the company's directors listed as knights. The list of knights is peppered with U.S. government officials, including cabinet members, ambassadors, and others.

Only the wealthiest of the wealthy can hope to become knights. The Black Nobility of Europe and the oldest and wealthiest European families constitute its members. Using an adapted version of the Jocist method of Catholic Action and Catholic Action itself (funded in the U.S. by the C.I.A. as a front, Wemhoff and others observe), along with a liberal application of Thomism, Morlion was able to distribute newsletters, books, and other articles, as well as host radio shows and seminars. His focus on public opinion clearly indicates he was using Masonic methods, with a "Catholic" twist; but that does not make them Catholic. Other indications taken from his work suggest he was actually promulgating Masonic teaching under the guise of Catholic belief. These include:

- The ideal, which Morlion aspired to all along, was to use:

    The traditions of the great world religions, and most completely through Christian tradition...[as] the moral norms 'written in the heart of man.' [the natural law] ...Pro Deo holds that the spirit of denominational controversy has to be kept out of the common concern for the reconstruction of temporal society on universal moral principles. It promotes measures which tend to organize world society through the practical recognition of the interdependence of all nations.[71]

This ideal places all religions on "an equal footing" (indifferentism) in order to enlist them in the service of the political economy and put them at the mercy of private, powerful interest groups. Notice that temporal society is no longer to be organized on Catholic moral principles guided by the Roman Pontiff, but "universal" ones, whatever those may be.

- Jacques Maritain is quoted as follows in Morlion's work, "Liberty, equality and fraternity" [the Masonic credo] are *"fundamentally of Christian inspiration."* [72] Morlion calls this slogan "noble."[73] Prior to his death, Pope Pius XII was preparing to excommunicate Maritain and Murray for their heresies (see Chapter IX, D of this work). According to Wemhoff, Rome officially forbade Murray to write on matters regarding Church and State in 1954, but the hierarchy failed to enforce the condemnation. [74]

- "Christians all over the world must devote their conjoint energies to the cultivation of a common political tradition inspired by moral and religious principles...Democracy can and must become the soundest guarantee for world peace."[75] The Catholic Church, on the other hand, following St. Thomas of Aquinas, prefers monarchy to other types of government.

- "The *Judaeo-Christian* revelation constitutes the core of the present tradition of the major part of mankind and is shared, more or less, by Mohammedan and Asiatic peoples." [76]

Fatima in the service of Pro Deo

Goncalves Cardinal Cerejeira of Lisbon, Portugal, who hosted Morlion in his city prior to his move to New York, is quoted by Morlion in his work:

> "What we want is a handful of specialists *trained in public opinion*...Militant Catholics must be schooled not only to repeat what bishops and priests have said, but also to bring the light of the Gospel into the furthest fields of human life..."[77]

What about what the *popes* have said? Is this the real reason Catholics never learned the Third Secret of Fatima? Apparently, Cerejeira was one of the first among the hierarchy to adopt the Luce/Murray, Pro Deo stance. Does this explain why Fatima was used so effectively as an anti-Communist vehicle to aid in spreading doctrinal warfare? Would the Third Secret have revealed that while Communism was indeed referenced in the Secret, the real enemies were those who intended to fulfill Holy Scripture, precipitating the Great Apostasy and installing a false pope as a true pope? Sister Lucia said it all by referring to Apocalypse chapters 8-13 as the source of the secret. Was the intended consecration of Russia *not* so much to deter them from spreading Communism but to prevent a fatal schism in the Church, historically one of Russia's most glaring errors?

Morlion recommends, "The creation of a void around evil influences; of a conspiracy of silence against lies is often the best method of combat." He calls it the "method of deflation..." [78] But given Morlion's outlook, who would he be conspiring against — those who were not Americanists? Catholics who wholeheartedly revered the pope and objected to his endorsement of Masonic ideals? Or perhaps it was the threat perceived in Sister Lucy, who could have herself revealed the Third Secret without hierarchical approval had she not been effectively silenced, possibly even murdered. (Certainly the woman presented to the world as Sister Lucy beginning in 1967 was not the true seer, as many have observed. According to one Internet report, the records of the Dorothean nuns in Coimbra, Portugal show Sister Lucy died in 1949, reportedly following a severe bout of bronchitis. And there does not appear to be any photos of Sister Lucy from the 1950s. A new, imposter Lucy seems to resurface again in 1967 at Fatima with Paul 6.) In fact, a saint had predicted the use of the "conspiracy of silence" technique and even named its source decades before. Pope St. Pius X wrote in his *Pascendi Dominici Gregis*:

> No wonder the Modernists vent all their gall and hatred on Catholics who sturdily fight the battles of the Church. But of all the insults they heap on them those of ignorance and obstinacy are the favorites. When an adversary rises up against them with an erudition and force that render him redoubtable, *they try to make a conspiracy of silence around him to nullify the effects of his attack*, while in flagrant contrast with this policy towards Catholics, they load with constant praise the writers who range themselves on their side, hailing their works, exuding novelty in every page, with choruses of applause; for them the scholarship of a writer is in direct proportion to the recklessness of his attacks on antiquity, and of his efforts to undermine tradition and the ecclesiastical magisterium... [79]

Catholics have long complained that somehow the Fatima message was compromised to represent something never intended by Our Lady or the seers. Their "Catholic sense" was right in this regard. These questions first surfaced following the replacement of "for many" (*pro multis*) by "for all" in the formula used for the consecration of the wine in the Canon of the true Latin Mass. Most telling was the prayer Our Lady reputedly gave to the seers as the second part of the secret, to be said between the Mysteries of the Rosary: "Oh my Jesus forgive us our sins, save us from the fires of hell. *Lead all souls to heaven* especially those most in need of Thy mercy." [80] It appears that the translation of the prayer quoted by nearly all those writing on Fatima was one of several and the one that best-suited their purposes, or the hidden motives of the superiors they consulted.

The easiest way to determine the true meaning of Our Lady in delivering this prayer is to examine the other two prayers given to the children, one by the Angel prior to the apparitions and the other by Our Lady herself, to say when making sacrifices for sinners. The Angel's prayer reads:

> Most Holy Trinity, Father, Son and Holy Ghost, I adore thee profoundly and offer the most precious Body, Blood, Soul and Divinity of Jesus Christ, [once] present in all the tabernacles of the earth, in reparation for the outrages, sacrileges and indifference with which He Himself is offended. And through the infinite merits of His Most Sacred Heart and of the Immaculate Heart of Mary, *I beg of thee the conversion of poor sinners.* [81]

The Angel used the same formula in his prayer that Our Lady would later use in hers. In asking the children to offer up their daily trials as sacrifices, Our Lady told them: "Oh my Jesus, it is for love of Thee, against the outrages committed against the Immaculate Heart of Mary *and for the conversion of poor sinners.*" Likewise, the prayers after Mass for Russia's conversion read: "graciously hear the prayers which we pour forth to Thee *for the conversion of sinners,* and for the freedom and exaltation of Holy Mother Church..." So instead of "lead all souls to heaven," shouldn't the prayer read, "Convert poor sinners…" since this appears to be consistent with the true intent of the Fatima message? Nothing in an apparition can even *appear* to be contrary to faith; an apparent contradiction shows the apparition to be false. The Church has declared the Fatima message to contain nothing contrary to faith and morals, however, so the prayer between the mysteries can only be interpreted as reflecting the primary Fatima message: prayer (especially for the conversion of sinners), reparation, repentance, and sacrifice. Our Lady's message to the children cannot be, must not be, perverted to support the heretical American proposition.

Morlion's *modus operandi* and the "new order"

Shining through all of Morlion's work is the great anticipation of a new world rising, a globalization of religion based on the natural law, an establishment of a new world order based on the sacrosanct "democracy" of the United States. So now it becomes clear how and why this effort was driven and from whom it came.

> Inspired by the spirit of brotherhood, ultimately based on the fatherhood of God, it promotes interest and understanding for the sound heritages and achievements of all peoples and further is a richer current of culture and a broader scope of progress by the interaction of West and East, North and South….It promotes measures which tend to organize world society through the practical recognition of all nations, which under divine Providence is becoming a fact in the present stage of civilization. [82]

One of the chapters in Morlion's book is entitled "Mobilization of the Laity." By redirecting Catholic Action from its true course and funding it with C.I.A. money, Morlion realized this mobilization and succeeded in creating a "collective conscience" among Catholics. Pope St. Pius X, again, answers the statement of Morlion above in *Pascendi Dominici Gregis*:

Note here, Venerable Brethren, the appearance already of that most pernicious doctrine *which would make of the laity a factor of progress in the Church.* Now it is by a species of compromise between the forces of conservation and of progress, that is to say between authority and individual consciences, that changes and advances take place. *The individual consciences of some of them act on the collective conscience, which brings pressure to bear on the depositaries of authority, until the latter consent to a compromise, and, the pact being made, authority sees to its maintenance."* [83]

Pope St. Pius X condemns the idea that "The Church...needs to be adjusted to contemporary historical conditions and to the forms of civil government publicly in vogue." Here, he aptly describes the process of thesis, antithesis and synthesis that socialists and Communists believed would bring about the changes needed to establish their dominions.

Already in the late 1800s, liberals calling themselves Catholics had begun demanding a greater share of power in ruling the Church, participatory roles in the liturgy (including lay deacons and lectors) and even advocated for relaxation of obedience in obeying papal and diocesan decrees. [84] Their efforts succeeded only in small part. It is clear Morlion very much intended, at the behest of his masters, to revive this strategy by using the laity as a "factor of progress" in the Church. He took great pains to mobilize them, then marched them left to the tune of the progressives. If one follows the thinking and teaching process as presented in Morlion's book, it is easy to see where he is going. First, he seizes the minds of his readers with the Catholic "take" on what it all means and what can be done. By his own admission, certain news and opinions are filtered out deliberately that do not fit in with Morlion's mindset. This is not honest journalism, but omission of the facts needed to make a balanced decision, now known as "fake news." True journalism tries to present both sides and lets the audience decide for themselves, while pointing out any discrepancies and/or factual errors. When corruption is involved, and it is verified as such, the perpetrators are presumed innocent until proven guilty, but this does not mean they have a "voice" in news reporting. The truth is presumed to be determined by means of the judicial process.

Morlion claimed his journalists "are chosen from among those who possess a general synthesis of the great principles of Christian philosophy and theology and are especially trained to apply scholastic logic to the treatment of current news. These rules are elaborated in a special course…for the formation of specialists." [85] But given his affiliations and the outcome, these principles were undoubtedly those of the then re-emerging Modernists, the liturgical and sacramental deconstructionists such as de Lubac, Congar, Schillbeeckx, Bernardin, Rahner, and others who would later dismantle Mass and Sacraments. His gospel of democracy as the only solution to the world's problems is soundly refuted by the scourge of the Modernists, Pope St. Pius X, in his *Our Apostolic Mandate* on the Sillon in France.

> We fear that worse is to come: the end result of this developing promiscuousness, the beneficiary of this cosmopolitan social action, can only be a Democracy which will be neither Catholic, nor Protestant, nor Jewish. [86] It will be a religion…more universal than the Catholic Church, uniting all men to become brothers and comrades at last in the 'Kingdom of God'. We do not work for the Church, we work for mankind…
>
> Further, whilst Jesus was kind to sinners and to those who went astray, He did not respect their false ideas, however sincere they might have appeared. He loved them all, but He instructed them in order to convert them and save them. Whilst He called to Himself in order to comfort them, those who toiled and suffered, it was not to preach to them the jealousy of a chimerical equality. Whilst He lifted up the lowly, it was not to instill in them the sentiment of a dignity independent from, and rebellious against, the duty of obedience…Leo XIII, [in his] Encyclical on political government which We have already quoted, [wrote]: 'Justice being preserved, *it is not forbidden to the people to*

*choose for themselves the form of government which best
corresponds with their character or with the institutions
and customs handed down by their forefathers.' And the
Encyclical alludes to the three well-known forms of
government, thus implying that justice is compatible with
any of them.* [87]

President John F. Kennedy seemingly warned Americans in his
address before the American Newspaper Publishers Association on
April 27, 1961:

The very word 'secrecy' is repugnant in a free and open
society; and we are as a people inherently and historically
opposed to secret societies, to secret oaths and to secret
proceedings. We decided long ago that the dangers of
excessive and unwarranted concealment of pertinent facts
far outweighed the dangers which are cited to justify
it...For we are opposed around the world by a monolithic
and ruthless conspiracy that relies primarily on covert
means for expanding its sphere of influence — on
infiltration instead of invasion, on subversion instead of
elections, on intimidation instead of free choice, on
guerrillas by night instead of armies by day. It is a system
which has conscripted vast human and material resources
into the building of a tightly knit, highly efficient machine
that combines military, diplomatic, intelligence, economic,
scientific and political operations. Its preparations are
concealed, not published. Its mistakes are buried, not
headlined. Its dissenters are silenced, not praised. No
expenditure is questioned, no rumor is printed, no secret is
revealed. It conducts the Cold War, in short, with a wartime discipline no democracy would ever hope or wish to
match. [88]

Was Kennedy not only talking about the Soviets but also sending
us a hidden message here? Internet reports and biographical sources
reveal that his relations with the C.I.A. were not always the most
agreeable. What other president in recent history has warned the

American public against secret societies? Did he pay for this attempt to alert Americans with his life?

By that time the work of Morlion, Luce, and Murray was almost accomplished. Once the false doctrine of religious liberty was proclaimed at Vatican 2, the project was complete. In 1963, Morlion would help John 23 and President Kennedy negotiate peace with Cuba during the Cuban Missile crisis, as Franco Bellegrandi reports in his work *Nikita Roncalli,* and others have likewise reported. Morlion also would continue to contribute in a major way to Rome's changed perspective on the Jews, participating in the negotiations described in a 1966 mainstream magazine article "How the Jews Changed Catholic Thinking." [89]

Morlion and his cohorts ruled out the application of anything but democracy as a legitimate form of government (although the Constitution of his INTERCIP organization claimed it supports no particular form of government or political party).[90] They attempted to construct, and succeeded in constructing, the very "Democracy" Pope St. Pius X had feared would result: the "universal" (read one world) religion of democracy, uniting "all men" as brothers and *comrades.* St. Pius X called this false religion the "Kingdom of God," and the V2 church calls itself the "People of God." Morlion promoted the Americanist Proposition by disseminating public opinion after the fashion of (his brother) Masons, those Masons concealed within the government and within the Knights of Malta (as well as other "Catholic" orders). These Roman-like traitors (*traditores*) funded their efforts with the thirty pieces of silver from government coffers, in collusion with Roncalli and Montini, among others, to betray Christ and His Church. They deceived American Catholics in order to advance their own political agenda and that of Freemasonry, just as those at Christ's trial by the Sanhedrin lied to convict Him. The Church had done nothing wrong, but they crucified Her anyway. And by operating the very mechanism for the Church's destruction from the Vatican itself, they effectively erected a type of the abomination of desolation in the holy place long before Roncalli's reign.

How did the Church enter Her Passion? In the very same manner Her Master did: "I was wounded in the house of them who loved Me." [91] By reorienting the Catholic Action groups that should have been trained to rush to protect the faith when the reign of the usurper popes occurred, the traitors robbed the faithful of any recourse to the "clean-up" crews sent in to "rescue" them. The Fatima Secret was being fulfilled, and the time had come for the Church to join Her Savior mystically in His Passion. Catholics became like the fox who agreed to carry the scorpion across the river. At one time they knew better and realized his deadly venom could kill. But deceived by the idea of false liberal charity, they believed "love" would remove the dangers. And so the faithful were poisoned by Masonic doctrine, forgetting the sect's hatred for the Church and their commitment to destroy Her in order to rule the world. This even though, up to the very end, the warnings of the clergy and lay authors such as Leon de Poncins were clear. Having dismissed them as the enemy and admitted them as friends, those yet calling themselves Catholic cannot — will not — see that Masonry's infernal blueprint for world destruction moves forward at an ever-increasing pace with the help and the blessing of what they have come to believe is the "Catholic" church.

D. Secret societies and the cult explosion

Following the dismantling of the Church by the false Vatican 2 council, American youth, bereft of true spiritual guides and exposed to increasingly liberal teachings on college campuses, began gravitating to the many cults that proliferated in the wake of a general breakdown in religion. They were joined by members of the older generation, suffering cultural shock after the many disruptions and social changes in the 1960s. Fundamentalist cults, Wicca, Satanic cults, survivalist cults, pagan cults, a flood of new age cults, suicide cults, organizations promoting Eastern mysticism, and even "Catholic" cults sucked in vulnerable and naïve young men and especially women. These groups isolated them from their families, derailed their dreams and too often left them bankrupt, disillusioned, depressed, and even mentally ill. Many of these cults required their members to keep their activities secret, at least on some level, or otherwise involved them in secret practices and rituals. Most of these groups were simply fads that died out of their own accord. Some lingered (such as Moon's Unification Church, the Hare Krishna Movement, EST, Scientology, The Way, and various Traditionalist groups) but were rocked by scandals that alerted the general public to the dangers they posed. New cults emerged on a regular basis. All used some form of mind control. But one group enjoyed a remarkable popularity that eventually earned them the ranking of America's third largest religion.

This group can be classified as a pagan cult that exists in a variety of related organizations spread across the U.S., all teaching some form of Tantric Buddhism. This type of Buddhism is not to be confused with the more traditional forms brought to this country by oriental immigrants over the years. It is best described by an ex-devotee and author, Christine Chandler, who spent 29 years in its clutches before realizing the alarming dangers it poses to true religious freedom in America:

> Hindu Tantra, Tibetan Tantra and new-age and amalgam 'new religious movements' previously known as cults [are destined] to be the Gaia handmaiden of international corporatism and a spiritualized world citizenship of austerity for the future — a purposeful influence to shift Western thinking from national sovereignty and the creative individualism and responsibility it depends on, to slide us into communitarianism [the new communism] with its 'whole is greater than its parts' viewpoint....The Dalai Lama [is] a self-declared Marxist....[His] *Kalachakra Tantra* teachings...include a prophecy about the coming of a World War III; a *Shambala* war that will destroy Semitic and other 'heretic' religions [including Christianity] after which a 1,000-year peace and [a great ruler] ...will come into being....In the Tibetan Lamaist Tantric cult, they are patiently waiting for Christians Jews and Muslims to destroy each other, as their Tibetan Kalachakra prophecy predicts. [92]

In her book, Chandler explains how the lamas running these groups exact strict obedience, are misogynistic while presenting as pro-woman, practice sex with minors and then exact obedience from devotees to keep the acts secret, hate westerners while pretending to "love" them, fleece their adoring devotees on a regular basis, present themselves as god-kings to be adored, and accomplish all this by reducing awareness and rational thought through constant meditation. She warns that over several decades, these Buddhist groups have insidiously penetrated the halls of academia, especially the ranks of those practicing psychology, by spreading the teaching of "mindfulness" or "contemplative psychology," which has raked in millions for the cult. It also has made its presence known in the education field and regarding religion, supports a "new ecumenicalism," which translates into a cultural and religious syncretism. Few are aware of the astonishing inroads made into this country and Canada by these Tantric sects, or the growing number of devotees who follow this lama-worship cult today. Tantric Buddhist centers dot the North American landscape from coast to coast — hundreds of them. And this does not count the thousands of charities, non-profit organizations, and other spinoff organizations the cult has generated, Chandler says. According to Wikipedia, between 1990 and 2008, 1.2 million became Buddhist followers, a 170 percent increase. Forty percent of these live in Southern California and many others in Colorado. And Chandler notes that the majority of those embracing Tantric Buddhism over the years are disillusioned Catholics and Jews.

What is remarkable about the cult phenomena is its predictable course. Kevin Orlin Johnson, Ph.D., a Novus Ordo author, provides a good assessment of cults in a booklet based on a live presentation he made, yet Johnson fails to see that what he is describing applies to his own sect as well. He sets out four criteria for cult involvement:

1) Distinction from mainstream society on the basis of some shared characteristic or condition, usually a weakness or a failure;
2) Bridge-burning — performance of some act not allowed by the conventions of mainstream society;

3) Replacing the norms of mainstream society with norms of its own;
4) Severing ties with mainstream society and embracing cult norms will provide relief. [93]

Johnson rightly identifies Protestantism as a cult, as well as Charismatics. But Charismatics are accepted by the Novus Ordo usurpers, although he fails to acknowledge this. Moreover, by substituting "the Church as a Divine society" for "mainstream society," the actions of the Novus Order church can be ranked as cultistic. The Novus Order is a cult because by Johnson's criteria: 1) Those who engage in it are bound together by their acceptance of the new liturgy and expanded lay rights, their belief in ecumenism, and their belief that the unchangeable Church can change; 2) they burned bridges with the true Church by changing both the appearance of the Church as well as her liturgy and doctrine, which was never permissible; 3) they created laws and new teachings of their own to replace the existing law and doctrine; and 4) they believed that by practicing liberal charity and shedding the "rigid" properties of the old Church, they would fit in with the rest of society and attract more members. But many of their churches have closed and church attendance has dwindled.

What is described above is precisely what the Tantric Buddhists and many other New Age sects have done. Most important to their dream of cultural and spiritual syncretism is destroying the old and replacing it with the new — erase and replace, as the popular liberal jingle goes. This is what we are seeing with the removal of the Confederate flag and statues; the banning of images and team names of Native Americans from school sports logos and gyms; and the prohibition of Nativity scenes, the Ten Commandments, religious statues, and crosses all over the country. All the emphasis on non-violence and abolishment of the death penalty, all the endless "peace" talks and dialogues with enemies of the U.S., all the slaps on the wrist for those in high places guilty of releasing classified information to the enemy or leaking it to the press — it is all a product of the Tantric Buddhist credo. In their teachings, Chandler explains, there is "no right or wrong." Facts are an "illusion," so fact-based research and the use of logic is worthless. "Mystical manipulation" or managing to state something in such ambiguous terms that it can be interpreted in multiple ways to suit the hearer (shades of all those "encyclicals" issued by the false popes) is a practiced art. And all is directed to effect the creation of a one-world Buddhocracy. This is being done with the aid of Communist China, which calls lama-worship and the refined thought control exercised by these gurus their "soft power," the preparation for the takeover of America without ever dropping a bomb. No wonder so many among the upper-class elite are telling their children to learn Mandarin — they have an inside track to what is going on.

So mainstream media should stop obsessing about the White Supremacists who at least are visible and identifiable. Certainly they are a dangerous bunch, but no right-thinking Catholic or God-fearing Christian would ever endorse them, far less join them (although many Traditionalists have leanings in this direction). But then why not? Traditionalism, like the neo-Nazi movement, is also a cult. All these groups work hand in hand with high-degree Freemasonry on many different levels and in many different religious groups; White Supremacists are only one of them. Ironically, Heinrich Himmler himself was an admirer of Tantric Buddhism. As Chandler notes in her work, many Buddhists object that Tantric Buddhism is not what Buddha taught, just as many Muslims object that what ISIS practices is not what Mohammed taught, and just as sincere Traditionalists reject the Novus Ordo for its many teachings not in harmony with the Deposit of Faith. None of these non-Catholic sects have escaped the inroads made by the enemies of the Church: their original teachings all have been attenuated by liberalism, the effects of double-speak and coercive persuasion to such a degree that their doctrines now are unrecognizable.

The Novus Ordo church has been very friendly to the Dalai Lama, and Rome and the Dalai Lama both desire that all be one under the same umbrella. Both endorse climate change and global warming, and Francis appears to join the Dali Lama in embracing the Gaia religion worshipping mother earth as a living being. The language of Francis and the language of the Dalai Lama differ little when it comes to world problems. Erase and replace has worked well. The church has even embraced the Buddhists and given them a podium to promote their cause.

In a *Catholic Family News* article printed in March 2004, Jacob Michael details such an incident. He relates how earlier that year, the Tibetan Monks of the Tashi Lhunpo Monastery in India presented an evening of religious prayers at St. Adelbert's Basilica in Grand Rapids, Michigan. Michael explained that it was just one stop along a three-month tour the monks were taking of the northeastern states, including Pennsylvania, Rhode Island, and New York as well as other locations. This was the second world tour that these monks had embarked on in two years. One of the Buddhists said they had been welcomed at universities, Masonic temples, Presbyterian, Lutheran, and Baptist churches, also several "Catholic" parishes. Their goal was to raise international awareness about Human Rights and to help free the "10th reincarnation of the Panchen Lama," age six, from his kidnappers — the Chinese government. They also hoped to expose others to the Buddhist culture and raise money to build a new monastery. The altar area of St. Adelbert's given over to the monks featured Buddhist signs and pictures, with a large photo of Panchen Lama so prominent on the main altar that it was barely visible. Signs on each side of the altar read "Free Tibet," and "Release the Panchen Lama," etc.

Chandler's work explains the circumstances surrounding this effort. C.I.A money fueled the spread of this Tantric cult, she observes, "funding the Dalai Lama for decades." That funding supported the Dalai Lama's counter-revolutionary forces fighting in Tibet purportedly to free that country from Communist rule and eventually to allow the Dalai Lama, exiled in 1959, to return to his native land.

In one tiny southern Colorado community dominated by Buddhist and Hindu temples, an experiment in global citizenship has been conducted for the past several decades by the various Buddhist gurus, courtesy of former United Nations member Maurice Strong and his Tantric Buddhist wife Hanne. [94] The Strongs donated the land on which many of these centers are built. They followed the blueprint for the U.N.'s Agenda 21, established through an executive order signed by President Bill Clinton, which calls for strict adherence to Environmental Protection Agency guidelines regarding endangered species, wetlands, forests and other federally protected areas. Smart Growth, initiated by President Barack Obama, is one of the programs promoted in Agenda 21. The Agenda itself seeks to direct land development, not on a local level, but as dictated by international organizations such as those spawned by Tantric Buddhists, new age advocates, the global warming crowd, et al. Basically it robs property owners of their rights and places decisions regarding use of their land in the hands of the Internationalists.

Interpreted widely, Agenda 21 forces people off their land to allow nature to take over and prohibits the use of motorized vehicles on that land. The use of eminent domain to enforce this is already at work in communities across America. In this tiny area in Colorado, where the experiment is being conducted, a system identified as "communitarianism" [95] has been developed that replaces democratic government with rule by a consensus prevailing in the community, which imposes on the local citizens the spiritual mores of the Tantric Buddhist and other new age centers that predominate there. The "consensus" is now lobbying the local governments in the town and surrounding areas to fund its plans to prepare for the coming catastrophe that will usher in the "prophesied" Tantric Buddhist 1,000-year reign of peace, estimated to occur sometime in 2020. This is how far along the plans of these pagan organizations have advanced.

Conclusion

Documenting Masonry's political origin is important. But separating it from the initial destruction of the Church — Masonry's most covert but cherished triumph — is akin to insisting that the Catholic Church played no real part in warning the world of the dangers secret societies pose, thereby staying the hand of Freemasonry. We cannot ignore cause and effect; we do so only by shutting down our rational thinking processes just as those promoting "mindfulness" intend. Freemasonry's victory has been directly linked to the advent of the Vatican 2 "popes" and their Masonic ecumenism, the whitewash of Freemasonry itself, and the promotion of Communist "soft power" under the guise of ecumenism and Catholic charity. The predicted reign of Antichrist as a king usurping the papal see and Antichrist's system as a series of spinoff usurpers is the only logical explanation for this success. But who will help those struggling to keep the Catholic faith, oppressed for so long and so few in number, and fight for the very survival of the true Catholic Church of all time — visibly headless and eclipsed, but invincible? Without help from those who know the truth from a political "Christian" standpoint at least, the truly heinous, Medusa-headed nature of Freemasonry's treachery in oppressing the freedom of the true religion will never come to light. And unless it comes to light today, the light of truth soon will be extinguished for all claiming to be Christians anywhere.

The next chapter of this work introduces readers to the anticipation of Antichrist's reign. It begins with the remarkable history of Pope Paul IV's bull, *Cum ex Apostolatus Officio*, and how this much-maligned pope predicted to a "T" some 558 years ago just how the papal see would be compromised, and by whom.

Chapter VI Endnotes

[1] Douay-Rheims edition of Holy Scripture, Isaias Ch. 8:13
[2] Douay-Rheims edition of Holy Scripture, Jude 1:4
[3] *Nostis et Nobiscum,* Dec. 8, 1849, http://www.papalencyclicals.net/Pius09/p9nostis.htm
[4] Vicomte Leon de Poncins, *Freemasonry and the Vatican*, Omni Publications, Palmdale, Calif., 1968, quote from the Masonic publication *La Massoneria,* Florence, 1945, 127
[5] Ibid., quote from O. Wirth's *La Franc-Maconnerie rendue untelligible a ses adeptes*, 128
[6] Ibid., 32
[7] Dom Prosper Gueranger, *The Liturgical Year,* Vol. XII, Briton's Catholic Library reprint, "Time After Pentecost," Bk. III, pg. 65

[8] Robert Cross, *The Emergence of Liberal Catholicism in America*, Swarthmore College Press, 1957, 170

[9] Henry Denzinger, *The Sources of Catholic Dogma*, 30th Edition, Marian House, Powers Lake, N.D., 1957, DZ 1839

[10] Revs. Stanislaus Woywod and Callistus Smith, *A Practical Commentary on the Code of Canon Law*, Joseph F. Wagner, Inc., New York and London, 1957

[11] *Humanum Genus*, April 20, 1884, http://w2.vatican.va/content/leo-xiii/en/encyclicals/documents/hf_l-xiii_enc_18840420_humanum-genus.html

[12] All quotes taken from a speech given by Msgr. Ernest Jouin, Dec. 8, 1930, reprinted under the title *Papacy and Freemasonry* by the Christian Book Club of America, Palmdale, Calif.

[13] William J. Whalen, *Christianity and American Freemasonry*, Bruce Publishing Co., Milwaukee, Wis., 1958, all quotes from Ch. VII, 88-99

[14] Ibid.

[15] Albert Pike, *Morals and Dogma*, printed at the behest of the Ancient and Accepted Scottish Rite Southern Jurisdiction, Charleston, W. H. Jenkins, Richmond, Va., 1871, 815

[16] Msgr. George Dillon's *Grand Orient Freemasonry Unmasked*, (first printed in 1950, reprinted by Christian Book Club, Palmdale Calif., in 1999), 94, 103

[17] Michael Bradley, *Secrets of Freemasons*, Metro Books, New York, N.Y., 2006, pg. 158

[18] Herbert W. Armstrong, *The United States and Britain in Prophecy*, Worldwide Church of God, 1980, 174-175

[19] Ibid.

[20] http://www.papalencyclicals.net/Leo12/l12quogr.htm

[21] Msgr. George Dillon's *Grand Orient Freemasonry Unmasked*, Christian Book Club of America, 1999

[22] Richard Brennan, *Life of Pope Pius IX*, Benziger Bros., New York, N.Y., Cincinnati, Ohio, Chicago, Ill., 1878, 116

[23] *Acta Sancta Sedis*, July 13, 1865

[24] Rev. Michael Muller, *God, the Teacher of Mankind*, Benziger Bros., New York, N.Y., Cincinnati, Ohio, Chicago, Ill., 1880, 143

[25] *Humanum Genus*, April 20, 1884, http://w2.vatican.va/content/leo-xiii/en/encyclicals/documents/hf_l-xiii_enc_18840420_humanum-genus.html

[26] Vicomte Leon de Poncins, *Freemasonry and the Vatican*, Omni Publications, Palmdale, Calif., 1968, 34

[27] https://w2.vatican.va/content/pius-xi/en/encyclicals/documents/hf_p-xi_enc_19370319_divini-redemptoris.html

[28] To view an illustration of Lady Queensborough's pyramid, go to http://www.betrayedcatholics.com/articles/a-catholics-course-of-study/traditionalist-heresies-and-errors/papal-teaching-on-church-and-state/the-amazing-secret-behind-freemasonrys-triumph/

[29] Vicomte Leon de Poncins, *Freemasonry and the Vatican*, Omni Publications, Palmdale, Calif., 1968, 38

[30] David A. Wemhoff, *John Courtney Murray, Time/Life, and the American Proposition: How the C.I.A.'s Doctrinal Warfare Program Changed the Catholic Church*; South Bend: Fidelity Press, 2015

[31] *Ibid.*, Chapters 33 and 34.

[32] Henry Denzinger, *The Sources of Catholic Dogma*, 30th Edition, Marian House, Powers Lake, N.D., 1957, DZ 1967, 1975, 1976; *Testem Benevolentiae*

[33] Stephen Goode, *The CIA*, Franklin Watts, New York, N. Y., 1982, 4

[34] *Ibid.*, 2

[35] *Ibid.*, 4

[36] http://www.military.com/ContentFiles/techtv_update_PSYOPS.htm

[37] Pope Pius IX's *Syllabus of Errors*, Henry Denzinger, *The Sources of Catholic Dogma*, 30th Edition, Marian House, Powers Lake, N.D., 1957, DZ 1755

[38] *Mirari Vos Arbitramur*, Pope Gregory XVI, Aug. 15, 1832, http://www.papalencyclicals.net/Greg16/g16mirar.htm

[39] http://www.vatican.va/archive/hist_councils/ii_vatican_council/documents/vat-ii_decl_19651207_dignitatis-humanae_en.html, para. 3

[40] Henry Denzinger, *The Sources of Catholic Dogma*, 30th Edition, Marian House, Powers Lake, N.D., 1957, DZ 1717, 1719, 1721, 1724, 1727, 1733

[41] Msgr. Joseph C. Fenton, *The American Ecclesiastical Review*, Catholic University of America Press, Washington, D.C., "Sacrorum Antistitum and the Background of the Oath Against Modernism," October 1960

[42] *Ibid.*

[43] *The Great Encyclical Letters of Pope Leo XIII*, Benziger Bros., New York, N.Y., 1908

[44] Henry Denzinger, *The Sources of Catholic Dogma*, 30th Edition, Marian House, Powers Lake, N.D., 1957, DZ 1975

[45] Msgr. J.C. Fenton, "The Catholic Church and Freedom of Religion," *The American Ecclesiastical Review*, Catholic University of America Press, Washington, D.C., October 1946, 298-99

[46] Rev. Amleto Cicognani, *Canon Law*, Dolphin Press, Philadelphia, Penn., 1935, Canons 19, 20

[47] Msgr. J.C. Fenton, "The Catholic Church and Freedom of Religion," *The American Ecclesiastical Review*, Catholic University of America Press, Washington, D.C., October 1946, 299

[48] *Summa Theologica, St. Thomas Aquinas, I-II*, q. 91, a. 2.; 1-11, q. 93, a. 2; *I-II*, q. 94, a. 2; *I-II*, q. 94, a. 2; *Supp.*, q. 65, a. 3. Quotes taken with permission from an unpublished essay by Lauri Brown.

[49] Robert Nugent, "The Censuring of John Courtney Murray, Part Two," *The Catholic World*, March/April 2008, Vol. 242, No. 1445

[50] Msgr. Joseph Fenton *Diary* begun Dec. 13, 1960, 2-4

[51] Thomas T. McAvoy, C.S.C, *The Americanist Heresy in Roman Catholicism*, 1895-1900, University of Notre Dame Press, Notre Dame, Indiana, 1963, 32

[52] Ibid., 169-171

[53] *Redemptor Hominis*, John Paul 2, United Sates Catholic Conference Publications Office, Washington, D.C., March 4, 1979

[54] Thomas T. McAvoy, C.S.C, *The Americanist Heresy in Roman Catholicism*, 1895-1900, University of Notre Dame Press, Notre Dame, Indiana, 1963, 168-169, 171. It was Pope St. Pius X who identified this synthesis as Modernism in his condemnation of the heresy found in *Pascendi Dominici Gregis.*

[55] *The Permanent Instruction of the Alta Vendita: A Masonic Blueprint for the Subversion of the Catholic Church*, John Vennari, editor, TAN Books and Publishers, Rockford, Ill., 1999, 7-9

[56] Msgr. Joseph Fenton *Diary* begun Oct. 25, 1960, 240-241 (Cardinal DiMeglio communication)

[57] John of Paris, *On Royal and Papal Power*, J. A. Watt, translator (and author of introduction), The Pontifical Institute of Medieval Studies, Toronto, Canada, 1971, 79, 242-243, 250

[58] Robert Cross, *The Emergence of Liberal Catholicism in America*, Swarthmore College Press, 1957, 220

[59] Albert Pike, *Morals and Dogma*, printed at the behest of the Ancient and Accepted Scottish Rite Southern Jurisdiction, Charleston, W. H. Jenkins, Richmond, Va., 1871, 90

[60] http://www.historyisaweapon.com/defcon1/bernprop.html

[61] Editor, Vincent A. Yzermans, *The Major Addresses of Pope Pius XII*, Vol. I, The North Central Publishing Co., St. Paul, Minnesota, 1961, 132

[62] *Acta Apostolica Sedis*, XLII, (1950), 251

[63] Martin A. Lee, "Their Will Be Done" in *Mother Jones* online magazine at http://www.motherjones.com/politics/1983/07/their-will-be-done.

[64] Michael Baigent, Richard Leigh and Henry Lincoln, *The Messianic Legacy*, Dell Publishing, New York, N.Y., 1989, 348-50

[65] Paul I. Murphy and R. Rene Arlington, *La Popessa*, Warner Books, New York, N.Y., 1983, 306

[66] Penny Leroux, *The People of God*, Penguin Books, New York, N. Y., 1989, 298-99

[67] Helen M. Peters, *One World*, Michigan, circa 1982

[68] *Paul VI — Beatified?* "Chiesa viva," September 2011, pg. 33, footnote

[69] Ernle Bradford, *The Knights of the Order: St. John Jerusalem, Rhodes, Malta*, Dorset Press, New York, N. Y., 1991, 227

[70] http://www.motherjones.com/politics/1983/07/their-will-be-done *Mother Jones* magazine; "Their Will Be Done"

[71] Felix Morlion, *The Apostolate of Public Opinion*, Fides Publishing, Montreal, Canada, 1944, 214

[72] Ibid., 155

[73] Ibid., 160

[74] David Wemhoff, *John Courtney Murray, Time/Life, and the American Proposition: How the C.I.A.'s Doctrinal Warfare Program Changed the Catholic Church*; South Bend: Fidelity Press, 2015, 458

[75] Felix Morlion, *The Apostolate of Public Opinion*, Fides Publishing, Montreal, Canada, 1944, 163

[76] Ibid., 151

[77] Ibid., 187

[78] Ibid., 174

[79] http://w2.vatican.va/content/pius-x/en/encyclicals/documents/hf_p-x_enc_19070908_pascendi-dominici-gregis.html , para. 43

[80] (See questions regarding translation of this prayer at http://www.holyromancatholicchurch.org/articles/FatimaPrayer.htm)

[81] Rev. John di Marchi, *Mother of Christ Crusade*, 1947, I. The Angel

[82] Felix Morlion, *The Apostolate of Public Opinion*, Fides Publishing, Montreal, Canada, 1944, 214-215
[83] http://w2.vatican.va/content/pius-x/en/encyclicals/documents/hf_p-x_enc_19070908_pascendi-dominici-gregis.html
[84] Robert Cross, *The Emergence of Liberal Catholicism in America*, Swarthmore College Press, Swarthmore, Penn., 1957, 167-70 (this is not a Catholic work)
[85] Felix Morlion, *The Apostolate of Public Opinion*, Fides Publishing, Montreal, Canada, 1944, 83
[86] Please see the supplement to this work written for non-Catholics at www.betrayedcatholics.com, available for order when purchasing this book.
[87] http://www.fisheaters.com/apostolicmandate.html
[88] https://archive.org/details/jfks19610427 The speech can be downloaded from this site. One of the comments posted to *Archive* agrees with this author's estimation of Kennedy's text: "Personally I think he may have made some implications where he spoke on the repugnance of secrets, secret societies, and secret oaths. I do not see any other reason he should have made such comments. They were not required to make his point, to me those words were 'extra.' Why he made the comments like that, only he knows, but the fact he made them the way he did, implies more than the rest of the speech states." In my opinion Kennedy made them as a Catholic, and yes, he *did* know.
[89] *Look* magazine, Jan. 25, 1966, http://www.fisheaters.com/jewsvaticanii.html
[90] Felix Morlion, *The Apostolate of Public Opinion*, Fides Publishing, Montreal, Canada, 1944, 215
[91] Douay-Rheims edition of Holy Scripture, Zach. 13: 6
[92] Christine Chandler, *Enthralled: The Guru Cult of Tibetan Buddhism*, Amazon Books, 2017, xxviii, 163
[93] Kevin Orlin Johnson, PhD., *What's a Cult?*, Capital Booklets, Dallas, Texas, 1994, 2
[94] Maurice Strong divorced his wife Hanne shortly before his death in 2015. She continues to live in the southern Colorado community she and her husband founded and to promote Tantric Buddhist teaching.
[95] See articles, #7, recent articles, Communitarianism at www.betrayedcatholics.com

Chapter VII — A Pope Predicts Antichrist's Coming
But his warnings were suppressed

A. Pope Paul IV — *Cum ex Apostolatus Officio*

When Catholics first began searching for answers in the fight to save the Church, none were more authoritative than Pope Paul IV's bull *Cum Ex Apostolatus Officio*, written in 1559 during the height of the Reformation by the very pope who, as a cardinal, first convened the Inquisition. This much disliked and very severe pope was burned in effigy at his death and his body was thrown into the Tiber River, later to be rescued and properly entombed. Considering the fact that he accurately predicted exactly how Antichrist would seize the papal see as a usurper, it is no wonder the devil and all his cohorts struck out so viciously against him. Before reading this chapter, readers are urged to carefully study the annotated version of Pope Paul IV's bull.[1]

Reverend Adolphe Tanquerey, whose texts were used worldwide in Catholic seminaries, taught:

> Divine Tradition, preserved and explained by the authentic teaching authority of the Church, is a source of revelation distinct from Scripture and is infallible. This thesis is *de fide* from the Council of Trent and of the Vatican... Scripture is not a complete rule of faith... It is not easily attainable by all... *Tradition is more essential to the Church than Sacred Scripture.*[2]

He goes on to explain that by the solemn magisterium of the Church is meant the *dogmatic definitions of popes and general councils,* professions of faith approved by the Church, and *theological censures* contrary to heretical or anti-faith propositions. From what will be presented below, it will become clear that *Cum ex Apostolatus Officio* is infallible. Therefore, Catholics must follow and obey it without question. Had this been the case from the beginning of the "troubles" surrounding the false Vatican 2 council, the restoration of the Church would now be complete.

A summary of the bull's main points follows:

Heresy rife

Paul IV makes it clear that dangers to the faith were very great at the time he wrote his bull. He clearly evidences his detestation for heresy and his determination to see that it does not pervert the faithful. He warns that Scripture is being falsified and Antichrist is threatening to enter the Holy Place.

All censures reinstated

He therefore reinstates all previous censures for heresy, apostasy, and schism and declares them reinstated "forever," censuring both those committing them in his own time and at any time in the future. Pope St. Pius V would later confirm the reinstatement of these censures in his *motu proprio Inter Multiplices* (December 21, 1566). Some maintain that the reinstatement of these older censures was abrogated with the issuance of the 1917 Code of Canon Law; but by applying Canon 6 §4, which advises adhering to the old law in cases of doubt, the old censures are seen to remain in place.

Heresy, apostasy, and/or schism must be manifest

All without exception, even Catholic leaders of nations, but especially clerics and religious, bishops, archbishops, patriarchs, cardinals, and even one appearing to be pope, are declared *ipso facto* excommunicated if they have publicly committed heresy, apostasy, or schism prior to election or promotion. These leaders or members of the hierarchy also automatically lose their offices. Since *Cum ex Apostolatus Officio* is the primary law governing the canons on heresy for the 1917 Code, and since the Code itself states in its governing principles that in a doubt of law one must return to the old law, this means that *Cum ex Apostolatus Officio* governs all the matters today regarding questions on heresy, apostasy, and schism. (For those who doubt that *Cum ex Apostolatus Officio* is indeed retained in the 1917 Code of Canon Law, see the articles cited in the endnotes. [3])

Heretical and/or schismatic clergy are reduced to the lay state

As a result of heresy, apostasy, or schism, all clerics become the equivalent of simple laymen (Canon 188, §4). They cannot be rehabilitated, nor can they participate in any future conclave or election. (Schism is the primary error found today among the many Traditionalist sects. But this schism also is shot through with heresy, especially concerning the nature of the papacy.)

No declaration is needed to suffer the effects of these censures

No declaration of this heresy, apostasy, or schism or the subsequent deposition of clerics is necessary. Even a man elected pope who committed heresy prior to his election is automatically deposed from his office. Bishops, archbishops and cardinals especially are held to a greater responsibility in these matters than the laity; to whom more is given, more is expected, as Holy Scripture teaches.

All acts of heretical usurpers null and void

Nothing a schismatic or heretical usurper "pope" does, says, orders is valid or licit; all of his acts are null and void, including his appointments and dismissals. Likewise null and void are the acts of any others mentioned above who became heretics, apostates and/or schismatics prior to their promotions. (So no question of deposing an "heretical pope" ever arises, since such a man was never validly elected to begin with. Such a "pope" was a heretic prior to his election, therefore one only deposes a lay usurper.)

Universal obedience/acceptance does not grant any validity

Such an election or promotion of heretics and/or schismatics cannot gain any validity by seeming possession of the office, enthronement, homage paid, or universal obedience rendered to a man believed to be a Roman Pontiff, or by passage of any length of time in such circumstances. Nor shall such a person obtain any sort of quasi-legitimacy. Francis' desperate attempt to provide such legitimacy by "canonizing" John 23, Paul 6 and John Paul 2 means nothing; as a false pope he can canonize no one. SSPX supporters most certainly do not owe Francis and his five predecessors any homage, nor can they be considered even quasi-legitimate according to some "material/formal" theory. No matter how many accept and acclaim Francis and no matter how long this imposture lasts, such a heretic cannot gain validity. The recent push by pseudo-traditionalist authors Robert Siscoe and John Salza to impose the "universal acceptance" idea and lure others to the Novus Ordo — despite the alleged Masonic background of one of these authors — has failed to meet the level of even a probable opinion. [4] These are the same men who have condemned *Cum ex Apostolatus Officio* as a mere disciplinary law and dismissed it. They promote the material/formal heresy, which has been soundly refuted (see the links provided in the endnotes section). [5] It should be noted here that the material/formal premise is based on the natural law (erroneously promoted by John of Paris, as discussed in the previous chapter, and eventually condemned as Gallicanism), not on Canon Law, which provides the only valid method for dealing with the scandal and heresy occasioned by the usurpers "reigning" since Pius XII's death. The Church is a divine, not a secular institution, with her own laws and teachings; and Her laws and doctrines cannot be set aside in the pursuit of a theory to explain how heretics can somehow be qualified to reign as popes.

Flee from heretics or share in their sins and censures

Those who accept or defend either a false "pope" whose heresy has been clearly demonstrated or anyone whom he has appointed as cardinal, bishop, etc., are also excommunicated *ipso facto*. Cardinals, other clerics, and laity who leave the service of a false pope or other heretic, if immediately upon realizing that these heretics' publicly demonstrated heresy requires denunciation, are not held accountable for having once obeyed them.

Permission to call a papal election

If a man usurping the papacy cannot be removed, "all" may implore the aid of the secular arm (Catholic lay leaders of civil governments, now non-existent and thus no longer available to the faithful) to remove him. No mention is made here of any "interim" government for the Church such as concocted by Traditionalists. Pope Paul IV assumes that the papacy will be re-established as soon as possible and the usurper (a layman) duly deposed. The permission to elect a new pope is implied, since surely if a usurper is ousted, a true pope must take his place. Unfortunately today for the Church, no true bishops who retained the Catholic faith remain to elect a true pope in lieu of the cardinals, as St. Robert Bellarmine and others would permit in such circumstances. And the faithful are forbidden under pain of excommunication to hold a papal election.

Only a Pope *canonically* elected is a true Pope

Obedience is owed only to the canonically established Roman Pontiff or those in obedience to him and appointed by him. Bishops not in obedience to the Roman Pontiff and priests and laity not in obedience to bishops under a true pope are forbidden to function in any sacramental or teaching capacity. (The bull defines how this true pope must be established, which is according to Canon Law.) It is actually a matter of faith to believe that for the Roman Pontiff to be validly elected, he must be *canonically* elected. [6] This means that his election must be held in strict accordance with the existing law on papal elections, which in this case is Pope Pius XII's *Vacantis Apostolicae Sedis;* [7] and all provisions of the law must be followed until a true pope is elected.

It is also of faith that "a pope *canonically elected,* who lived for a time after having expressed his own name, is the successor of blessed Peter, having supreme authority in the Church." This was an article of faith proposed for belief to the Armenians and to Wycliffe and the Hussites. Monsignor J. C. Fenton states that these articles are to be considered as dogmas of faith. [8] Pope Paul IV's *Cum ex Apostolatus Officio* reads: "Subjects [are] bound in fealty and obedience to future Bishops, Archbishops, Primates, Cardinals and the *canonically established* Roman Pontiff," even though they are allowed to depart "with impunity" from a man only appearing to be pope who is schismatic and/or is teaching heresy.

Infallible decrees must be observed and obeyed
Pope Paul IV commands Catholics to avoid heretics, apostates, and schismatics as "warlocks, heathens, publicans, and heresiarchs." He warns all who would infringe his bull that they will incur the wrath of the Holy Apostles Peter and Paul.

It is quite clear that any and all who have publicly set up Traditionalist chapels and attended these chapels are in schism. And clearly those who recognize Francis and his five predecessors as partly legitimate in order to assert their purported jurisdiction favor the usurpers and are excommunicated. Paul IV reminds Catholics they must not associate with those outside the Church on pain of sin. If Traditionalists truly recognize the infallibility and indefectibility of the papacy, if they honestly believe that *Cum ex Apostolatus Officio* is infallible, then they have no choice but to bring their beliefs and actions in line with this bull and obey it if they wish to escape excommunication; this according to both Pope Paul IV *and* Pope St. Pius V, as will be seen below. That Traditionalists have not done so in the forty years that *Cum ex Apostolatus Officio* has been available is proof positive that their pretensions to unity and reverence for the papacy are nothing more than empty words. Under Canon 1325, their manner of acting alone constitutes heresy and schism.

B. A Cardinal is disqualified as *papabile* for suspected heresy

Before exploring the characteristics of *Cum ex Apostolatus Officio* that qualify it as infallible teaching, it is necessary to delve into the history behind the bull. Pope Paul IV suspected one of his cardinals, Giovanni Morone, of heresy, owing to his sympathy with the Lutherans. It should be remembered that Martin Luther was the heretic who burned the papal bull announcing his condemnation before his former monastery in Wittenburg, Germany. He then wrote a treatise entitled: "Against the Execrable Bull of the Antichrist." [9]

Luther's hatred of the Mass and the papacy and his private interpretation of Scripture were important tenets of his heretical belief system. In the preamble to *Cum ex Apostolatus Officio*, Paul IV specifically condemns those who "against the rule of right Faith...strive to rend the Lord's seamless robe *by corrupting the sense of the Holy Scriptures with cunning inventions.*" In the very next paragraph, Paul IV speaks of his intention to impede "the abomination of desolation, standing in the holy place," which frames the content of the entire bull.

Regarding Morone's sympathies with Lutheranism, the *Catholic Encyclopedia* relates:

> During these early years in Germany, and indeed throughout his life, Morone remained a conspicuous member of a little group of moderate and intellectual men who saw that in the deadly struggle with Lutheranism, the faults were not all on one side. When Cardinal Sadoleto in 1537 for addressing a courteously worded appeal to Melanchthon was denounced by many of his own side as little better than a traitor and a heretic, Morone wrote the cardinal a letter of sympathy [noting that] to show charity to heretics was a better way than to overwhelm them with abusive language....[U]nder the pontificate of Paul IV, Morone, owing to his wide and liberal views had the misfortune to awaken the pope's suspicions when the latter presided over the Roman Inquisition....[He] was arrested by the pontiff's order, confined in the Castle of Saint Angelo (31 May, 1557), and made the object of a formal prosecution for heresy, in which his views on justification, the invocation of saints, the veneration of relics, *and other matters* were incriminated and submitted to rigid inquiry. [10]

Morone's attitude toward heretics, that they should be shown kindness and charity, would later be modeled by one Angelo Roncalli (John 23), as will be demonstrated below. For his liberal views on this and other matters, Morone was tried for heresy and imprisoned. But even before Paul IV died, Morone was promoting himself for the papacy. At the conclave, he managed to garner a good portion of the votes until he ran full force into Cardinal Ghislieri, the future Pope St. Pius V. The historian Hergenrother in his *The History of the Popes* reports that Morone's campaign as *papabile* (a cardinal eligible for election) was "quashed by the intervention of Cardinal Ghislieri, who pointedly remarked that *Morone's election would be invalid owing to the question mark hanging over his orthodoxy."* [11] And this is the opinion not only of a great pope, but also of a great saint.

Pope Paul IV's successor Pope Pius IV later exonerated Morone of all guilt. After the case against him was resolved in his favor, Morone would eventually contribute much to the founding of the important Collegium Germanicum in Rome, a work in which he was closely associated with St. Ignatius Loyola. Morone also became the Cardinal Protector of England.

While the encyclopedia article states that "under...succeeding pontiffs his credit was in no way impaired," and this includes the pontificate of Pope St. Pius V, it appears that Pope St. Pius V nevertheless wanted to make it clear to the faithful that should anything suspicious once again arise concerning those previously accused of heresy, they had recourse. In his *motu proprio Inter Multiplices,* [12] Pope St. Pius V ratified *Cum ex Apostolatus Officio,* "*confirm(ing) it as inviolable and wish(ing) and command(ing) that it be observed to the letter, according to its contents and wording"* (see below).

Pope Paul IV himself was convinced of Morone's guilt. The following is taken from author Glenn Kittler's *The Papal Princes*: "If I discovered that my own father was a heretic, I would gather the wood to burn him," Paul IV said. During the trial of Cardinal Morone, Kittler says that *Paul IV "decreed that any cardinal accused of heresy could not be elected pope."* [13] And there is to be no exception concerning those who deviated from the faith "secretly" before their election-- that is, committed some pre-election heresy that became public only after the election. They too are automatically deposed. Here we have a perfect reflection of the mind of the lawgiver concerning an election, worth its weight in gold. In response to Morone's attempt to promote himself as pope, Paul IV also penned the apostolic constitution *Cum Secundum Apostolum* on December 15 or 16, 1559. The constitution decrees extreme penalties against those who discuss the election of the future pope, behind the back and without permission of his predecessor while he is still alive, a crime now punished by Pius XII with the highest possible excommunication on the books: a *latae sententiae* penalty reserved in a most special manner to the Holy See. This means that only the pope can dispense from such a censure, should he choose to do so.

Rabid Protestants were running amok when Pope Paul IV reigned. Luther was the very heretic who dared to proclaim that if he could overthrow the Mass, he could overthrow the papacy; thus, Luther understood well the connection between the Mass and the papacy. As Adrian Fortescue explains in *The Catholic Encyclopedia* article on the Mass, the center of unity in belief in the Catholic Church is the papacy, but the Holy Sacrifice is the expression of that unity. The Great Apostasy had begun, and the Inquisition was ordered in the attempt to stay it.

Few recognize the significance of Paul IV's use of Scripture in the first paragraph of his bull, probably because they are so certain that this decree has become an irrelevant artifact. But what he says not only defines this phrase of Scripture — a rare event throughout the papacy, Pope Pius XII says — it also addresses and settles a controversy that rages yet today, the very controversy that relates to the "falsifying of Scripture" that Pope Paul IV referred to in his preamble. For the Protestants have revived in full force their accusations that the pope is Antichrist, or at least that the *office* of the papacy is Antichrist (the current view of the Lutherans). The phrase in question is "abomination of desolation," which Pope Paul IV uses to denote would-be heretical usurpers of the Roman See:

> 1. ...The Roman Pontiff, who is Vicar of God and our Lord Jesus Christ on earth, holds the fullness of power over kingdoms and kings, and who judges all, but can be judged by no one in this world, (even he) may be corrected if *he is apprehended straying from the Faith ... Lest it befall us to see in the Holy Place the abomination of desolation, which was spoken of by Daniel the prophet,* We wish, as much as

possible with God's help, in line with our pastoral duty, to trap the foxes that are busily ravaging the Lord's vineyard and to drive the wolves from the sheepfolds, lest We seem to be silent watchdogs, unable to bark, or lest We come to an evil end like the evil husbandmen or be likened to a hireling.[14]

Pope Paul IV's definition of this phrase was indeed prophetic, anticipating as it did the very situation we face today. That such a definition is infallible in itself is explained by Henry Cardinal Manning:

> The Council of Trent (Sess. IV) declares that to the Church it belongs to judge of the true sense and interpretation of Holy Scripture. Now the sense of the Holy Scripture is two-fold; namely, the literal and grammatical, or, as it is called, the *sensus quis*; and the theological and doctrinal, or the *sensus qualis*. The Church judges infallibly of both. It judges of the question that such and such words or texts have such and such literal and grammatical meaning. It judges also of the conformity of such meaning with *the rule of faith*, or of its contradiction to the same. The former is a question of fact, the latter of dogma. That the latter falls within the infallible judgment of the Church has been denied by none but heretics. [15]

The first paragraph of *Cum ex Apostolatus Officio* seems to provide a theological and doctrinal explanation, for Pope Paul IV specifically mentions those rebelling "against the rule of right faith" in the preamble to his bull. His concept of the abomination also includes bishops and cardinals in their own Sees. This is because, as Manning further explains in his work:

> Secondly, it is a matter of faith that the *Ecclesia docens* or the Episcopate, to which, together with Peter, and as it were, in one person with him, the assistance of the Holy Ghost was promised, can never be dissolved; *but it would be dissolved if it were separated from its head*. Such

separation would destroy the infallibility of the Church itself. The *Ecclesia docens* would cease to exist; but this is impossible, and without heresy cannot be supposed...Even though a number of bishops should fall away, as in the Arian and Nestorian heresies, yet the Episcopate could never fall away. It would always remain united, by the indwelling of the Holy Ghost, to its head; and the reason of this inseparable union is precisely the infallibility of its head. Because its head can never err, it, as a body, can never err. How many soever, as individuals, should err and fall away from the truth, the Episcopate would remain, and therefore never be disunited from its head in teaching or believing. Even a minority of the Bishops *united to the head*, would be the Episcopate of the Universal Church. They, therefore, and they only, teach the possibility of such a separation, who assert that the Pontiff may fall into error. But they who deny his infallibility do expressly assert the possibility of such a separation.

The promises '*Ego rogavi pro te*,' and '*Non praevalebunt*' [the gates of hell shall not prevail], *were spoken to Peter alone*. The promises, 'He shall lead you into all truth,' and, 'Behold, I am with you all days,' were spoken to Peter with all the Apostles. *The infallibility of Peter was, therefore, not dependent on his union with them in exercising it; but, their infallibility was evidently dependent on their union with him. In like manner the whole Episcopate gathered in Council is not infallible without its head.*[16] [...] It is also a matter of faith that not only no separation of communion, but even no disunion of doctrine and faith between the Head and the Body, that is, between the *Ecclesia docens and discens*, can ever exist. Both are infallible; the one actively, in teaching, the other passively, in believing and both are therefore inseparable, because necessarily, united in one faith.[17]

In other words, when the pope is alive, in the event of a widespread falling away from the faith, at least a few bishops will always exist who still hold the faith and are loyal to the pope. When the pope is not alive, there is no guarantee that the bishops will not fall into error because they are separated from their head, and he alone is the guarantee of infallibility. This is why the Church insists a papal election must be held almost immediately and not delayed when the pope dies.

It was Pope Benedict XV who instructed Catholics in no uncertain terms to cling closely to the teaching of St. Jerome in scriptural matters, in order to "retain and guard the Catholic doctrine of the Divine inspiration of the Scriptures." So what does St. Jerome tell us concerning the abomination? In the Roman Breviary, he is quoted as follows:

> It is possible to apply this text easily to either the Antichrist... [or to the idols placed in the Jewish Temple]. In the Old Testament, however, the term abomination is applied deliberately to idols. To identify it further, 'of desolation' is added to indicate that the idol was placed in a desolate or ruined temple. The abomination of desolation can be taken to mean as well every perverted doctrine. When we see such a thing stand in the Holy Place, we should flee. [18]

During the time of the Jewish antichrist Antiochus, the Roman soldiers erected an altar in front of the main altar and set upon it a statue of Jupiter Olympus to be worshipped. This remarkably prefigured the erection of altars facing the people, set in front of the main altar during the reign of Giovanni Montini (Paul 6). But before these sacrilegious altars were ever placed in front of the main altar, Churches across the world were stripped of their tabernacles, side altars, statues, stations, holy pictures, and were modernized or rebuilt in modern fashion. So the definition of St. Jerome concerning "of desolation" also was fulfilled. And Montini did not limit his reforms to the liturgy; the destruction he wrought throughout the Church touched dogma, discipline, Tradition, social problems, the faithful, the clergy, and every other possible facet of Catholic existence.

Four centuries prior to Pope Paul IV's reign, St. Bernard also designated the antipope Anacletus as the abomination of desolation and an antichrist, demonstrating that the Church has always considered any false pope reigning from Rome as a true pope to be the abomination. In supporting Pope Innocent II, St. Bernard wrote the following in a letter to Hildebert, archbishop of Tours:

> Behold, Innocent the Christ, the anointed of the Lord, is 'set for the fall and the resurrection of many.' For they that are of God willingly adhere to him, whilst opposed to him stand Antichrist and his followers. We have seen 'the abomination of desolation standing in the holy place' (Matt. 34: 15). He persecutes Innocent and with him all innocence. [19]

Reverend Culleton recorded that St. Francis of Assisi shared the opinions of St. Bernard concerning Antichrist usurping the papal see. In Vol. III of the *Catholic Encyclopedia,* St. Bernard's opinions are mentioned in contradistinction to those of the Protestants, who taught not that a *usurper* would be the Antichrist but that Antichrist is always embodied in the Pope and the Church persecuting.

Pope Clement XIII also warned that the abomination "might even be brought into the Holy Place" (*Summa Quae,* 1768), alerting the faithful to the danger of intruding Masonic bishops. This further relates to what was said above, that true bishops in communion with a canonically elected pope alone can be said to teach unerring doctrine. Reverend Bartholomaus Holzhauser (1613-1658) entitled a chapter of his interpretation of the Apocalypse: "Of the Abominable Antipope and the Idolatrous Scoundrel Who Will Tear Up the Church of the West and Cause the First Beast to be Adored." Certainly the following excerpts from the Council of Florence prove the Church considers all antipopes antichrists.

> For our part, as soon as we were aware from the reports of trustworthy people that so great an impiety had been committed [installation of an antipope], we were afflicted with grief and sadness, as was to be expected, both for the great scandal to the church and for the ruin of the souls of its perpetrators, *especially Amadeus that antichrist* whom

we used to embrace in the depths of charity and whose prayers and wishes we always strove to meet in so far as we could in God....We exhort, beg and beseech *the antichrist Amadeus* and the aforesaid electors, or rather profaners, and whoever else believes in, adheres to, receives or in any way supports him, straightaway to stop violating the church's unity for which the Saviour prayed so earnestly to the Father....Within fifty days immediately following the publication of this letter, *the antichrist Amadeus* should cease from acting anymore and designating himself as the Roman pontiff and should not, in so far as he can, allow himself to be held and called such by others, and should not dare hereafter in any way to use papal insignia and other things belonging in any way to the Roman pontiff. [20]

Clearly, the Church has always associated the abomination with all those things St. Jerome detailed above, thus his opinion cannot be discounted. The abomination is precisely what Pope Paul IV defined it would be: a usurper pope perverting the doctrines of the Church — and this perversion is inextricably linked with the worship of false idols.

Had Montini confined his destruction to doctrine, it might not be difficult to understand how he could seduce so many. But when he not only perverted doctrine and modernized the Church but also abrogated the Tridentine Mass, he then should have been revealed for what he truly was. Because the pope is Christ's representative on this earth, and is revered as such, any usurper would be setting himself up as an idol, to be revered as possessing a Christ-granted power he never possessed, earning the title "abomination of desolation." The same is true of a fruitless liturgy — whether that of the Novus Ordo or Traditionalists — with "clergy" incapable of validly consecrating. The "eucharist" they offer, then, is only a "bread idol," a term found in several places in Holy Scripture.

In his book *Divine Armory,* the greatly-esteemed Reverend Kenelm Vaughan lists both Christ's and Daniel's prophecies under the heading "False Christs in the Temple of Christ." Further down, under the heading "Names and Types of the False Christs," he lists alongside the appropriate Scripture passage:

> Bread idols, bread of lying, bread of wickedness, wheat bringing forth thorns, profitless wheat, vine without grapes, wine of iniquity, bitter wine, the wine of the condemned, the two iniquities [bread and wine], Maozim who our fathers knew not (Dan. 11:38), a strange god, idols without life, an idol moving the God of the Eucharist to jealousy, altars unto sin, a sin graven on the horns of the altar, sin of the sanctuary, unacceptable holocaust, a conspiracy, vain sacrifices, throne of iniquity, sin of the desolation (Dan. 8:13), falsehood personified, a lying vision, the abomination of desolation (Dan. 11:31).[21]

This can only refer to our own times, since the Jewish sacrifice involved only animals.

Had *Cum ex Apostolatus Officio* been analyzed and properly publicized as the answer to the Great Apostasy in 1978, when it was first released in Latin and Spanish by Dr. Carlos Disandro, the damage to the Church could have been minimized. But it was not, and as a result, the bull is still assailed to this day as non-infallible, abrogated, and dismissed as a disciplinary law. This error will be refuted below.

C. *Cum ex Apostolatus Officio* per the Vatican Council's definitions

The Vatican Council provided all the qualifications by which a papal utterance can be determined infallible in its own documents. [22] The following analysis presents the criteria for papal infallibility laid down by the Council in bold, followed by one or more excerpts from *Cum ex Apostolatus Officio* that fulfill each particular criterion.

The Pope is infallible when:

(a) He speaks in his capacity as the ruler and teacher of all Christians.

Cum ex Apostolatus Officio, paragraph 1:

215

The Roman Pontiff, who is Vicar of God and of Jesus Christ on earth, holds fullness of power over kingdoms and kings...We wish, as much as possible with God's help, in line with our pastoral duty, to trap the foxes that are busily ravaging the Lord's vineyard and *to drive the wolves from the sheepfolds...*lest we come to an evil end like the evil husbandman... (Pastors teach, among other things. – Ed.)

(b) He uses his supreme apostolic authority.

Cum ex Apostolatus Officio, paragraph 2:
Now therefore, having thoroughly discussed these matters with Our venerable brothers the Cardinals of the Holy Roman Church, upon their advice and with their unanimous consent, We approve and renew, *by Our Apostolic authority*, each and every sentence, censure or penalty of excommunication, suspension and interdict, and removal, and any others whatever in any way given and promulgated against heretics and schismatics by any Roman Pontiffs Our Predecessors...

Cum ex Apostolatus Officio, paragraph 3:
Through this Our Constitution, which is to remain forever effective, in hatred of such a crime the greatest and deadliest that can exist in God's Church, *We sanction, establish, decree and define, through the fullness of Our Apostolic power,* that although the aforesaid sentences, censures and penalties keep their force and efficacy and obtain their effect...(all these persons) are also automatically and without any recourse to law or action, completely and entirely, *forever deprived of,* and furthermore disqualified from and incapacitated for their rank...

(c) The doctrine on which he is speaking has to do with faith and/or morals.

Cum ex Apostolatus Officio, paragraph 1
We must see attentively to driving away from Christ's fold those who, in Our time more consciously and balefully

than usual, driven by malice and trusting in their own wisdom, rebel against the rule of *right faith*.

(d) He issues a certain and definitive judgment on that teaching.

> *Cum ex Apostolatus Officio*, paragraph 1:
> The Roman Pontiff, who...judges all, but can be judged by no one in this world — *(even he) may be corrected if he is apprehended straying from the Faith.* Also, it behooves us to give fuller and more diligent thought where the peril is greatest...*lest it befall Us to see in the holy place the abomination of desolation spoken of by Daniel the prophet...*

> *Cum ex Apostolatus Officio*, paragraph 6
> If ever at any time it becomes clear that any Bishop, even one conducting himself as... a Roman Pontiff, [who] before his promotion or elevation as a Cardinal or Roman Pontiff, has strayed from the Catholic Faith or fallen into some heresy, or has incurred schism, then *his promotion or elevation shall be null, invalid and void.*

(e) He wills that this definitive judgment be accepted as such by the universal Church.

> *Cum ex Apostolatus Officio*, paragraph 7:
> *No one at all, therefore, may infringe this document of our approbation, reintroduction, sanction, statute and derogation of wills and decrees, or by rash presumption contradict it.* If anyone, however, should presume to attempt this, let him know that he is destined to incur the wrath of Almighty God and of the Blessed Apostles, Peter and Paul.

For those believing that this document is only disciplinary and therefore cannot be judged infallible, please see Chapters III and IV above on the infallible nature of certain disciplinary decrees. (And remember, as stated above, no proof is admissible against verified documents of the Roman Pontiff in legal matters.) For those now teaching that this infallible document was a disciplinary decree abrogated by the 1917 Code of Canon Law, please read the articles written on *Cum ex Apostolatus Officio* cited in the endnotes. [23] These articles have circulated on the Internet for nearly 10 years, so they certainly are not new.

Notice in (b) above that Pope Paul IV *infallibly decrees* that such heretics are *forever disqualified* from holding office in the Church and *can never reassume* their previous rank. Many have asked why there is such a drive of late by several groups of Traditionalists to totally discredit and impugn *Cum ex Apostolatus Officio*. The answer to this is they know full well that it is infallible and retained in the Code, and that it destroys all hope of promoting their material-formal papacy "solution" (that an antipope or false pope can "convert" and become a true pope, returning the Church to her former glory, when *Cum ex Apostolatus Officio* and other papal decrees teach such a person never became pope and can never be restored to any office he previously possessed in the Church). This is nothing more than the denial of Catholic dogma and the resurrection of the Gallicanist heresy, which the Vatican Council set out to destroy once and for all. It also echoes the beliefs of the Old Catholics, who like the Gallicanists refused to accept the definition of infallibility.

In the second citation (on the abomination of desolation) under (d) above, it is important to note that not only does Pope Paul IV define a Scripture phrase, but this definition also has important implications for Catholics today. *For here Paul IV is specifically pointing to a usurper as the abomination of desolation, not to the introduction of a false liturgy, which could not be instituted unless the usurper was in place.* So in defining this Scripture phrase, he also resolved the controversy still raging today of the true definition of the abomination of desolation: *It is not (primarily) the cessation of the Holy Sacrifice, but the striking of the shepherd that the flock may be dispersed.* [24]

Therefore, one can see why Traditionalists are so anxious to discredit *Cum ex Apostolatus Officio* and have gone to such great lengths to do so. The most recent attacks against Pope Paul IV's bull are countered below.

D. St. Robert Bellarmine and the heretical pope controversy

A recent work translated from the Latin endeavors to show that St. Robert Bellarmine, who was fully aware of *Cum ex Apostolatus Officio,* taught that a (true) pope could never be or become *the* Antichrist, and this is true. A man who is canonically elected and whose election has not been disputed in any way could never be Antichrist, because Antichrist is not a member of the Church. Nor could any pope, in his public capacity, err in faith or morals, for this is the very guarantee of infallibility defined at the Vatican Council. However, a man whose election is doubtful for sufficiently grave reasons cannot be considered a valid pope, if we are to learn any lessons from the Western Schism. St. Robert Bellarmine writes:

> This principle is most certain. The non-Christian cannot in any way be Pope, as Cajetan himself admits (ib. c. 26). The reason for this is that he cannot be head of what he is not a member; now he who is not a Christian is not a member of the Church, and a manifest heretic is not a Christian, as is clearly taught by St. Cyprian (lib. 4, epist. 2), St. Athanasius (Scr. 2 cont. Arian.), St. Augustine (lib. de great. Christ. cap. 20), St. Jerome (contra Lucifer.) and others; therefore, the manifest heretic cannot be Pope. [25]

St. Robert then goes on to explain what happens when it appears that a man elected pope has become a heretic:

> Then two years later came the lapse of Liberius, of which we have spoken above. Then indeed the Roman clergy, stripping Liberius of his pontifical dignity, went over to Felix, whom they knew [then] to be a Catholic. From that time, Felix began to be the true Pontiff. For although Liberius *was not a heretic,* nevertheless he was considered one, on account of the peace he made with the Arians, and by that *presumption* the pontificate could rightly [*merito*] be taken from him: for men are not bound, or able to read hearts, but when they see that someone is a heretic by his

external works, they judge him to be a heretic pure and simple [*simpliciter*] and condemn him as a heretic. [26]

The presumption that St. Robert speaks of above is that stated in Canon 2200:

> The evil will spoken of in Canon 2199 means a deliberate will to violate the law and presupposes on the part of the mind a knowledge of the law and on the part of the will freedom of action. Given the external violation of the law, the evil will is *presumed* in the external forum until the contrary is proven. [27]

St. Bellarmine is not concerned with whether *internally* such a man is a heretic or not (is guilty of the *mortal sin* of heresy), but only the external appearance of any deviation from the faith, in order to safeguard the public welfare. What St. Bellarmine is concerned about is heresy itself and the *danger* it represents. Whether it occurred before or after the event is not important to him. Both St. Bellarmine and Canon Law are saying that where heresy is concerned, if it quacks, walks, and acts like a duck and you really think it is a duck, then it is a duck, even if you later discover it's a goose.

St. Bellarmine's treatise on "Antichrist" from *de Romano Pontifice* clearly shows that he does not believe that a true pope could ever become Antichrist. This is precisely because Antichrist is a heretic, and a heretic could never become a true pope, as the saint stated above, and as Pope Paul IV teaches in *Cum ex Apostolatus Officio*. But St. Bellarmine's *Antichrist* does not treat the specific case in point considered here: that of a series of men never validly elected pope who are mistaken for true popes, and the false church that they concocted being (erroneously) accepted as the true Church established by Christ. Instead, St. Bellarmine was treating the reverse case in his *Antichrist*, refuting the Protestants' false teaching that the popes throughout history were Antichrist. He was *defending* a line of men validly elected to the papacy whose elections were never questioned and who were, without a doubt, the legitimate heads of the true Church. Although quoted for decades by Traditionalist clergy as supporting the idea that a pope could publicly commit heresy, as pope, this is not what St. Bellarmine taught. Monsignor J.C. Fenton confirms that St. Bellarmine supported as "probable" the opinion of Pighius in his day, that the pope could not err in matters of faith and morals even *as a private person;* and unlike modern works lacking Church approval, Monsignor Fenton's works are entirely reliable. He comments on this topic as follows:

> St. Robert Bellarmine (died 1621), who contributed more than any other individual theologian to the formation of the thesis on papal infallibility, characterized the teaching of Gerson and Allemain [proponents of what was later condemned as the Gallicanist heresy, which taught the pope is fallible and could be judged] as 'entirely erroneous and proximate to heresy' (*De Romano Pontifice*, Lib. IV, cap. 2, "De controversiis christianae fidei adversus huius temporis haereticos," Ingolstadt, 1586, I, col. 975). On the other hand, he accepted the opinion of Pighius as [only] 'probable,' and defended it, (Ibid., Cap. 5, col. 988). His essential teaching on infallibility is summed up in three propositions.

> I. Under no circumstances can the Supreme Pontiff be in error when he teaches the entire Church on matters of faith and morals.

> II. The Roman Church [the pope and bishops together, the Holy Office speaking with the pope's express consent] as well as the Roman Pontiff is exempt from the possibility of error in faith (Ibid., cap. 3, col. 975).

> III. The Roman Pontiff is incapable of error, not only in decrees of faith, but also in precepts of morals which are prescribed for the whole Church and which deal with matters necessary for salvation or with matters good and evil in themselves (Ibid., cap. 5, Col. 987). [28]

Here is the end, finally, to the fallacious and irresponsible assertions by certain Traditionalists claiming St. Robert Bellarmine taught that a *canonically elected* pope could fall into heresy. Even had he so taught, he would not have erred, since infallibility was not defined until 300 years later. Theologians attending the Vatican Council would later specify that the privilege of infallibility does not reside in the pope personally and exists only transiently when he speaks publicly on matters of dogma. In other words, he lacks the charisma of infallibility when speaking privately, for then he is not speaking to the whole Church and any heresy that he might hold either would not be broadcast publicly or could be corrected prior to the release of a written document.

During the Vatican Council deliberations, the nature of the pope's charism of infallibility was defined in detail. This is reported by the historian Reverend Philip Hughes (whose pre-V2 works can be considered reliable because they were approved and generally accepted by the Church.) [29] Hughes writes that the Archbishop of Bologna, Cardinal Guidi, a Dominican, proposed,

> ...to make the title of the decree [on infallibility] more exact, not to use in such a document the loose phrase, 'the pope's infallibility,' which might be taken to mean a permanent quality in the pope. The divine assistance which preserves the pope from error as universal teacher is a transient divine act, he pointed out, making the pope's act infallible but not his person. Therefore, let the title be 'The infallibility of the Pope's dogmatic pronouncements.' [30]

Hughes remarks in a footnote that Pope Pius IX was not particularly pleased with Guidi's conduct, but allowed the distinction to stand, nevertheless. Cardinal Manning describes the distinction between personal infallibility and the charism of infallibility in almost identical terms in his work, *The True Story of the Vatican Council*. In a work by Reverend E. S. Berry, St. Bellarmine is quoted as follows:

A doubtful pope is no pope…Therefore, if a papal election is really doubtful for any reason, the one elected should resign, so that a new election may be held. But if he refuses to resign, it becomes the duty of the bishops to adjust the matter, for although the bishops without the pope cannot define dogmas nor make laws for the universal Church, they can and ought to decide, when occasion demands, who is the legitimate pope; and if the matter be doubtful, they should provide for the Church by having a legitimate and undoubted pastor elected. That is what the Council of Constance rightly did (Bellarmine's *De concilio*, ii, 19). [31]

It must be remembered that the validity of papal elections is a dogmatic fact, and as such comes under the heading of the secondary object of infallibility. In other words, such a fact could not be contradicted without calling into question the authority of the popes, so it simply cannot be questioned without rock-solid proofs. We also see reiterated here the principle of Canon 2200: no absolute certainty need exist as to whether the individual accused actually is guilty of committing heresy or not. A seemingly heretical person is to be judged so externally to safeguard the faith, as Canon 2200 explains; but in the case of a pope, this means only that if such heresy actually occurred, it happened pre-election; or it was unmistakably manifested after the election, indicating it was held at some point prior to election. The deviation or straying from the faith referred to in *Cum ex Apostolatus Officio* suggests this. Cardinal Zabarella taught this same principle at the time of the Western Schism. And in fact, he went so far as to say that if the bishops did not act to address the situation, the faithful had the duty to compel them to act. But those who saw Roncalli as a doubtful pope felt helpless to do anything; the momentum that was the false Vatican 2 council precluded this. And those who may have suspected it certainly did nothing about it. It is questionable whether anything at that time *could* have been done, given that nearly all the bishops were professed liberals and either infiltrators or Modernist sympathizers themselves.

Henry Cardinal Manning's nephew, Reverend Henry Ryder, echoes Bellarmine's opinion in his work:

> The privilege of infallible teaching belongs only to an undoubted Pope; on the claims of a doubted, disputed Pope, the Church has the right of judging [as occurred at the Council of Constance]....During a contested papacy, the state of things approximates to that of an interregnum. The exercise of active infallibility is suspended. [32]

And according to the opinions of seven different theologians cited by Reverend Ignatius J. Szal on fulfilling the requirements of Canon 20 for canonical provision:

> *There is no schism involved...*if one refuses obedience [to a pope] *inasmuch as one suspects the person of the Pope or the validity of his election...* [33]

Notice that one need only *suspect* that the Pope is a heretic or invalidly elected (Canon 2200). What Szal presents, then, is a solidly probable opinion, and according to the laws of the Church it may be followed at will. But again, positive doubt must exist to justify such suspicions. So much, then, for the material/formal papacy hypothesis. And so much for the idea that St. Bellarmine's work on Antichrist somehow contradicts *Cum ex Apostolatus Officio*. Even if there was put forth any question of who was to be believed and followed, Bellarmine or Pope Paul IV, all Catholics know the answer to this question. However great a saint, doctor, and theologian Cardinal Bellarmine may have been, his teaching could never be preferred to an infallible papal document. A slew of recent articles easily found on the Internet continues the attack on Pope Paul IV's bull as non-infallible, and in typical fashion offers no credible Scholastic proofs of these claims whatsoever. While the analysis of these arguments is too lengthy to include in this work, the reader is encouraged to view the author's refutation of these claims. [34]

Conclusion

The savage attacks launched against Pope Paul IV's *Cum ex Apostolatus Officio* from the 1970s when it was first published until the present proves that those relentlessly attacking this law know only too well its true import and the destruction it spells for their own plans. Those writing against it cite this bull in support of their false beliefs that true popes can become heretics while holding office, even though the bull itself clearly dispels this heresy. They dare to cite St. Robert Bellarmine, who lived during Pope Paul IV's time, to vindicate their theory as if Bellarmine himself held the same beliefs as they. This is a false evaluation of St. Bellarmine's true teachings and a direct and reprehensible denial of the Vatican Council's infallible definition regarding the inability of St. Peter's faith to ever fail. The next chapter will examine the writings of other popes who also warn of Antichrist's approach, including one pope who confirms without exception Pope Paul IV's bull *Cum ex Apostolatus Officio*.

Chapter VII Endnotes

[1] http://www.betrayedcatholics.com/free-content/reference-links/4-heresy/annotated-guide-to-cum-ex/

[2] *Manual of Dogmatic Theology*, Desclee Co., New York, Tournai, Paris, Rome, 1959, Vol. 1, 171, 173

[3] www.betrayedcatholics.com, Archives, #6, Canon Law

[4] John Salsa and Robert Siscoe, *True or False Pope?: Refuting Sedevacantism and Other Modern Errors*, STAS Editons, St. Thomas Seminary, Winona, Minn., 2015

[5] To read a refutation of the material/formal and universal acceptance theories, please see http://www.betrayedcatholics.com/articles/bombshell-basis-for-the-material-pope-theory-why-traditionalists-never-left-the-novus-ordo-church/; http://www.betrayedcatholics.com/material-formal-hypothesis-contradicts-papal-teaching/

[6] Henry Denzinger, *The Sources of Catholic Dogma*, 30th Edition, Marian House, Powers Lake, N.D., 1957, DZ 570d, 650, 652, 674; *Cum ex Apostolatus Officio*, Can. 147, Can. 160

[7] *Vacantis Apostolicae Sedis*, paras. 1-3, Ch. 1; Pope Pius XII, 1945, http://www.betrayedcatholics.com/free-content/reference-links/1-what-constitutes-the-papacy/apostolic-constitution-vacantis-apostolicae-sedis/
[8] Msgr. J.C. Fenton, *The Concept of Sacred Theology*, Bruce Publishing Co., Milwaukee, Wis., 1941,132-33
[9] (Found in the work by Roland H. Bainton, *Here I Stand: A Life of Martin Luther*, Hendrickson Classic, 1950; pp. 153-155 http://law2.umkc.edu/faculty/projects/ftrials/luther/againstexecrablebull.html
[10] http://www.newadvent.org/cathen/10575a.htm (Giovanni Morone)
[11] *Briton's Catholic Library Letters*, Vol. 3, Letter no. 4, July 1985, 233
[12] http://www.betrayedcatholics.com/pope-st-pius-vs-inter-multiplices-confirms-cum-ex/
[13] Glenn Kittler, *The Papal Princes*, Dell Publishing Co., New York, N.Y., 1961, 254
[14] http://www.betrayedcatholics.com/free-content/reference-links/4-heresy/annotated-guide-to-cum-ex/
[15] *The Vatican Council and Its Definitions: A Pastoral Letter to the Clergy*, D. and J. Sadlier, New York, N.Y., 1887, 75
[16] Ibid., 96
[17] Ibid., 113
[18] *Roman Breviary in English*, (Autumn); edited by Rt. Rev. Msgr. Joseph Nelson, Benziger Bros., New York, N.Y., Cincinnati, Ohio, Chicago, Ill., Breviary Lesson for the 24th and Last Sunday after Pentecost
[19] Rev. Albert Luddy, *The Life and Teaching of St. Bernard*, M.H. Gill and Son, Dublin, Ireland, 1950, 238
[20] Council of Florence, Session 9, 23 March 1440 http://www.ewtn.com/library/COUNCILS/FLORENCE.HTM
[21] Rev. Kenelm Vaughan, *The Divine Armory of Holy Scripture*, B. Herder Book Co., London, 1939
[22] Henry Denzinger, *The Sources of Catholic Dogma*, 30th Edition, Marian House, Powers Lake, N.D., 1957, DZ 1839
[23] www.betrayedcatholics.com, Archives, #6, Canon Law
[24] Douay-Rheims edition of Holy Scripture, Zach. 13:7; Matt. 26:31
[25] *De Romano Pontifice*, lib. II, cap. 30
[26] Ibid.

27 Revs. Stanislaus Woywod and Callistus Smith, *A Practical Commentary on the Code of Canon Law*, Joseph F. Wagner, Inc., New York and London, 1957

28 Msgr. J. C. Fenton, *American Ecclesiastical Review*, Catholic University of America Press, Washington, D.C., "The Necessity for the Definition of Papal Infallibility by the Vatican Council," December 1946, 451

29 Philip Hughes, *The Church in Crisis: A History of the General Councils*, Hanover House, Garden City, N. Y., 1960

30 Ibid., 361

31 E. Sylvester Berry, *The Church of Christ: An Apologetic and Dogmatic Treatise*, B. Herder Book Co., St. Louis Mo., 1927, 402

32 *Catholic Controversy*, The Catholic Publication Society, New York, N.Y., 1882, 30-31

33 Rev. Ignatius J. Szal, A.B., J.C.L., *The Communication of Catholics with Schismatics*, (A Canon Law dissertation); The Catholic University of America Press, Washington, D.C., 1948, 2

34 See www.betrayedcatholics.com/ , Free Content, no. 4. Heresy, I and J

Chapter VIII — Succeeding Popes Echo Paul IV
Papal warnings and visions of future desolation

A. Pope St. Pius V — *Inter multiplices*

Pope Pius IV may have exonerated Morone of all charges of heresy leveled by Pope Paul IV; yet Pope St. Pius V says in his *motu proprio, Inter Multiplices,* that previous popes were deceived by men such as Morone, and the letters exonerating them, *"even from Roman Pontiffs who were our predecessors,"* were to be considered null and void. (Please reread the explanation in Ch. VII, A (3) above explaining how later popes are able to abrogate even a law that seems to be perpetual, given certain conditions.) The Pope writes:

> While We, in our assignment at the Most Holy Office of the Roman and Universal Inquisition, were dealing with matters in lesser affairs against heretical perversity, We learned at length from long custom and the teaching of experience that many indicted accused parties — parties who had been indicted even in the aforesaid Holy Office or elsewhere before a local bishop, parties who had been tried by inquisitors for heretical perversity and investigated for heretical perversity for causing false witnesses to be examined in their defense...were enjoying the assistance and testimony of corroborating character witnesses little informed of their life and teaching, and...by various other illicit means, were deceiving and deluding through guileful justifications and roguery the aforesaid sacred Office of the Most Holy Inquisition, other judges, *and even Roman Pontiffs.*...We, in like manner, *wish and command*, through the agency of the aforesaid Holy Office of the Holy Inquisition and the Cardinals of the Holy Roman Church (our beloved present-day sons and those who will emerge over the course of time as inquisitors of heretical perversity, appointed now and in the course of time over said Office), that *the same accused, denounced, and investigated individuals can and should be investigated and tried again, even if they were or are Bishops,*

Archbishops, Patriarchs, Primates, Cardinals of the same Holy Roman Church. [1]

Clearly this was a vindication of Pope Paul IV's suspicions of Morone expressed in *Cum ex Apostolatus Officio* by the very *saint* who prevented Morone's election as pope. Yet it appears that Morone gave no cause to reopen his investigation, at least in his or Pope St. Pius V's lifetime. Pope Pius IX would later declare that any time those seeing a papal command do not follow it, they are to be considered schismatic. But that was not all Pope St. Pius V commanded to be observed.

> And closely following upon the footsteps of Our predecessor of happy memory Paul IV, We renew, in accordance with this *motu proprio*, the constitution against heretics and schismatics previously issued by the same predecessor Paul, namely the one dated at Rome at St. Peter's, in the year of our Lord's Incarnation, February 15, 1558 [sic], in the fourth year of his pontificate, and We also confirm it as inviolable and wish and command that it be observed to the letter, according to its contents and wording."

> [The translator of *Inter Multiplices* notes that this same year is given in several different editions of the Bullarum. Other sources on the Internet give the year of *Cum ex Apostolatus Officio* as 1559. Lancelotti's Bullarum prints *Cum ex Apostolatus Officio* with the year of 1558 and a date of 16 (not 15 as in *Inter multiplices*) days before the Kalends of March, or February 14. Professor Carlos Disandro's translation from the Latin original reads *15 Kalend Martii, Pontifficatis Nostri anno 4 texto Magnum Bullarium Romanum, a B. Leone Magno ad Innocentium X.*] [2]

This command convicts those who would impugn or minimize *Cum ex Apostolatus Officio* in any way as guilty of heresy. A rational man could not fail to conclude that a great saint and pope would not confirm a bull with such a weighty provision for re-investigation of heretics without grave reasons. Those who dismiss *Cum ex Apostolatus Officio* as abrogated by the 1917 Code of Canon Law or as non-infallible are not just questioning a "disciplinary" law written by an unpopular pope whom even some historians fail to favor; they also bring into disrepute the decision of a man they turn to for the validation of their "right" to say the Latin Mass, since Pope St. Pius V also authored *Quo Primum*. And like *Cum ex Apostolatus Officio*, *Quo Primum* also ends with calling down the wrath of Sts. Peter and Paul on any who would violate it. [3] Of course there are some who claim *Quo Primum* is not infallible. But given the proofs offered in Chapter II on papal authority, they are in error.

This *motu proprio* would not be so remarkable if some had not claimed that because cardinals are able to avoid censure for excommunication (Canon 1557 §1, 2227), [4] they cannot be considered excommunicated for heresy (although this is clearly not the case during an interregnum if one reads Pope Pius XII's *Vacantis Apostolicae Sedis* [5]). However, unless they are expressly mentioned as censured in the law, Canon 2227 states that cardinals of the Holy Roman Church are exempt from penal law. *Cum ex Apostolatus Officio*, of course, overrides this provision as the old law now in effect, for it explicitly mentions not only cardinals but also bishops and archbishops. In addition, *Vacantis Aposotolicae Sedis* also governs all actions of clergy and laity in this time period, essentially forbidding them to act against papal law and teaching and forbidding even cardinals to usurp any papal powers under pain of invalidity of such acts. *Vacantis Aposotolicae Sedis* is the only other law that can or does apply, seeing that it is the last papal election law written before the reign of the false popes; and Pope Pius XII *specifically changed it* to make these provisions infallible. Pope St. Pius V allows even a doubt concerning the orthodoxy of any previously suspected or censured heretic or schismatic to serve as grounds for (re)investigating them and (re)trying them. This is later explained in the 1917 Code by Canon 2200, which tells us that those accused of heresy, apostasy, or schism are presumed guilty until proven innocent, placing them sufficiently outside the Church until such

231

investigation and trial take place. Any case may be opened according to civil law on the discovery of previously unknown (new) evidence. Canon 2198, which so many have relied upon to dismiss the guilt of so-called clerics who celebrated the Novus Ordo and conducted themselves as clerics — without any proof of valid ordination — also comes into play here: "In order for a crime to be called public, it is necessary that the fact be publicly known as a criminal or morally imputable act — in other words, that the act is known as a crime..." Canon 2197 no. 3 preceding this canon defines as *public*: "The Code calls an offense public when knowledge of it has been spread among the people [as few as six in a small community] *or when it was committed under circumstances which make it practically impossible to keep the offense secret.*" [6] Who could argue that this was true in the case of cardinals who unblinkingly elected a man known to have, at the very least, sympathized with heretics prior to his election and who, in reality, actually espoused heresy?

Less than 200 hundred years following the promulgation of *Cum ex Apostolatus Officio*, the popes would begin to warn the faithful that Antichrist's plan to overthrow the papacy was in motion and being actively disseminated by the secret societies. The popes warned about this repeatedly until their voices were silenced. Pope Leo XIII wrote the definitive work *Humanum Genus* condemning the sect, and he also provided Catholics with a powerful prayer to restrain Satan and his minions, even then encircling the Church.

B. Pope Leo XIII, light in Heaven

A prophetic event

Pope Leo XIII's coat of arms portrays a comet streaking through the heavens, causing some to refer to him as "light in heaven." In his famous encyclical on Freemasonry *Humanum Genus*, Pope Leo XIII introduces the topic of Freemasonry by referring to the sect as the City of Satan described in St. Augustine's work, juxtaposed to the City of God. He quotes St. Augustine as follows: "Two loves formed two cities: the love of self, reaching even to contempt of God, an earthly city, and the love of God reaching to contempt of self, a heavenly one." Pope Leo continues: At every period of time, each has been in conflict with the other, with a variety and multiplicity of weapons, and of warfare, although not always with equal ardor and assault. At this period however, the partisans of evil seem to be combining together, and to be struggling with united vehemence, led on or assisted by that strongly organized and widespread association called the Freemasons.

In his conclusion of this encyclical, he sums up the war led by Freemasonry as follows:

> Their chief dogmas are so completely and manifestly opposed to sane reason that it is difficult to imagine deeper perversion. In reality is it not the peak of madness and of the most audacious impiety to be so presumptuous as to want to destroy the religion and the Church created by God himself and assured of his perpetual protection; and after 18 centuries to want to replace it with the customs and institutions of pagans? [7]

Incredibly, what once was deemed the "peak of madness" by sane Catholics later became the standard for rationality, allowing the customs and institutions of pagans to appear to be sanctioned by the Vatican 2 "popes." This was demonstrated in the heretical admission of "all men" as worthy of salvation regardless of any effort on their part, even though they worshipped idols! How many photos do we presently find circulated on the Internet, showing these false pontiffs engaged in the ceremonies of these pagans? Have Catholics forgotten what St. Paul said about sacrifices made to idols? "The things which the heathens sacrifice, they sacrifice to devils and not to God" (I Cor. 10).

It is no wonder that having written this encyclical, witnessing in his day the takeover of Rome by the Masonic sect, Pope Leo XIII would be favored by God with a vision concerning the final battle St. Michael would win over his eternal foe. Many have wrongly condemned this vision as false, or the product of papal legend, but we must remember that it directly resulted in the addition of the St. Michael's Prayer to the end of the Latin Mass in 1886. This in itself reveals its importance since nothing even so much has been appended to the Mass since the fifth century. Pope Leo XIII later wrote a longer version of the St. Michael's Prayer (in 1888) to be used by priests for private devotion. It appeared in the *Raccolta* until 1934. All editions of the *Raccolta* issued from 1934 on, carry the short prayer, but omit the long prayer issued *motu proprio* by Pope Leo in 1888 with its telling paragraph, highlighted below. This omission is particularly revealing when one considers the content of this prayer. The full text of the prayer as initially found in the *Raccolta* follows:

Prayer to St. Michael

"O GLORIOUS Archangel St. Michael, Prince of the heavenly host, be our defense in the terrible warfare which we carry on against principalities and Powers, against the rulers of this world of darkness, spirits of evil. Come to the aid of man, whom GOD created immortal, made in his own image and likeness, and redeemed at a great price from the tyranny of the devil. Fight this day the battle of the LORD, together with the holy angels, as already thou hast fought the leader of the proud angels, Lucifer, and his apostate host, who were powerless to resist thee, nor was there place for them any longer in Heaven. That cruel, that ancient serpent, who is called the devil or Satan who seduces the whole world, was cast into the abyss with his angels. Behold, this primeval enemy and slayer of men has taken courage. Transformed into an angel of light, he wanders about with all the multitude of wicked spirits, invading the earth in order to blot out the name of GOD and of his CHRIST, to seize upon, slay, and cast into eternal perdition souls destined for the crown of eternal glory. This wicked dragon pours out, as a most impure flood, the venom of his malice on men of depraved mind and corrupt heart, the spirit of lying, of impiety, of blasphemy, and the pestilent breath of impurity, and of every vice and iniquity. These most crafty enemies have filled and inebriated with gall and bitterness the Church, the spouse of the immaculate lamb, and have laid impious hands on her most sacred possessions.

In the Holy Place itself, where has been set up the See of the most holy Peter and the Chair of Truth for the light of the world, they have raised the throne of their abominable impiety, with the iniquitous design that when the Pastor has been struck, the sheep may be scattered. Arise then, O invincible Prince, bring help against the attacks of the lost spirits to the people of God, and give them the victory. They venerate thee as their protector and patron; in thee holy Church glories as her defense against the malicious power of hell; to thee has GOD entrusted the souls of men to be established in heavenly beatitude. Oh, pray to the GOD of peace that He may put Satan under our feet, so far conquered that he may no longer be able to hold men in captivity and harm the Church. Offer our prayers in the sight of the Most High, so that they may quickly conciliate the mercies of the LORD; and beating down the dragon, the ancient serpent, who is the devil and Satan, do thou again make him captive in the abyss, that he may no longer seduce the nations. Amen.

V. Behold the Cross of the LORD; be scattered ye hostile powers.
R. The Lion of the tribe of Juda has conquered the root of David.

V. Let thy mercies be upon us, O LORD.
R. As we have hoped in thee.

V. O LORD, hear my prayer.
R. And let my cry come unto thee.

Let us pray.
O GOD, the FATHER of our LORD JESUS CHRIST, we call upon thy holy name, and as suppliants, we implore thy clemency, that by the intercession of Mary, ever Virgin immaculate and our Mother, and of the glorious Archangel

St. Michael, thou wouldst deign to help us against Satan and all other unclean spirits, who wander about the world for the injury of the human race and the ruin of souls. Amen." [8]

+ + + + + + + + + + + +

Clearly Leo perceives the "Holy Place" spoken of by Daniel the prophet to be the Vatican itself, or remotely, Rome. But Rome would not hold Her (the Church's) most sacred possessions; only the Vatican would hold them, for there is located Peter's chair, the Vatican archives, the Sistine Chapel, etc. Pope Leo uses the language of Daniel (Holy Place, abominable) and St. Paul (iniquitous). He is describing the infiltration into the City of Rome by the agents of Antichrist, who already had begun their drive to capture the papacy. One Traditionalist, citing the necessary documentation, notes that the "throne of abominable impiety" raised up in "the Holy Place itself, where there has been set up the See of the most holy Peter and the Chair of truth for the light of the world" referred to the throne of the excommunicated King of Italy, Victor Emmanuel, set up in the Quirinale Palace in 1870. Previously it had been the principal palace in Rome where papal conclaves were conducted. It also was here that the pope, sitting on the papal throne, often held court. This usurpation still prevailed when Pope Leo wrote his long St. Michael's Prayer in 1888. The short St. Michael's Prayer was added to the Mass in 1886, not 1888 as some have erroneously reported. Later in 1902, this same Traditionalist writes, the long prayer was modified by Pope Leo as a courtesy to King Umberto of Italy, who was then peacefully negotiating with the Holy See.

It is not unreasonable, then, to conclude that the part of the prayer referring to the throne of impiety and striking the shepherd was later removed from the *Raccolta* in deference to the Lateran Treaty and these negotiations in 1933. That there most likely were other reasons for this removal should be obvious today, considering the destruction of the Church and its perceived (but temporary) disappearance as an institution. Traditionalists attempting to minimize the prayer's import and even cast doubt on its true meaning are loathe to believe that a pope could have foreseen what we view today or that such a thing could even occur. They refuse to accept the reality of the reign of Antichrist in our time because it effectively negates their authority.

Despite their attempts, reliable sources cited in several Internet articles on the vision demonstrate there is proof it actually occurred, although the details have suffered in translation over the years. In 1947 Father Domenico Pechenino related what he had witnessed over six decades before:

> I do not remember the exact year. One morning the great Pope Leo XIII had celebrated a Mass and, as usual, was attending a Mass of thanksgiving. Suddenly, we saw him raise his head and stare at something above the celebrant's head. He was staring motionlessly, without batting an eye. His expression was one of horror and awe; the colour and look on his face changing rapidly. Something unusual and grave was happening in him. (Later Pope Leo would relate that Satan asked God to give him 100 years to influence the world more than he had ever influenced before. He also saw St. Michael appear and cast Satan and his legions into the abyss of Hell.)
>
> Finally, as though coming to his senses, he lightly but firmly tapped his hand and rose to his feet. He headed for his private office. His retinue followed anxiously and solicitously, whispering: 'Holy Father, are you not feeling well? Do you need anything?' He answered: 'Nothing, nothing.' About half an hour later, he called for the Secretary of the Congregation of Rites and, handing him a sheet of paper, requested that it be printed and sent to all the ordinaries around the world. What was that paper? It was the prayer that we recite with the people at the end of every Mass. It is the plea to Mary and the passionate request to the Prince of the heavenly host (St. Michael: 'Saint Michael the Archangel, defend us in battle...') beseeching God to send Satan back to hell. [9]

Cardinal Giovanni Batista Nassalli Rocca di Corneiliano wrote in his *Pastoral Letters on Lent*:

> The sentence, 'The evil spirits who wander through the world for the ruin of souls' has a historical explanation that was many times repeated by his private secretary, Monsignor Rinaldo Angeli. Leo XIII truly saw, in a vision, demonic spirits who were congregating on the Eternal City (Rome). The prayer that he asked all the Church to recite was the fruit of that experience. He would recite that prayer with strong, powerful voice: we heard it many a time in the Vatican Basilica. Leo XIII also personally wrote an exorcism that is included in the Roman Ritual. He recommended that bishops and priests read these exorcisms often in their dioceses and parishes. He himself would recite them often throughout the day. [10]

So there are two accounts of the vision and resulting prayer:

1. Pope Leo XIII attending a Mass where "something [appeared] above the celebrant's head" (that something is not identified) causing "horror and awe;" the Prayer to St. Michael being written 30 minutes later, when the pope went to his office (Father Pechenino's account, often associated with a report of a possible 100-year period of unprecedented satanic influence); and
2. Pope Leo XIII seeing demons in Rome (is this what he saw over the celebrant's head at the Mass he attended?) The resulting prayer, then, was described as "the fruit of that experience" (Monsignor Angeli's account).

There is yet another account which appears in Reverend Carl Vogl's *Begone Satan.* [11] Father Vogl relates that one day following Mass, Pope Leo was in conference with his cardinals and suddenly collapsed. Doctors summoned to the scene could find no pulse or heartbeat. Yet suddenly Pope Leo recovered and recounted a vision he had seen while unconscious. Satan had gained the upper hand in the entire world and was poised for triumph when suddenly St.

Michael appeared "just in the nick of time" and cast him into the abyss with his cohorts.

Vogl also reports another interesting fact in his work. He tells his readers that Reverend Theophilus Riesinger, who successfully drove out the demon in the 1928 Earling possession case, [12] predicted that Judas soon would appear as the Antichrist, who would be accompanied by the False Prophet. It is the contention of this work that this is precisely what has happened in these times.

Some maintain that after his death, Cardinal Mariano Rampolla was discovered by Pope St. Pius X to have been a Freemason. When presented with the papers proving this, Pope St. Pius X allegedly said: "The unhappy man! Burn them..." (This would most likely have been sometime in 1914. Rampolla died December 16, 1913 and Pope St. Pius X died August 20, 1914.) Rampolla was Pope Leo XIII's secretary, and perhaps he had somehow used his influence with the pope to have the most damning elements of the prayer removed. The real reason for the prayer's modification cannot be absolutely verified, although the historic background just provided is one explanation. It must be remembered what a ruthless smear campaign the Freemasons had launched against the La Salette seer Melanie Calvat, who was hounded her entire life for daring to expose their plans at the command of the Mother of God! Biographies of Melanie confirm this. Pope Leo XIII's vision and resulting prayer confirms it. What if someone was able in 1902 to convince the aging pope, who died in 1903, that his vision was not so much prophetic as it was personal; that he had given it too much credence and actually even allowed his first impression of the vision to adversely affect progress that could yet be made with the civil government of Rome? Is not that just as plausible as the previous explanation? And why do Traditionalists insist on de-emphasizing the urgency of the papal warnings on Freemasonry, which reveal the undeniable inroads made into the Vatican even in Pope Leo XIII's day?

The *Alta Vendita's* reference in their documents to the "pope of their wants" reigning on the "throne of the prostitute of Babylon" in itself indicates their intention to capture the See. What about the reference to the Pastor being struck and the sheep scattered in the last line of Leo's prayer? We find these words first uttered by an Old Testament prophet and later by Christ at the beginning of His passion. [13] Orchard's commentary refers to Zacharias' mention earlier of the "foolish shepherds" who would forsake the flock, and the shepherd who would be struck is said to be one of these foolish shepherds. [14] Reverend Bullough explains that this shepherd would be both King Antiochus IV (in Zacharias' day) and Antichrist in the latter days. Pope Leo's intention seems to be that a true pope would be removed or was about to be removed, in order that a foolish shepherd might be installed. This is the sense that Christ intended in quoting Zacharias, since He could not have been referring to Himself as an "evil" or "foolish" shepherd. This once again indicates that the abomination would be a false pope ruling as a true Pope. St. Paul foretold that this reign of Antichrist could not come "...unless there come a revolt first." [15]

The sheep would first need to be scattered. In Daniel 12:7, we read of "...the scattering of the band of the holy people." We learn from the documents of the first Vatican Council:

> We judge it to be necessary for the protection, safety, and increase of the Catholic flock... to set forth the doctrine on the...nature of the Sacred Apostolic Primacy, in which the strength and solidarity of the whole Church consist. [16]

The pope is the center of all unity. If he is taken away, the flock can then be scattered. Surely then, "he who withholdeth" – the obstacle preventing the advent of Antichrist – can only be the pope, the "Supreme Pastor," the "Good Shepherd's vicar," who rules from the Holy See. Thus have two previous popes understood the phrase, since the entire thrust of Paul IV's bull was to ensure that no man not canonically elected could ever be considered a valid successor of St. Peter. Henry Cardinal Manning, in his work *The Temporal Power of the Vicar of Christ*, explains in great detail how "he who withholdeth" is none other than a true pope. And if "he who withholdeth" is Christ's true vicar, then when he "is taken out of the way," the "man of sin" will be revealed. Thus does the removal of the obstacle (a true pope) signify the rule of the "abomination of desolation." The two are tied inextricably together, since only the falling away of the withholding power can usher in the desolation. This will be explained later in more detail.

C. Pope St. Pius X — Restoring all things in Christ

In his first encyclical, *E Supremi Apostolatus*, Pope St. Pius X officially adopted his papal motto: To restore all things in Christ. Perhaps he embarked on this daunting task because he also identified in this encyclical, at the very inception of his papacy, the advent of Antichrist.

> Society is at the present time, more than in any past age, suffering from a terrible and deep-rooted malady which, developing every day and eating into its inmost being, is dragging it to destruction. You understand, Venerable Brethren, what this disease is — apostasy from God, than which in truth nothing is more allied with ruin, according to the word of the Prophet: 'For behold they that go far from Thee shall perish' (Ps. lxxii., 17)....When all this is considered there is good reason to fear lest this great perversity may be as it were a foretaste, *and perhaps the beginning of those evils which are reserved for the last days; and that there may be already in the world the 'Son of Perdition' of whom the Apostle speaks* (II. Thess. ii., 3). Such, in truth, is the audacity and the wrath employed everywhere in persecuting religion, in combating the dogmas of the faith, in brazen efforts to uproot and destroy all relations between man and the Divinity! While, on the other hand, and this according to the same apostle as the distinguishing mark of Antichrist, man has with infinite temerity put himself in the place of God, raising himself above all that is called God; in such wise that although he cannot utterly extinguish in himself all knowledge of God, he has contemned God's majesty and, as it were, made of the universe a temple wherein he himself is to be adored. 'He sitteth in the temple of God, showing himself as if he were God' (II. Thess. ii., 2). [17]

Here is yet another definition of a scriptural phrase: *secular humanism directly identified with the prophecy concerning Antichrist showing himself in the temple as though he was God, Himself.* Perhaps this prediction regarding the Son of Perdition would not be so striking were it not for the fact that six days prior to the delivery of Pope St. Pius X's encyclical, Giovanni Battista Montini, the future Paul 6, turned six years old. And it would be Paul 6 who would promote secular humanism, constructing altars of abomination standing in the sanctuary, the holy place where the Blessed Sacrament is enthroned, solely to please man. Thus did Pope St. Pius X devote himself to shoring up the Church as much as he could, before his heart was broken by the declaration of World War I. It was a war he had told his papal secretary, Cardinal Merry del Val, would come after his death. "I pity my successor," he told him in the spring of 1914. "I shall not see it, but it is only too true that a great conflict is coming nearer and nearer." [18] Was he speaking perhaps of two events at once — the war and the conflict in the Church? We shall never know, but certainly this demonstrates Pius X had the gift of foresight, for he accurately predicted not one, but two key events long held as indicators of the last days.

The saintly pope did all he could to prepare the faithful for these catastrophes, living up to his motto by attempting to restore as much in the Church as he could possibly manage in the time God had allotted him on this earth. The reform of the curia was needed, Pope St. Pius X said in his *E Supremi Apostolatus* (October 4, 1903), to put it into "a position to more easily perform its work for the pontiff and the Church." His concerns about widespread ignorance among Catholics was addressed in *Acerbo Nimis* (see below). And he also must have had the less than desirable state of the laity in mind when he reformed the Breviary. From his biography *The Great Mantle*, we read:

> His object in reforming the Breviary, as had been that of various popes before him, was to restore the proper celebration of the seasons of the Church, for the observance of the feast of various saints had displaced in

great part the offices of the ecclesiastical year which were the basis of Christian devotion. [19]

The condemnation of the pervasive error of Modernism, with its twisted and convoluted method of propagation, was his greatest triumph, for it was no easy task to nail down the slippery methods and insidious doctrines of these devils. Modernism he called the "synthesis of all heresies," and this has easily been borne out by its resurgence in modern times.

Formation of the clergy

Pope St. Pius X also taught at length on the importance of proper priestly training and holiness during his reign in order to safeguard the faithful from ignorant clerics. In the first encyclical of his pontificate, he wrote:

> "How great must your solicitude be for the formation of the clergy to sanctity!...When the time comes for the promotion of candidates to Holy Orders, never forget the words of Paul to Timothy: *Do not impose hands hastily on anyone*; ponder deeply on the truth that, in the majority of cases, *the faithful will be such as those you admit into the priesthood*. Take no count, therefore, of personal considerations; consider only God, the Church and the eternal welfare of souls, lest as the Apostle says *you should share in the sins of others.* [20]

So this pope well knew the dangers posed to the faithful by ill-formed priests. Pope Pius XI would later expand on his predecessor's teaching in *Ad Catholici Sacerdoti:*

> The man who wants to be a priest for the noble motive of giving himself to the service of God and the salvation of souls, and at the same time possesses solid piety, proved chastity, and has or is trying to acquire sufficient knowledge, as we have already explained, that man is clearly called to the priestly state....*Superiors of seminaries...should, without any regard for human*

considerations order those who are unsuitable or unworthy to leave the seminary. ...In deciding these cases, the safer view should always be followed. [21]

Pope Pius XII also expressed his concerns about priestly formation in *Sedes Sapientiae*, teaching:

The Roman Catechism teaches us that 'they are said to be called by God who are called by the lawful ministers of the Church'....Those who aspire [to the priesthood] ...must possess every quality necessary to constitute this many-sided vocation. [22]

Safeguards against ill-trained and unworthy priests are framed within the 1917 Code of Canon Law, safeguards all but discarded following the death of Pope Pius XII. For then no lawful bishops remained to call men to the priesthood, and Traditionalist bishops who pretended to call them were "consecrated" by schismatics and heretics, rendering their offices invalid. (See *Etsi Multa* in Chapter III, B.)

Codification of Canon Law
The codification of Canon Law was a great blessing for many poor priests and bishops, who for years had struggled first to learn the basics of the science from an antiquated and sometimes contradictory set of laws, then to apply what they knew to problems not in existence when some of these laws were first made. It was Pope St. Pius X who first entered upon the massive task of codifying the law, purging many useless laws and fine-tuning others to the circumstances of the 20th century. This task had never before been accomplished. It should have served the Church well for centuries to come, according to one author:

Since 1317, no official collection of the laws of the Latin Church had been promulgated....Law is intended to subsist for *an indefinite period of time*; it must give the society of the Church the element of stability...essential to good

order and the common good,...[However] every
ecclesiastical law which is not based on the divine law,
positive or natural, must be adapted to the varying
circumstances of each successive period,...When
circumstances so require, it must be possible to revise laws
which have become unsuited to their time and
place....Benedict XV...to prevent the Code from fast
becoming obsolete, decree[d] the creation of a permanent
commission charged to interpret the Code...incorporating
in it such modifications as may come to seem necessary....
But in no case will the numbering of the old canons be
changed. The Code itself has not been changed by these
numerous decrees and instructions. More than forty years
after its promulgation, modifications of detail have been
made in only a few of its canons. [23]

It is remarkable that Traditionalists, who claim to march under
the anti-modernist banner of Pope St. Pius X, have somehow
mustered the audacity to ignore the very law that would have kept
them in communion with their holy patron. Their disgraceful
rejection of Canon Law puts them in closer company with members
of the new church than they perhaps care to admit.

It is interesting to note that as a monsignor, the future Pope Pius
XII, Eugenio Pacelli, then working on the code under the direction of
Pope St. Pius X, favored the application of Canon Law to the person,
not the territory. Metz explains that a personal application would
mean that

"laws must bind those subject to them wherever they
might go, even should they leave the territory for which the
laws had been enacted...The territorial system [held] laws
ought only to have binding force within the boundaries of
that territory for which they were promulgated...The
conception of territoriality prevailed." [24]

Today all territories are basically erased because all offices have
been vacated, since Traditionalists (whether claiming to be bishops
or priests), never received an office from the Pope or a true and
unquestionably valid bishop. Therefore, this law has ceased to exist

because no one governs the territory. It can apply only personally in the current situation.

Since Pope Pius XII was in favor of giving the law a more universal character not dependent on the laws of the various episcopal territories and since legitimate bishops no longer exist, it seems that we can invoke the known mind of the last lawgiver to reverse the application of this law. This would successfully prevent those wishing to operate outside Her laws who simply claim that the laws no longer bind from prevailing in this matter. They are right insofar as the ones who enforce them no longer exist, but they are not correct in claiming that the current laws do not now apply personally to Catholics. Metz notes that "territorial application is presumed; personal application is not." This is thus reflected in Canon 8, which states: "Laws become effective by their promulgation [and] are not presumed to be personal, but territorial, unless the law indicates it is a personal law." [25]

"*Pontifical* laws of a universal character," however, Metz says, "bind all Catholics," since the Church is spread throughout the entire universe. So according to Canon 18 on what to do in a doubt of law, the known mind of the last lawgiver the Church possessed — Pope Pius XII — can be followed safely. Metz says that the future pope published an important study on the subject of laws applying personally in 1912 which ran into several new editions even after he became pope. Had he wished to withdraw this work he could easily have done so, but he did not. When in doubt about any law, the 1917 Code refers us to Canon 18, which states:

> "If the meaning of the terms [of law, in this case Canon 8] remain doubtful or obscure, one must have recourse to parallel passages of the Code (if there are any) or to the purpose of the law and its circumstances, *and the intention of the legislator.* [26]

Papal election law

Another sort of codification achieved by Pope St. Pius X was the collection, all into one place, of the laws regarding papal election.

All previous legislation concerning the conclave was codified and renewed by Pius X's bull, *Vacante Sede Apostolica* (December 25, 1904), which abrogates the earlier texts except Leo XIII's constitution *Praedecessores Nostri* (May 24, 1882), authorizing occasional derogations in circumstances of difficulty, e.g. the death of a pope away from Rome or an attempt to interfere with the liberty of the Sacred College. *The bull of Pius X is rather a codification than a reform.* [27]

This would scarcely be worthy of mention if it had not played such an important role in current affairs. This constitution gathered up all papal election laws from previous centuries and kept the best and most pertinent portions of each one. It nullified the right of any layperson to participate in the conclave or veto a candidate during the conclave. Such a veto is thought to have saved the Church from possibly electing an unworthy pastor during Pope St. Pius X's own election, when the man rumored to be a Freemason, Mariano Cardinal Rampolla, was almost elected. The Austria-Hungarian Archduke Franz Ferdinand vetoed Rampolla as a candidate, and some believe it later cost him his life and ignited the First World War. Others speculate that high-level Masonic officials ordered Ferdinand's assassination. The seer Berthe Petit was said to have warned Pope St. Pius X of the Archduke's assassination and the coming war. Many believe that the sainted pope died of a broken heart after doing all he could to prevent it.

D. Pope Pius XI and Pope Pius XII

In his encyclical on the Sacred Heart, [28] Pope Pius XI also referred to the near approach of Antichrist. After detailing a host of atrocities endured by the Church during his pontificate, he identified them as "the dawn of the beginning of sorrows that will bring 'the man of sin' arising against all which is called God and is honored by worship."

Following Pope Pius XI's death, Pope Pius XII's first encyclical, *Summi Pontificatus* characterized his own generation as one "tormented...by spiritual emptiness and deep-felt interior poverty," referencing a telling passage of the Apocalypse: "Thou sayest: I am rich, and made wealthy, and have need of nothing: and knowest not, that thou art wretched, and miserable, and poor, and blind, and naked." [29]

Author Francis Panakal, who includes the above quotes in his work on Antichrist, [30] observes that Catholic Scripture commentators generally relate this Apocalypse passage (addressed to the Laodicia church, described above) with the entire time of Antichrist's reign. Christ knocking at the door [31] is interpreted by Reverend H. B. Kramer as the announcement that His final coming is "imminent." [32] And so Pope Pius XII was backhandedly implying above that this age had already begun, after commenting as a cardinal that the Church was facing a dark night when Her people would appear to question their faith. Later, in 1945, Pope Pius XII revamped Pope St. Pius X's papal election constitution, retaining it in almost all its particulars, but adding some pertinent changes, including a two-thirds plus one voting requirement (to preclude that any candidate could win the election by voting for himself). Hefty verbiage also was added to the document, rendering it infallible. This was no coincidence, but a deliberate addition made to protect the Deposit of Faith based on what Pius XII knew was already occurring. As will be demonstrated below, it would be this very document which would prevent the Church from experiencing Her ultimate ruin.

Conclusion

Each of the popes above contributed valuable information regarding the identity of Antichrist. As we have learned from this, we are bound to accept even their opinions in such matters because they are based on Church teaching and tradition. And yet Traditionalists refuse to believe that we could be living in such times, and think little of these predictions made by the popes. They pretend the Church can exist without a true head when the Church Herself has taught this is not the case. Even though a quick look at the state of the world today tells a rational person that never before in the history of the post-Christian era has there been such a general perversion of morals and lack of faith — corresponding identically to the Great Apostasy and coming of Antichrist — Traditionalists will argue that it is simply not the end times. Even though seers at La Salette and Fatima warned that the Church would experience a terrible crisis in this very time period, many, rather than believe in these Church-approved apparitions, are now debunking Fatima and are wrongly asserting that the La Salette message was proscribed by the Popes. They are immersed frighteningly deep in the river of denial, and yet they have no clue that they are even in danger of drowning. Nor, given St. Paul's evaluation of the operation of error, is it likely they will come to their senses before going under. As Reverend John Kearney says in his work, *Our Greatest Treasure*: "The Gift of Faith may be lost. This is an undoubted fact. It is also a fact that once lost the Gift of Faith is seldom regained." [33] He refers to the words of St. Paul in Hebrews 6: 4-6 where he teaches that it is "morally impossible" for those who have once had the truth, participated in the Sacraments, and been properly instructed, yet have fallen away, to be saved without a "miracle of grace." Thankfully many today never received all the true Sacraments and were *not* properly instructed. We can only pray that this miracle of grace is somehow granted to those of good will ready and willing to accept the truth.

The next chapter will cover the prelude to the death of Pope Pius XII and the many incidents indicating that the Church was inevitably heading towards the very crisis Our Lady had warned would engulf the faithful. But they did not see the warning signs, most likely because they did not spend enough time in prayer and making reparation. And so the flood came and swept nearly all of them away spiritually.

Chapter VIII Endnotes

[1] http://www.betrayedcatholics.com/pope-st-pius-vs-inter-multiplices-confirms-cum-ex/
[2] Ibid.
[3] http://papalencyclicals.net/Pius05/p5quopri.htm
[4] Revs. Stanislaus Woywod and Callistus Smith, *A Practical Commentary on the Code of Canon Law*, Joseph F. Wagner, Inc., New York and London, 1957
[5] http://www.betrayedcatholics.com/free-content/reference-links/1-what-constitutes-the-papacy/apostolic-constitution-vacantis-apostolicae-sedis/
[6] Revs. Stanislaus Woywod and Callistus Smith, *A Practical Commentary on the Code of Canon Law*, Joseph F. Wagner, Inc., New York and London, 1957
[7] http://w2.vatican.va/content/leo-xiii/en/encyclicals/documents/hf_l-xiii_enc_18840420_humanum-genus.html
[8] (Raccolta, 1934, Benziger Bros.).
[9] http://traditioninaction.org/Questions/B649_Leo13.html
[10] http://the-american-catholic.com/2014/09/29/pope-leo-and-saint-michael-the-archangel-2/
[11] Rev. Carl Vogl, *Begone Satan,* first published in the early 1900s by the Rev. Celestine Kapsner, O.S.B.; reprinted by TAN Books, 2010
[12] This 1928 exorcism, which occurred in Earling, Iowa, involved the possession of Anna Ecklund with multiple entities. The exorcisms lasted for 23 days and included three sessions.
[13] Douay-Rheims edition of Holy Scripture, Zach.13:7, Matt. 26:30
[14] Dom Bernard Orchard's *A Catholic Commentary on Holy Scripture,* S. Bullough, O.P., Zach. 13:7, Thomas Nelson and Sons, New York, N.Y., 1953
[15] Douay-Rheims edition of Holy Scripture, II Thess. Ch. 11:3
[16] Henry Denzinger, *The Sources of Catholic Dogma*, 30th Edition, Marian House, Powers Lake, N.D., 1957, DZ 1821

[17] https://w2.vatican.va/content/pius-x/en/encyclicals/documents/hf_p-x_enc_04101903_e-supremi.html

[18] Katherine Burton, *The Great Mantle*, Longmans, Green and Co., New York, N.Y., 1950, 215

[19] Ibid., 168-69

[20] http://w2.vatican.va/content/pius-x/en/encyclicals/documents/hf_p-x_enc_04101903_e-supremi.html para. 11

[21] http://w2.vatican.va/content/pius-xi/en/encyclicals/documents/hf_p-xi_enc_19351220_ad-catholici-sacerdotii.html

[22] *The Pope Speaks Magazine*, Joseph Sprug editor, Washington, D.C., Winter, 1956-57, Vol. 3, no. 3

[23] Rene Metz, *What is Canon Law?*, Hawthorn Publishers, New York, N.Y., 1960, 40, 56, 62, 64

[24] Ibid., 53-54

[25] Revs. Stanislaus Woywod and Callistus Smith, *A Practical Commentary on the Code of Canon Law*, Joseph F. Wagner, Inc., New York and London, 1957

[26] Ibid.

[28] See the *Catholic Encyclopedia Dictionary* at: http://encyclopedia.jrank.org/COM_COR/CONCLAVE_Lat_conclave_from_cum_.html

[28] *Miserentissimus Redemptor,* http://www.papalencyclicals.net/Pius11/P11miser.Htm

[29] Douay-Rheims edition of Holy Scripture, Apoc. 3:17

[30] Francis Panakal, *The Antichrist* (date unknown; probably the 1970s) — self-published

[31] Douay-Rheims edition of Holy Scripture, Apoc. 3: 20

[32] H.B. Kramer, *The Book of Destiny*, Apostolate of Christian Action, Fresno, Calif., 1972, 110

[33] Rev. John Kearney, *Our Greatest Treasure*, Benziger Bros., New York, N. Y., 1942, 107.

Chapter IX — *Fatima and Two World Wars*
Prayer and penance sadly lacking

A. The Church on "one world"

The war Pope St. Pius X predicted came to pass, and with it came also heavenly warnings. The seeress Berthe Petit predicted that the Archduke Ferdinand would be assassinated and that this would spark World War I. Our Lady came to Fatima to predict the end of World War I and request prayer and penance to prevent World War II, to no avail.

President Woodrow Wilson (1913-1921) attempted to short-circuit the intent of the Founding Fathers, bypassing the Declaration of Independence principle stating people are 'endowed by their Creator with certain unalienable rights.' He wished to replace this instead with Hegelian syncretism and dialectics, believing perfection and unity could be had from any and all systems, even those excluding God. All would be under state control sans Declaration of Independence and Constitution. His first attempts to create a United Nations-like organization to achieve this goal began with the Treaty of Versailles and an organization which would later be known as the League of Nations. Despite his energetic efforts to overcome senate opposition to his desired participation in founding the League, the plan was tabled; and the U.S. never joined. Later Wilson cited failure to approve America's entry into the League of Nations as the reason for the Second World War.

Honoring St. Joseph, universal patron of the Church, Pope Benedict XV on July 25, 1920 warned of the evils of one-world government and the suppression of individual freedoms:

> The advent of a Universal Republic, which is longed for by all the worst elements of disorder, and confidently expected by them, is an idea which is now ripe for execution. *From this republic, based on the principles of absolute equality of men and community of possessions,* would be banished all national distinctions, nor in it would the authority of the father over his children, or of the public

power over the citizens, or of God over human society, be any longer acknowledged. *If these ideas are put into practice, there will inevitably follow a reign of unheard-of terror.* [1]

Pope Pius XII was well aware of Pope Benedict XV's teaching on such matters, having worked with him to secure a true and lasting peace following WWI. "Benedict was highly in favor of a league of nations, but not one in which conquerors drunk with power were to favor themselves." [2] Pius XII was much of the same mind some 30 years later, and his points for peace following WWII were very similar to Benedict's. It is a well-known fact that the U.N., both in practice and in policy violates nearly every principle that Pope Pius XII requested world leaders to consider in establishing this organization. While this pope may have been reluctant in the beginning to pronounce judgment on their undertaking, observing patience in political matters to allow such a massive work the time and effort it needs to develop, by 1956 Pius XII was well aware that the Church was not on the same page as the U.N. In that year, he wrote in his Christmas message:

> Although the program which is at the foundation of the United Nations aims at the realization of absolute values in the coexistence of peoples, the recent past has shown that a false realism is making headway among not a few of its members, even when it is a question of restoring respect for those values of human society which are openly trampled upon. The unilateral view, which tends to work in the various circumstances only according to personal interest and power, is succeeding in bringing about accusations of destroying the peace. [3]

Pope Pius XII did not believe in a world union of any kind unless such an agreement was freely entered into by all nations. He spoke only of that sort of union that would protect state sovereignty, not subjugate states in such a way that they would lose their freedom of action. The Novus Ordo church attempts to make it appear that

Pope Pius XII favored the U.N. by quoting only those documents which encouraged leaders to found it on principles of the natural law, but the NO church fails to note the pope's reservations about the formation of the U.N. That he had reservations about the U.N. is clear from addresses on this subject issued by Pius XII at the time. The various points for peace from these addresses were summarized in an address delivered by Reverend E. A. Conway, S.J., at Immaculate Conception Cathedral in Denver, Colorado on April 11, 1943. The following is an abbreviated version of Conway's summary of Pope Pius XII's points for peace cited in *Pius XII on World Problems* by Reverend James Naughton, S.J. Reverend Naughton's work is a collection of excerpts from various encyclicals of Pope Pius XII. Because it is intended for the laity, Naughton explains in his preface that he has paraphrased some of Pope Pius XII's teaching in his work for ease of reading. Regarding the prerequisites for a true world order, he references Father Conway's following summary of points taken from four Christmas addresses delivered by the pope:

1. Assurance of the right to life and independence of all nations.
2. All governments must respect the rights of racial and religious minorities.
3. Repudiation of power politics, which generates wars.
4. Suppression of cold national egoism — narrow nationalism, state absolutism
5. Establishment of permanent international institutions to guarantee fulfillment of all peace conditions and supervise any revisions.
6. Sincere, honest, mutually agreed upon progressive disarmament (in his 1953 address *Ci Riesce*, Pope Pius XII twice emphasized the need for any international cooperation on all levels, not just disarmament, to be free and not to be imposed arbitrarily, "whether these nations want it or not." Instead Pius XII was considering the possibility that such

states, "remaining sovereign [could] freely unite into a juridical community.")

7. International collaboration to assure a proper standard of living for all peoples and prevent hoarding of economic resources and materials destined to be used by all.

8. Every government must guarantee its citizens the right to work, to worship, to marry, and freely choose one's state of life.

9. Achievement of social unity in each nation among various classes and groups in the interests of the common good.

10. Restoration of the integrity and validity of the family as the basic unit of society.

11. Practical recognition of the dignity of work, the rights of labor as expounded in the social encyclicals (particularly *Rerum Novarum*), with special reference to the right to a living wage and the widest possible diffusion of private property.

12. Banishment of all hatred between nations.

13. Universal recognition of an order of rights and obligations called the juridic order, free of human whim, pressure, or expediency; and repudiation of the principle that utility is the basis of law; also repudiation of "might makes right."

14. Development of a deep sense of responsibility, which measures all human statutes according to the law of God — either the Ten Commandments or the natural law, which the Church teaches is written on the hearts of all men; a hunger and thirst for justice; and the exercise of true Christian charity. (The Pope's mention of the natural law as a basis for such a plan certainly cannot be construed in the same manner intended by John Courtney Murray and Reverend Felix Morlion, for this would deny Christ His rights as King.)

15. Recovery by statesmen and people, both employers and employees, of faith in a personal God "which is the only source...of that maximum courage and moral strength

needed for the reconstruction of a new Europe and a new world." [4]

As Father Naughton comments, the "dawn of a new era" as Pope Pius XII anticipated it, and whether or not it would actually be better, depended on

> "whether the political, economic and social disorders and differences between countries will actually be smoothed out. [This] will depend upon whether or not statesmen and governments will be willing to recognize and put into practice the Peace Plan of the Pope." [5]

To these principles need to be added Pius XII's clarifying remarks in the address from which the above summary is taken, *On the "New" World Order:*

> Because if it is true that the ills which beset present-day humanity are partly caused by economic imbalance and the struggle between interests for the equitable distribution of the goods which God has conceded to man to use for his sustenance and progress, it is no less true that their root is more profound and internal. It is found in religious faith and moral convictions, which have been perverted by the progressive detachment of peoples from the unity of doctrine and faith, and from customs and morals, once fostered by the unceasing beneficent labor of the Church. The re-education of humanity, if it wishes to have any effect, must above all be spiritual and religious; and, therefore, it must arise from Christ as its indispensable foundation, be realized by justice, and be crowned by charity. [6]

Rather than adopting the points urged by Pope Pius XII, the U.N. embraces notions such as "sharing the wealth" (a far cry from the idea of property rights and the obligation to work); "the right to choose" whether or not to end the life of a fetus or a young child (instead of ensuring that positive right-to-life laws prevail); and "power politics" (which is the stock in trade not only of Communist leaders and other foreign powers, but also of the political system in this country as well). Particularly during the administration of U.S. President Barack Obama, world affairs declined to such a dismal extent that no one could pretend that Pope Pius XII's points listed above ever applied or could apply.

B. The Church battles anti-Semitism

In 1914, Pope Benedict XV wrote in *Ad Beatissimi*:

> Never perhaps was there more talking about the brotherhood of men than there is today; in fact, men do not hesitate to proclaim that striving after brotherhood is one of the greatest gifts of modern civilization, ignoring the teaching of the Gospel, and setting aside the work of Christ and of His Church. But in reality, never was there less brotherly activity amongst men than at the present moment. Race hatred has reached its climax; peoples are more divided by jealousies than by frontiers; within one and the same nation, within the same city there rages the burning envy of class against class; and amongst individuals it is self-love which is the supreme law overruling everything. [7]

Sadly, Benedict was mistaken about race hatred having reached its climax. That would come in the pontificate of his two successors, Popes Pius XI and XII.

Nazism was based on race hatred, as none are likely to forget. Reverend Denis Fahey tells Catholics how they must comport themselves where the Jews are concerned in order to walk that fine line between anti-Semitism and the championing of the rights of Christ the King. Father Fahey writes that while addressing Belgian peasants over the radio one day, Pope Pius XI read a prayer from the Canon of the Mass (prayer following the Consecration, beginning "And this deign…") remarking:

> Anti-Semitism is incompatible with the sublime ideas and truths expressed in this text… We Christians can take no

part in such a movement... No, it is impossible for Christians to take part in anti-Semitism. We acknowledge that everyone has the right to defend himself, in other words, to take the necessary precautions for his protection against everything that threatens his legitimate interests. But anti-Semitism is inadmissible. Spiritually we are Semites. [8]

According to a cardinal who witnessed the address, the Pope wept as he read the words from the Canon. This was in September 1938, after the Fascist government of Italy issued the anti-Semitic laws stripping Jews of their rights and civil liberties, including rights to inheritance, land ownership, marriage with Aryans, and service in teaching posts.

Fahey comments on the passage above:

The Church condemns race hatred in general and the hatred of the Redeemer's race in particular... Thus we find in this pronouncement of Pope Pius XI the two currents, which, down through the centuries, run through the official declarations of the Holy See concerning the Jews. On the one hand, the Sovereign Pontiffs strive to protect the Jews from physical violence and to secure respect for their family life and worship, as the life and worship of human persons. On the other hand, they aim unceasingly at protecting Christians from the contamination of Jewish Naturalism and try to prevent Jews from gaining control over Christians. [9]

Fahey then mentions the duty of Christians, as explained above, to refrain from those attitudes concerning the Jews which the popes have forbidden. Generally, yes, Catholics are bound to oppose Naturalism; but Fahey wrote at a time when a war against this great evil could possibly have been launched. Yet it wasn't launched, and Catholics did not realize the true extent of the dangers. Instead many of them willingly embraced Jewish Naturalism in accepting the Novus Ordo church. As might be expected, this action caused a reaction — many Traditionalists overcompensated and developed an actual racial hatred for the Jews; some of them even sympathized with neo-Nazi groups and individuals, and still do today. They blamed the Jews for destroying the Church, but that blame rested far more with negligent Catholics than it ever did with the Jews or even the Freemasons.

A never released encyclical

But the most definitive exposition of the Church on anti-Semitism, never officially released, would not be discovered until the 1960s. A Jesuit seminarian, Thomas Breslin, accidentally uncovered a "lost" encyclical, bearing the official title, *Humani Generis Unitatis.* Its discovery is detailed in the work *The Hidden Encyclical of Pope Pius XI.* [10] It tells the amazing story of how Pope Pius XI commissioned an American Jesuit priest, John LaFarge, S.J., to write an encyclical on anti-Semitism, which he did with the help of two friends. Cardinals Eugene Tisserant and Domenico Tardini both are quoted in the work as testifying that the draft encyclical was ready to be published at the time of Pope Pius XI's death in 1939, something historians had known for many years. Correspondence between Father LaFarge and a Father Talbot also confirmed that the draft of the encyclical was before Pius XI for review. Although the pope reportedly left explicit instructions to release the encyclical in the event of his death, for some reason, Pius XI's Secretary of State Eugenio Pacelli, who would succeed him as Pius XII, never fulfilled his dying wish. Perhaps he felt that because Pope Pius XI had not had a chance to properly revise and approve the draft, since it was not his own work, the instructions of his predecessor were not binding. In any event, Pope Pius XI had stated his views in other documents, and Pope Pius XII later reiterated his teaching in Pius XI's unofficial encyclical in works of his own.

The commencement of World War II only months after Pius XI left this earth certainly would have made fulfilling his predecessor's wish problematic for Pope Pius XII, for the very reasons that Pius XI himself states in his encyclical. Still, no official explanation was ever offered concerning its suppression. The unpublished encyclical taught that although the Church could never discriminate against the

Jews or deprive them of their rights, She could however issue reproaches and limit pre-existing favors if they infringed on the rights of Catholics. Under no circumstances could the Church appear to approve of their religious beliefs or endorse them, nor could She dismiss their animosity to the Church throughout the centuries.

Given the later concessions made to the Jews at Vatican 2, the fact that LaFarge was a Jesuit who wrote for *America* magazine, and that he just happened to know Pius XII's personal assistant Robert Leiber, S.J., places a rather different cast on the matter. Was LaFarge complicit in the suppression of the draft of the encyclical he wrote for Pius XI, as reported by the authors of *The Hidden Encyclical...* and if so, was its suppression an early attempt at appeasing the Jews? Had LaFarge perhaps undertaken this work on behalf of those working with John Courtney Murray, Henry Luce, and others to lay the groundwork for the future? This cannot be ruled out, and the fact the encyclical was never released seems to be proof that it had not met with approval, perhaps, from curial members. Nevertheless, even though Pius XII did not release it, he honored his predecessor's wishes by his published works, his actions, and his later observations.

In his last unpublished encyclical, Pope Pius XI addressed the evils of modern technology and established the Church's official attitude regarding anti-Semitism. Anticipating the tidal wave inexorably headed for Europe during those dark days prior to his death, the Pope's words would have done much to enlighten Catholics inundated with Nazi racial propaganda, unsure where to draw the lines according to Catholic dogma. For as Father Fahey also notes, Pius XI taught that while the Church had at different times condemned Jewish practice and at other times had protected them, he denies that the Church's true position on the Jews is contradictory. He points out the Holy See has censored Jewish persecution of Christians on several occasions. Yet, he roundly condemns open anti-Semitism and the unjust oppression of the Jews. He holds the Jews responsible for their attitudes toward Christianity and does not fail to teach that especially the Sanhedrin or Jewish high court, in collusion with the pagan authorities, were responsible for Christ's crucifixion.

He also asks the faithful to pray for their conversion. This confirms that the Church primarily blames the Jewish *leaders*, not the Jewish people themselves, for Christ's arrest and death. And this teaching is no contradiction; rather, it reflects the mercy of God upon the Jews as explained in Reverend Leo Haydock's commentary on Matthew 27:25:

> All the people answered: 'his blood be upon us and upon our children,' which continues, saith St. Jerome, to this day. Still, the God of all mercies did not literally comply with their impious prayer.... For, of these children He selected some for himself... [11]

The final words of Pope Pius XI encourage Catholics to be merciful to the persecuted and defend their rights. He reminds them that past popes have encouraged this, and therefore it is the constant teaching of the Church. This should be a wake-up call for Traditionalists, who since 1963 and the circulation of *The Plot Against the Church* [12] at Vatican 2, have laid the blame for all the Church's woes squarely on the backs of the Jews, refusing to examine their own consciences.

Calumny against Pope Pius XII

Such is the official position of the Catholic Church concerning the Jews and there is no need here, despite any "politically correct" stance demanded by the liberal press or the Novus Ordo church, to depart from Pius XI's assessment of the situation. Recent attempts to indict Pope Pius XII as an anti-Semite, or for failing to do all he could do for the Jews, has been ably refuted by competent historians. The proofs cited in such works as *A Question of Judgment: Pius XII and the Jews*, and a booklet written by the Director for the International Affairs Department of the Anti-Defamation League, distributed in 1963, disproves the accusation that Pope Pius XII was an anti-Semite. [13] The author demonstrates, rather, that the Pope did all he could to assist the Jews in their hour of need, just as Pius XI promised and the papacy has done historically. Although the encyclical was never promulgated, Pope Pius XII verified its content in his actions. Moreover, it expresses the mind of Pius XI in such matters, as contained in other documents such as the encyclical *Mit Brennender Sorge*, and this cannot be overlooked.

In 1950, Reverend Senan, O.F.M., Cap., wrote:

> Over and over again the Holy Father has stressed that no Catholic worthy of the name can be an anti-Semite, for anti-Semitism is a violation of Christian charity. His Holiness made a remarkable pronouncement in favor of the Jews in January 1945 when he said: 'They (the Jews) are the people whose country God chose to be the birthplace of his Son. Our God is their God, and our lawgiver is their lawgiver. For centuries, they have been most unjustly treated and despised. It is time they were treated with justice and humanity. God wills it and the Church wills it. St. Paul tells us that the Jews are our brothers. Instead of being treated as strangers, they should be welcomed as old friends. It is not by our own merit that we have had the heritage of the Lord. We are all entitled to see the light of Faith... Their entry into the Church will mark the spiritual renovation of the world,' (January 1945). Again, towards the end of the same year, when addressing a group of Jews who had come because *'they wished the supreme honor of being able to thank the Holy Father personally for his generosity on their behalf during their persecution,'* [Pope Pius XII] said: 'Your coming before us gives an intimate testimony of the gratitude on the part of those men and women who, in times of their agony and deadly dangers, have experienced how the Catholic Church and her true followers in the exercise of charity could rise above all narrow and arbitrary limits created by human selfishness and racial passions.' [14]

The chief Rabbi of Rome no less, Isaac Herzog, as well as other Jewish leaders worldwide following the war, confirmed this testimony. Yet none of these events are ever cited; the statements that would vindicate Pope Pius XII are never quoted. Pope Pius XII spoke the truth; and as stated above, the testimony of history would bear him out. But as Joseph Bottum has observed in the introduction to his edited work *The Pius War,* [15] the voices of his numerous enemies were both louder and more readily believed than any facts not modern enough to suit today's hearers. Bottum blames this on the anti-Catholicism specific to America, "a papaphobia that has turned against the entire idea of authority." And David Dalin, Bottum's co-editor, attributes it to "an intra-Catholic fight over the future of the papacy." [16]

Before leaving this subject, there is another matter to address. In addition to all the other charges leveled against Pope Pius XII, he also has been accused of being the enemy of religious toleration, of encouraging sedition, and of forcing conversions to Catholicism. Yet in an effort to do all in his power to facilitate a lasting peace, Pope Pius XII made it clear that the Church was ever the champion of religious tolerance, insofar as Catholic teaching allowed, and would not tolerate intolerance from Her members. Certainly there was no toleration where modern errors were concerned, as will be seen below.

C. The popes on Communism and ecumenism

In analyzing Pope Pius XII's condemnation of Communism issued in 1949, Reverend William Conway identifies those individuals Pius XII included in his condemnation: "Those, who by words or conduct externally manifest that they personally accept the doctrine of Communism are apostates...and incur excommunication *ipso facto.*" [17]

It is unthinkable that Roncalli could have effectively ignored this decree replete with censures. But certainly his words and most especially his conduct can be said to have expressed his true internal disposition. In order that no doubt remain in the minds of the readers concerning the nature of Pius XII's decree on Communism, an official decree from the Holy Office follows in its entirety, along with a lengthy excerpt from a commentary on the decree published in the *Homiletic and Pastoral Review.*

Holy Office decree on Communists

This Supreme Sacred Congregation has been asked:

1. Is it lawful to join *or to show favor* to Communist groups?

2. Is it lawful to publish, disseminate or read books, periodicals, newspapers or leaflets which uphold Communist doctrine and practice, or to write in them?

3. May the faithful who knowingly and willingly perform the actions referred to in nn. 1 and 2 be admitted to the Sacraments?

4. Do the faithful who profess, *and above all those who defend and spread*, the materialistic and anti-Christian doctrine of the Communists *ipso facto*, as apostates from the Catholic faith, fall into an excommunication reserved *speciali modo* to the Holy See?

The Most Eminent and Reverend Fathers, charged with the safeguarding of matters of faith and morals, after having previously received the opinion of the Very Reverend Consultors, in a plenary session held on Tuesday, the 28th of June 1949, decided the response should be:

1. In the negative: because Communism is materialistic and anti-Christian. Though Communist leaders verbally profess not to oppose religion; nevertheless, in fact, both by teaching and action, they show themselves to be the enemies of God and the true religion and the Church of Christ.

2. In the negative: for they are forbidden by law itself (cf. Canon 1399, C.I.C.)

3. In the negative, according to the ordinary principles as regards the denial of the Sacraments to those who are not disposed.4. In the affirmative. On the following Thursday, the 30th of the same month and year, his

265

Holiness Pius XII, Pope by divine Providence, in the customary audience granted to his Excellency, the Most Reverend Assessor of the Holy Office, approved the aforementioned resolution of the Most Eminent Fathers and ordered it to be promulgated in the official journal, the *Acta Apostolicae Sedis*. Given in Rome, July 1, 1949 (Peter Vigorita, Notary). [18]

Homiletic and Pastoral Review editors' comments
No decree of the Holy See has received such lengthy notices in the daily press as that of the Holy Office regarding Communist affiliation and support. We have even witnessed earnest efforts to provide a canonical commentary. The sensational and seemingly political overtones of the Decree should not lead us to overlook its careful wording and the clear-cut distinctions it makes. Communism is materialistic and anti-Christian. That has been known long since to anyone who has followed its successive condemnations, notably, that of Pope Pius XI in *Divini Redemptoris*. It is confirmed by the frankness of Communist writers and, above all, by the activities of Communist leaders the world over. As a consequence, any Catholic who subscribes to true Communist doctrine, whether or not he carries a card of the Communist party, is an apostate from the Church, and; therefore, automatically excommunicated. His case is reserved to the Holy See, though once he abjures his perverse doctrines, the apostate can be absolved from the excommunication in the external forum by the local Ordinary, if his crime has been or is made public. (Canon 2314.) Occasionally, Catholics have lapsed into Communism and thus, apostatized from the church.

Without accepting Communism, there are some who have become identified with its activities or else have lent support to them. The Holy Office now further clarifies the dictum of Pope Pius XI, in his encyclical *Divini Redemptoris*: "Communism is intrinsically evil, and no one desirous of saving civilization can collaborate with it." *It is strictly forbidden to join the Communist Party or any truly Communist group. It is likewise, strictly forbidden to show it favor, for example, by defending its activity, giving it financial support, failing as a public official to check it when such is one's duty.* It is seriously wrong to publish or disseminate, or even to contribute to Communist publications, which support either Communist doctrines or policy. The Decree does not indicate how far a publication must support Communism in order to come under this ban. That is a question of fact to be decided in the individual case on the basis of the regular content of the publication. Furthermore, the faithful are forbidden to cooperate with Communism by reading any of its publications. Those who have need of doing so by reason of their profession, or in order to expose its pernicious errors, must seek the required permission from the local Ordinary, who is empowered by law to make exceptions in individual cases. (Canon 1402, 1.)

All who openly disregard the foregoing restrictions are publicly disobedient to the law of the Church, and; therefore, publicly unworthy of receiving Her Sacraments. But to be so penalized, a person must act *scienter* and *libere* — (knowingly and freely). Obviously, one who is duped into acting wrongfully should not suffer for his action because of his good faith. The meaning of the term *libere*, however, is more difficult to determine and undoubtedly will require further clarification. Perhaps we can say tentatively, that the action in question must not only be "free" in the ordinary sense of the term, but also free of grave fear, necessity and grave inconvenience. (cfr. Canon 2205, 2.) In other words, to be barred from the Sacraments, a person must not have been coerced into cooperating with Communism by circumstances, or by the wrongful action of others.

[…] The Catholic Press carried the text of a subsequent Decree of the Holy Office, dated August 11, 1949, explaining further how far Communists and cooperators with Communism are to be denied the Sacraments. The Degree states that those who adhere to the tenets of Communism, being apostates, are to be denied all sacred rites on the occasion of their marriage, which as a mixed marriage, is not to be celebrated in church. The parties in question are to sign the customary guarantees. However, those who belong to a Communist group or cooperate with Communism in the ways already mentioned are, on the occasion of their marriage, *to be treated as members of a forbidden society or public sinners, respectively.* (Canons 1065-1066.) [19]

Directive on Religious Unity, *Mortalium Animos*

In Pope Pius XII's directive on religious unity in March 1949, the good Pope lays down guidelines to be observed mainly by bishops in conducting conferences and meetings with non-Catholics. Commenting on this document, Reverend William Conway writes:

> The second general directive... is that in all efforts toward reunion, there is no question of restoring a unity...lost, but simply of a return by non-Catholics to a unity which has always existed and which can never cease to exist. [20]

Roncalli's comment in Venice in 1954 on this subject can hardly be said to conform to this norm laid down by Pius XII, for Roncalli speaks of "that which unites rather than that which divides." [21] No wonder his audience in Venice was shocked, for as Conway writes: *"The Instruction explicitly condemns that method of approach which concentrates on stressing points of doctrine on which Catholics and non-Catholics are agreed, rather than those on which they disagree."* [22] Again, this demonstrates Roncalli's contempt for the authority of the Holy See. Here is what Pope Pius XI had to say about teachings like Roncalli's:

Pope Pius XI, *Mortalium Animos* (1928)

Is it not right, it is often repeated, indeed, even consonant with duty, that all who invoke the name of Christ should abstain from mutual reproaches and at long last be united in mutual charity?...*These things and others that class of men who are known as pan-Christians continually repeat and amplify*; and these men, so far from being quite few and scattered, have increased to the dimensions of an entire class, and have grouped themselves into widely spread societies, most of which are directed by non-Catholics, although they are imbued with varying doctrines concerning the things of faith...How so great a variety of opinions can make the way clear to effect the unity of the Church We know not; that unity can only arise from one teaching authority, one law of belief and one faith of Christians. *But We do know that from this it is an easy step to the neglect of religion or indifferentism and to modernism, as they call it. Those, who are unhappily infected with these errors, hold that dogmatic truth is not absolute but relative, that is, it agrees with the varying necessities of time and place and with the varying tendencies of the mind, since it is not contained in immutable revelation, but is capable of being accommodated to human life.* Besides this, in connection with things which must be believed, it is nowise licit to use that distinction which some have seen fit to introduce between those articles of faith which are fundamental and those which are not fundamental, as they say, as if the former are to be accepted by all, while the latter may be left to the free assent of the faithful: for the supernatural virtue of faith has a formal cause, namely the authority of God revealing, and this is patent of no such distinction....

For the teaching authority of the Church, which in the divine wisdom was constituted on earth in order that revealed doctrines might remain intact forever, and that they might be brought with ease and security to the knowledge of men, and which is daily exercised through the Roman Pontiff and the Bishops who are in communion with him, has also the office of defining, when it sees fit, any truth with solemn rites and decrees, whenever this is necessary either to oppose the errors or the attacks of heretics, or more clearly and in greater detail to stamp the minds of the faithful with the articles of sacred doctrine which have been explained. But in the use of this extraordinary teaching authority no newly invented matter is brought in, nor is anything new added to the number of those truths which are at least implicitly contained in the deposit of Revelation, divinely handed down to the Church: only those which are made clear which perhaps may still seem obscure to some, or that which some have previously called into question is declared to be of faith...Furthermore, in this one Church of Christ no man can be or remain who does not accept, recognize and obey the authority and supremacy of Peter and his legitimate successors. [23]

Those who contend that Roncalli was at liberty to disregard the directives of Pope Pius XI because his teaching was consistent with an "older Christian tradition" than that promulgated in *Mortalium Animos* will find themselves running afoul of Pope Pius XII's teaching on Antiquarianism:

Pope Pius XII, *Mediator Dei* (1947)
50. The sacred liturgy does, in fact, include divine as well as human elements. *The former, instituted as they have been by God, cannot be changed in any way by men.*

58. It follows from this that the Sovereign Pontiff alone enjoys the right to recognize and establish any practice touching the worship of God, to introduce and approve new rites, as also to modify those he judges to require modification.

59. The Church is without question a living organism, and as an organism, in respect of the sacred liturgy also, she grows, matures, develops, adapts and accommodates herself to temporal needs and circumstances, *provided only that the integrity of her doctrine be safeguarded. This notwithstanding, the temerity and daring of those who introduce novel liturgical practices, or call for the revival of obsolete rites out of harmony with prevailing laws and*

rubrics, deserve severe reproof. It has pained Us grievously to note, Venerable Brethren, that such innovations are actually being introduced, not merely in minor details *but in matters of major importance as well. We instance, in point of fact, those who make use of the vernacular in the celebration of the august eucharistic sacrifice; those who transfer certain feast-days — which have been appointed and established after mature deliberation — to other dates; those, finally, who delete from the prayer books approved for public use the sacred texts of the Old Testament, deeming them little suited and inopportune for modern times....*

63. *Clearly no sincere Catholic can refuse to accept the formulation of Christian doctrine more recently elaborated and proclaimed as dogmas by the Church, under the inspiration and guidance of the Holy Spirit with abundant fruit for souls, because it pleases him to hark back to the old formulas. No more can any Catholic in his right senses repudiate existing legislation of the Church to revert to prescriptions based on the earliest sources of canon law.* Just as obviously unwise and mistaken is the zeal of one who in matters liturgical would go back to the rites and usage of antiquity, discarding the new patterns introduced by disposition of divine Providence to meet the changes of circumstances and situation.

64. This way of acting bids fair to revive the exaggerated and senseless antiquarianism to which the illegal Council of Pistoia gave rise. *It likewise attempts to reinstate a series of errors which were responsible for the calling of that meeting as well as for those resulting from it, with grievous harm to souls, and which the Church, the ever-watchful guardian of the "deposit of faith" committed to her charge by her divine Founder, had every right and reason to condemn.* For perverse designs and ventures of this sort tend to paralyze and weaken that process of sanctification by which the sacred liturgy directs the sons

of adoption to their Heavenly Father of their souls' salvation. [24]

An instruction from the Holy Office, December 20, 1949, also reiterated the points made above by Pope Pius XI in *Mortalium Animos*. [25] Therefore, it is impossible for anyone to claim that these errors were not specifically condemned prior to the reign of John 23, or that Catholics were insufficiently taught, and therefore no one committed heresy in introducing liturgical innovations. As will be seen below, Roncalli's public comments branded him as a pan-Christian, since his comments were almost identical to what Pope Pius XI forbid.

D. Pope Pius XII's vision

Various papal biographies report that several years before his death, Pope Pius XII suffered a protracted health crisis that nearly ended his life. His physician treated, then monitored, a gastric illness that began with exhaustion in 1953 and worsened in the early months of 1954, bringing him close to death later that year. The illness, according to one unidentified source, was attributed to his repeated use of a chromic acid preparation left in the papal bathroom "accidentally" by his dentist. Intended for a one-time application only, it is suggested that the preparation caused the hiccups and inability to eat, resulting in weight loss, which also was troubling the Pope. However, many other serious medical issues could have caused this condition, issues that went undetected by the Pope's doctors at the time. Pope Pius XII was surrounded by enemies, and as noted elsewhere, the C.I.A. operatives already operating in the Vatican could have made him one of the guinea pigs for their ongoing drug experiments. But not so coincidentally, other factors were at work that greatly affected Pius' health.

According to a work by the British author Piers Compton, [26] Pope Pius XII became increasingly concerned over the direction the Christian Democrat political party had taken following the 1948 elections. When the Christian Democrat Alcide De Gasperi assumed leadership of the Italian government after World War II in 1945, it did not take long for Pius XII to realize that concessions, however gradual, would be made to the Communists. De Gasperi and Giovanni Montini were good friends. Montini's father had long been involved with the Christian Democrats. In 1948 the Vatican, the Knights of Malta, the British Office of Strategic Services (O.S.S.), and the C.I.A. funded the Italian elections in which the Christian Democrats, Montini's father's party, played a key role. In 1954, a Protestant Archbishop from Sweden advised Pius XII that Montini had been embroiled in conciliatory correspondence with the Soviet Union after gaining access to certain intelligence reports. The pope immediately opened an enquiry into the matter, which revealed that Montini's private secretary, the Jesuit Alighiero Tondi — who later abandoned the priesthood — was the Russian agent responsible for notifying the KGB concerning the identities of priests and bishops secretly sent behind the Iron Curtain by Pope Pius XII. The betrayal hit especially close to home as Secretary of State under Pope Pius XI, then-Cardinal Eugenio Pacelli (who became Pius XII) had dealt with almost identical circumstances. The incident was obliquely mentioned in the 1973 work *The Jesuit*, a fact-based novel written by a former Jesuit. [27]

A copy of a purported O.S.S. document declassified in the 1980s, Compton reports, confirmed this account and stated that the meeting between Montini and Palmiro Togliatti, a Ukrainian politician and leader of the Italian Communist Party, was held at the home of a Christian Democrat minister in July of 1944 (Montini's brother Lodovico? Or Don Luigi Sturzo, the Sicilian activist priest who co-founded the Christian Democrats with the elder Montini?) This meeting, the document states, initiated the alliance of the Christian Democrats with the Socialists and Communists in Italy in order to obtain a majority vote in the 1948 Italian election, won by the elder Montini's Christian Democrat party. Once Roncalli ascended the throne, the Christian Democrats formally aligned themselves with the left, throwing the Italian government into chaos.

Then there was another incident involving Montini's family (also Pope Pius XII's nephew) in the early 1950s. Several Vatican and government officials were implicated in the death of a young woman; and the incident, known as the Montesi Affair, was linked to orgies and black masses celebrated at a lodge frequented by Rome's "Black Nobility." The pope cannot help but have been pained and mortified by the associations revealed in the prolific publicity surrounding Wilma Montesi's death. Reporter Reynolds Packard, special correspondent of THE NEWS, reported under a Rome dateline June 30, 1954: "Pope Pius XII, deeply upset at police disclosures of an aristocratic dope ring that may also have celebrated orgiastic black masses is considering formal excommunication of the bluebloods, authoritative sources said." [28]

In 1972, a former student of the Jesuits forwarded author Piers Compton a document composed by a group dedicated to defending the faith. Written by Reverend Joaquin Saenz y Arriaga of Mexico, at the order of the Jesuit Superior-General Arrupe, it dealt with the shady past of Paul 6. It solemnly stated that Montini was prominently involved, from 1936 to 1950, in "a vast network of espionage that covered some of the countries, on both sides, involved in the Second World War." [29] The document also stated that Montini was the principal shareholder of a chain of brothels in Rome. According to Robert Neville's *The World of the Vatican*, Pope Pius XII, still in the care of physician Riccardo Galeazzi-Lisi, took a turn for the worse shortly after receiving a letter from a young woman who had initially been part of the scandal but had repented and retired to a convent. Her confessor had ordered her to tell all she knew about Montesi's death. Anna Maria Caglio "wrote anxiously to the Pope, warning him that there were people around him that might do him harm." [30] After receiving her letter, Pius XII remained incommunicado for the next five months. Much of this time the Pope was in seclusion at Castel Gondolfo, according to Paul L. Murphy's *La Popessa.* But his failing health did not prevent Pope Pius XII from attending to urgent matters.

At about the same time the Montesi scandal erupted in Rome, Montini also was busy siding with his friends Angelo Roncalli and Yves Congar in the worker-priest affair. This scandal erupted in France while Roncalli was nuncio, a position Montini had secured for him by reportedly pressuring Pius XII. For evangelization purposes, Cardinal Suhard allowed Catholic priests to use a novel approach to effect conversions by working alongside lapsed Catholics in the factories and markets in hopes of attracting them to religion. Instead, many of these priests began neglecting their priestly duties and joined in with Marxists and Communists agitating for social and political changes. Some even left the priesthood to marry. Roncalli sat on the situation and failed to address it. Montini endorsed a book written by Congar sympathizing with the movement. As a result of this and other infractions, the Holy Office listed Congar and others as suspect of heresy (see below).

In October of 1954, it was discovered that Montini had failed to inform the Pope of a schism involving bishops in China. For Montini, time had run out. The monsignor had blatantly overstepped his bounds and breached the Holy Father's trust. French Traditionalist Rene Rouchette, writing for the German publication *Einsicht* in June 1980, related that from 1945 on, Montini had been designated as the successor to Pope Pius XII by the heads of the secret societies. But when the pope became gravely ill, and especially after his rift with Montini deepened, Roncalli was prepared to succeed Pius XII sometime in 1954. By December of 1954, the pope was near death; and it is not idle speculation to assume that it was as much a spiritual and mental anguish that afflicted him as it was an actual physical condition itself. The pope later would explain the event that preceded his miraculous recovery — a vision of Christ.

Following the arduous canonization ceremony for Pope St. Pius X in May 1954, and despite a lengthy sojourn at Castel Gondolfo, where he wrote no less than 22 carefully crafted speeches, Pius XII was in a greatly weakened condition by the end of November. He had been gravely ill for nearly a year. He had lost 40 pounds. He was hiccupping as before and could not keep food down. In short, he appeared to be a man close to death. Numerous physicians were called in on consultation, all with different scenarios of what was wrong with the pope. But no one had any suggestions for a cure.

> On the evening of Dec. 1, Pope Pius XII requested that no physicians be in attendance: he was expecting a vision that

arrived that same evening. On the morning of Dec. 2, he awakened very early, feeling even weaker than before. He began reciting the *Anima Christi* (Soul of Christ). At the very moment that he reached the part, "At the hour of my death call me," Pius XII saw Our Lord standing by his bedside, "silent in all His eloquent majesty." *It was the first time he knew of Our Lord appearing in such a way to a Pope since St. Peter asked, "Quo Vadis, Domine?"* Like St. Peter, when he was first called, Pius XII thought Our Lord was inviting him to "Follow Me." With joy in his heart, the Holy Father said, with what strength he had: *"O bone Jesu! O bone Jesu! Voca me; iube me venire ad Te!"* (O good Jesus! O good Jesus! Call Thou me; order me to come to Thee!) But alas, Our gentle Savior had not come to summon Pius XII home, but to comfort him. And after a little while He went away. [31]

Over the next few days, the Pope seemed much better and resumed his normal activities. While he acknowledged he had received the vision after it was made public, much to his embarrassment, it is quite possible he omitted certain pertinent details. According to Internet reports, at least one Italian magazine claims the pope did indeed receive a "divine message" during the vision, a message that Roncalli was supposed to open following Pius XII's death. Like the Fatima message, however, the message was never released. Shortly before Pius XII's vision, on November 1, the pope had informed his pro-secretary of State Giovanni Montini that he was appointing him Archbishop of Milan, sans the cardinal's hat that customarily accompanied the appointment. The words Pius XII directed to Montini on that day in November are innocent enough, but in retrospect are the most chilling words imaginable: "One day my son," he told him prophetically, "you will return." [32] It was shortly after this act that the pope's condition greatly worsened.

And who is to say these details did not determine the events that followed? For in the wake of Montini's dismissal, Sister Pascalina insisted that Pope Pius XII limit his schedule severely due to his health problems. She personally screened all his visitors, prelates and cardinals included. [33] Until his death, various authors have reported that he would trust no one except Sister Pascalina. He wrote his own encyclicals, left key positions unfilled, no longer held meetings with his department heads, and even failed to appoint an acting Cardinal Camerlengo, responsible for calling the next papal election when Pius XII died. Domenico Cardinal Tardini, a conservative, greatly chafed under these restrictions and severely criticized the pope. He even wrote a book portraying Pius in a negative light and labeled him a "weak" pope. He especially decried his failure to communicate with the hierarchy and the Holy Office. [34] During this time period Sister Pascalina believed she was doing all she could to safeguard the pope's health, but the nun came under great criticism from all sides for her fierce protectiveness.

Unable to deal successfully with his subordinates, Pope Pius turned to the lay people, addressing various groups on a wide range of topics. Frequently, he spoke to scientists and their colleagues, explaining how Christian teachings related to scientific discoveries and results. He wrote thoughtful evaluations of the different occupations the laity were engaged in. And he addressed moral questions in a world where such matters were growing increasingly complicated, and already morality in general, even among Catholics, was beginning to wane. Church teachings on ethics also were explained to professional societies. It was as though the pope, in these last years, turned his mind entirely to the lambs of his flock, disillusioned by his dealings with his demanding, increasingly liberal hierarchy. Some believe, based on writings and teachings existing even before his 1954 vision, that Pius XII possessed the gift of foresight, which guided his writing. And in 1954 Our Lord Himself may even have informed him that the hierarchy was a lost cause, and any hope that remained would be found in the laity. A look at his pre-1954 actions below will confirm this.

Battening down the hatches on St. Peter's Barque

Many Traditionalist and Novus Ordo *literati* have insinuated that Pope Pius XII paved the way for all the changes that later came in the Church and even planned a second Vatican Council, but this is not substantiated by his life's work and the massive teaching legacy he left for those who care to read it. We have seen above that both Pope Pius XI and Pius XII had been warned not to call a council because of the many Modernists already holding high positions in the Church. Those criticizing Pius XII base their claim primarily on one particular Traditionalist work, *The Undermining of the Catholic Church*, by Mary Ball Martinez. which they contend shows that Papa Pacelli was favorable to the changes in the Church and even put them into motion. This work, written by an accredited journalist employed by the Vatican Press Corps in the 1970s and 1980s, relies primarily on information gained from Traditionalist and Novus Ordo sources via interviews and private conversations, also works generally attributed to authors writing after the death of Pope Pius XII, (written by Novus Ordo and Traditionalist clerics as well as secular authors). Certainly Martinez's work can contribute to the general knowledge of what occurred *after* Pope Pius XII's death, but are statements made to a reporter by people who are not even members of the Catholic Church — members likely to have only disdain for Pius XII's papacy — really likely to be factual and trustworthy? Not according to *Cum ex Apostolatus Officio*, which bars unrepentant heretics from acting as witnesses in ecclesiastical courts. [35] A recent work on Pope Pius XII written by Novus Ordo author Robert A. Ventresca does not portray this pope in the same light in which the Vatican Press Corps correspondent mentioned above portrayed him. In fact, Ventresca relates the following:

> Tensions within the church of Pius XII over doctrinal matters intensified through the late 1940s and reached a crescendo after the publication of the papal encyclical *Humani Generis,* (August 1950). In it, Pius XII condemned what he saw as the "false theories" of modern philosophies that were affecting the work of Catholic thinkers — whose adherents were labeled by critics as exponents of a *nouvelle théologie*, a "new" theology that threatened to undermine the very foundations of the church's teaching...The pope...was concerned near the end of his life that he had written and said too much during his

pontificate. Speaking in May 1957 to Father Antoine Wenger, then editor of the French Catholic newspaper *Le Croix*, Pius XII admitted to worrying that perhaps by issuing so many letters and speeches over the course of a long pontificate he had contributed to an 'inflation of the papal word.' Some critics at the time agreed that Pius XII perhaps was speaking too frequently and too expansively on matters far beyond his competency. The result was not so much the inflation of papal words as their trivialization...*Many of Pius XII's advisors and admirers admitted that in the latter part of his pontificate especially the papal court exhibited a tendency toward inertia, stagnation, and reaction. For a faithful critical thinker like Jacques Maritain, it was especially lamentable that Pius XII gave free rein to the "archaic methods" and mentality of the men of the Holy Office.* [36]

In a *Forbes Magazine* online review of Ventresca's work in 2014, [37] writer John Farrell quotes Professor Don O'Leary as follows:

Catholic scholarship was severely curtailed in the latter half of Pius's pontificate. Some theologians were forbidden by Vatican authorities to teach or publish on the basis of guidelines such as those laid down in *Humani Generis*. Those who were censured for their views, or who were very restricted in expressing their views, included, most notably the French Dominicans Yves Congar and Marie-Dominique Chenu, and the Jesuits Henri de Lubac, Karl Rahner, Pierre Teilhard de Chardin, Jean Daniélou, [Joseph Ratzinger] and John Courtney Murray." [38]

This also is noted by Ventresca and is supported by Reverend Robert Nugent's work *Silence Speaks*, which details communications between the censured theologians and the ecclesiastical authorities and describes how the disciplinary actions taken against them affected them both personally and spiritually. [39]

So how does what Maritain says above square with Pope Pius XII secretly supporting the coming changes? Ventresca, in his work, disparages the notion the pope was veering left; and some of his reviewers criticize him for it. The problem is that those who demonize Pius XII in this way never read his encyclicals or addresses; instead, they listen to those who "interpreted" and continue to interpret Pius XII's writings to their own liking at a much later date. Pope Pius XII had to be portrayed as paving the way for Vatican 2 by those who were promoting the Americanist Proposition because any perceived breach or apparent break with (true) Tradition would have sounded the alarm. Scholastic study and demonstration are far removed from journalistic methods. Journalism has its place, but not in treating theology. And if journalism operates on the basis of Henry Luce's and Felix Morlion's *Apostolate of Public Opinion,* as may very well have been the case, it is not credible anyway.

Martinez does not cite one papal document or Canon Law, only the false Vatican 2 council papers. As far as Pope Pius XII goes, she may have known what his enemies thought of him; and perhaps she was imbued to some extent with that pervading mistrust of all the popes, which poisoned the minds of so many Traditionalists following the takeover by the usurpers. But she did not know what Pius XII actually taught, how he commanded others to believe, the many decisions and infallible statements he made in his numerous documents. As already noted, in actuality, he was tying up any loose ends in the last years of his life to protect and defend the Church he so ardently loved. If he seemed to reach out even to those among the hierarchy who were erring, as Ventresca indicates, so what? The popes have always tried to reason with those in error and to bring them back into the fold, even Martin Luther and Leonard Feeney. Many believe he assented to the "democratization" of the Church and gave full consent to Morlion's (read the C.I.A.'s) presence in the Vatican, and perhaps he did. Perhaps he believed the dissemination of democracy, in this particular time period, was the only way to save the world from Communism and assure a semblance of peace. He may have looked to the U.S., based on its cooperation with the Vatican during World War II, as a protector and believed they would continue protecting the Church. Is this any different than his predecessors' often misguided reliance on the emperors of various nations for protection in earlier ages?

Pius XII seemingly lent his support, at least at first, to the ongoing experiment with democracy and its application to Church government. At that time, the pope was relying on the guidance of Montini and others in Montini's entourage for advice and direction regarding this new idea. It was Pope Pius XII's understanding that the principles guiding this experiment were to be applied to governments, not the Church. He seemed unaware of the true nature of the entire plan; he was certainly unaware of the underlying goal of Doctrinal Warfare operatives to seize the government ruling Vatican City and ultimately the world, the choicest prize of them all. When he began to discover the true nature and extent of the corruption in the Church, degree by degree as described above, he retreated. Already he had refused to appoint a new head for the Knights of Malta, despite his longstanding friendship with Francis Cardinal Spellman. Pius XII must have perceived Montini's ambitions to become pope, and he deflected this by declining to appoint him a cardinal. The pope obviously realized that his own cardinals and other assistants were working against him, and so he refused to fill many vacancies in the Holy See. He devised a list of those posing a danger to the Church, among them Jacques Maritain, John Courtney Murray, and others mentioned above, citing them as suspected Modernists. Roncalli may well have been on this list, given his involvement in ventures disapproved of or disbanded by Pius XII.

Never mentioned in any of his biographies, at least the ones examined for this work, was Pius XII's relationship with his personal assistant from his days as papal nuncio in Germany, Robert Leiber, S. J. According to author David Wemhoff, Leiber was one of the O.S.S.'s primary agents during WWII, passing information to American operatives regarding the activities of Adolph Hitler. He continued to forward information following the war, including details of personal conversations with the Pope. One of these conversations relayed to Murray via Leiber reportedly indicated that as a private theologian at least, Pius XII sympathized with Murray and did not share Ottaviani's views on the Americanist proposition. Monsignor

Fenton challenged this assertion; and in his diaries, he indicates his belief that the Jesuits were selling out the Church and precipitating the great apostasy. [40] Still, Wemhoff indicates that Fenton believed it was possible that Pius XII sympathized with Murray. Certainly Fenton believed Pope Pius XII was a weak pope, as his diaries explain, but there is no indication in Pope Pius XII's formal teachings that he supported Murray's position. What Piers Compton wrote in his work, without naming any source for the material, may well be true:

> It was during the pontificate of Pope Pius XII that a number of priests, then working at the Vatican, became aware that all was not well beneath the surface. For a strange kind of influence, not to their liking, was making itself felt, and this they traced to a group who had come into prominence as experts, advisors and specialists...who surrounded the pope so closely he was spoken of, half humorously, as their prisoner....Those priests more seriously concerned set up a series of investigations...their spokesman was Fr. Eustace Eilers...of Birmingham, Alabama....That the hand of the Illuminati was definitely involved became clearer when Fr. Eilers, who announced that he was publishing those facts, was suddenly found dead... [41]

Wemhoff carefully notes that to this day, the correspondence and activities of Leiber remain classified information. According to one website, Lieber helped Nazis escape from Germany via the infamous "Ratlines" by falsely portraying himself as acting in his official capacity as a papal advisor. Reportedly, Cardinal Giuseppe Siri was another cooperator in facilitating the Nazis' escape. The same site also relates that Lieber destroyed all his personal records related to his time as an assistant with Pope Pius XII because he was afraid it would "cast Pius in an unfavorable light." [42] Certainly, given the fact that Pius XII was in the company of known spies and traitors from his own ranks, one could easily believe he was being manipulated at least, and probably was being intimidated and coerced, even drugged.

And it seems that Pope Pius XII *knew* he had been surrounded. After recovering from his illness, he retreated and devoted the rest of his years to penning those addresses and radio broadcasts geared primarily to the faithful. One seasoned journalist relayed the following impression of the Pope in the mid-1950s:

> Only by the most strenuous means had Pius XII, an extraordinary being, maintained the prestige of the Church. This tall frail man with piercing black eyes had for 25 years conducted an almost incredibly arduous reign. He had literally thrown open the huge bronze doors of the Vatican and invited people to come to him...He had made a good start toward adapting ancient principles to modern times...He had severely condemned racialism, anti-Semitism and totalitarian doctrines...Possibly his greatest achievement was recognition of the need for a fresh appeal to the workingman...But the Pope may have felt the Church had gone far enough. [43]

Pius XII already had stated his position in many prior documents of both the ordinary and extraordinary magisterium. And the gist of his teachings, summarized below, is proof of his real doctrinal intent.

- In 1943 came *Mystici Corporis*, defining that bishops may function as bishops only with the jurisdiction granted by the Roman Pontiff and in communion with him; they do not receive their jurisdictional faculties directly from Christ. This encyclical also condemned that "unhealthy" quietism which excludes Catholic Action; condemned the idea of an invisible or pneumatological Church; reaffirmed Christ as the true Head of the Mystical Body; condemned acceptance of Christ as the Head without the Pope as the Church's visible head on earth; and also condemned the belief that prayers may only be addressed to God the eternal Father, not to Jesus Christ (a Protestant and Novus Ordo heresy).

- Two years later, Pope Pius XII "reform[ed] some points of the Constitution *Vacante Sede Apostolica* of Pope Pius X, December 25, 1904, and the *Motu Proprio* of Pope Pius XI, March 1, 1922, and adopt[ed] the remaining provisions of these two documents." [44] His constitution was duly entered into the *Acta Apostolica Sedis*. One of the most notable points reformed by the pope was a one-sentence addition to paragraph three that forever changed the nature of this document. In that paragraph, both Pope St. Pius X and Pius XII state:

> During the vacancy of the Apostolic See, regarding those things that pertained to the Sovereign Roman Pontiff while he lived, the Sacred College of Cardinals shall have absolutely no power or jurisdiction of rendering neither a favor nor justice or of carrying out a favor or justice rendered by the deceased Pontiff; rather, let the College be obliged to reserve all these things to the future Pontiff. We declare invalid and void any power or jurisdiction pertaining to the Roman Pontiff in his lifetime, which the assembly of Cardinals might decide to exercise... [45]

And if even the cardinals could not exercise it, certainly the bishops could not presume to do so. Then in paragraph three Pope St. Pius X wrote in 1904:

> The laws issued by Roman Pontiffs in no way can be corrected or changed by the assembly of Cardinals of the Roman Church while it is without a Pope, nor can anything be subtracted from them or added or dispensed in any way whatsoever with respect to said laws or any part of them. This prohibition is especially applicable in the case of Pontifical Constitutions issued to regulate the business of the election of the Roman Pontiff."

Pope Pius XII added to the above paragraph in 1945:

> In truth, if anything adverse to this command should by chance happen to come about or be attempted, *We declare it, by Our Supreme Authority, to be null and void.* [46]

This one sentence successfully hamstrings anyone trying to hijack the laws and rights of the Church during an interregnum and nullifies all acts of those who would attempt such treachery. Why did Pope Pius XII add this infallible statement? No doubt he was well aware of exactly what had happened in the past, and what could easily happen again, given the rise of liberalism, neo-modernism, and paganism in the world. This statement is repeated later in this constitution.

> This present document and whatever is contained in it can by no means be challenged... we command those individuals to whom it pertains and will pertain for the time being to vote, that the ordinances must be respectively and inviolably observed by them, and if anyone should happen to try otherwise relative to these things, by whatever authority, knowingly or unknowingly, *the attempt is null and void.* [47]

Nothing could be clearer than these paragraphs. As such they nullify the exercise of all episcopal offices during an interregnum for lack of a papal mandate, which is required under pain of excommunication in *Ad Apostolorum Principis*, [48] (also entered in the AAS). This is clearly a usurpation of papal jurisdiction, for only the pope can approve bishops. And the exercise of tonsure [49] necessary to validly assign priests to a diocese and enroll them in their studies, by bishops who in reality never became bishops at all according to this infallible decree, was likewise worthless. Pius XII also nullifies a papal election of a suspected or even secret heretic attempted in violation of *Cum ex Apostolatus Officio* and Pope St. Pius V's *Inter Multiplices*, such as Roncalli's. These important papal laws pertain directly to the election and who is qualified to be elected, meaning it corresponds with Pope Pius XII's command that "this prohibition is especially applicable in the case of Pontifical Constitutions issued to regulate the business of the election of the Roman Pontiff," (VAS above).

- In 1947, *Mediator Dei* [50] condemned in advance many of the proposed liturgical abuses Pius XII is accused of sanctioning. Reading this encyclical gives one a clear picture of exactly what those lobbying for liturgical reform were demanding.
- In 1949, *Suprema Haec Sacra*, [51] citing *Mystici Corporis*, declared that those not members of the Catholic Church yet united to Her in a certain way can be saved without water Baptism by a desire animated by perfect charity, if it is joined by supernatural faith. This would apply to those who are invincibly ignorant. It had long been a teaching of the Catholic Church, but at that time was being challenged by an American Jesuit, Leonard Feeney, who was later excommunicated. No one at that time would have ever foreseen the possibility that a person willing to administer water Baptism with the intention of the Church would be difficult to find. Nor could they have envisioned a time when such great confusion would prevail because there would no longer be a visible Catholic Church on earth. Longing to be or to remain a member of the Church even though it is no longer a juridic entity is the plight of remnant Catholics today.
- In 1950, *Humani Generis*[52] cleared the controversy concerning the infallibility of documents issuing from the ordinary magisterium, for all the good it did for Traditionalists. For most believed that only *ex cathedra* documents were infallible without even knowing the definition or context in which *ex cathedra* was used by the Vatican Council. (See Chapter II above.) Other topics in the encyclical were dogmatic relativism, where the pope condemns the contempt of doctrine and those things agreeing "... with the varying necessities of time and place and with the varying tendencies of the mind, since it is not contained in immutable revelation, but is capable of being accommodated to human life." [53]

This of course is exactly where the Vatican 2 church is today, and is why they embrace false charity, indifferentism, salvation of all men, and many of their other errors. On this same topic, the pope explained that no one may presume to replace with conjectural notions "the things composed through common effort by Catholic teachers over the course of the centuries…[by] men endowed with no common talent and holiness, working under the vigilant supervision of the holy magisterium." [54] And in "revising" all these wonderful works, those who embarked on the Vatican 2 changes did just that.

Relativism leads, Pius XII said, to *eirenism*, a setting aside of opinions that divide men, in order to reconcile dogma, which cannot be compromised. This error is also known as minimalism. The pope teaches that removing these "road blocks" to reunite Christians would unite them alright, *"but only to their destruction."* [55] He calls efforts to effect such a false union widespread among some theologians, the clergy, and the laity. He cautions that this eirenism and relativism originate from a love of novelty, and "are not always advanced in the same degree…terms or with the unanimous agreement of their authors." He warned that over time, they would become openly and audaciously promoted, which was certainly the case. He also condemns errors involving Sacred Scripture, already condemned by several popes, which deny that Holy Scripture was divinely inspired.

He then rakes over the coals those who show disdain and even contempt for scholastic theology and philosophy and the terms used to express it, calling it "supreme imprudence" and explaining that it weakens speculative theology, which is based on theological reasoning. These men do so, the pope said, because they consider speculative theology devoid of true certitude, an error common to Modernists. He also condemns *historicism*, a form of secular humanism which gives value only to the events of man's life, "overthrow[ing] the absolute foundation of all truth and absolute law, both on the level of philosophical speculation and especially to Christian dogmas." [56] *Evolution* also is addressed in this encyclical. On this subject, the pope condemns this belief as Communist, pointing out that all must hold souls as created immediately by God and must not teach that some men took their origin through natural generation from men not proceeding from Adam (polygenism). The pope warns that false teaching on evolution gives rise to the new philosophy known as *existentialism*, a dangerous new false philosophy that emphasizes the existence of things to the neglect of their immutable essence.

- Also in 1950, *Munificentissimus Deus* infallibly defined the dogma of the Assumption of the Blessed Virgin Mary. [57]
- In 1954, *Ad Sinarum Gentum* [58] further elaborated on the inability of bishops to function independently of the Holy See as defined in *Mystici Corporis Christi.* [59]
- In 1958, shortly before his death, *Ad Apostolorum Principis* shored up Pope Pius XII's statements in *VAS* (1945), forbidding bishops be appointed to sees in China without papal confirmation. He attached a special excommunication to this encyclical forbidding these bishops to function unless absolved by the Pope himself. [60] This automatically excludes any so-called Traditionalists from functioning until such absolution can be conferred by a truly canonically elected pope. In this encyclical Pius XII refers to *Ad Sinarum Gentum* and the inability of bishops to function outside the authorization of the Holy See.

And in *Ad Apostolorum Principis*, Pius XII tellingly describes the very methods used by the C.I.A. to destroy the Church — Chinese thought reform, or psychological warfare — while never referencing the C.I.A. or the American proposition. The pope wrote:

> In these meetings, the unwilling are forced to take part by incitement, threats and deceit. If any bold spirit strives to defend truth, his voice is easily smothered and overcome and he is branded with a mark of infamy as an enemy of his native land and the new society....An almost endless series of lectures and discussions, lasting for weeks and months, so weaken and benumb the strength of mind and will that by *a kind of psychic coercion*, an assent is extracted which contains almost no human element, an

assent which is not freely asked for as should be the case….All men of good sense cannot refrain from raising their voices with Us in real horror from uttering a protest deploring the deranged conscience of their fellow men. [61]
And there were many other addresses and allocutions.

From the above, it is clear that what Pius XII predicted was precisely how those who protested the changes in the Church were treated and how the enemy successfully weakened the mind and spirit of Catholics. And even today, all raising their voices against these abuses are crushed by the opposition on both sides as disseminators of conspiracy theories, lies, fake news, and are accused of vicious calumnies.

Alpha and Omega

It is difficult to imagine how much more thorough Pope Pius XII could have been in warning the faithful what lurked in the murky beyond. But clergy and faithful were not listening. They connected none of what happened after his death to his warnings in life. Few indeed even attempted to abide by the teachings he imparted or even realized it was required of them to do so in order to remain Catholic.

In the October 20, 1958 issue of *Time* magazine, one correspondent stated:

> In his preoccupation with the world at large and with his diplomat's tendency to avoid sharp edges, Pope Pius often neglected the Vatican itself. He seemed to shrink from making much-needed appointments to the central machinery of the church. Result, at the time of his death: 15 vacancies in a superannuated College of Cardinals, no Secretary of State, no governor for Vatican City, no [cardinal] camerlengo [in charge of electing the next pope]... Said one of his closest advisers sadly last week: 'He provided badly for his successor.' [62]

Those chronicling his death at the time know that this pope, who gave his all to the Church before he died, would never have carelessly left Her without the means to continue Her mission. He did what any good householder would do on leaving his place of residence for an unspecified amount of time: he locked all the doors and barred the windows; he took the keys with him, forbidding anyone to enter his residence until his return, or the return of Our Lord Himself or His assigns; he bequeathed detailed instructions to his servants, the faithful, in order that they might carry on until that time; he made certain that no decisions could be made in his name; and he demonstrated by his actions that the Church would experience an interruption in her normal processes.

Christ indeed must have conveyed to him the future of the Church in his 1954 vision, a future already predicted in the Fatima Secret and by Our Lady at La Salette; a future clearly outlined in Chapters 8-13 of St. John's Apocalypse. It also is possible that contrary to popular belief, the pope read the contents of the third secret of Fatima. For clearly Pope Pius XII was chosen to know the contents of the little scroll [63] that would taste sweet in his mouth *but make his belly bitter*; he *lived* that prophecy in his earthly sufferings! St. Anthony Mary Claret reveals in his autobiography that Our Lord told him in a vision that he (St. Anthony) was the "angel" in this passage of Apocalypse. It was Pope Pius XII who canonized St. Anthony Mary Claret on May 7, 1950, during the Holy Year. In his commentary on Apoc. 10:7, Reverend E. Sylvester Berry tells us that the phrase "time will be no more" in this verse means that the time for the judgment against obstinate sinners has come, the time that Our Lady of Fatima predicted would happen if enough people did not pray and do penance. Father Berry continues, "This judgment shall be the great persecution of Antichrist and its attendant evils." [64]

In 1939, while burying Pope Pius XI beneath St. Peter's Basilica, an accident led to the discovery of an unknown section of the catacombs. Pope Pius XII approved the excavation of the newfound catacomb and it was there that St. Peter's tomb was eventually discovered, modestly wedged between two magnificent pagan mausoleums. Across from the first pope's tomb stood an empty niche. Pius XII would not live to see the completion of all the many archaeological finds in those catacombs. But because he had approved the excavation, it was in the empty niche opposite St. Peter's tomb that Pope Pius XII was laid to rest, whether intentionally — to entomb his "doctrinal intransigence" along with his papacy — or simply as a gesture to commemorate his devoted service. Either way, his resting place is a powerful and inescapable indicator of the *alpha* and *omega* (beginning and end) of the juridical Church established on earth by Jesus Christ, and the re-entry of the Church into the catacombs she inhabited in the early centuries of Her existence.

Conclusion

Pope Pius XII's death was the logical separation point between the old and the new. Even Protestants who were not favorable to the Church noticed the marked difference between the reigns of Pacelli and Roncalli. Not even three months after his election, Roncalli would call the false Vatican 2 council. He also would approve the new consecration formula, *for all men*, for private use by the faithful. There are those who call Pope Pius XII a false pope, throwing him in with the usurpers and making it appear as though there was every indication that he paved the way for the changes. But what has been presented above is proof that this was not the case, nor is there any evidence that pre-election he was anything but solidly Catholic. Those making these claims have never succeeded in providing scholastic proofs; they have not taken into account the purpose of these laws or the grave circumstances surrounding them. Nor have they referred integrally to the entire body of works — the mind of the lawgiver — produced by Pius XII, as Canon Law teaches. And that body of works is considerable. It even seems they have forgotten the words of Sister Lucy regarding the year 1960. Certainly by then, all could see for themselves the path laid out for the destruction of the Church and the true character of the man purportedly elected to take the place of Pope Pius XII. Part II below will chronicle the actual takeover of the Church and the entrance of the abomination into the holy place.

Chapter IX Endnotes

[1] Motu proprio *Bonum sane*, quoted by Rev. Denis Fahey, *The Kingship of Christ According to the Principles of St. Thomas Aquinas,* reprinted by Christian Book Club of America, Palmdale Calif., (first printed in 1931); 171

[2] Walter H. Peters, *The Life of Pope Benedict XV*, Bruce Publishing Co., Milwaukee, Wis., 1959,

[3] *The Pope Speaks Magazine*, Joseph Sprug editor, Washington, D.C., "The Contradiction of Our Age," Dec. 23, 1956, Spring 1957, Vol. 3, no. 4

[4] Rev. James Naughton, S. J., *Pius XII on World Problems*, The America Press, New York, N.Y., 1943, 49-50

[5] Ibid.

[6] *The Pope Speaks*, Michael Chinigo Editor, Pantheon Books, New York, N.Y., 1957, 168-69

[7] http://w2.vatican.va/content/benedict-xv/en/encyclicals/documents/hf_ben-xv_enc_01111914_ad-beatissimi-apostolorum.html

[8] Rev. Denis Fahey, *The Kingship of Christ and the Conversion of the Jewish Nation*, Christian Book Club of America, Hawthorne, Calif., reprinted 1987, 82

[9] Ibid., 82-83

[10] George Passelecq and Bernard Suchesky, *The Hidden Encyclical of Pope Pius XI*, Harcourt Brace & Co., New York, N.Y., San Diego, Calif, London, UK, 1997

[11] *Douay-Rheims New Testament* translated from the Latin Vulgate, 1859; Edward Dunigan and Brother, New York, N.Y.

[12] Written in 1962 under the pseudonym "Maurice Pinay," the authorship of *The Plot Against the Church* was later claimed by Anacleto Gonzales-Flores, a Mexican physician and son of a Cristero martyr. It is believed Gonzales-Flores teamed with the Mexican priest and canon lawyer Fr. Joaquin Saenz-Arriaga to write the book. Gonzalez-Flores later told this author in a typewritten letter sent from Mexico in the early 1980s: "I am Maurice Pinay." The book focuses on the Jews as practically the sole cause of the Church's subversion, ignoring the role played by Freemasonry, the C.I.A (not known at that time) and apostate/heretic Catholics. It spawned the creation of a right-wing segment of Traditionalists affiliated with Aryan

nations and certain militia groups, here and abroad — a faction still active today.

[13] https://www.jewishvirtuallibrary.org/a-question-of-judgment-pius-xii-and-the-jews

[14] Fr. Senan, O.F.M., Cap., *Angelic Shepherd*, Capuchin Annual Office, 1950, 88-89

[15] *The Pius War: Responses to the Critics of Pius XII*, edited by Joseph Bottum and David Dalin, Lexington Books, Boulder, Colo., New York N.Y., Toronto, Canada, 2004

[16] Ibid., p. 8

[17] Rev. William Conway, *Problems in Canon Law*, Brown and Nolan, LTD, Richview Press, Dublin, 1956, 322

[18] *Homiletic and Pastoral Review*, Vol. 50, No. 1, Oct. 1949

[19] Ibid.

[20] Rev. William Conway, *Problems in Canon Law*, Brown and Nolan, LTD, Richview Press, Dublin, 1956, 331

[21] Alden Hatch, *A Man Named John: The Life of Pope John XXIII*, Hawthorne Books Inc., New York, N.Y., 1954

[22] Rev. William Conway, *Problems in Canon Law*, Brown and Nolan, LTD, Richview Press, Dublin, 1956, 331

[23] Pope Pius XI's *Mortalium Animos*, Jan. 6, 1928, http://w2.vatican.va/content/pius-xi/en/encyclicals/documents/hf_p-xi_enc_19280106_mortalium-animos.html

[24] Pope Pius XII, *Mediator Dei,* Mediator Dei (November 20, 1947) | PIUS XII - Vatican.va

[25] *The Canon Law Digest,* Vol. 4, T. Lincoln Bouscaren, S. J., LL.B., S.T.D., and James I. O'Connor, S.J., A.M., S.T.L., J.C.D., Bruce Publishing Co., Milwaukee, Wis., 1958, (AAS 42-142)

[26] Piers Compton, *The Broken Cross: The Hidden Hand in the Vatican*, Veritas Publishing CO., Party LTD, Australia, 1984, 51-55

[27] John Gallahue, *The Jesuit*, Stein and Day Publishers, New York, N.Y., 1973

[28] https://www.newspapers.com/newspage/161048779/

[29] Piers Compton, *The Broken Cross: The Hidden Hand in the Vatican*, Veritas Publishing Co., Party LTD, Australia, 1984, 110

[30] http://samurailearntorock.blogspot.com/2010/11/illuminati-and-catholic-church.html

[31] Alden Hatch and Seamus Walshe, *Crown of Glory*, Hawthorne Books, New York, N.Y., 1957, 234-35

[32] Andre Fabert, *Pope Paul VI*, Monarch Books, Inc., Derby, Conn., 1963, 44

[33] Paul I. Murphy and R. Rene Arlington, *La Popessa*, Warner Books, New York, N.Y., 1983, 284-85

[34] Ibid., 281-82

[35] "Further, whoever knowingly presumes in any way to receive anew the persons so apprehended, confessed or convicted [of heresy, apostasy or schism], or to favor them, believe them, or teach their doctrines shall *ipso facto* incur excommunication, and, become infamous" (para. 5).

[36] Robert A. Ventresca, *Soldier of Christ: The Life of Pope Pius XII,* The Belknap Press of Harvard University Press, Cambridge, Mass., and London, 2013, Ch. 7, p. 272

[37] http://www.forbes.com/sites/johnfarrell/2014/08/11/the-cautious-pope-and-the-evolution-encyclical/#619abfb87c0a

[38] *Roman Catholicism and Modern Science,* p. 154; *see also* http://www.traditioninaction.org/ProgressivistDoc/A_001_CondemnationRatzinger.htm

[39] See also Nugent's comments in "The Censuring of John Courtney Murray," Part II, *Catholic World*, March/April 2008, http://novusordowatch.org/wp-content/uploads/censuring-murray2.pdf

[40] Fenton Diaries, Vol. 4, 109-10

[41] Piers Compton, *The Broken Cross*, Veritas Publishing Co., Pty, Ltd, Australia, 1984, 37

[42] https://ipfs.io/ipfs/QmXoypizjW3WknFiJnKLwHCnL72vedxjQkDDP1mXWo6uco/wiki/Robert_Leiber.html

[43] Melton S. Davis, *All Rome Trembled*, G. Putnam's Sons, New York, N.Y., 1957, 101

[44] *A Practical Commentary on the Code of Canon Law*, Rev. Callistus Smith and Stanislaus Woywod, Joseph F. Wagner, New York, N.Y., 1957; commentary on Can. 160

[45] http://www.betrayedcatholics.com/free-content/reference-links/1-what-constitutes-the-papacy/apostolic-constitution-vacantis-apostolicae-sedis/

[46] Ibid., para. 3

[47] Ibid., para. 108

[48] http://w2.vatican.va/content/pius-xii/en/encyclicals/documents/hf_p-xii_enc_29061958_ad-apostolorum-principis.html

[49] See http://www.betrayedcatholics.com/free-content/reference-links/6-traditionalists/why-traditionalist-clerics-never-received-valid-orders/ which explains the necessity of jurisdiction for valid tonsure

[50] Mediator Dei (November 20, 1947) | PIUS XII - Vatican.va

[51] The Canon Law Digest, Vol. III, T. Lincoln Bouscaren S.J., S.T.D., LL.B., Bruce Publishing Co., Milwaukee, Wis., 1954, 525-530

[52] : http://w2.vatican.va/content/pius-xii/en/encyclicals/documents/hf_p-xii_enc_12081950_humani-generis.html

[53] http://w2.vatican.va/content/pius-xi/en/encyclicals/documents/hf_p-xi_enc_19280106_mortalium-animos.html

[54] http://w2.vatican.va/content/pius-xii/en/encyclicals/documents/hf_p-xii_enc_12081950_humani-generis.html

[55] Ibid.

[56] Ibid.

[57] http://w2.vatican.va/content/pius-xii/en/apost_constitutions/documents/hf_p-xii_apc_19501101_munificentissimus-deus.html

[58] AD SINARUM GENTEM - Papal Encyclicals Online

[59] http://w2.vatican.va/content/pius-xii/en/encyclicals/documents/hf_p-xii_enc_29061943_mystici-corporis-christi.html

[60] Revs. Stanislaus Woywod and Callistus Smith, *A Practical Commentary on the Code of Canon Law*, Joseph F. Wagner, Inc., New York and London, 1957, Can. 953; also Can 2333

[61] http://w2.vatican.va/content/pius-xii/en/encyclicals/documents/hf_p-xii_enc_29061958_ad-apostolorum-principis.html

[62] October 20, 1958 issue of *Time* magazine, "The Succession"

[63] Douay-Rheims edition of Holy Scripture, Apoc., Ch. 10

[64] E. Sylvester Berry, *The Apocalypse of St. John*, John W. Winterich, Columbus, Ohio, 1921

PART II: THE ABOMINATION OF DESOLATION REVEALED

Chapter X — Because Then It Will Seem Clearer
The false prophet fulfills his mission

A. Fatima and the present crisis

On May 17, 1955, Cardinal Ottaviani repeatedly asked the Fatima seer Lucia dos Santos why the Third Secret committed to the children by Our Lady was not to be opened before 1960. She told him, "Because then it will seem clearer." [1] Sister Lucy expressed that it was the Blessed Virgin's wish that the Secret would be read to the world at her death, but in no event later than 1960. By then it should have been apparent to the shepherds and even the laity that the man reigning as pope planned to dismantle the Church. On January 25, 1959, John 23 announced he would call a council. It was the 21st anniversary of the sign Our Lady told Sister Lucia she would send to warn the world of the approach of the second great war. On January 28, 1959, an imprimatur was given to missalettes for the laity to follow the dialogue mass. In those missalettes, the words in the Canon of the Mass for the consecration of the wine read in English: "for all men." The terrible crisis in the Church had come about precisely as Our Lady predicted.

It is as Sister Lucy allegedly told Father Fuentes, "Father, we should not wait for a call to the world from Rome on the part of the Holy Father to do penance. Nor should we wait for a call for penance to come from the Bishops in our Dioceses, nor from our Religious Congregations. No, Our Lord has often used these means, and the world has not paid heed. So, now each one of us must begin to reform himself spiritually and each one has to save not only his own soul, but also all the souls that God has placed on his path." [2] While it is possible and even likely that the true Sister Lucy died in the late 1940s, these words still remain true and could be her own, even if

297

uttered by her imposter successor. After all, the replacement Sister Lucia had to at least sound like the genuine article, maybe even paraphrasing Lucia's own words from her writings, until the actual events transpired that forever changed the Church.

So many believing themselves members of the Church — "clergy" and "faithful" alike — desire today to be recognized as "Catholic," while holding beliefs, in public or in private, that are heretical or proximate to heresy. From other accounts of her conversation with Father Fuentes, Sister Lucy stresses that we live in the last times and Catholics are in imminent danger of losing their souls; Fatima was bound to reflect this fact. For those who wish to know, the Secret is opened here for all to see according to papal teaching, not only from an apparition many have since questioned. For those who do not wish to know, it is "shut up," just as the teachings of the seven thunders were sealed up. [3] Those seven thunders very possibly were the last seven Popes — Gregory XVI through Pius XII. The Sons of the Immaculate Heart of Mary, St. Anthony Mary Claret's sons, duly reiterated their teachings. They preached prayer and mortification to prepare the way for Fatima. The word they spread was that of the Gospel, but also that of their founder St. Anthony Claret, the Apocalyptic angel. [4] That which was "sealed up" is the very heart of the Fatima secret, for it is the final woes (WWI and WWII) and the key to the "sea and earth" beasts,[5] the coming of Antichrist. For these are the beasts of Apocalypse 13, and as Lucia dos Santos has said, the Third Secret is about the last times. Our Lady was only explaining to the simple what the popes had been saying for decades. Much of the Fatima message and its true meaning would only be understood long after the fact.

Our Lady's own words concerning Russia's errors, in the plural, indicate that the full meaning of what she said was not made known. Russia's primary error was schism, NOT Communism. Russia also was the first country to be granted permission to use a liturgy in the vernacular. Quoting from De Maistre, Tito Casini relates that Russia's gradual alienation from Rome began 200 years before her departure from the Church.

In the ninth century Pope John VIII over-indulgently allowed the Slavs their own tongue in the celebration of the liturgy. But on reading a later letter of the Pontiff's, the 95th, one hardly wonders at his admission of the many drawbacks of such a dispensation. In fact, Gregory VII revoked it, but too late — too late to save the Russians — with what ultimate results only became evident in the course of time; Russia's separation from Rome and the people falling under the sway of a succession of 'popes,' all of whom, Stalin included, succeeded in being at the same time heads of state and heads of Church, despotically ruling Godless multitudes....*Schisms and heresies have always been against Latin — always pro-vernacular, nationalistic...* [6]

Fatima facts that point to the Third Secret

The numbers and dates discernible in the Fatima apparitions and events subsequent to the apparitions can be viewed as signposts which foretell much of what has happened and is happening today.

- Some hold that Pope Pius XII did not consecrate Russia to Our Lady in the manner she desired, or as quickly as she desired. Nor did all the bishops unite with him in this consecration. As Lucia predicted, Pope Pius XII suffered the same fate then as the French King Louis XIV, who failed to heed the requests of St. Margaret Mary Alacoque regarding the Sacred Heart of Jesus: *he died surrounded by his enemies and his throne was overthrown immediately following his death*. Still, it seems, Lucia harbored the hope that Our Lady would somehow accept what Pope Pius XII did do as at least an attempt at fulfillment. Was he instructed in his 1954 vision that it was Christ's will he go down with the ship — the Barque of St. Peter — as its captain?
- The resignation of the little seers to their fate, their eagerness to offer sacrifices, their constant belief in what Our Lady revealed to them, and their devotion to the Rosary is the template for what we must imitate most faithfully today.

- The Angel's Spiritual Communication of the children is a clear indicator that this form of Communion would become common during the chastisements Our Lady predicted. This can only be a prophetic warning that the Sacrifice and most of the Sacraments would cease. Indeed, little Jacinta died without receiving the last rites.
- The future rise of Islam is predicted in Our Lady's choice of places to appear, but also her wish that these people convert. Her role in the victory at Lepanto prefigures her intercession in the situation today.
- The number 13 (the date upon which Our Lady chose to appear six times from May to October 1917, with the exception of the month of August) is undeniably linked to the founding of America. But it is especially identified with the practice of Freemasonry and predicts its temporary triumph. *Communism is one of the errors counted among the top degrees of Freemasonry: it can only be properly understood and appreciated as an actual arm of Freemasonry.* This number also symbolizes rebellion and apostasy in Holy Scripture. In addition to the number 666, it is the sign of Antichrist's arrival on earth, *since the 13th course of the pyramid, its very capstone, is Antichrist.*
- Three is a number also identified with Fatima and with Christ's Passion; it points to the Passion of His Mystical Body.
- The dates chosen by Our Lady to appear highlight special truths of faith taught by certain saints and also events that many have long forgotten.
- May 13 is the feast day of St. Robert Bellarmine, the author of the teaching, "a doubtful pope is no pope." In his *de Concilis*, he taught that in the event of a vacancy of the papal throne accompanied by an absence of the cardinals, true bishops could call an Imperfect Council to elect a pope. He also taught that:

> "Heretics, already before being excommunicated are outside the Church and deprived of all jurisdiction. For they have already been condemned by their own sentence, as the Apostle teaches (Tit. 3:10-11), that is, they have

been cut off from the body of the Church without excommunication, as St. Jerome affirms.... All the ancient Fathers...teach that manifest heretics immediately lose all jurisdiction." [7]

Also on this day the role of Our Blessed Mother as the Queen of All Saints and Martyrs was celebrated in certain locations in times past.

- June 13 is the Feast of St. Anthony of Padua, Hammer of Heretics and patron of things lost, whose miracles and intercession would be greatly needed in these times of lost faith.
- July 13 in 1865, Pope Pius IX issued a condemnation of Freemasonry, emphasizing the dangers of this accursed sect. The Vatican Council also took its first vote on the definition of infallibility on this date in 1870, a definition that would eventually provide the key to unraveling the crisis in the Church announced at Fatima. St. Anthony Mary Claret was one of the key advisors for the council, and his life and works are predicators in and of themselves of what would happen if men did not do penance and amend their lives. St. Anthony Claret was a great example of what every bishop should be and would *not* be in our times.
- August 19 (the date upon which Our Lady appeared when the August 13 apparition date was interrupted by Freemasons who seized and detained the children) is the feast of St. John Eudes, who first promoted devotion to the Sacred Hearts of Jesus and Mary. August 20 is the feast of St. Bernard, another great lover of Mary, who spent much of his life fighting the antipope Anacletus and championing the cause of the true pope, Innocent II. His life's work for this cause should have served as an example of what good clergy and religious were obliged to do when the usurpers seized the seat of St. Peter following the death of Pope Pius XII.
- September 13 is the date immediately preceding the feasts of the Exaltation of the Holy Cross and Our Lady of Sorrows. These two close dates tie the Fatima apparitions more intimately to the

Passion of the Mystical Body. It is also the date Pope Leo XIII penned *Apostolicae Curae*, [8] a constitution which set down norms for how to determine the validity of ordinations. This constitution would later become increasingly relevant in determining the validity of Traditionalists and the validity of the "new" Novus Ordo rites of the Sacraments.

- October 13 is the feast of St. Edward the Confessor. St. Edward was a model Catholic monarch and a fierce enemy of injustice. In this he imitated Christ, the Sun of Justice. He refused to levy taxes and was loyal to the papacy. He was the model for all Catholic monarchs, reminding the world that its only hope for a true peace and favor in God's eyes lies in its conversion and recognition of the Roman Pontiff as the one, true spiritual head of Christ's kingdom on earth: one flock and one only shepherd. On this date, also, King Phillip the Fair of France seized all the Templars, exciting the animosities that later fueled the establishment of Freemasonry. Many also believe that on this day Pope Leo XIII saw the vision of Satan attacking the Church that inspired the issuance of the St. Michael's Prayer after Mass and the longer version to be said by priests privately.

These highly relevant dates cannot be written off as coincidences. In selecting them, Our Lady was providing the uneducated masses of Catholics with the clues they would need in order to understand what would happen to the Church. She was pointing us in a direction if we but take the time to go there. Freemasonry, using atheistic Russian Communism as the hammer to forge a new world religion and Islam as the symbolic crescent-shaped sickle to reap the whirlwind, would seek to destroy the faith and plunge the world into the darkness of unbelief. Just as it had in Russia, it would begin with the Liturgy. The papacy could have halted its progress, but only Pius XII seems to have at least attempted to do so. Devotion to Our Lady's Immaculate Heart and to the Rosary, prayer and sacrifice, all know the recurring themes. The attempts to pervert the true meaning of the Fatima apparitions and redirect attention to the salvation of "all souls" (see below), followed in the 1990s by Russia's pretended "conversion" — not to mention the anti-Church's release of the falsified third secret — were used as a smoke screen to obscure the true mystical meaning of Our Lady's message.

Entirely missing from these misdirections, of course, was any reference to her triumph over paganism, the peril to the papacy, the approaching tidal wave of heresy, the Passion of the Mystical Body, and the overriding dangers of Freemasonry. The long St. Michael's Prayer and Pope Leo XIII's vision place all into perspective. But the Miracle of the Sun, taken at face value and never regarded as a portent of what might come, was Our Lady's most valuable warning. It lies in the future and may well be the culmination of what all the popes and Our Lady, in her many visits to earth, warned against. While many expect a physical chastisement to cleanse the earth, and one could well still arrive at the conclusion of this time period, Catholics have undergone a spiritual chastisement of unprecedented length and intensity. It began with the reign of Angelo Roncalli, false prophet, which indeed commenced just before the year 1960.

B. Roncalli's pre-election heresy

> For years the Holy Office had maintained a dossier on Roncalli which read, "suspected of Modernism." The file dated back to 1925, when Roncalli, who was known for his unorthodox teachings, was abruptly removed from his Professorship at the Lateran Seminary in mid-semester (he was accused of Modernism) and shipped off to Bulgaria. This transfer to Bulgaria began his diplomatic career. Of particular concern to Rome was Roncalli's continuing, close association with the defrocked priest, Ernesto Buonaiuti, who was excommunicated for heresy in 1926. [9]

Further evidence of Roncalli's true orientation can be found in his activities as papal nuncio to Paris. His true internal dispositions are confirmed by entries made in his private journal. All the years of Roncalli's sojourn in Istanbul, all his years as a nuncio in Paris, were years in which Montini was Vatican secretary of ecclesiastical affairs. Had Montini omitted telling details of Roncalli's behavior in his reports to Pius XII? Did he act as another Mariano Rampolla, suspected of secretly working as a change agent and perverting the clergy? Pius XII fell ill early in 1954, shortly after Roncalli's appointment as cardinal. Montini's "refusal" of the red hat of a cardinal in 1946 and again in 1953 is said to have been a polite way of expressing Pius XII's wishes that Montini not become a cardinal. Until 1953, it had been rumored that Pius XII was grooming Montini to be his successor. Yet, his decision to send Montini to Milan (a cardinalitial see) without making him a cardinal has been viewed by many as a pointed rebuke and a temporary guarantee that Montini would not become Pope, at least not as a successor of Pius XII.

As mentioned earlier, Pius XII came very near to death in December of 1954. After his recovery, he ran the Vatican literally by himself, and notably, without a secretary. He also did not appoint a cardinal *camerlengo*, who directs papal elections on the death of the pope. Montini's treason in betraying those sent secretly into Russia, resulting in the death of these bishops and clergy; his conciliatory overtures through certain channels to Soviet officials; and also his association with a Roman brothel have been cited as sufficient reasons for Pius XII's decision. All this seems ominous, indeed, in view of the fact that Montini was the first cardinal created by John 23. While it is unknown what prompted Pius XII to make Roncalli a cardinal given his prior listing as a suspected Modernist, some speculate that it could have been to keep a better eye on him. Others opine that Roncalli was reputed to have made errors not owing to maliciousness, but simplicity, and Pope Pius XII was simply not aware of his true character. It also has been suggested he wished to contain a scandal brewing in the Knights of Malta, particularly the American branch. Whatever the reason, Roncalli's true intentions would be revealed only later; his appointment as cardinal would not change his liberal outlook.

The attitudes and behavior of Nuncio Roncalli have been well expressed by his biographer:

> Roncalli's...public silence on the dangers of Communism at the time of the Cold War; his refusal to comment on the much-publicized experiment of the worker priests, or on other burning issues, is in itself evidence of an attitude different from what was expected of a representative of Pius XII....Had he not become Pope and pursued a policy of 'openings to the left,' what he said or did not say in France would by now be forgotten. [10]

But it *cannot* be forgotten, and, indeed, it was only an indication of what to expect from the Patriarch of Venice. We need only remember that one of the ways to express heresy, as defined in Canon 1325, is by *"silence,* subterfuge, or manner of acting." [11] Truth be known, Roncalli exhibited all three, as will be further demonstrated below.

As a cardinal, Roncalli outdid himself as a liberal. While outwardly he was careful to appear as a lamb, as was also Montini, author Lawrence Elliott tells us: "Both were loyally following directives of Rome. *Their separate papacies are perhaps better evidence of their true beliefs...*" [12] In other words, Elliot is implying that both men were occult heretics; and had Catholics not been so slothful, they would have realized that Roncalli's and Montini's heresies were expressly manifest long before their respective elections. Roncalli was not in the least shy about making his true beliefs known, even though these heterodox beliefs were a cause of scandal to Venetians. In August of 1956, both Montini and Roncalli termed any coalition with the Left "a very grave doctrinal error." But upon his arrival in Venice in 1953, Roncalli had addressed the Mayor and Council of Venice, many of them Socialists and Communists, and uttered these telling lines:

> I am happy to be among busy people, for only the man who works to good purpose is a true Christian [...] the only way to be a Christian is by doing good [...] there may be some here who do not call themselves Christians, but who can be acknowledged as such on account of their good deeds [...] I give my paternal blessing to all without distinction. [13]

Author Alden Hatch reports that in 1954 Roncalli shocked the faithful with his "Christian" ideas concerning unity in a series of conferences delivered on the subject. Roncalli emphasized in his speeches "that which unites rather than that which divides...The road to unity of the various Christian confessions is charity, so little observed on either side...My heart is big enough to enfold all the people of the world in my desire for unity." [14] Hatch writes: "It is said that those gathered in the great ornate hall were astonished." [15]

So also were Venetians shocked by Roncalli's welcome of the Socialists' Congress in August of 1956. "The archbishop had had posters erected all over the city welcoming these socialists, and in his personal greetings, urged them to "...improve living conditions and social well-being" [16] Roncalli told one reporter seeking an explanation for his strange behavior the following: *"Along-side purity of doctrine, there open up fields for the exercise of charity, which begins with respect and courtesy."* Elliott notes that "...the controversy in Venice was nothing compared *with the silent disapproval that surged from the Vatican."* [17] Our good Roncalli had done it again. And that was not all. "Perhaps Roncalli's greatest friend was the grand old socialist and anti-clericalist Edouard Herriot." [18]

This smacked of a similar friendship when Roncalli was accused of suspected Modernism and shipped off to Bulgaria, where he began his diplomatic career. "Of particular concern to Rome was [his] continuing, close association with the defrocked priest, Ernesto Buonaiuti, who was excommunicated for heresy in 1926." [19] And when Roncalli was the nuncio to France, he appointed yet another close friend, the thirty-third degree Freemason Baron Yves Marsaudon, as head of the French branch of the Knights of Malta, a Catholic lay order. [20] This happened in 1950. For years, Pope Pius XII had been receiving disturbing reports about the activities of the Knights of Malta as an order, particularly in America, through his housekeeper, Sister Pascalina. Following Roncalli's appointment of Marsaudon, Pius XII appears to have had no choice but to act.

A year later, in 1951, Pope Pius XII refused to appoint a new head for the Knights of Malta, suspending its operations and appointing a commission of cardinals to investigate the group.

> On November 14, 1951, Ludovico Chigi Albani della Rovere, Grand Master of the Order of Malta died in Rome. Normally, the Knights would have then convened to elect a successor; but they did not do so. They were unable to do so: Pius XII formally forbade them to do so. The Pope appointed a commission of Cardinals charged to reform (or suppress) the Order of Malta, and for the rest of the days of Papa Pacelli, the Knights would not have a Grand Master. All of that changed on June 24, 1961. On that date, the feast of Saint John the Baptist, patron of the Order (and of Masonry), John XXIII received the Knights at the Vatican, and to their great satisfaction, publicly issued the Brief by which the Commission of Cardinals instituted by Pius XII was suppressed. [21]

This online article offers additional proofs of Roncalli's "reconciliation" of the Church with Freemasonry. Roncalli had proven his muster and fulfilled his mission as False Prophet for his co-conspirator, Paul 6. For according to numerous sources, he already had been designated as the next pope.

A L'Osservatore Romano staffer's expose

Franco Bellegrandi was at one time on the staff of Rome's *L'Osservatore Romano* (The Roman Observer) newspaper, the "semi-official" publication of the Holy See. It was initially funded to print in June 1861 by Pope Pius XII's grandfather, with Pope Pius IX's permission. Bellegrandi served in his position through the reign of several popes. The following, taken from his work on Roncalli and the post-V2 church, is enough to convince even those hesitating to make a "rash" judgment that Roncalli was a Freemason:

> Of that French period is an incident, unknown to most, which raises for a moment the curtain on Roncalli's alleged membership in the Masonic sect. His most eminent

highness, prince Chigi Albani della Rovere, then Great Master of the Sovereign Military Order of Malta, had received in the Gran Magistero's Rome office a letter from cardinal Canali, heavy as a massive boulder: *Pius XII, protector of the Order, had just learned, with great pain, that the minister of the Order of Malta in Paris was a freemason.* They hastened, in the Magistral palace of the Via dei Condotti, to rummage through the file of Baron Marsaudon, recently appointed in place of Count Pierredon, whom had been retired. It was discovered, with a certain relief, that he had been made 'Grand Cross of Magistral Grace' at the suggestion of his predecessor and, above all, appointed minister on recommendation by the nuncio in Paris, Roncalli. The outcome of that first investigation was immediately reported to the Vatican, to cardinal Canali, who was heard crying: "Poor Roncalli! I'm sorry I have to embarrass him and I hope that this would not cost him the cardinal's hat!" The Vatican arranged in the strictest reserve that the Order send a trusted person to Paris at once, to carry out in depth the delicate discovery. The Great Magisterium was in an awkward situation. All three personages involved in the story had indeed to be treated with regard. The nuncio, for his precious contribution to the Order of Malta in the closing of certain business deals in Argentina; Count Pierredon for his lengthy services, first at Bucharest, and then at Paris; Baron Marsaudon himself for his meritorious commitment in order to obtain the official recognition of the Order by the French government.

Monsignor Rossi Stockalper, who was also canon[ic] of Santa Maria Maggiore and thus in [the] Vatican's hands... left for Paris at once. He had been advised to begin his discovery with father Berteloot, of the Company of Jesus, and an expert in Masonic issues. The Jesuit, consulted in the strictest discretion, confirmed to him that Baron Marsaudon not only was a Freemason, but 'thirty-third level' of Masonry and life-member of the Council of the Great Lodge of the Scottish Rite. Monsignor Rossi

Stockalper continued his tour. He learned very little from the archbishop of Paris Monsignor Feltin, who sent him instead to his general vicar, Monsignor Bohan, "who knew the baron more closely." Here, for the envoy from Rome, was another surprise: the general vicar had pulled out of a safe and scattered over the table a series of incontrovertible documents, among which was an issue of the *Journal Officiel de l'Etat francais*, published in Vichy during the (German) occupation, in which Yves Marie Marsaudon was indicated among the followers of Freemasonry; three or four copies of the Masonic magazine *Le Temple* containing a few of his articles, and an informative profile of the subject. No document existed relating to an [abjuration].

The Magistral Visitor, with his heart in pain, dragged on to 10 Avenue President Wilson, residence of the nuncio. He asked Roncalli, tactfully, for circumstantial information about the mason-baron. The sturdy priest from Sotto il Monte, between a smile and a joke, sent the chaplain of the Order of Malta back to the secretary of the nunciature, Monsignor Bruno Heim. This priest, today the apostolic legate in Great Britain, ended up startling the envoy from Rome, first with his clergyman and the smoking pipe in his teeth, then with his amazing statements on Freemasonry, defined as 'One of the last forces of social conservation in today's world, and, therefore, a force of religious conservation,' and with an enthusiastic judgment on Baron Marsaudon who had the merit of making the nunciature grasp the transcendent value of Freemasonry. Precisely for this his merit, the Nuncio of Paris, Angelo Giuseppe Roncalli, had sustained and approved his appointment to minister of the Order of Malta in Paris. Monsignor Stockalper at that turn had remained dumbfounded, and received the ultimate blow when, protesting that Canon 2335 of the Canon Law calls for the excommunication for the affiliated to Freemasonry, he was told by his interlocutor, between a puff and another at the scented smoke of his big pipe, that "the nunciature of Paris was working in great secret to reconcile the Catholic Church with Freemasonry." (!!!)

It was 1950! This episode seems to expose the connivance of Roncalli with Freemasonry. The post-conciliar Church will indeed reconcile with the secret sect. I wish to wrap up this subject, reporting a revelation made to me a while ago, by Count Paolo Sella of Monteluce. This figure, an economist, politician, writer and journalist, who was a close friend of Umberto of Savoy, and who boasts a direct descent from the founder of the Italian Historical Right, senator Quintino Sella of Biella, shared with me, in the quiet of his Roman home on the slopes of Monte Mario, the evidence in his possession, of the assault by Freemasonry on the Catholic Church. I had found in his drawing room Vaticanist Gabriella di Montemayor, who had been the go-between for our encounter. Count Sella was reorganizing some papers on the low table in front of him. The sunset burst in from Monte Mario and gilded the shelves loaded with ancient volumes with their spine of parchment, and the reddish beams of the sun, filtering through the curtains barely moved by the evening breeze, enlivened the portraits of the ancestors watching severe, from the walls that learned descendant of theirs, sitting in an armchair, before me. Then the count, raising his face and staring at me, he began to speak:

In September 1958, about seven or eight days before the Conclave, I was at the Sanctuary of Orope, attending one of the usual dinners at Attilio Bottoís, a Biellese industrialist who fancied gathering around him competent from various branches, to discuss the different issues. That day had been invited a character I knew as a high Masonic authority in contact with the Vatican. He told me, driving me home, that, 'The next Pope would not be Siri, as it was murmured in some Roman circles, because he was too authoritarian a cardinal. They would elect a Pope of conciliation. The choice has already fallen on the patriarch of Venice, Roncalli.'

"Chosen by whom?" I rejoined surprised. "By our Masonic representatives in the Conclave," responded placidly my kind escort. And then it escaped me:

"There are freemasons in the Conclave?"

"Certainly," was the reply, "the Church is in our hands." I rejoined perplexed: "Who, then, is in charge in the Church?" After a brief pause, the voice of my escort uttered precise: "No one can say where the upper echelons are. The echelons are occult."

The following day, Count Sella transcribed in an official document, now kept in the safe of a notary, the full name of that character and his stunning statement complete with the year, month, day, and hour. Which days later would turn out absolutely exact. [22]

It must be remembered that Bellegrandi's work, his memoirs as it were, came to light only much later, long after the damage had been done. How much of what he reported had been known to Pope Pius XII is a mystery.

A lay canonist speaks

The above information also was addressed by lay canonist and medical doctor Cyril Andrade writing from India in the 1970s:

A French writer, Pier Carpi, in his book Les Properties de Jean XXIII, (1976), states that Angelo Roncalli took the name John XXIII, last used (1410-1415) by anti-Pope Baldassare Cossa, probably because under the name (i.e., Baldassare Cossa) he (Roncalli) joined the Masonic Rosicrucians in Turkey (1935). Further, Charles Riandey, a Masonic Sovereign Grand Master, contributed the following preface to Ecumenism as seen by a Traditionalist Freemason (Paris, 1969) by Yves Marsaudon, State Minister of the Superior Council of France (Scottish Rite): "To the memory of Angelo Roncalli, priest, Archbishop of Messamaris, Apostolic Nuncio in Paris, Cardinal of the

Roman Church, Patriarch of Venice, Pope under the name of John XXIII, *who has deigned to give us his benediction, his understanding and his protection.* [23]

As Andrade points out, there is no doubt concerning the Church's seriousness regarding Freemasonry; over a 214-year span "nine Constitutions, six Encyclicals, two Allocutions and some 200 other documents were issued against Freemasonry by eight Popes." [24] All declared that those embracing Freemasonry were excommunicated for heresy and apostasy. Those professing, defending or propagating Communism are condemned as apostates, [25] a decision handed down by the Holy Office in 1949.

Catholic author Leon de Poncins later confirmed that Roncalli was a mole with the intent to reconcile the Faith with Freemasonry, as if such a horrid thing was possible. In his *Freemasonry and the Vatican,* De Poncins writes:

> The campaign for closer relations between Freemasonry and the Church remained quiescent while Pius XII was Pope; obviously... the Progressives, who by this time enjoyed a considerable influence in the Church realized that they had little chance of success during the Pope's lifetime. With the accession of Pope John 23 and the growth of the new conceptions of ecumenism which followed this event, something like an explosion took place. A sudden flowering of works devoted to Freemasonry blossomed forth from a variety of authors...in favor of a reconciliation between the Catholic Church and Freemasonry....

> After the manner of Communism, Freemasonry no longer sets itself up as the declared adversary of the Church. Instead of openly attacking her, *it is seeking to infiltrate and penetrate her in order to impose its own humanitarian, naturalistic and anti-traditional conceptions.* The success of the general penetration of the forces of subversion was made possible by the support, which at times attained a fanatical pitch, of progressive elements in the Church, and

the last council [referred to throughout this work as 'V2' because it was not a true council of the Church] revealed to the whole world the strength and extent of their ascendancy. We are confronted here with a new and absolutely unprecedented situation in the history of Christianity, which would now appear to be in a state of permanent civil war. Subversion has entered the very heart of the Church, and all her traditional doctrines are being questioned. This is a state of affairs the gravity of which cannot be concealed. [26]

So Roncalli's whitewash of Freemasonry alone, once he sat as usurper in the Vatican, was enough to prove his previous clandestine affiliation. Pope Clement XII had written on Freemasonry:

We command the faithful to abstain from intercourse with those societies in order to avoid excommunication...which will be the penalty imposed upon *all* those contravening this, Our order. None, except at the point of death, could be absolved of this sin except by...the then existing Roman Pontiff. [27]

Commenting on Pope Clement's statement, the Freemasonry expert Monsignor Ernest Jouin wrote: "Not only is the condemnation by Pope Clement XII extended to Masonic sects, but it applies also to all...who, although they are not members of societies called Freemasonic, favor them in any manner." [28]

It is rumored that Roncalli was a high-degree Rosicrucian himself, and this of course would automatically place him outside the Church as an apostate. It is said the Marquis de la Franquerie was well aware of Roncalli's Masonic associations. Barring that however, Roncalli's fostering of Freemasonry while "pope" and his close association with French Masons while nuncio to France is sufficient. Serious doubt is all that is needed to withdraw allegiance from one claiming to be a validly elected pope. As St. Robert Bellarmine taught: "A doubtful pope is no pope." Once any of the faithful became aware of Roncalli's Masonic affiliations, yet continued to consider him a pope without fully investigating the matter, they ceased to be Catholic per Pope Clement XII's decree.

C. Other heretical acts post-election

Roncalli initially promulgated "for all" in the Canon

In January of 1959, a new "people's mass" appeared, substituting "for all men" vs. "for many" in the English translation of the Canon. [29] These dialogue mass booklets were widely distributed and used throughout the U.S. and even abroad until the Novus Ordo was established in 1969. They came into the hands of the faithful almost immediately following Roncalli's election and shortly after the consistory met that appointed Montini cardinal. So in essence, the most devastating change made in the liturgy and the one that proves Roncalli's denial of divine law and Scripture — falsifying Our Lord's very own words and His meaning of redemption — occurred not in 1969 during the reign of Paul 6, or in 1962 with Roncalli's insertion of St. Joseph into the Canon, but in 1959. This proves that Roncalli was as much a secular humanist as his dear friend Montini. And truth be known, Montini was every bit as responsible for these missalettes as Roncalli.

Whatever the reason for the retention of "for many" in Latin in the 1962 altar Missal — and some opine that it had to be retained to avoid alerting priests to Roncalli's true orientation — his intentions here are clear. Roncalli operated on the principal that *the laity would come to believe as they prayed*, and he was correct. The most abominable violation of the Latin Tridentine Mass was the insertion of "for all men" *right into the text of Pope St. Pius V's liturgy.* Because in these mass booklets, not one iota of the Tridentine Rite is changed except the Canon. This is a far greater insult to Our Lord than even Paul 6's official promulgation of the NOM would later be. But it follows a pattern logical to Modernists: If the people have no objection to the change, it becomes a rule of faith in the minds of the new theologians. This then paved the way for the official promulgation of even bolder changes in the rites of the Sacraments *and* the liturgy. And if any objections are made, all that needs to be said is that it has been done with the knowledge and consent of the "People of God."

But in his *Mediator Dei*, issued in 1947, Pope Pius XII infallibly condemned this error well in advance of its later appearance:

> On this subject, We judge it Our duty to rectify an attitude with which you are doubtless familiar, Venerable Brethren. We refer to the error and fallacious reasoning of those who have claimed that the sacred liturgy is a kind of proving ground for the truths to be held of faith, meaning by this that the Church is obliged to declare such a doctrine sound when it is found to have produced fruits of piety and sanctity through the sacred rites of the liturgy, and to reject it otherwise. Hence the epigram, *"Lex orandi, lex credendi"* — the law for prayer is the law for faith… [But] if one desires to differentiate and describe the relationship between faith and the sacred liturgy in absolute and general terms, it is perfectly correct to say, "Lex credendi legem *statuat supplicandi" — let the rule of belief determine the rule of prayer.* [30]

The insertion of the false wording into the Canon in these missalettes is a classic example of the Communist concept of gradualism, or "boil the frog slowly." Its timing proves Roncalli's heretical intent. How many people used the booklets is not known, but no hue and cry ever went up at the time from those later proclaiming themselves "Traditionalists." Until this insertion was discovered sometime in 2008, few, if any, even knew it existed. In ten years' time (1959-1969), a sufficient number had used the books and accepted the change without ever saying a word. Regardless of any other considerations, Roncalli's tolerance of "for all men" alone must drastically alter how we view the entire makeup of the Church from that point forward. Did priests really continue to say "for many" at the altar, while the faithful silently read "for all? What does it matter? *They were reading and believing heresy — we know who was working behind the scenes and what would later become the NOM.* And as Reverend Garrigou LaGrange, O. P., states: "The one thing that suffices for formal heresy is an obstinate denial of any truth which has been infallibly proposed by the Church for belief. *It is not necessary that the individual believer realizes that the truth in jeopardy has been revealed.*" [31] For 15 centuries, the Church had proposed Her canon as inviolate, enshrining Christ's sacred words. The liturgy is sacred Tradition, and this portion of the liturgy safeguarded the inspired words of Holy Scripture. All those using these mass booklets and praying from them were, at the very least, material heretics, no matter how galling that may be to those considering themselves true Catholics today.

The Canon was *first* violated in October 1958

Was the Canon valid, if said correctly by the priest? For other reasons it was not, as one Traditionalist later would amply demonstrate. From the moment of Roncalli's election the Canon was destroyed. This fact would not be acknowledged until the 21st century, and to this very day very few Catholics indeed have assimilated its full implications.

As the Traditionalist Donald Sanborn rightly pointed out several years ago, and Reverend Saenz-Arriaga first noticed, the insertion of the name of a false pope into the Canon of the Mass — not actually the Consecration *per se*, but the sacrosanct Canon, nevertheless — is a definite indication that all are in union with whatever "papal" name is inserted. He then quotes the actual wording of this portion of the Canon, found in every 1940s-1950s Catholic missal:

> ...which in the first place we offer up to Thee for Thy Holy Catholic Church, that it may please Thee to grant her peace, to protect, unite and govern throughout the world, together with Thy servant N. our Pope, N. our Bishop, and all true believers and professors of the Catholic and Apostolic Faith." In Latin, the phrase "together with" is rendered by *una cum*.

Sanborn then quotes the following from Pope Benedict XIV (born 1675, died 1758):

But whatever can be said about this controverted point of ecclesiastical learning, it is sufficient for us to be able to affirm that the commemoration of the Roman Pontiff in the Mass as well as the prayers said for him in the Sacrifice are considered to be, and are a certain declarative sign, by which the same Pontiff is recognized as the head of the Church, the Vicar of Christ, and the Successor of Saint Peter, and becomes of profession of a mind and will firmly adhering to Catholic unity....Nor is this any less proven by the authority Ivo Flaviniacensis (in Chronicle, p. 228) where it reads: "Let him know that he separates himself from the communion of the whole world, whoever does not mention the name of the Pope in the Canon, for whatever reason of dissension; nor [by the authority of] the well-known Alcuin, who, in his book *De Divinis Officiis* (chap. 12) wrote this: 'It is certain, as Blessed Pelagius teaches, that those who, for whatever reason of dissension, do not observe the custom of mentioning the name of the Apostolic Pontiff in the sacred mysteries, are separated from the communion of the whole world.'" (Pope Benedict XIV then lists comments by several priests and theologians, among them the distinguished Reverend F. Lucius Ferraris): "First the priest offers the sacrifice for the Church, then in particular for the Pontiff, in accordance with an extremely old custom of the Churches, for the purpose of signifying the unity of the Church and the communion of the members with the head."

This quote from Pope Benedict XIV alone is enough to convince any believing Catholic that to insert the name of an actual false pope into the Canon immediately invalidates the Mass, if indeed it is not already invalidated in some other way. It also constitutes the crime of *communicatio in sacris* — communicating with non-Catholics in sacred rites — resulting in *ipso facto* excommunication for schism/heresy (Canon 2314 §3; Canon 1258).

The 1962 addition of St. Joseph to the Missal

Inserting St. Joseph's name in the Canon may appear to be a slight change or minor inroad to most. Yet it was the first *official* "change" in the Canon of the Mass for 1500 years, although a minute change was made about 1,400 years ago to a part of the Mass outside the Canon (Reverend Daniel de Rops). Roncalli was an avowed ecumenist long before his election and this was no secret. His "encyclical" on religious liberty, *Pacem in terris*, clearly states that all are free to practice the religion they see fit to practice. "Where he was absolutely adamant was in his insistence on total liberty of conscience...*Here he demolished orthodox and traditional Catholic teaching."* [32] While such liberty of conscience is allowed to all Catholics, it can never leave the confines of Catholic faith and morals. Catholics can never "choose" what to believe as Catholics: this was the contention of Murray, Morlion, and Luce. Adding St. Joseph's name to the Canon was not an expression of Roncalli's devotion to St. Joseph, or a liturgical concession. It was a clear signal to the Anglicans that Rome finally blessed their reunionist activities in cooperation with Catholics, which Pope Pius IX had condemned in 1864 when these same reunionists first proposed adding St. Joseph's name to the Canon. And Roncalli's final blessing of these activities was to grant at last their many petitions. As Roncalli's biographer Paul Johnson commented, John 23 had no qualms in overturning the decrees of his predecessors.

In fact, the acceptance of the 1962 missal, whether Lefebvrites and others realized it or not, was the first step to the full acceptance of Benedict 16 (B16) and his antichurch, which welcomed into its big tent those SSPX adherents who bought into that. B16 announced in his infamous *"motu proprio"* that the Tridentine was never abrogated, and this is true: the 1962 mass they called "Tridentine" — John 23's missal — was the one being celebrated in 1969 when the Novus Ordo Missae (NOM) was instituted. Roncalli's missal was never intended as abrogated by Paul 6; *the actual abrogation of the* immemorial *Latin (Tridentine) Mass had already taken place during Roncalli's reign when Roncalli's 1962 Missal replaced that of Pope St. Pius V.* It was *Roncalli's* missal which departed from the

Tradition of the Church in Her liturgy by adding St. Joseph to the Canon and "all men" to the mass booklets. Reverend Thomas Kinkead and all other theologians list liturgy as part of revealed Tradition.

> The Church finds the revealed truths She is bound to teach in the Holy Scripture and revealed traditions…The Church finds the revealed traditions in the decrees of its Councils; *in its books of worship*; …in the lives of its saints, the writings of the Fathers and in its own history. [33]

It must be remembered that the actual Consecration words, however, are taken from Holy Scripture itself, and all Bibles, even the oldest and newest Protestant editions among them dating back to the 1960s, report Christ's stated words as "for you and *for many*." The remainder of the canon is revealed Tradition. Revealed Traditions are faithfully preserved and handed down; they do not permit innovation. So those supporting the 1962 missal err if they believe themselves to be *Traditionalists*. And no, it does not matter that the false "pope" Benedict 16 returned the wording of the canon to "for many," for he had no papal power to either change that wording or restore it.

Author C. Leroux comments that the introduction of St. Joseph into the Canon:

> "was absolutely contrary to the meaning of the Mass, which is the Sacrifice of the New Covenant, St. Joseph having died before the public life of Jesus and before His Passion was part of the Old Testament, whatever we may wish. At the Canon of the Mass, only the names of martyrs and defenders of the Faith must appear, and those who are charged with maintaining orthodoxy… From then on, decisions ruinous to our faith continued to accumulate… [34]

The weak reflexes exhibited by Catholics in allowing this monumental change to slip by unnoticed is proof of the gradual decline of Faith over many years. As Patrick Omlor wrote:

> On December 8, 1962, through the influence of the then nascent Robber Church, the Canon of the Mass, the ancient Roman Canon, was officially destroyed. With the insertion of the name of St. Joseph into it, a change which went into effect on that day, the "Canon" of the Mass ceased to be a canon. Derived from a Greek word meaning a *rigid rod* or rule, *kanon*, it is a thing, inflexible and unchangeable. By definition, therefore, the Canon of the Mass is unchangeable. Due to the emphasis many of us have recently placed upon the decree *Quo Primum* (1570) of Pope St. Pius V, which decree forbade *in perpetuity* any additions or changes whatsoever in the Roman Missal, under the penalty of incurring 'the wrath of Almighty God, and of the Blessed Apostles Peter and Paul,' there are some who now harbor the incorrect notion that the Roman Canon dates only from the year of *Quo Primum*, 1570. In truth this Canon, which St. Pius V took the formidable measures of *Quo Primum* to protect from change, actually is substantially the same as that used by the Roman (or Western) Church *from the very beginning*; that is to say, it quite probably dates from apostolic times. It is believed that St. Gregory the Great (died A.D. 604) perhaps rearranged the order of certain prayers in the Canon; and this much is an absolute certainty: 'Since the seventh century our Canon has remained unchanged.'" (*Cath. Encyc.,* Vol. III, p. 256). In *The Question of Anglican Ordinations Discussed* (London, Burns & Oates, 1873), the esteemed author E. E. Estcourt, then the canon (pastor) of St. Chad's Cathedral, Birmingham, gives the following account:

> "What, then, is the Canon of the Mass? And what claims has it on our respect? Let us hear Sir William Palmer, as a writer whose testimony is beyond suspicion. After stating various facts and arguments on the subject, he says:

'Combining these circumstances together, there seems nothing unreasonable in thinking that the Roman liturgy, as used in the time of Gregory the Great, may have existed from a period of the most remote antiquity; and perhaps there are nearly as good reasons for referring its original composition to the Apostolic age, as there are in the case of the great Oriental liturgy.'

"The care taken to preserve the Canon in its original authentic form we learn from other writers. 'In ancient times,' says Muratori, 'although the liturgy of the Roman Mass was observed generally in the churches of Italy, France, Germany, Britain, and other countries, yet there was no small variety in their Missals; but this did not affect the substance of the mystery, or the chief and essential rites of the Mass. The difference ran in adding collects, sequences, and special feasts, which each Bishop might insert in his own missal. *But to change the sacred words of the Canon was a crime.*' By the laws of Charlemagne, it was ordered that only men of full age should be employed to transcribe it; and the Councils of York and Oxford in the twelfth century decreed that the Archdeacon should examine in every church whether there were errors or defects in the Canon, either by the faults of transcribers or the books being old. Always too the Canon was written in different and larger characters than the rest, and sometimes in gold letters throughout, as an offering of reverence." (End of the quotation from Estcourt, pp. 279-280; emphasis added.) [35]

How could Roncalli possibly escape the anathemas of the Council of Trent, which pronounce him excommunicated for saying that the Canon of the Mass contains errors and should be abrogated (missal) or that the Mass should be celebrated in the vernacular, for which all his liturgical renewal friends heartily advocated? [36]

Does this make Roncalli "the" Antichrist, and not Montini? The answer is no, for several reasons, although certainly Roncalli qualified as *an* antichrist among many others. Antichrist proper is the mirror reverse of Christ; in a perverse way he must resemble Him in all things. Just as Christ had as his precursor St. John the Baptist, who prepared the way for Him, so did Montini have a John, who also prepared the way. The reference to Antichrist having his own false prophet is found in Apocalypse. [37] Haydock's commentary treats it in the footnote for verse 11, noting the false prophet is also referred to in subsequent verses. [38] Many other Scripture commentators also mention the false prophet. Without Roncalli, Montini would not have been made a "cardinal" and could not have become "pope." Montini had to be eased into his "papal" role because he was a known liberal, and Roncalli helped pack the college of cardinals that elected him.

"Cardinal" Montini and Roncalli then worked together on everything that was done, especially those things involving the new mass and the false council. Roncalli laid all the groundwork for the changes in the Mass, defiling its canon with additions, but he did not change the consecration formula in the Roman Missal itself. Only Paul 6 actually changed that formula formally, by "papal" decree, effectively forbidding the celebration of any other Mass. It was Paul 6 who presided over the most destructive years of the council. He was the one who finally removed the St. Michael Prayers at the end of the Mass. Only Paul 6 saw the culmination of all the changes, commissioned the heretical new 1968 Sacrament formulas, rewrote the papal election constitution, and was listed as the 666th pope in the *Annuario Pontificio*. He continually used the number six for all he did. This will be thoroughly examined in the next chapter.

**Suppression of St. Michael's Prayer,
prayers for Russia's conversion**

Already on March 9, 1960, during Roncalli's reign, the Sacred Congregation of Rites had ruled that the Leonine prayers could be omitted after a *dialogue mass* said on Sundays and feast days. [39] These consisted of three Hail Mary's, the Hail Holy Queen, and the short St. Michael's Prayer. These prayers were said for different intentions over time; but following the apparition of Our Lady at Fatima and the signing of the Lateran treaty, they have been recited for the conversion of the people of Russia. Pope St. Pius X approved the addition of the ejaculation, "O Sacred Heart of Jesus." In 1964, prior to the close of the false Vatican 2 council, the Holy Office (sic) issued a liturgical instruction which read: "The Last Gospel is omitted; the Leonine Prayers are suppressed." [40] This clearly reflects both Roncalli's and Montini's openness to Communist countries and constitutes their proclamation that having seized the Holy See, there was no longer any need or desire for St. Michael's protection.

D. Why Roncalli was never pope

Ineligibility for election

There are several requirements that must be fulfilled in order for one to be elected pope. The one elected must be a baptized male Catholic, free from all suspicion of heresy, and there must be no evidence of insanity. As St. Robert Bellarmine teaches, it is not possible that one not a Catholic could rule the Church, a doubtful pope is no pope, and even the *appearance* of heresy is sufficient to presume the delict has been committed (see Chapter VII, A. 3 above). Pope Paul IV confirms this in his bull. A candidate for election to any office in the Church cannot be under any excommunication for heresy, apostasy, schism, or even lesser sins against the faith, as papal election laws state and as *Cum ex Apostolatus Officio* specifically defines. It must be remembered that it is the teachings of the popes we are to follow as the only saving guidelines in these matters, and both *Cum ex Apostolatus Officio*, which tells us that no one professing heresy pre-election can be elected, and Pope Pius XII's papal election Constitution *Vacantis Apostolicae Sedis* are infallible documents. Both likewise exclude from the conclave those *ipso facto* deposed for heresy pre-election, as did the previous election law of Pope St. Pius X.

In Roncalli's case, there was far more than just *suspicion* of heresy. According to C. Leroux, the future John 23 had plenty of time to plot his course as "pope." Quoting a French work called *Echoes of the Supernatural,* Leroux writes:

> As to the Council, I wrote to Cardinal Roncalli, (former Nuncio to Paris, to whom I was an advisor) on August 14,

1954, to announce his future election (to the papacy).... I asked for a meeting with him...to study his first work, the Council. [41]

In the work *Nikita Roncalli*, the editor of the semi-official publication of the Vatican *Osservatore Romano*, Italian author Franco Bellegrandi states:

> The election of the patriarch of Venice at the Conclave of 1958 was known in advance.... Cardinal Eugenio Tisserant [wrote] to an abbot professor of Canon Law, in which the French cardinal declares illegal the election of John XXIII, because [it was] 'wanted' and 'arranged' by forces 'extraneous' of the Holy Spirit" (Cfr. *Vita* of September 18, 1977 pg. 4 "Le profezie sui papi nell'elenco di San Malachia", by "Il Minutante"). [42]

Italian journalist Gabriella Montemayor, who was a close friend of Archbishop Arrigo Pintonello, reports the following in her unpublished work, *I'll Tell My Cat*:

1) Dr. Elizabeth Gerstner, Vatican employee and a German countess, revealed after the fact that the name of Roncalli as Pius XII's successor was on everyone's lips when she worked at the Vatican, even while Pius XII was yet alive (Chapter 1, "Rome").
2) Tadeusz Breza in his *The Walls of Jericho* reports that the election of Roncalli was carefully planned so Montini, the candidate favored by the leftwing cardinals and Italian politicians, could be appointed cardinal.

In his *Are Papal Elections Inspired by the Holy Ghost?*, Indian author and lay canonist Cyril Andrade, M.D., wrote in 1976:

> The late 'Cardinal' Heenan of England — a true-blue product of Vatican II, in his book *A Crown of Thorns* (p. 360) makes this remarkable statement: "There is no great mystery about Pope John's election. He was chosen

because he was a very old man. His chief duty would be to make Monsignor Montini of Milan a cardinal so that he could be elected Pope at the next conclave. This was the policy of the cardinals and it was carried out precisely. That will present no problems to posterity. [43]

It is impossible to escape the conclusion that having actually succeeded in attaining election (unlike Morone, the cardinal who was accused of heresy by Pope Paul IV), Roncalli, working silently throughout his pontificate with Montini, became what Paul IV identifies as *"the abomination of desolation standing in the holy place"* — a usurper gaining control of the Holy See after professing pre-election heresy and unlawfully campaigning for election.

Canon 2330 reads:

With regard to the penalties enacted against offenses which may be committed in the election of a Roman Pontiff, the only law to be considered is the Constitution of Pope Pius X…. (Commentary by Revs. Woywod-Smith: "The Constitution *Vacantis Apostolicae Sedis*, of Pope Pius XII, December 8, 1945 revised and supplanted the constitution of Pope Pius X….The name of Pope Pius XII should now be substituted in the Canon in the place of Pope Pius X….) *All of these excommunications are reserved to the Supreme Pontiff so that nobody, (not even the Major Penitentiary), can absolve them except in danger of death.* These excommunications are as follows: […] (6) The discussion of a successor to the Roman Pontiff while he is still living and without consulting him; the promise to vote for such future candidate; and all deliberations and discussion on this subject at private gatherings (V.A.S., no. 93) …" […] (8) Agreements, compacts, promises or any other obligations made or assumed by Cardinals which may restrict their freedom of voting or not voting for some one or several candidates (V.A.S., no. 95). [44]

A footnote to this canon states that the sentences are most likely *latae sententiae* and *cannot* be absolved from in urgent cases (Canon 2254) in the absence of a true pope. This is because Canon 2330 itself states that only the constitution governs the censures exclusively, not the Code, because papal election law is considered special law. When there is no Pope during an interregnum, the one in question must wait until the election is concluded for the absolution and in the meantime, could not be elected. Reverend Anscar Parsons, O.F.M, notes that men in ecclesiastical elections who are considered unfit or unworthy of election are "those who are *legally infamous* or laboring under censure [also] notorious *heretics, apostates, schismatics* ...public sinners and persons whose conduct is sinful or scandalous." [45] Roncalli qualifies as unfit on all counts. It should be noted here that Canon 2314 §3 declares those who have participated in non-Catholic services as infamous, resulting from the excommunication incurred for heresy, apostasy, or schism. Communism and Freemasonry both are considered as non-Catholic (apostate) sects and are actually two halves of a whole. At the very least Roncalli favored them and this encouraging and favoring is further condemned by Pope Paul IV:

> All and sundry Bishops, Archbishops, Patriarchs, Primates, Cardinals...who in the past have, as mentioned above, strayed or fallen into heresy or have been apprehended, have confessed or been convicted of incurring, inciting or committing schism or who, in the future, shall stray or fall into heresy or shall incur, incite or commit schism or shall be apprehended, confess or be convicted of straying or falling into heresy or of incurring, inciting or committing schism, being less excusable than others in such matters, in addition to the sentences, censures and penalties mentioned above, (all these persons) are also automatically and without any recourse to law or action, completely and entirely, forever deprived of, and furthermore disqualified from and incapacitated for their rank.... Further, whoever knowingly presumes in any way to receive anew the persons so apprehended, confessed or convicted, *or to*

favor them, believe them, or teach their doctrines shall *ipso facto* incur excommunication, and, become infamous. [46]

Moreover, Pope Paul IV's bull addresses even those who are at least *suspect* of heresy/schism at the end of section 6:

> The persons themselves so promoted and elevated shall, *ipso facto* and without need for any further declaration, be deprived of any dignity, position, honor, title, authority, office and power, [without any exception as regards those who might have been promoted or elevated before they *deviated* from the faith, became heretics, incurred schism, *or committed or encouraged any or all of these.*] [47]

Notice that "deviated from the faith" is distinguished from actual heresy or schism as a "lesser" offense, indicating that it is a separate offense suggestive of these. This would include suspicion of heresy, those things proximate to heresy, or those things "smacking" of heresy. And here also we see that this extends to those who encourage all these acts, even though they may not be guilty of such acts themselves. Because the laws on heresy are in question today, *Cum ex Apostolatus Officio* is the prevailing law and must be followed to the letter, as Canon 6 §4 prescribes.

Deposition as a disqualifier for papal election

Since Roncalli apparently participated in planning for his future election, he was never eligible for election as pope. This censure excluded him from voting in the 1958 election (see paragraphs 94, 96 and 98 in Pius XII's *Vacantis Apostolicae Sedis*), so therefore he could never have been validly elected. The language in *Vacantis Apostolicae Sedis* makes it clear that even an attempt to violate any of the precepts laid down by Pope Pius XII in his election constitution renders the act itself null and void, and here we are speaking of an infallible document. Although other censures do not apply to cardinals according to the 1917 Code and VAS itself (para. 34), *remember there is doubt concerning Roncalli's membership in the Church long before he became a cardinal, and that doubt requires the use of Canon 6§4 as the prevailing law in this case.* This Canon reads: "In case of doubt whether some provisions of the Canons differ from the old law, one must adhere to the old law." *Cum ex Apostolatus Officio* is clearly listed as the old law under several different canons on heresy in the *Fontes*, or footnotes to the canons. Cardinals are definitely mentioned as capable of incurring heresy in *Cum ex Apostolatus Officio*. And this principle is echoed in the history of ecclesiastical elections: "The election is automatically invalid, only if the lacking quality is required for the validity of the election..." [48] The quality lacking in Roncalli's case is unquestionable orthodoxy, which is certainly required for the valid election of a pope.

There are many points regarding Roncalli's eligibility for election that deserve scrutiny besides his ineligibility for being promoted as Pope Pius XII's successor during the pope's lifetime. Pius XII's constitution on papal elections states that deposed cardinals may not participate in the election; they have automatically forfeited their office as cardinal under one of the very laws footnoted by *Cum ex Apostolatus Officio* [49] And Roncalli, as even a material heretic, was deposed.

> **Canonically** deposed Cardinals, or those who have renounced the cardinalitial dignity with the Roman Pontiff's consent, have no legal right at an election. On the contrary, during the vacancy of the See, the Sacred College cannot restore or bring back to their former state Cardinals stripped of this right or deposed by the Pope. [50]

Canon 188 §4 states only that any cleric is considered *ipso facto* deposed if he has "publicly lapsed from the Catholic faith." This canon does not require that a cardinal be guilty of notorious apostasy, heresy or schism to be excluded from the conclave, for deposition requires an even lower threshold than heresy. The deposition for publicly lapsing from the faith (Canon 188 §4) refers to more than just heresy. In his papal bull *Cum ex Apostolatus Officio,* the parent law for Canon 188 § 4 found in the footnotes or *fontes* to this Canon, Pope Paul IV refers to it as "deviating from the faith," as noted in the previous section. The best way to explain this is to cite the Vatican Council:

> But since it is not sufficient to shun heretical iniquity unless these errors also are shunned which come more or less close to it, we remind all of the duty of observing also the constitutions and decrees by which base opinions…not enumerated explicitly here, have been proscribed and prohibited by this Holy See.

This warning is repeated as Canon 1324 in the Code. In other words, those who have shown a definite leaning in any direction that would suggest they are not in line with the teachings of the Roman Pontiff on any given subject (especially if this resulted in a detriment to souls) would lose their office. This is the opinion of two other modern-day commentators on Canon 188 § 4. We must remember that Roncalli was already a suspected Modernist early in his career. He also supported Communists and hobnobbed with Freemasons and other questionable characters. He also was rumored to be a Freemason. Later Roncalli promoted liturgical renewal and ecumenism, and he lost no time after his "election" in inserting "for all men" into English missalettes intended for use by the faithful in this country. This occurred only three days after the announcement that he was calling the false Vatican 2 council. Roncalli obviously had a following prior to election who favored these same ideas. While it may not have been full-blown heresy or schism to start out with, it didn't need to be. Those promoting and supporting Roncalli, also Roncalli himself, were deprived of their offices as cardinals and could not legally vote, (returning to the old law).

Those who incur the penalties of Canon 2314 §1-3 also automatically incur those of Canon 188 §4, and both canons have as their fontes *Cum ex Apostolatus Officio*. They also incur the vindicative penalty of infamy of law. This too deprives them of all dignities, benefices, and offices, as well as the right to validly posit ecclesiastical acts, (Canon 2294, Woywod-Smith). What Reverend Anscar Parsons tells us above indicates Roncalli was already classified in this category as unfit for election; and while a legitimate election devoid of any doubts concerning the faith of the candidate would nullify certain *minor* instances of unworthiness, this "benefit of the doubt" does not apply to heresy, apostasy, or sins amounting to a contempt of faith. Pope Pius XII would not have included this in addition to paragraph 36 of his constitution, lifting excommunications, suspensions, etc., unless he had a serious reason and the two were mutually exclusive.

Those so-called "Traditionalists" advancing the erroneous assertion that Roncalli was legitimately elected because such instances could be erased by the actual election and subsequent acceptance by the faithful do not consider that the majority of those voting for Roncalli, not just Montini, were *invalid electors*, for many different reasons. The actions of the cardinals for whom the paragraph on deposition was intended need only be public and discoverable. Such cardinals must be proven to be guilty of sins and activities that result in a detriment to souls or contempt of faith. Those conducting the election are guilty of not bringing these facts to light, as well as not barring from the conclave those involved in the conspiracy to elect Roncalli. This may have been more difficult to detect at the time of the conclave, but today the fruits of their deplorable works are easily known. Pope Paul IV specified no time limit for how long it might take the faithful, and even the hierarchy, to deduce that the man claiming to be pope was a fraud (*Cum ex Apostolatus Officio*, para. 7). This will be addressed below.

Were the cardinals Catholic in 1958?

It is difficult to understand how anyone might think the cardinals electing John 23 were possibly true Catholics, given the fact they elected Paul 6 and cast votes as bishops approving the schemas of Vatican 2. Many of them were the same cardinal bishops appointed by Pope Pius XII. The following illustrates how far gone the Church was already in the 1920s.

> As early as May 23, 1923, Pope Pius XI had wanted to convoke an Ecumenical Council to condemn the modern errors of Communism and Modernism. The Cardinals at

that time voiced strong opposition to the idea, stating that *so many bishops had been imbued with Modernist and liberal ideas that such a Council would do more harm to the Church than good.* Cardinal Billot said: 'The worst enemies of the Church, the Modernists...are already getting ready...to bring forth a revolution in the Church, like that of 1789 [in France].' [51]

Due to the dangers involved, Pope Pius XI gave up on the idea of an ecumenical council. He had to be content with condemning the errors of his time in his encyclicals, like *Quas Primas* (December 11, 1925) restating the rights of Christ the King, *Mortalium Animos* (January 6, 1928) condemning false ecumenism, *Casti Connubii* (December 31, 1930) condemning the errors of divorce, artificial birth control and abortion, *Mit Brennender Sorge* (March 14, 1937) condemning certain errors of Nazism, and *Divini Redemptoris* (March 19, 1937) condemning Communism.

Pope Pius XII decided to resume the project of an Ecumenical Council in 1948, (Fr. R. Dulac, p. 10) because new errors had spread in the Church. But he too had to abandon the idea because *by this time ideas of revolution and rebellion had spread to even more bishops and the apparent necessity of such a Council was outweighed by the dangers.* Pope Pius XII had to be content with condemning the errors of his time in his encyclicals, like *Humani Generis* (August 12, 1950) where he condemned several modern errors, including the evolutionary errors of Teilhard de Chardin, and *Ad Sinarem Gentem* (October 7, 1954) where he condemned certain errors of the Communists. [52]

Monsignor J.C. Fenton confirms the above in his diaries, where he writes:

Undated entry, 1960
"Our Maltese friend (who was born in Alexandria) told us that he saw Spelly [Cardinal Francis Spellman] coming out of the [1958] conclave looking white and shaken."

November 5, 1960
"To me the condition here in Rome is an evidence of the existence of the Church as a miracle of the social order. In general it is being run by men who have no concern whatsoever for the purity or the integrity of the Catholic doctrine. And yet, when the chips are down, the doctrine of Christ always comes through."

"The council will not be allowed to fail. This trip has taught me one thing: I definitely am a believer. It has also shown me that some of the leaders in the Church appear not to believe."

October 31, 1962
"The sense or feeling of this gathering seems to be entirely liberal. I am anxious to get home. I am afraid that there is nothing at all that I can do here. Being in the council is, of course, the great experience of my life. But, at the same time, it has been a frightful disappointment. I never thought that the episcopate was so liberal. This is going to mark the end of the Catholic religion as we have known it. There will be vernacular Masses, and, worse still, there will be some wretched theology in the constitutions."

November 23, 1962 (writing about the V2 council)
"If I did not believe God, I would be convinced that the Catholic Church was about to end."

September 24, 1963
"[Fr.] Ed Hanahoe gave me two books on Modernism. In one of them I found evidence that the teaching in the first chapter of the new schema on the Church [the one that became the Vatican II dogmatic constitution *Lumen gentium*] and the language are those of [the

excommunicated Modernist Fr. George] Tyrrell. May God preserve His Church from that chapter. If it passes, it will be a great evil. I must pray and act."

May 11, 1963
"Liberal Catholicism as understood by these men was and is the system of thought by which the teachings of the Catholic Church were represented as compatible with the maxim that guided the French Revolution."

March 27, 1969
Thoughts for writing: 1) The 'for all men' [as an English translation of *pro multis* in the canon of the Mass]; 2) Perjury & the Anti-Modernist Oath; 3) Only the historian can judge heresy – a statement by a pretender in the field of theology" *This was the last entry in Monsignor Fenton's diary. He died on July 7, 1969.* [53]

Monsignor Fenton was an admirer of Billot; he references him often in his works. Fenton also was a well-respected theologian, a winner of a coveted papal award from Pope Pius XII, and a papal chamberlain. These men are trusted witnesses to this in their own right. It is interesting how Fenton references the French Revolution just as Billot had done, and like him also, makes pointed reference to the liberals and Modernists. His last entry is most revealing, for he singles out as topics for refutation the falsified Canon of the Mass, those who perjured themselves after taking the Modernist oath, and the idea that heresy can only be detected from an historical distance. *By 1958, not only bishops had been infected by liberalism and Modernism, but by then these two heresies had also spread to the cardinals. After all, cardinals are only bishops themselves.*

The Oath Against Modernism is not the only oath to consider here. Cardinals created after 1945, before the conclave begins, are to read the constitution and take a special oath swearing to "scrupulously preserve" the things decreed in the election constitution. According to Canon 506 §1: "...each and every member must take an oath to vote for those only for whom he believes before God he should vote." [54] Similarly, cardinals also take an oath before depositing their ballots. This oath, contained in Pius XII's *Vacantis Apostolicae Sedis* (*VAS*), reads: "I call to witness Christ the Lord, Who will judge me, that I choose the man that, according to God, I conclude ought to be elected." And in paragraph 108, Pope Pius XII infallibly states:

> Since the entire business has been seriously considered, and moved by the examples of Our Predecessors, We therefore ordain and prescribe these things, decreeing that this present document and whatever is contained in it can by no means be challenged ...(T)hese same documents are manifestly and will be always and perpetually true, valid, and effective...(W)e command those individuals to whom it pertains and will pertain for the time being to vote, that the ordinances must be respectively and inviolably observed by them, and if anyone should happen to try otherwise relative to these things, *by whatever authority, knowingly or unknowingly,* the *attempt is null and void.* [55]

Whether these men *knew* Roncalli had been called on the carpet by Pope Pius XII or suspected he favored heresy doesn't matter; they violated their oaths and violated Pius XII's constitution by failing to uphold it. *By voting for Roncalli they favored a heretic and thus deprived themselves of office.* But most importantly the entire election, even without such deposition, was voided by Pius XII himself in the above paragraph (and also in paragraph 96) when the cardinals, influenced by those engaging in doctrinal warfare, conspired to elect Roncalli. Paragraph 96 also declares excommunicated *latae sententiae* anyone who would allow lay people to interfere with the election in any way. This could be said of nearly every American cardinal accepting the American proposition regarding religious liberty, if not all of them. According to Revs. Woywod-Smith, [56] these *latae sententiae* penalties, including those for promoting oneself as pope during the reigning pope's lifetime, can be lifted only by the Roman Pontiff, for VAS forbids anyone to usurp his jurisdiction during an interregnum. What is not understood at all here is that once Roncalli was "elected," given his heretical unworthiness, all cardinals taking that oath and voting in the election also lost their right to posit *another* election under Canon 2391§1. This Canon reads: "A college which *knowingly* elects an unworthy person is automatically deprived, for that particular election, of the right to hold a new election." [57] Reverend Anscar Parsons comments:

> In normal cases, it is presumed that the chapter made its choice with full deliberation and knowledge, *because it is their duty to investigate the qualities of the person whom they elect* [...] if the majority elect someone who is unworthy, all the voters, *even those who are innocent,* are deprived of the right to vote in this instance. [58]

Reverend Timothy Mock agrees with Parsons, writing: "...the burden of proof...will be upon the electors to show that they did not know of the defect in the candidate. The electors are presumed to know the qualifications required by law." [59]

Because Pope Pius XII states "knowingly or unknowingly" above, the electors in *a papal* election are not even able to plead ignorance; their actions are simply voided by the pope. *Roncalli was not elected*, nor could they proceed to a new election. Most of the same cardinals who elected Roncalli elected Montini (Paul 6), when by law they were barred from positing another election. Parsons comments on this canon: "Is the election of an unworthy person void from the beginning? It seems that it is, for the law says that the chapter is deprived of the right to proceed to 'a new election.' In making this disposition, the legislator seems to suppose that the original choice was null and void." And Parsons assures readers that there is no doubt that the laws governing ecclesiastical elections apply here, for he writes: *"The election of the Holy Father has been the prototype for the election of inferior prelates."* [60]

In the end Roncalli was unworthy because he was a heretic, and this we have on the authority of Pope Paul IV's infallible bull. But what results is the most important part. For both Paul IV's *Cum ex Apostolatus Officio* and Canon 2391 §1 relieve us of the responsibility of determining whether or not those elected after Pope Pius XII were possibly valid. In cases of doubt one must adhere to the old law. *Cum ex Apostolatus Officio* tells us concerning those elected or appointed by heretics who appear to possess an office:

> Every one of their statements, deeds, enactments, and administrative acts, of any kind, and any result thereof whatsoever, shall be without force and shall confer no legality or right on anyone. The persons themselves so promoted and elevated shall, *ipso facto* and without need for any further declaration, be deprived of any dignity, position, honor, title, authority, office and power, without any exception as regards those who might have been promoted or elevated before they deviated from the faith, became heretics, incurred schism, or committed or encouraged any or all of these. [61]

The prohibition in paragraph 36 of VAS regarding cardinals "canonically deposed" refers to those mentioned in Canon 188 § 4, who have publicly lapsed from the Catholic faith. Canon 192 states the loss of an office "may be incurred either *according to the law itself* or through the act of a legitimate superior." Actual deposition is a separate event, but is presumed as following the loss of office if the offender fails to repent. Canonical deposition is the loss of office declared in the law itself. Why else would the pope distinguish between the two? The question is this: Does defection from the faith exclude one from voting, and hence, from being elected? Obviously it does, since it is listed fourth among the causes of loss of office mentioned in Canon 188; and Pope Pius XII clearly states that the canons themselves effect the deposition. The official Latin declaring loss of office reads: "*A fide Catholica publice defecerit.*"

Webster's Seventh Collegiate Dictionary interprets *deficerit* as 1) a failing or deficiency; and under defection, no. 2) a conscious breach of allegiance; desertion. Cassell's Latin Dictionary agrees. Unworthiness or a "failing" is definitely indicated in this canon. The Pope would hardly make contradictory comments, one in paragraph 34 and one in 36, as some have insinuated. The lifting of excommunications by Pius XII in paragraph 34 does not apply because deposition involves loss of office only; it is not an excommunication. This privilege granted cardinals by Pope Pius XII applies only to papal elections; in ecclesiastical elections, those under censure or infamy of law inflicted by a declaratory or condemnatory sentence are banned from voting as are heretics, apostates, and schismatics. Deposition deals with unworthiness for office, not excommunication. The *office* is lost *ipso facto*; the person is not *ipso facto* excommunicated, but is able to be deposed. After listing *all* the many types of deposition, including the one in Canon 188 §4, Reverend H. A. Ayrinhac explains:

> Deposition…creates an inability for future promotion [such as elevation to the papacy]… The Church, like every complete society, must have the power to depose from office unworthy incumbents and pronounce them unfit for the same position in future. She claimed and exercised this power from the beginning. [62] If they have become formally affiliated with a non-Catholic sect or publicly adhered to it, they incur *ipso facto* the note of infamy; clerics lose all ecclesiastical offices they might hold (Canon 188 no. 4) and after a fruitless warning they *should* be deposed [re Canon 2314]. [63]

Doubts about the application must be directed to *Cum ex Apostolatus Officio* for clarification. In paragraph 6 of the bull, Pope Paul IV states there is no need for the warning to be issued in order for the deposition to automatically take place. And Canon 2391 rejects all those electing an unworthy person even should a new election be held. "A college which knowingly elects an unworthy person is automatically deprived for that particular election of the right to hold a new election." The unworthiness in this case is loss of office, and this the college cannot supply for according to VAS. Pope Pius XII holds the cardinals responsible for their actions, whether performed "knowingly or unknowingly."

While Canon 2390 specifically states that particular canon does not apply to papal election law, Canon 2391 does not contain this clause. Add to this the fact that VAS declares null and void any acts requiring papal jurisdiction performed during the interregnum, even by Cardinals, (including lifting those censures reserved to the Roman Pontiff); and the election is null and void for usurping papal jurisdiction. So the question on whether the censures for discussing the election prior to the pope's death has answered itself. But there is yet another point to be made here.

> The laws issued by Roman Pontiffs in no way can be corrected or changed by the assembly of Cardinals of the Roman Church while it is without a Pope, nor can anything be subtracted from them or added or dispensed in any way whatsoever with respect to said laws or any part of them. This prohibition is especially applicable in the case of *Pontifical Constitutions* issued to regulate the business of the election of the Roman Pontiff. [64]

The above is from paragraph 3 of Pope Pius XII's *Vacantis Apostolicae Sedis*, which does not mention the unworthy *per se* in the constitution, but only implicitly in paragraph 36 by referring to Canon 188 §4. Parsons points out that old papal election law was used to create the laws on ecclesiastical elections, so the canon laws on these elections already reflect the practice in the history of the Church concerning papal elections. If any doubts remain that the current law differs from the old law, one is to follow the old law. [65] This applies mainly to *Cum ex Apostolatus officio* regarding Canon 2314 and the treatment of heretics, apostates, and schismatics who occupy the offices of bishops, cardinals, and even the Roman Pontiff. In regard to simple doubt about the terms of ecclesiastical law, as Canon 18 states, one is to consult parallel passages of the Code, the purpose of the law and its circumstances, and the intention of the lawgiver (in this case Pius XII). This is demonstrated above concerning Pope Paul IV's intent in writing his bull. The laws on ecclesiastical elections are the only parallel passages in the Code which treat of elections at all other than the papal election law, Canon 160 and Canon 2391. *The Catholic Encyclopedia*, in the article on elections, also designated the election of an unworthy candidate as invalid. According to certain ancient canons (can. "Oportet," 3; can. "Nullus," 4, dist. 79), only cardinals should be chosen pope. However, Alexander III decreed (cap. "Licet", 6, "De elect.") that "he, without any exception, is to be acknowledged as pontiff of the Universal Church who has been elected by two-thirds of the cardinals... Of course, the election of a heretic, schismatic, or female would be null and void." [66] The one elected *must* be a Catholic, as St. Robert Bellarmine teaches, one cannot rule a society of which he is not a member.

As noted above, "For years the Holy Office had maintained a dossier on Roncalli which read, "suspected of Modernism." Roncalli proved these suspicions to be well grounded by his later actions. Not only that, he fit the bill laid out in *Cum ex Apostolatus Officio* in every way, more than qualifying as the front man for and collaborator with the abomination of desolation.

Conclusions drawn from Roncalli's ineligibility

Pope Paul IV's bull declares that anyone appearing to be pope, who teaches or even encourages something apostatic, heretical or schismatic, is *by that fact* considered to have been a secret heretic pre-election, and thus was never elected (in the case of the pope). Nowhere does Paul IV specify that this heresy must be professed '*ex cathedra,*' nor does he demand that it be "manifest" per se. He says only that it must *"become clear"* that such a person has strayed from the faith or fallen into heresy, apostasy or schism. So what would constitute the clarity to which the bull refers?

- When anyone openly fosters something such as Freemasonry, which the Catholic Church has considered a heresy for over two centuries — and this is attested to by credible witnesses (approved authors writing prior to the death of Pope Pius XII) and other proofs — then it cannot be discounted as unsubstantiated. The Church has rules regarding such proofs. She teaches that no one elected to an office, including the pope [67] is *validly* elected unless the ones electing are competent and the election is conducted in strict compliance with the canons (Canon 147; papal election law, Canon 160). According to the binding decrees found in DZ 570d, 650, 652, 674, [68] also *Cum ex*

Apostolatus Officio, it is of faith that "a pope *canonically elected*, who lived for a time after having expressed his own name, is the successor of blessed Peter, having supreme authority in the Church," (DZ 674). This is an article of faith proposed for belief to the Armenians and to Wycliffe and the Hussites. The article proposed to the Armenians asks them to hold that "*all* the Roman Pontiffs who...succeeding Blessed Peter have entered canonically and *will* enter canonically," will possess the same plenitude of jurisdiction Christ granted to St. Peter. Monsignor J. C. Fenton states that what was proposed to the Armenians is to be considered a dogma of faith. [69] In accepting this truth of faith, Catholics bind themselves to the belief that *future pontiffs can be true popes only if they are elected canonically according to the laws and teachings of the Church.*

• Reverend Adolphe Tanquerey, whose works were used as seminary texts, reminds us:

> The power [of supreme jurisdiction] over the universal Church is given immediately by God to the Roman Pontiff once he is [canonically] elected and accepts his office [Canons 109, 219]; *this power comes to an end at the time of his death* or of his resignation. [70]

So following the death of Pope Pius XII, the true power of the papacy came to an end. Please read and study Pope Pius XII's constitution *Vacantis Apostolicae Sedis* [71] that backs this up: No one may usurp papal jurisdiction during an interregnum, and this declaration is infallible.

• In this case there are doubts not only concerning the one elected but also concerning the integrity of the election itself, as well as the Catholicity of the ones electing. Pope Pius XII specifically stated in *Vacantis Apostolicae Sedis* that without a two-thirds plus one majority the election was invalid. He assumed, of course, that those voting would be Catholic, but we know from their acceptance of the Americanist heresy and acquiescence to the likes of the Knights of Malta, John Courtney Murray and Felix Morlion that this is not the case. These cardinal-bishops elected then pledged obedience to Roncalli. They later went on to vote at the false Vatican 2 council and endorse Murray's heretical teachings expressed in *Dignitatus Humanae* (On Religious Liberty). They stood by while Roncalli pandered to Freemasons, ecumenists and the Communists, tolerating heresy, and violating the Oath Against Modernism that they are required to take on becoming cardinals, as well as the cardinal's oath itself. They proved their *previous heretical disposition* by their actions. According to *Cum ex Apostolatus Officio*, this means that either *prior* to their appointment as cardinals or sometime afterward they became heretics. As such they were subject to the same penalties as Roncalli, laid down in *Cum ex Apostolatus Officio.* For that bull states that "anyone who admits or encourages" heresy, schism or apostasy *is likewise deprived of all office,* authority and power as well — this is the parent law of Canon 188 § 4. And certainly in electing Roncalli, they, at the very least, encouraged these heresies, condemned by numerous popes as shown above.

• John 23 filled the 19 vacancies for cardinals left open by Pope Pius XII and then some; Montini was his first appointment. All in all, he (invalidly) created 55 new cardinals in three years. [72] The total number of cardinals entering the conclave for Paul 6 was a record 80 cardinals, out of a total of 82. And this number was down from an original 88. For comparison, only 51 cardinals elected Roncalli (according to author Lawrence Elliot, this count was down 19 from the usual 70 cardinals, with two having died at the conclave and several others prevented from attending by Communist regimes). The number had remained set at 70 for the previous four centuries. Elliot notes: "Of the 51, only 16 had been cardinals when Pius XII was made pope in 1939; thus, only these men had ever participated in a papal election." [73] *If only 51 voted, only 16 or fewer cardinals did not vote for Roncalli (the remaining one-third minus one). Is it possible that those 16 or so cardinals, or a majority of them, were the ones appointed by Pope Pius XI? If among the remaining 35 or more electors, even a few were not Catholic, i. e., had lost their offices under Canon 188 §4 for publicly lapsing from the faith, Pope Pius XII infallibly declares the election invalid, because the two-thirds plus one needed for validity would not have been achieved.* Even in secular elections, the vote count is adjusted during the canvass to exclude disqualified electors per the prevailing laws.

Theologian and philosopher Alice von Hildebrand, wife of Professor Dietrich von Hildebrand told one magazine interviewer:

> Bella Dodd, the ex-Communist who reconverted to the Church, openly spoke of the Communist Party's deliberate infiltration of agents into the seminaries. She told my husband and me that when she was an active party member, she had dealt with no fewer than four cardinals within the Vatican 'who were working for us.' [74]

And given the positions of the cardinals as described in David Wemhoff's work on doctrinal warfare, several of them, not just one, had already endorsed Murray's heresy regarding religious liberty, which certainly was likewise endorsed by Roncalli pre-election.

- One version of what actually occurred at the conclave is offered by journalist and author Benny Lai, who was the Dean of Journalists accredited to the Holy See at the time of his death in 2013. Lai had been accredited by the Holy See since 1952. He wrote a work entitled *The Pope Who Was Not Elected*, and a translation of Chapter 8 of this work was sent to this author by Nellie Villegas, a teacher living in Canada, prior to her death. Lai speculated that Giuseppe Cardinal Siri was the intended candidate, but states in Chapter 8: "After the death of Pius XII Cardinal [Gaetano] Cicognani, who was secretary, sent me to Siri to offer him the candidacy. Cicognani thought that Siri was the only one who was able to continue Pacelli's magisterium...Siri refused saying that he was not in good health. (Interview from the archbishop José Sebastian Laboa with the author (10/10/1989)." Lai also adds:

> Siri rejected the multiple invitations to accept the candidacy... Many candidates were spoken of, but in reality only two cardinals enjoyed a discreet number of preventative consensus: the seventy-seven-year-old Angelo Giuseppe Roncalli, Patriarch of Venice [11]; and Gregorio Pietro XV Agagianian, a sixty-three year old born in the Soviet Caucasus [Mountains], Patriarch of the Armenians....

Wikipedia styles Agagianian as a theological liberal and reports at least one journalist suggested Agagianian was elected, but did not accept the papal office. [75] According to Lai, only one-third of the cardinals attending the conclave were Italian. Three of the cardinals, Lai relates, none of them Italians, needed assistance at the conclave. He insinuates that even Siri voted for Roncalli.

• A doubt concerning the *fact* of a pope's actual election is sufficient to call it into question, especially when that doubt involves the Catholicity of the one elected, as shown above. The election of a true pope is a dogmatic fact, and one cannot believe something to be dogmatic that is in fact not true. The canonist Reverend Francis Miaskiewicz says a doubt of fact arises when one is not certain that the fulfillment of a law has been satisfied in some affair (laws governing papal election) or that someone is actually competent to perform certain acts. [76] He goes on to explain on this same page that there must be some good objective reason and real basis for this belief, some serious objections as foundation for such a doubt. Miaskiewicz notes that according to moralists, positive doubt is equivalent to a probable opinion. Under the laws of Catholic morals, there isn't even an obligation to search out whether the contradictory opinion is "more, or less, or equally probable." [77] Such are the laws of the Catholic Church.

- Nor is there any need to fear one would be in schism for refusing "obedience" to Roncalli or any of his "successors" (which *Cum ex Apostolatus Officio* says, is not rightfully owed anyway). As stated above, seven notable theologians, sufficient to establish the very probability Miaskiewicz mentions (Vermeersch-Creusen, Reiffenstuel, Schmalzgrueber, Ferraris, Vechiotti and Szal) all agree that: *"There is no schism involved...*if one refuses obedience [to a pope] *inasmuch as one* suspects *the person of the Pope or the validity of his election.* [78] Here we see the principal of doubt concerning a matter necessary to salvation put into practice. If there is even well-founded doubt, one need not be *certain* that such a man was not pope, because the principle of probability cannot be applied to the Sacraments *or to those things necessary to salvation* (see sources below).

We know from the decree of Pope Boniface VIII that in order to be saved, all must be subject to the pope. Some have said the faithful in Roncalli's day would need to have objected to his election *at that time*, and since they did not, then it was valid — but this is not true. Pope Paul IV teaches in paragraph 7 of his bull that despite the amount of time that has passed, anyone may withdraw obedience from such a person. And he also teaches such a man never validly elected cannot be considered quasi-legitimate. Papal decrees issued either from the ordinary or extraordinary magisterium and the teachings of ecumenical councils are what bind Catholics, not the teachings of laymen or even theologians.

Modern day histories and encyclopedias, in print and online, tell their readers there is no basis for questioning Roncalli's election; various religious forums debate the topic. A 700-page book now denies any valid objection can exist. Some even maintain that in order for Paul 6 to be considered as Antichrist, Roncalli would need to have been validly elected. This, however, does not fit the *Catholic Encyclopedia* definition of Antichrist or Pope Paul IV's warnings regarding the identity of the Abomination of Desolation. Let them prove scholastically, beyond a reasonable doubt, the actual validity of Roncalli's election — not just the phenomenalistic *appearance* of its validity — and then perhaps they might be able to present a believable argument. Catholics serious about their faith cannot and do not proceed from secular standards or resort to dialogue of the questionable ecumenical kind to resolve these matters. They are bound to obey the Roman Pontiffs in order to be saved and salvation is everything to them. When in doubt concerning a matter that affects this salvation, they must take the safer course, which means they cannot risk obeying a man that would endanger that salvation, even if they cannot gain formal certitude regarding his heresy (Bd. Pope Innocent XI, DZ 1151, [79] Reverend Dominic Prummer, [80] and Canon 15, 1917 Code. [81]). As a consequence, they have every right to know and to question the election of such a person whenever credible evidence is provided — from both a testimonial and a canonical/faith-based standpoint — indicating there is reason to doubt such validity. True Catholics belong to a Divine society founded by Jesus Christ; *no one* has the right to dictate to them what they must do or believe concerning the practice of their faith when the infallible heads of that ancient society decree otherwise.

Conclusion

No rational human being would deny that there is more than enough here to constitute doubt; in fact, what is provided here should result in formal certitude. But then many of those presenting as Catholics seem unaware they even need to obtain certitude; in fact few indeed appear to be rational today. Well-founded positive doubt, however, is all that is needed to disenfranchise Roncalli and his "successors," although the dismantling of the Church following the false Vatican 2 council should have been all that anyone needed in way of proof. And the time has long since passed when one could hope for the election of a true pope; that must be a miracle God will need to work, if He sees fit, to restore His Church. If not, then the world can expect the final conflagration and ensuing General Judgment. In the meantime, those who wish to be worthy of the name Catholic, if they are to save their souls, must divest themselves of any commitment to the teachings of men (or women) that is not in strict accord with the laws and teachings of the Catholic Church. For as Pope St. Pius X taught in his condemnation of the Sillon, it was the stated aim of those working to establish the Novus Ordo that they would *"not work for the Church, [but] for mankind."* We, then, are tasked with obeying God, not man, and working for what remains of Christ's Church on earth until He restores the Church miraculously, or comes for the Final Judgment. For Antichrist, the Abomination of Desolation, has already made his appearance on the world stage; we are merely waiting for our Lord to reign as King. The next chapter will explain how Antichrist's reign over the Church and the world has already come and gone.

Chapter X Endnotes

[1] Frere Michel de la Sainte Trinite of the Little Brothers of the Sacred Heart, *The Whole Truth About Fatima, Vol. 3, The Third Secret,* Immaculate Heart Publications, Buffalo, New York, N.Y., 1986, 725

[2] Ibid., 747-48

[3] Douay-Rheims edition of Holy Scripture, Apoc. 10:6

[4] Ibid., Apoc. 11:2

[5] Ibid., Apoc. 10:8-9

[6] Tito Casini, *The Torn Tunic*, Christian Book Club of America, Hawthorne, Calif., 1967, 15

[7] *De Romano Pontifice,* lib. II, cap. 30, http://www.cmri.org/02-bellarmine-roman-pontiff.html

[8] http://www.papalencyclicals.net/Leo13/l13curae.htm

[9] Lawrence Elliot, *I Will be Called John,* Readers Digest Press, E. P. Dutton and Co., N.Y, 1973, 90-92

[10] Meriol Trevor, *Pope John*, Doubleday and Co., Inc., New York, N.Y., 1967, 207

[11] Revs. Stanislaus Woywod and Callistus Smith, *A Practical Commentary on the Code of Canon Law*, Joseph F. Wagner, Inc., New York and London, 1957

[12] Lawrence Elliot, *I Will be Called John,* Readers Digest Press, E. P. Dutton and Co., New York, N.Y, 1973, 228

[13] Ibid., 209

[14] Alden Hatch, *A Man Named John: The Life of Pope John XXIII,* Hawthorne Books, New York, N.Y. 1963, 114

[15] Ibid., 114.

[16] Lawrence Elliot, *I Will be Called John,* Readers Digest Press, E. P. Dutton and Co., New York, N.Y, 1973, 228

[17] Ibid., 229

[18] Alden Hatch, *A Man Named John: The Life of Pope John XXIII,* Hawthorne Books, New York, N.Y. 1963, 114

[19] Lawrence Elliot, *I Will be Called John*, Readers Digest Press, E. P. Dutton and Co., New York, N.Y, 1973, 90-92

[20] Paul I. Murphy and R. Rene Arlington, *La Popessa,* Warner Books, New York, N.Y., 1983, 332-33

[21] "The Pope of the Council," Part 19, *Sodalitum,* October-November 1996 http://www.angelfire.com/journal2/post/pope_mason.html

[22] Franco Bellegrandi, *Nikita Roncalli,* 1995, (translated and made available in PDF format by Australian Traditionalist Hutton Gibson)

[23] Dr. Cyril Andrade, *Was Pope John XXIII Really a Pope?* 1976, http://www.betrayedcatholics.com/free-content/reference-links/5-antipopes/was-pope-john-xxiii-really-a-pope/

[24] Ibid.

[25] Revs. Stanislaus Woywod and Callistus Smith, *A Practical Commentary on the Code of Canon Law*, Joseph F. Wagner, Inc., New York, N.Y. and London, 1957, Can. 2314 §2

[26] Vicomte Leon de Poncins, *Freemasonry and the Vatican*, Omni Publications, Palmdale, Calif., 1968, 13

[27] *In Eminenti*, 1738; renewed by Pope Leo XIII in *Humanum Genus*, 1884

[28] Msgr. Ernest Jouin speech given Dec. 8, 1930; reprinted in booklet form as *Papacy and Freemasonry*, various publishers

[29] *Our Parish Prays and Sings,* Order of St. Benedict, Collegeville, Minn., first edition printed in January 1959; *The People's Mass*, Paulist Press

[30] Mediator Dei (November 20, 1947) | PIUS XII - Vatican.va

[31] *The Theological Virtues*, Vol. I, *On Faith,* B. Herder Book Co., 1965, (written during the reign of Pope Pius XII but translated afterwards), 432

[32] Paul Johnson, *Pope John XXIII*, Little, Brown and Co., New York, N.Y., 1974, 153

[33] Rev. Thomas Kinkead, *Kinkead's Baltimore Catechism #3*, reprinted by TAN Books, Rockford, Ill., 1974 from the 1885 original, Q. 557 and 560

[34] C. Leroux, *The Son of Perdition*, Calais, France, 1982, translated by Dolores Rose Morris, 20

[35] Patrick Henry Omlor, *The Robber Church*, The Collected Writings, 1968-1997 (PDF), 180-81

[36] Henry Denzinger, *The Sources of Catholic Dogma*, 30th Edition, Marian House, Powers Lake, N.D., 1957, DZ 953 and 956

[37] Douay-Rheims edition of Holy Scripture, Apoc., 13:11.

[38] Ibid., Apoc. 16:13, 19:20 and 20:10

[39] *Canon Law Digest*, Vol. V, T. Lincoln Bouscaren, S. J., LL.B., S.T.D., and James I. O'Connor, S.J., A.M., S.T.L., J.C.D., Bruce Publishing Co., Milwaukee, Wis., 1963, 136

[40] Rubrics, *Inter oecumenici* 1964, Chapter II, Mystery of the Eucharist, *I. ORDO MISSAE* (SC art. 50); (j)

[41] C. Leroux, *The Son of Perdition*, Calais, France, 1982, translated by Dolores Rose Morris

[42] Franco Bellegrandi, *Nikita Roncalli*, 1995, (translated and made available in PDF format by Australian Traditionalist Hutton Gibson)

[43] Dr. Cyril Andrade, *Was Pope John XXIII Really a Pope?* 1976 (see 22 above for link)

[44] Revs. Stanislaus Woywod and Callistus Smith, *A Practical Commentary on the Code of Canon Law*, Joseph F. Wagner, Inc., New York and London, 1957

[45] *Canonical Elections*, Catholic University of America Press, Washington, D.C., 1939

[46] *Cum ex Apostolatus Officio,* para. 5, http://www.betrayedcatholics.com/free-content/reference-links/4-heresy/annotated-guide-to-cum-ex/

[47] Ibid., para. 6

[48] Rev. Timothy Mock, *Disqualification of Electors in Ecclesiastical Elections*, (Canon Law dissertation) Catholic University of America Press, Washington D.C., 1958, 135

[49] Can. 188 no. 4

[50] *Vacantis Apostolicae Sedis*, para. 36, http://www.betrayedcatholics.com/free-content/reference-links/1-what-constitutes-the-papacy/apostolic-constitution-vacantis-apostolicae-sedis/

[51] Fr. R. Dulac, *Episcopal Collegiality of The Second Vatican Council*, (French publ.), pp. 9-10

52

http://www.catholicapologetics.info/modernproblems/vatican2/renew2.html

⁵⁴ Revs. Stanislaus Woywod and Callistus Smith, *A Practical Commentary on the Code of Canon Law*, Joseph F. Wagner, Inc., New York, N.Y. and London, 1957

⁵⁵ http://www.betrayedcatholics.com/free-content/reference-links/1-what-constitutes-the-papacy/apostolic-constitution-vacantis-apostolicae-sedis/

⁵⁶ Revs. Stanislaus Woywod and Callistus Smith, *A Practical Commentary on the Code of Canon Law*, Joseph F. Wagner, Inc., New York, N.Y. and London, 1957, (footnote to Can. 2330)

⁵⁷ Ibid., Can. 2391 §1

⁵⁸ Rev. Anscar Parsons, O.F.M., Cap., J.C.L., *Canonical Elections: An Historic Synopsis and Commentary*, Catholic University of America Press, Washington D.C., 1939, 197

⁵⁹ Rev. Timothy Mock, *Disqualification of Electors in Ecclesiastical Elections*, (Canon Law dissertation) Catholic University of America Press, Washington D.C., 1958, 135, 137

⁶⁰ Rev. Anscar Parsons, O.F.M., Cap., J.C.L., *Canonical Elections: An Historic Synopsis and Commentary,* Catholic University of America Press, Washington D.C., 1939, 197

⁶¹ http://www.betrayedcatholics.com/free-content/reference-links/4-heresy/annotated-guide-to-cum-ex/

⁶² Rev. H. A. Ayrinhac, *Penal Legislation in the New Code of Canon Law*, Benziger Bros., New York, N.Y., 1920, nos. 168-169, 170

⁶³ Ibid., no. 201c

⁶⁴ http://www.betrayedcatholics.com/free-content/reference-links/1-what-constitutes-the-papacy/apostolic-constitution-vacantis-apostolicae-sedis/

⁶⁵ Can. 6 §4

⁶⁶ http://www.newadvent.org/cathen/11456a.htm

⁶⁷ T. Lincoln Bouscaren S.J. and Adam Ellis, S.J., *Canon Law, A Text and Commentary*, The Bruce Publishing Co., Milwaukee, Wis., 1946, Can 145 §1, no. 2 and Can. 147 §1 and §2

⁶⁸ Henry Denzinger, *The Sources of Catholic Dogma*, 30ᵗʰ Edition, Marian House, Powers Lake, N.D., 1957

⁶⁹ Msgr. Joseph C. Fenton, *The Concept of Sacred Theology,* The Bruce Publishing Co., Milwaukee, Wis., 1941,132-33

[70] Rev. Adolphe Tanquerey, *Manual of Dogmatic Theology*, Vol. I, Desclee Co., New York, N.Y., Tournai, Paris, Rome, 1959, 152

[71] http://www.betrayedcatholics.com/free-content/reference-links/1-what-constitutes-the-papacy/apostolic-constitution-vacantis-apostolicae-sedis/

[72] Lawrence Elliot, *I Will Be Called John*, E. P. Dutton and Co., New York, N.Y., 1973, 283

[73] Ibid., 5

[74] *The Latin Mass Magazine*, "Pope Paul VI and the Slippery Slope," Ramsey, N.J., Thursday, July 12, 2011

[75] https://en.wikipedia.org/wiki/Gregorio_Pietro_Agagianian

[76] Rev. Francis Miaskiewicz, *Supplied Jurisdiction According to Canon 209*, (Canon Law dissertation), Catholic University of America Press, Washington D.C., 1940, 210

[77] Ibid., 181

[78] Rev. Ignatius Szal, A.B., J.C.L., *The Communication of Catholics with Schismatics,* (Canon Law dissertation) Catholic University of America Press, Washington D.C, 1948, 2

[79] Henry Denzinger, *The Sources of Catholic Dogma*, 30th Edition, Marian House, Powers Lake, N.D., 1957

[80] Rev. Dominic Prummer, *Handbook of Moral Theology,* P.J. Kenedy and Sons, New York, N.Y., 1957, no. 149, 64

[81] Revs. Stanislaus Woywod and Callistus Smith, *A Practical Commentary on the Code of Canon Law*, Joseph F. Wagner, Inc., New York, N.Y. and London, 1957

Chapter XI — Paul 6, Man of Sin
Son of Perdition, Lawless One

A. Defining Antichrist

In *The Church*, a collection of addresses compiled in 1963 by (Cardinal) Giovanni Battista Montini, later elected "pope" as Paul 6, the point was driven home that those who brought about the changes enacted by the (false) Vatican 2 council, which first convened in 1962 under John 23, were fully aware of what they were doing and exactly how the faithful would react. In this work Montini predicts: "We may anticipate that a great many of these reforms will hardly be noticed by the majority of the faithful.... [But] more than a few *innovations* will be introduced by the council and noticed favorably by the faithful, too." [1] So they had prepared for those who would stay in the Vatican 2 church as well as those who would protest the changes and depart from it. They had plans for handling both. They knew the value of gradualism and just how far to go with their selected audience without appearing to go too far.

And those perceived as the faithful, most of whom had fallen victim to secularism and modernism long before Vatican 2, were not praying and watching as cautioned by Our Lord. They were reveling in the many concessions made to the laity and their newfound importance in their church, making them equal with their Protestant contemporaries. And like their Protestant friends, they had a total misconception of Antichrist and what would mark his coming; or they believed it to be too far in the distant future to be worthy of their attention. If they thought about it at all they accredited it to some yet-to-appear political figure along the lines of a Stalin or a Hitler who would persecute the free world. It never occurred to them that such an important figure in Holy Scripture, destined to seduce and cruelly crush the entire Church, must above all be a spiritual leader who would persecute and seduce primarily in a spiritual manner, not just physically. They envisioned Antichrist's false miracles as some sort of particularly clever magic tricks, and his mark as a physical brand of sorts along the lines of concentration camp ID tattoos. Or they agreed with other non-Catholics that it could well be a microchip implanted to monitor their every move.

John Henry Cardinal Newman and St. Hilary had different ideas. Newman describes Antichrist in the following terms:

> That Antichrist is one individual man, not a power — not a mere ethical spirit, or a political system, not a dynasty, or succession of rulers — was the universal tradition of the early Church....Far be it from any of us to be of those simple ones who are taken in that snare which is circling around us! Far be it from us to be seduced with the fair promises in which Satan is sure to hide his poison! *Do you think he is so unskillful in his craft, as to ask you openly and plainly to join him in his warfare against the Truth?* No; he offers you baits to tempt you. He promises you *civil liberty*; he promises you *equality*; he promises you trade and wealth; he promises you a remission of taxes; he promises you *reform*. This is the way in which he conceals from you the kind of work to which he is putting you; he tempts you to rail against your rulers and superiors; he does so himself, and induces you to imitate him; or he promises you illumination — *he offers you knowledge, science, philosophy, enlargement of mind. He scoffs at times gone by*; he scoffs at every institution which reveres them. He prompts you what to say, and then listens to you, and *praises you, and encourages you.* He bids you mount aloft. *He shows you how to become as gods.* Then *he laughs and jokes with you,* and gets intimate with you; he takes your hand, and gets his fingers between yours, and grasps them, and then you are his. [2]

St. Hilary says much the same:

> But nowadays, we have to do with a disguised persecutor, a smooth-tongued enemy, a Constantius who has put on Antichrist; who scourges us, not with lashes, but with caresses; who instead of robbing us, which would give us spiritual life, bribes us with riches, that he may lead us to eternal death; *who thrusts us not into the liberty of a*

prison, but into the honours of his palace, that he may enslave us: who tears not our flesh, but our hearts; who beheads not with a sword, but kills the soul with his gold; who sentences not by a herald that we are to be burnt, but covertly enkindles the fire of hell against us. He does not dispute with us, that he may conquer; but he flatters us, that so he may lord it over our souls. *He confesses Christ, the better to deny him; he tries to procure a unity which shall destroy peace; he puts down some few heretics, so that he may also crush the Christians; he honours Bishops, that they may cease to be Bishops;* he builds up Churches, that he may pull down the Faith.... I say to thee, Constantius, what I would have said to Nero, or Decius, or Maximian: You are fighting against God, you are raging against the Church, you are persecuting the saints, you are hating the preachers of Christ, you are destroying religion, you are a tyrant, not in human things, but in things that appertain to God. Yes, this is what I should say to thee as well as to them; but listen, now, to what can only be said to thyself: Thou falsely callest thyself a Christian, for thou art a new enemy of Christ; thou art a precursor of Antichrist, and a doer of his mystery of iniquity; thou, that art a rebel to the faith, art making formulas of faith; thou art intruding thine own creatures into the sees of the Bishops; thou art putting out the good and putting in the bad.... By a strange ingenious plan, which no one had ever yet discovered, thou hast found a way to persecute, without making Martyrs. [3]

Newman captures the totality of the seduction process: its reliance on bribes and flattery; its appeals to greater liberty (for the laity and in deciding doctrinal matters) and equality (for women and for the lay people in general as regards the liturgy); its call for reform, that catchword use by Protestants to destroy the Church in the 1500s. He details the saccharine-sweet chumminess exhibited by Francis, John Paul 2, and to some extent even John 23 — the "new charity" extended to the "people of God" to better assure them of equal status with their superiors, giving them little reason to revere and obey them. St. Hilary notes this same false charity, so important for deception to succeed. He especially notes the false unity these usurpers try to engender among those fooled by this pretense of charity, also the resultant destruction of true members of the clergy, in order to intrude false bishops. He refers to false formulas of the faith and the ability of Antichrist to do all these things without physically making martyrs. In short, he describes what has occurred for the past six decades. This extension of false charity to the faithful by the usurpers is what convinced them these men bore them no ill will and because they refrained from outright cruelty, could not be considered evil men. This is why so few believed that Paul 6 could possibly have been the Antichrist.

The Catholic writer William Strojie, who believes Montini was the Abomination, explains this phenomenon as follows:

> That the Antichrist might have come and gone with no recognition of his person seems impossible to most people, such has been the influence of Protestant apocalyptic fantasy writers. It is, on the contrary, in accordance to God's acknowledged way of working with men by types and analogy, that the Antichrist would pass by almost entirely unrecognized, as with Christ Himself. This is also the opinion of St. Paul who predicted the "operation of error" and a spiritual blindness that would cause the Antichrist to be received by the majority of Christians as their very own. This also follows from St. Paul's prediction of a Great Apostasy to accompany the Antichrist, of which he will be partly the cause and partly an effect. How else could this most evil of men all but destroy the Catholic Church and loose upon the whole world the growing disorder we see in our time? How else but by deceit from the highest place. The Antichrist must appear to be that which he is not, otherwise the necessary deceit is not possible. And he must usurp the highest spiritual office. The "perfection in evil" (St. Thomas Aquinas, St. John's 666, symbolic of "perfect imperfection") of this man must be that spiritual perfection in evil of Lucifer, of pride and envy behind the mask of goodness and of concern for all humanity. [4]

The very meaning of Antichrist in the *Catholic Encyclopedia is* "A king who reigns during an interregnum," a man reigning as a pagan Pontifex Maximus of old rather than a true Catholic Pontiff. [5] Reverend H. B. Kramer, commenting on Apoc. 13: 11-18, writes:

> This false prophet, possibly at the behest of Antichrist, usurps the papal supremacy.... His assumed spiritual authority and supremacy over the Church would make him resemble the Bishop of Rome.... He would be Pontifex Maximus, a title of pagan emperors, having spiritual and temporal authority. Assuming authority without having it makes him the False Prophet.... Though he poses as a lamb, his doctrines betray him. [6]

Although Kramer's designation of a usurper as the false prophet is correct as far as Roncelli goes, it also is correct in the case of Paul 6, who succeeded him. Not all biblical commentators always see the entire picture. Reverend Carl Vogl, in his *Begone Satan,* tells his readers that Reverend Theophilus Reisinger, who successfully drove out the demon in the Earling possession case, predicted that Judas soon would appear as the Antichrist and would be accompanied by the False Prophet, as already explained. The prophet Daniel and St. Hippolytus also style Antichrist as a king. But the Church Father, St. Irenaeus says it all:

> And not only by the particulars already mentioned, but also by means of the events which shall occur in the time of Antichrist is it shown that he, being an apostate and a robber, is anxious to be adored as God; and that, although a mere slave, *he wishes himself to be proclaimed as a king. For he (Antichrist) being endued with all the power of the devil, shall come, not as a righteous king, nor as a legitimate king, [i.e., one] in subjection to God*, but an impious, unjust, and lawless one; as an apostate, iniquitous and murderous; as a robber, concentrating in himself [all] satanic apostasy, *and setting aside idols to persuade [men] that he himself is God, raising up himself as the only idol, having in himself the multifarious errors of the other idols.* [7]

"Count the number of the beast, for it is the number of a man... 666."[8] As Francis Panakal wisely observes in his booklet, "the number of a man implies very definitely *that he is really one among several men*, each of whom will have a number, the beast in the prophecy being the one with the number 666."[9] Here, Panakal refers to the fact that in the *Annuario Pontificio*, published since 1954, the names of all the popes are listed (after the first 22) according to the date of election, coronation as pope, and the date on which his pontificate ended. Panakal notes that a few numbers on this list occur more than once, but Montini's number appears only once; and that in the 1974 edition, his number reads 666 - VI for Paulus VI; VI for the month of June (his election); VI for the month of his coronation (June). On the back cover of his work, Panakal provides a copy of the page from the 1974 edition of the *Annuario Pontificio* listing Montini as proof, noting: "From 1964 to 1978, 15 editions of the *Annuario Pontificio* corresponding to the entire 15-year course of Paul VI's pontificate indicated his number as 666. However, in the 1979 edition as well as in subsequent editions, his number is 668."

Although these Roman numeral VI's are the only ones St. John could have identified in his vision, since he could not read Arabic numbers, the sixes do not stop there. Further instances of the use of '666' can be seen reflected in Montini's papal coat of arms. *The World Book Encyclopedia*, under the heading heraldry, [10] lists the fleur-de-lis as a symbol of the "sixth son" in a family. Montini's coat of arms displays three fleurs-de-lis; hence, 6-6-6. Montini's papal coat of arms also shows six mountains resembling pillars, (the name Montini means mountain). Panakal lists several other instances of six: six names (Enrico Antonio Maria Giovanni Battista Montini); Montini's number in the conclave was six; he was 66 at the time of his election; the 264th pope; elected at the sixth conclave held in this century, in the sixth month of the year at 6 p.m. in the evening. Panakal points to Pope St. Pius X's first encyclical, *E Supremi Apostolatus* [11] where Pius X wrote: "So extreme is the general perversion that there is room to fear...that the Son of Perdition, of whom the Apostle speaks, has already arrived upon earth." In 1903, Montini was six years old. Moreover, Paul 6 signed his name in such an unusual way that when the signature is turned upside down, it reads "666." [12] All this, given what has already been written about Montini's betrayal of the faith in the chapter above, would be enough. Yet there is more to be found in the pages of Holy Scripture.

The Book of Daniel

- "He shall think himself able to change times and laws." [13] This Montini did, destroying the liturgical calendars and displacing many saints; rendering canon law of little effect and planning its revision; doing away with many of the time-honored rituals, the sacraments, the Mass, the tiara — the list is endless.
- "He shall...obtain the kingdom *by fraud*...and craft shall be successful in his hand." [14] Done. Everyone thinks Montini was a legitimate pope and John Paul 2, Benedict 16, and Francis are his legitimate successors. The world yet believes that the Catholic Church in Rome is the same Church as that of St. Peter to Pope Pius XII; that it can accommodate itself to the age. A greater fraud is unimaginable.
- "[H]e shall destroy...the people of the saints...and shall crush [overcome] the saints of the Most High." [15] Done, as all who care to see are well aware. And what do those who insist we shall forever have Mass and Sacraments think this verse means? Surely they cannot believe the Scriptures could be in error. But then those who do not accept that they live in the end times and have seen the abomination of desolation are laboring under the operation of error, and many will not be able to escape it.

St. Paul

- "Let no man deceive you... For unless there come a revolt first, so that the Man of Sin be revealed, the Son of Perdition..." [16]
- Antichrist "opposeth, and is lifted up above all that is called God, or that is worshipped, so that he sitteth in the temple of God, showing himself as if he were God..." [17] Paul 6 opposed many tenets of the true faith, particularly those that had anything to do

with the Church as the sole channel of salvation. His followers placed all he said and did above all that had been the constant teaching of the Church.

- The designation of this Temple, described by the commentators as either the Jewish Temple or the Church itself, has not been clear until the actual fulfillment of the prophecy. According to the Catholic writer William Strojie, both St. Jerome and St. John Chrysostom teach "'He will enthrone himself in the temple of the Church.'" Some Catholics and many Protestants believe this temple is the Jewish temple, but the early Fathers teach, "under Christ and in Christ, the Church is her own temple and altar." [18] In this is included the Continual Sacrifice, and Christ as the altar upon which that Sacrifice was offered. This passage from St. Paul thus refers to three things at once: a) the violation of the Holy Place, the Christian Temple, by one who had no right to stand there in Christ's place as His Vicar; b) the desecration of the altar by removing the tabernacle to a table facing the people; and c) elevating man above God by falsifying the Consecration of the wine in the true Sacrifice of the Mass.

- The *Catholic Encyclopedia* article "Antichrist" summarizes what St. Paul says in 2 Thess. 2: 3-10, as follows:

> Briefly, the 'day of the Lord' will be preceded by the 'man of sin' known in the Johannine Epistles as Antichrist; the 'man of sin' is preceded by 'a revolt,' or a great apostasy; this apostasy is the outcome of the 'mystery of iniquity' which already 'worketh,' and which, according to St. John, shows itself here and there by faint types of Antichrist. The Apostle gives three stages in the evolution of evil: the leaven of iniquity, the great apostasy, and the man of sin. But he adds a clause calculated to determine the time of the main event more accurately; he describes something first as a thing (*to datechon*) [the papacy], then as a person (*ho katechon*), [the pope himself], preventing the occurrence of the main event: 'Only he who now holdeth, do hold, until he be taken out of the way.' [19]

Once Pope Pius XII died, the floodgates were opened. The revolt, which began with the Protestant Reformation and continued with the French Revolution, culminated in Montini's efforts to promote Liberalism, Americanism, and Modernism — to bring the Church "up to date." The Great Apostasy's true author and dispenser was Montini, "the man of sin," aided and abetted by his false prophet Roncalli.

- Henry Cardinal Manning teaches that Antichrist (also referred to in Holy Scripture as "the lawless one")

> shall introduce disorder, sedition, tumult and revolution both in the temporal and spiritual order of the world.... [He] is not subject to the will of God or of man but whose only law is his own will.... [In] Daniel there is a prophecy almost identical in terms [where he foretells the rise] of a king 'who shall do according to his own will.' [20]

It was Paul 6's intention to revise the law to his own liking before Roncalli ever announced the calling of the false Vatican 2 council; this is found in Montini's own writings. [21] He did not care that a large number of Catholics were opposed to the introduction of the Novus Ordo Missae and the false council teachings. It was his way or no way. The Pauline passage "He who withholdeth" — the one who restrains the lawless individual known as Antichrist — is, Manning concludes, after assaying the teachings of the Fathers, *"Christendom and its head; the Vicar of Jesus Christ."* In that twofold authority, temporal and spiritual, the Supreme Pontiff *"is the direct antagonist to the principle of disorder."* [22] This will be treated in greater detail in the next chapter.

The Book of Apocalypse

- The great sign in the heavens (Apoc. 12: 1-5), a woman clothed with the sun in labor to give birth, is interpreted by Revs. E. S. Berry and H. B. Kramer to be the Church laboring to elect a pope. When the pope-elect is born, he is taken up to God and his throne. Some commentators interpret this as martyrdom; others say it means a special protection. But if "he who withholdeth" is "taken out of the way," it must mean martyrdom. The man God intended to be pope is not elected and suffers at least a dry or white martyrdom. Among those mentioned above as possible candidates for papal election in October 1958, and there were several, none appear to be martyr material. One who did not attend the conclave, however, might have qualified as a "white" martyr —Josef Cardinal Mindszenty. The journalist Benny Lai reports that the cardinals asked that he be released to attend the conclave; although the American embassy in Budapest, Hungary would have released him, the Communist Hungarian government refused. Were the cardinals asking for his release to consider him as a candidate, or simply to allow him to attend the conclave?

Mindszenty did not attend the false Vatican 2 council. After being released from his long imprisonment at the American embassy in Budapest in 1971, he went to Rome, although he remained there only a month. There, it is reported, "Paul VI embraced Cardinal Mindszenty and leads him to the papal residence. The Pope takes off his pectoral cross and his ring and gives them to the Cardinal." [23] Later, he also would gift Mindszenty with his papal cope, according to other reports. What is to be gathered from these exceedingly strange gestures? Is it possible that Montini was admitting that in truth Mindszenty was pope, since he was not? Why else give to him the Fisherman's ring? Three years later, much to the cardinal's sorrow, Montini would betray Mindszenty by stripping him of his primatial see in Hungary, to placate the Communists. It is not known if Mindszenty ever said the Novus Ordo Missae, or followed the 1968 revision of the Sacraments. But barring these disqualifiers, it would seem he very likely could have been the intended pope-elect.

- In Apoc. 13:1, the first beast is generally taken to be Antichrist, Reverend Haydock says. He becomes the abomination by betraying the Church (which Montini did), even before the false prophet (Roncalli) enters on the scene.

- In Apoc. 13: 2, the dragon (Satan) gives Antichrist his own strength and power, the mirror reverse of divine jurisdiction and infallibility.
- The death wound that is healed in Apoc. 13:3 is considered to be paganism, according to Haydock and others. The earth is in admiration after the beast, just as all the world governments and the non-Catholic religions were enamored with Paul 6, because he pandered to them. As stated elsewhere, these usurpers were out to engage the people, after the fashion of movie stars and rock stars. They do not have faithful subjects, but rather "fans" and "groupies."
- The earthlings adored the dragon and the beast (Apoc. 13:4). Many welcomed the new liturgy and accepted the Vatican 2 changes. They adored Paul 6 literally because his name was inserted into the false liturgy, where they paid him tribute in the Canon of the Mass. They adored him as God's true representative when he was not.
- Many take the 42 months of Apoc. 13:5 literally, but Haydock says more than once that it refers to only a "brief time." Note here that what is brief to the faithful is not necessarily brief as God understands it.
- The next verse (Apoc. 13:6) explains that Antichrist blasphemes the Church and the saints. Paul 6's most notable blasphemy was aimed at the tabernacle, in the use of "for all men" in the consecration of the wine found in the Canon of the Mass. His very usurpation of the papacy was a blasphemy. But every act he performed which detracted in any way from the honor of God, and such acts easily number in the hundreds of thousands, was a blasphemy. Montini "demoted" St. Philomena, St. Expedite, and St. Christopher and lessened the honors accorded other saints. He wiped out the existing Catholic calendar, changing the times and classes of the Church's feast days and laws regarding no meat on Friday, fasting before Communion, fasting during Lent, and many others.
- In undertaking his cutting-edge role in doctrinal warfare, Paul 6 truly can be said to have "made war" with the saints (Apoc. 13:7)

and to have overcome them with his subsequent election as "pope." In that role, he was assumed to have power (as "pope") over every single human being on earth; the Vatican Council proclaims this teaching. [24] "And tongue" in this verse may refer to the fact that Paul 6 gave all peoples the right to celebrate the New Order mass in their own language.

- "Another beast" in Apoc. 13:11 refers to the false prophet according to Haydock. This false prophet is distinct from the "beast whose wound was healed" (Apoc. 13:12), and the wound can be interpreted as paganism according to Haydock and others. As will be explained in greater detail below, the first beast and false prophet co-exist, but one could not exist without the other. Roncalli made it possible for Montini to officially reintroduce paganism proper by making sure the captured Church could be perceived as the Babylonish whore described in Holy Scripture.

It was definitely in the 1960s that paganism fully came back into vogue, as evidenced by the deterioration of morals during that time period. This officially came with the election of Roncalli in October 1958 as Montini's false prophet. Roncalli had to make sure the groundwork was laid to fulfill Scripture prophecy. Now Catholics know the Roman Pontiff is the bishop of the Diocese of Rome. This diocese is attached to the Supreme Pontificate through the apostle St. Peter by divine constitution. Now as Bishop of Rome, the Pope has jurisdiction as local ordinary over the Diocese of Rome, which contains six hills. The seventh hill, located in one of the suburbicarian dioceses, was not included under "papal" jurisdiction until the 1960s. In a *motu proprio* promulgated by the false pope Angelo Roncalli (John 23) on April 11, 1962, the ordinary jurisdiction over the suburbicarian sees was transferred by Roncalli from the cardinal bishops to himself. By taking ordinary authority over all seven hills of Rome, Roncalli appears to have fulfilled the prophecy of Apoc. 17:9, for those who have wisdom to understand. For prior to this event, the cardinals presided as the legitimate heads of these six suburbicarian sees, and the pope's ordinary jurisdiction as Bishop of Rome extended over territory including only six hills. Incorporating the seventh hill into the territory under the jurisdiction of the Bishop of Rome by taking the jurisdiction of the "cardinals" away ties this biblical verse directly to Rome in a way that could never have applied previously.

It is explicitly revealed in Apoc. 17:9 that the "seven heads" spoken of in Apoc. 13:1 are actually seven mountains or hills, ruled by seven kings. Not cardinals, for these men are not truly cardinals, but lesser kings under Pontifex Maximus, "king" of Vatican City. This description does not refer to the Catholic Church, which forever remains a virgin doctrinally, but to the "whore of Babylon," the prostituted version of the true Church. This prostituted "church" is a new creation based on an ancient model, not a continuation of what went before, so Protestant commentators cannot call the Catholic Church throughout the ages the whore of Babylon. The identity of the ruler of these seven kings is laid out in Apoc. 17:11. The beast was a cardinal, then was not a cardinal, becoming the eighth king, a bogus pope heading them all. The kings remain kings, but the ultimate exercise of their power rests with the eighth king. This applies to both Roncalli and Montini. The inevitable result was the advent of that *great harlot,* the Novus Ordo church, sprawled in serpentine fashion across the seven hills and ruled from across the Tiber River by the eighth head usurping the Vatican.

• In Apoc. 13:12, the second beast (False Prophet) exercises his power in the sight of the first beast (Antichrist proper). Haydock says this means the first beast exercises his power already while the false prophet is still alive. This passage may have been fulfilled in the influence Montini exerted over the "pontificate" of Roncalli who preceded him, for it is known that both Roncalli and Montini worked hand in hand on many projects even before Roncalli's "election."

• It is curious that Apoc. 13:13 should be the verse announcing great signs, since the number 13 is so reminiscent of Fatima. The explanation of these signs leads one back to the book of Kings, for it speaks of fire coming down from heaven on earth in the sight of men. "And the God that shall answer by fire, let him be

God...And he [Elias] built with the stones an altar to the name of the Lord...Then the fire of the Lord fell and consumed the holocaust." [25] This verse refers to the contest on Mt. Carmel between the prophet Elias and the priests of Baal. The fire from heaven ignited the true sacrifice offered then only by the Israelites. The fire that falls from heaven at the hands of the *false* prophet is the reversal of this miracle, making it appear that he had the power to change the words of the consecration of the wine in the sacrifice, and, being pope, could exercise that power. Remember, it was Roncalli who first changed the words of consecration of the wine in 1959 in the missalettes issued for use by the faithful.

- The signs that the False Prophet performs (Apoc. 13:14) are *given* to him to perform in the sight of the beast. This refers to two things. 1) Liturgical reform was to be the culmination of the works of the council. Roncalli had favored it decades before becoming "pope." He began the process and Montini officially crowned his efforts by replacing the Latin Mass with the Novus Ordo Missae. 2) Roncalli and Montini both collaborated in convening Vatican 2; it was Montini who pushed the idea of redefining the papacy and infallibility. The suggestion leaned toward the idea of a greater inclusion of the bishops in defining truths of faith. [26] As noted above, the two collaborated in writing *Pacem in terris*, which simply upheld all John Courtney Murray was teaching as part of the doctrinal warfare efforts. Later Murray's heresy would be included officially in Vatican Council documents. Montini was made "an image of the beast" by Roncalli, whose first official act was to create him a cardinal.

- In Apoc. 13:15, the image of the beast is given a voice, or "speaks officially" when Montini is elected. This imagery continued especially in John Paul I and II as well as Ratzinger and Bergoglio (Benedict 16 and Francis). Those who do not adore him are slain spiritually because they realize once the Novus Ordo Missae is introduced, they can no longer remain in the "church" of Rome. They exit that church only to be delivered into the hands of yet another enemy.

- The mark of the beast (Apoc. 13:16) is understood by many commentators as a type of hellish baptism, meaning no one can be included in this "church" without it and without participating in the NOM. The mark on the forehead is the new rite of baptism; the mark on the hand may well relate to the phrase in the NOM which calls the sacrifice "the work of human hands." In Apoc. 14: 9-10 the Angel proclaims that those who receive this mark and thereby adore the beast will not be saved. Tellingly, the Angel also refers to those who "drink the wine of the wrath of God," which may be a reference to sacrilegious corruption of the NO formula for the consecration of the wine.
- The name of a man — 666. This is explained above.

The notes on these Scripture verses, where they are not verified by the opinions of the commentators, are merely the author's observations, which appear to strengthen the likelihood Paul 6 was indeed Antichrist. Catholics are asked to read and understand. Commentators note that prophecy can be understood only closer to the event, and, in this case, posterior to those events. No one is bound to believe these observations. But all are required to read the signs of the times and search the Scriptures, to see if these things are truly so.

B. Montini's reign as priest and king

In his *Golden Bough,* [27] author Sir James Frazer relates that the god Jupiter Olympus was honored on the Capitoline Hill in Rome. The Roman emperors, hailed also as gods, were worshipped as Jupiter and even borrowed the vestments used in the god's rituals to wear on special occasions. Freemasons would later revere Jupiter as "the morning star rising in the East," emblem of, "the ever-approaching dawn of perfection and Masonic light." [28] Lucifer (and by association Montini, as will be explained) is referred to as this star in Holy Scripture, Is. 14:12-15, Luke 21:18 and Apoc. 9:1-2. For those who have difficulty believing the cultus of this god has been revived, J. R. Church, in his *Guardians of the Grail,* made the connection between Jupiter worship and the all-seeing eye atop the pyramid — that same eye we daily honor with each and every financial transaction. He identifies it as signifying that man can become God through "mind power." [29] Piers Compton in his work *The Broken Cross* also associated the all-seeing eye with the worship of Baal, Jove (Jupiter), Apollo, and the sun god Horus. [30]

According to Frazer, June, the month Montini was elected and crowned pope, was probably the traditional month during which Jupiter, "heavenly bridegroom," wed the goddess Juno, "heavenly bride" for whom June is named. This ritual, Frazer writes, was "intended to quicken the growth of vegetation." Montini's June bride was the Church, whom most yet perceived to be the spouse of Christ. To "father" his apostate "church" and ensure that it thrived, Montini chose the very month his pagan ancestors celebrated this feast to begin his pontificate. Fulfilling Daniel's prophecy concerning Apadno [31] Montini (whose name means "little mountain") would fix his apostate tabernacle "between two seas" (the Tyrrhenian to the west and Adriatic to the east of Italy), "upon a glorious and holy mountain" (the Church), "and he shall come even to the top." Frazer says, "The sanctuary of the god (Jupiter) on the top of the mountain was the religious center of the Latin League." [32] This is a visual image not only of a mountain, but of a pyramid as well. Montini climbed the steps of this pyramid by moving up through the various Masonic rites or degrees. He ascended "even to the top," and indeed Lady Queensborough, who wrote at length on Freemasonry, placed the Antichrist at the top of the pyramid, constituting the capstone.

The footnote to the passage in the Douay-Rheims translates Apadno (now Mt. Olivet) as "his palace" (which probably refers to the building called the Aula *Nervi,* commissioned by Paul 6 in 1963 following his election and filled with Satanic symbols). But its etymological sense implies that the word could mean, "departing from or off the [one or right] path," (a = away from, against, up on, apart from, off; (the) pad = path, or fraudulent addition; no = not one, not so, not any). [33] Montini first "fix(ed) his tabernacle" even before his "election" as pope, for he climbs the mountain to reach it. Because all that he accomplished was by way of "fraudulent addition," he needed little help to ascend the papal throne to establish his new palace, just as Holy Scripture foretells. Montini would cause the revived image of the god Jupiter to "speak" from Rome once again, healing the death wound dealt the pagan gods and the Roman Empire by the rapid spread of Christianity. [34] The first beast's (Apoc. 13:1) deadly wound was healed (Apoc. 13:12) This was the head that was slain in Apoc. 13:3, interpreted by several commentators, including Cardinal Manning, as the pagan Roman empire. Montini re-established that empire; he was the reincarnation, as it were, of that empire, complete with its democratic political affiliations. He had to pay homage to its god to receive a voice in order to fulfill his mission. Some commentators do not believe that the first beast can be both Antichrist and the head whose wound was healed at the same time; they hold it must be one or the other. The difficulty seems to be resolved if it is understood that such a man can be identified as Antichrist precisely because he is able to rule Vatican City as a king who is not a pope and who worships the gods of old, as well as the God of the Jews.

Paul 6's Jewish heritage

Concerning the Jewish nationality of Antichrist, Reverend P. Huchede insists that "...it is certain that [Antichrist] will be of the Jewish race. Tradition bears us out on this point." [35] Reverend Lehman, in his *L'Antichrist,* [36] does not agree, calling it "an undecided question." In support of Huchede's opinion, Reverend Joaquin Saenz-Arriaga quotes *The Golden Book of Noble Italian Heritage*, which states that Paul 6 was descended from the deBenedictus family and lists this family as "...of Hebrew origin." [37] The book lists Montini's ancestor as the great-grandfather of Pier deLeoni, the anti-pope Anacletus II of St. Bernard's day. In *The Plot Against the Church*, pseudonymous author Maurice Pinay (Saenz-Arriaga collaborating with Traditionalist Anacleto Gonzalez Flores) quotes the Jewish/Spanish Encyclopedia to document the fact that Baruz Leoni (a Jew) had himself baptized and took the Christian name of Benedict. The final sentence of this quote reads "...in spite of baptism and mixed marriages, the descendants of deBenedictus were connected down the centuries with the Jewish community." [38] So it would seem that Montini was a Jew. But to exemplify the height of imperfection to be realized by Antichrist, he must also have been a baptized Catholic. For Zacharias wrote: "I was wounded in the house of them that loved me." [39] No betrayal is so painful or so reprehensible as that perpetrated by close friends or relatives. Christ was crucified by His own, and in this, the passion of His Mystical Body, He once again suffers persecution by members of the Church He entrusted to St. Peter.

Montini's public appearance garbed in the symbols of the Kabbalistic priesthood wearing the ephod and breastplate of the high priest Caiphas should strengthen belief in his Jewish ancestry and the mission he was to fulfill to his brethren as a fellow Jew. A photo of Montini wearing these vestments was published in an excerpt of Saenz-Arriaga's *The New Montinian Church* distributed by the editors of the periodical *Veritas* in the 1980s. The photo credit reads: "Paul 6 wearing the ephod of Caiphas at the conclusion of the V2 liturgy at Yankee stadium, October 4, 1965." In his *The New Montinian Church,* Saenz quotes from Albert Mackey's *Dictionary of Freemasonry* to the effect that the ephod was seized during the captivity and was never returned to the Jews. [40] Worn by King David and exclusively by the Jewish high priest, it was a piece of embroidered cloth approximately nine inches square bearing 12 jewels representing the 12 tribes of Israel. Called the "breastplate of judgment," it was placed over the high priest's tunic as a symbol of unquestionable authority. [41] Another Masonic reference work sheds further light on the real implications of Montini's vesture in the ephod: "The Jews had a peculiar suspicious regard for this garment. *[They] employed it in connection with idolatrous worship,* and held that no worship, true or false, could subsist without its presence." [42] So Montini's adornment with the ephod can be given a dual meaning: for not only did the ephod ensure the Novus Ordo was idolatrous, it also may have confirmed it as the (new) true worship of Montini's church. Robert Bergin quoted Ven. Mary of Agreda on this subject as follows: "The Jews will finally bring a costly crown and a kingly garment as well as a scepter and declare him [Antichrist] their king." [43]

A special modernistic-style tiara resembling a bullet or warhead (designed by Montini himself) was custom made by artisans in Milan for his coronation, according to one Montinian biography. [44] The coronation ceremony began at 6 p.m. In November 1964, after wearing it off and on for a while, Montini laid his unusual headgear on the altar at St. Peter's Basilica. He never placed it on his head again. This was said to symbolize his abandonment of any pretensions to temporal power. In order to fulfill his diabolic mission, Montini had to present as both high priest of Catholicism *and* the Jewish religion, rolled into one, while reigning as King. Given the quotes at the beginning of this chapter there can be no doubt: *Paul 6 reigned solely as king of Rome, not the Church universal, although he arrogated the power of a true pope over all Catholics and really "all men" on earth!*

C. Roncalli, principal agent

It must be remembered that Roncalli's reign was simply that of a "transition pope," as so many have referred to him. His mission was to prepare the way for Montini, just as *St. John* the Baptist prepared the way for Our Lord. While Roncalli could not yet do publicly what Montini would later do, he laid the foundation for all that Montini hoped to accomplish; and this with Montini's constant input and cooperation (Montini co-authored *Pacem in terris* and other "encyclicals"). Montini was the true power behind the throne as biographies on both of these imposters reveal. So, in reality, in both truth and in fact although covertly, *Montini's reign commenced almost from the day that Roncalli began his usurpation of the Holy See*. His "baptism" as Antichrist came when he became the first cardinal Roncalli created following his election.

In civil law, accomplices are usually considered just as guilty as the primary perpetrators of a major crime. This principle is reflected in Canon 2209: "Persons who conspire to commit an offense and also physically concur in the execution of the same are all guilty in the same degree, unless circumstances decrease or diminish the liability of some individual." [45] In fact, Roncalli, by definition, was the principal agent in charge of the destruction of the Church, as C.

Leroux maintains. Revs. Woywod-Smith, in their definition of a principal agent under this Canon, write: "The *mandans* [principal agent] is one who either commands another over whom he has authority or commissions a person as his agent to perpetrate an offense. He is considered the principal author of the offense;" [46] and Roncalli commissioned Montini and others. But was Roncalli commissioned by Montini first? Canon 2315, which levies the penalty for those who incur suspicion of heresy for helping to propagate heresy under Canon 2316, confirms this. After allowing enough time to make sure that the offense was not the result of force, fear or ignorance, Canon 2315 declares, the offender is considered guilty of heresy. *Cum ex Apostolatus Officio* is listed as one of the sources for Canon 2316 (also Canon 2315 by inference) in the Latin version of the Code. [47] (This is only one of several Canons where *Cum ex Apostolatus Officio* is listed as a source.) If, after six months' time, the offender has not recanted or objected that the offense was the result of force, fear or ignorance, Canon 2315 declares the offender guilty of heresy. These disqualifiers don't apply to Roncalli for reasons explained below.

Montini finished Vatican 2, begun by Roncalli. He was both his partner and his accomplice, and later also became the principal agent in his own right. Both, under the definitions of the law, are equally guilty of heresy, apostasy and schism during Roncalli's "papacy." According to the rules of conscience, a doubt is sufficient to cause one to discount Roncalli's validity. Could Roncalli's act be contributed to ignorance? Not if we rest on presumption as a reflex principle. As the rule of law quoted by Reverend Cicognani concerning presumption states: "Whoever is once bad is presumed to be so always (in the same delict)." [48] And as we shall see below, Roncalli already had been designated as a suspected Modernist in his early years. Also, cardinals are presumed to possess "exceptional learning" according to Canon 232, so ignorance is no excuse. Under Canon 2316, we turn to the old law on what happens to one who is presenting as a true pope yet is propagating heresy: he automatically loses his office. There can be no exceptions to laws made to protect against a common danger unless it is absolutely certain that in a particular case the danger has ceased. [49] Valid popes alone can direct the faithful to salvation, and so in this, as with the Sacraments, Catholics must decide in favor of safeguarding the faith. There are numerous documented doubts concerning Roncalli's validity, cited in this work and elsewhere, so there is no excuse to fail to form certainty in this matter.

So far, this seems to be a spiritual destruction, corresponding to Zacharias 13:7: "Strike the shepherd, and the sheep shall be scattered..." But physical destruction cannot be ruled out, since hundreds of thousands of Catholics already had perished at the hands of the Communist masters later supported by Montini. Also, soul-murder is worse by far than physical death; and in this Montini excelled, by deceiving Catholics into believing that his schismatic "church" was the true Church. The "abomination of desolation" spoken of by Daniel has already been discussed in Chapter VII above; the cessation of the continual sacrifice will be covered later in Chapter XIII. Here, we have addressed the kingdoms and their present-day signification. But it cannot be denied that Daniel certainly spoke of kingdoms in reference to his own day, and he even speaks of conflicting bloodlines himself. Of course, the claim to Christ's "bloodline" is both vile heresy and the height of power-lust, but the bloodlines have certainly been sedulously cultivated by those claiming to be descendants of Christ and Mary Magdalene (the Mormons and the Priory of Sion, who some refer to as "Catholic masonry.") Roncalli is said to have belonged to the Priory, as well as Lefebvre and others. The prime progenitor of these blasphemous sects is *Satan* and his descendants, not Christ's. Christ tells the Pharisees: "You are of your father the devil ...truth is not in him ...for he is a liar, and the father, thereof." [50] No greater lie has ever been told than that upon which the "papacies" of the usurpers are founded. Already in the early centuries of Christianity, these conniving types of men had begun to attack Christians of the primitive Church. St. Jude wrote: "For certain men are secretly entered in, ...ungodly men, turning the grace of Our Lord God into riotousness and denying the only sovereign ruler, and Our Lord Jesus Christ...these men...despise dominion and blaspheme majesty..." [51] They have been with us always, and always their method of operation and their aims have been the same.

"He who withholdeth" (the true pope) and the wicked one who will come "in all power, signs and lying wonders" [52] (Antichrist, as a false pope) has been thoroughly covered. But what are these signs and lying wonders? Reverend P. Huchede asserts: "The greater part of these miracles will be optical *illusions* and diabolical charms. *Men shall be deceived by appearances*; hence, the reason why the Scriptures say he will work miracles before the eyes of man and not in the sight of God." [53] This is precisely the definition of "phantom," given on the title page of this work. St. Thomas of Aquinas writes: "As Augustine says...the works of Antichrist may be called lying wonders...because he will deceive men's senses by means of *phantoms*, so that he will not really do what he seems to do, or because, if he works real prodigies, *they will lead those into falsehood who believe in him.*" [54] His assumed position and acts will appear valid to all when they are nothing but pretensions, since they arise not from legitimate election and the granting of Divine power, but usurpation, and the grant of Satanic power.

John 23 and Paul 6 each had a calling unique to themselves. That calling was their pseudo-papacy. Both men received two horns: one of the "successor" of St. Peter and one as the successor of the hidden Satanic Pontiff. Thus is the Gnostic/dualist notion of God as both good and evil represented in reality. In this, the last days of the Church have become as the first, since the Gnostics have plagued the Church from Her inception. (It is important to note the Masonic implications of the names "John" and "Paul." Both Sts. John and Paul served the Templar order as dual patrons. The Rosicrucian chronicler Julius Sperber says Rosicrucians believe the greater mysteries of Christianity were revealed to St. John and St. Paul. [55] And recall that Roncalli has been styled as a high-level Rosicrucian.) The subsequent "canonization" of all three of these men by Francis is only an attempt to enter them into the record as a perverse form of Masonic "saint," since they certainly cannot be considered saints of the Catholic Church.

In retaining the "papal" names of both Roncalli and Montini, their successors in iniquity John Paul 1 and John Paul 2 signified that they were continuing the line of the usurpers. Apoc. 13:15 verifies just such a transfer of power, for it reads: "And it was given to him to give life to the image of the beast, that it should speak...." An echo of this transfer is also seen in Apoc. 17:8: "The beast which thou sawest was, and is not, and shall come up out of the...pit and go into destruction." [56] The line of false popes which began with Roncalli give life to the beast, that he may appear to speak infallibly as true popes do.

For Antichrist must resemble Christ as closely as he possibly can. If Christ's Vicars descend in unbroken succession from Our Lord to St. Peter, then Antichrist's pseudo-vicars must also descend in the same manner. If Christ's Vicars are infallible in matters of faith and morals, Antichrist's vicars must be infallible in matters of deception and connivery. There is the continual magisterium of the one, true Church and the continual magisterium of the anti-Church. There is Antichrist proper in that one man, Paul 6, and his partner in crime, Roncalli, (who first usurped the papacy and began the process of dismantling the Continual Sacrifice). But there also are the four successors of these two men in whom Antichrist incarnate was reborn with all the powers of their wicked predecessors. If the pope is said to reign until the consummation, so also the final successor to this malevolent line will live until thrown into the lake of fire. Just as each legitimate pope is fully St. Peter's successor and Christ's Vicar, so also each imposter pope. The first of Roncalli's successors, Paul 6, was personal Antichrist, the Man of Sin, who the ancient Fathers say must reign in addition to his system. Paul 6's successors are likewise Antichrist, albeit not *personal* Antichrist, because they pledge to do his bidding; and there can be only one head of Satan's Mystical Body. These men are Antichrist because they pose as the official heads of that perfidious system until Our Lord sees fit to destroy it and deliver us.

But couldn't Francis be the personal Antichrist?

In short, no. Francis was not the one who *initiated* the changes, the departure from Tradition, the false Vatican Council 2, the new rites of the Sacraments, the Novus Ordo Missae, abrogating the true Latin Mass. If a truly objective evaluation of all Paul 6 was is undertaken, the rational man will have no doubt Paul 6 was personal Antichrist. Francis and all who have usurped the See of Peter also are antichrists as explained above, just not *the* antichrist). The imposters also can be classified as collective antichrist and his system continuing to persecute Catholics. But only Paul 6 was *the* Man of Sin, the Lawless One.

D. Heresies pre-election and post-election

As explained above, for many reasons, Giovanni Battista Montini could never have been validly elected. First of all, he was a heretic pre-election, as both his pre-election and post-election conduct proved. Formally abrogating the Latin Mass of the ages alone and replacing "for many" with "for all men" is sufficient proof of heresy. In reality, he could never have been elected per pope Pius XII's *Vacantis Apostolicae Sedis*, [57] for those electing him were mainly appointed by a false pope and the Church historically has never accepted the validity of false popes and their appointees, rendering them automatically deposed, as *Cum ex Apostolatus Officio* teaches. To avoid future schisms, it was first laid down in the Third Lateran Council that no one was to be regarded as Roman pontiff unless he had been elected by two-thirds of the cardinals (Canon 1), and all appointments by antipopes were deemed invalid (Canon 2). The context for this teaching is as follows: After Pope Hadrian IV died in 1159, the cardinals nominated two men together, namely Roland of Siena, who took the name of Alexander III upon election, and Octavian of Rome, who though he was nominated by fewer cardinals, nevertheless with the support of the emperor Frederick, usurped the name of Pope Victor IV. The council thus invalidated the appointment of these antipopes as follows:

That person shall be held as Roman pontiff who has been chosen and received by the two thirds. But if anyone trusting to his nomination by the third party assumes the name of bishop, *since he cannot take the reality,* both he and those who receive him are to incur excommunication and be deprived of all sacred order, so that viaticum be denied them, except at the hour of death, and unless they repent, let them receive the lot of Dathan and Abiron, who were swallowed up alive by the earth....Renewing the decision taken by our predecessor of happy memory, Innocent, we decree that the ordinances made by the heresiarchs *Octavian* {2} and *Guido* {3}, and also by *John of Struma* {4} who followed them, and by those ordained by them, are void; and furthermore that if any have received ecclesiastical dignities or benefices through the aforesaid schismatics, they are to be deprived of them.[58]

To the two-thirds Pope Pius XII later added a plus one to prevent any cardinal from voting for himself. Already prior to *Cum ex Apostolatus Officio*, these ancient laws concerning the invalidity of popes not canonically elected were in place, as well the necessity of a two-thirds majority for validity.

- Religious liberty — Montini co-authored *Pacem in terris* with Roncalli. "Many took it for granted that the Cardinal Archbishop of Milan had a hand in preparing [*Ad Petri cathedrum*]... Montini's collaboration became even more obvious in...the encyclical *Pacem in terris*, where many of the ideas expressed by Montini could be found in paraphrases." [59] "Pope John's arresting address which opened the Council sounded much like the Montini 'Discorsi'.... Correspondents had commented, too, on the sound of Montini in *Pacem in terris*," [60] Religious liberty has been condemned by many popes, but most notably in Pope Pius IX's *Syllabus of Errors.*
- In a general audience held Jan. 23, 1973, Paul 6 announced: "The search and expectation of further revelations is not complete." [61] Catholic author William Strojie, writing in the 1970s, says this is a heresy *any* Christian should recognize as such.
- Modernism as expressed by Montini:

The Church...help[s] us share in...the elaboration of a social doctrine. Both human and receptive, this doctrine acknowledges that the changes which modern life brings about in social structures *are both right and inevitable*...For doctrine is founded on *experience*, in this case the Church's social constitution...The Church does not maintain closed and impenetrable positions, nor does it threaten and issue anathemas...The Church, through the forthcoming council, ...will take care to "*bring itself up to date.*" [62]

It takes only *one* heresy to exclude one as a member of the Church and the work quoted here is riddled with pre-election heresies. Pope St. Pius X condemned the idea that changes, even in the Church's social doctrine are, "right and inevitable." And Pope St. Pius X particularly condemned the notion that doctrine can be identified in any way with experience. Imagine anyone maintaining that the Church does not issue irrevocable anathemas or hold irretractable positions! As stated above, the Church infallibly teaches Her dogmas are unchangeable and immutable.

- Montini also stated publicly, "*The Church will have to reconcile Catholic Tradition with the* humanism *of modern times,*" [63] another example of Modernist ideology.
- Montini likewise collaborated with Roncalli in promoting Communism, ecumenism, and Freemasonry, in word as well as in action, both before the death of Pope Pius XII and also during his usurpation, as demonstrated above. According to both Pope Paul IV's *Cum ex Apostolatus Officio* and Pope St. Pius V's *Inter Multiplices*, those cooperating in the heresy of another are just as guilty of it as they are. Current Canon Law for those cooperating with Communists reflects this. And under Canon 6 §4 in the 1917 Code, *Cum ex Apostolatus Officio*, retained as an official footnote to the law, must be followed as the "old law," since all other laws on heresy have been called into doubt by Traditionalists.

Montini's primary heresy was Communism

Here we must pause to elaborate on exactly *how* Montini favored Communism pre-election as an archbishop and "cardinal," because the identification of this as his primary heresy is important in decisively qualifying him as a double agent and ultimate instrument of destruction in the Church. For remember — all the while he was quietly courting Communism under the auspices of his father's Christian Democrat party, he was openly espousing Americanism as the greatest weapon to fight Communism. And this he did as the co-founder of Pro Deo and while accepting funds from the C.I.A to promote Catholic Action! During his time as a young priest in Rome, Montini befriended convert Jacques Maritain, who later became his mentor. At that time Montini was involved in Catholic Action activities, heading CUCR, a club for Catholic university students in Rome. Pope Pius XI later appointed him national moderator of this group's parent organization — the Italian Federation of Catholic University Students, better known as FUCI. In the hostile Fascist environment then existing, and especially considering the antagonism encountered from the Fascist youth groups, Montini had license to operate his organizations more along political than spiritual lines. The result was conflict between the two youth groups that eventually ended in bloodshed, but Pope Pius XI exonerated Montini in the affair. Later, however, Cardinal Pacelli, while acting as Pope Pius XI's secretary of state, relieved Montini of his position, neither praising nor blaming him for his work. As the then Vatican undersecretary, Montini warmly praised his friend's literary works and penned an enthusiastic introduction for the edition of Maritain's book on integral humanism released in Italy.

As defined by French theologian Maurice Caron, "Integral humanism is a universal fraternity among men of good will belonging to any religion or to none." Caron states that in Maritain's humanism, "The Church is to be the inspiration and the 'big sister.'" Atheistic humanism is the Marxist philosophy behind the Communist political system. Maritain attempted to graft humanistic philosophy onto Thomism, an endeavor attempted by others whose systems were later condemned by the Church. According to author Mark Fellows:

Maritain tried to blend humanism with Thomism...[He] argued that secular forms of humanism were actually anti-human, for they failed to recognize the spiritual dimension of man. Instead he explored a 'new' Christendom. He sought to have Christianity inform political discourse and policy in a pluralistic age through a theory of cooperation, believing people of different intellectual, political and religious positions could nevertheless cooperate to achieve common practical aims. Its errors are 'distortions' of the truth, as opposed to blunt errors. It is an incorrect emphasis on truths and a false ordering of ends, (these subtle deceits are the means used to create a "counterfeit" Faith. I would summarize his error as *ad majorem hominis gloriam.* He lays an über-emphasis on promoting the dignity of man, who is made in the image and likeness of God...Humanism leads to a "cult of man." [64]

In other words, integral humanism is not all that different from the tenets of Freemasonry. This unholy alliance can be recognized primarily as the Liberalism and ecumenism condemned by Pope Pius IX in his *Syllabus* and by Pope St. Pius X in his letter to the Sillon. Pope Pius XII, in his condemnation of non-denominational religious unity meetings (1949), also touched on Maritain's errors. While Pius XII seems to have endorsed Maritain's philosophy and activities in the beginning, that enthusiasm eventually waned over time when he realized the direction in which Maritain was heading. According to Fellows, Pius XII's friend, Reverend Reginald Garrigou-Lagrange, O.P., most likely was among those alerting him that Maritain was trouble. Pius XII's hatred of Communism alone would have alienated him from Maritain, who regularly dialogued with Communists to exercise the tenets of his philosophy. Maritain especially courted one self-professed Communist — a name familiar to those in the political sphere today — who would later help plot the course of the Novus Ordo church.

The anarchist Saul Alinsky is often defended today as a non-conformist who embraced neither Christianity nor Marxism. But Alinsky simply chose to peddle the more appealing type of

Communism which evolved by necessity from the iron hammer approach used by Stalin. (Following the Stalinic purges, Moscow decided that a non-violent, gradualistic approach was better suited to Communist purposes.) Alinsky was a Russian-born Marxist Jew, who in his later years de-emphasized his commitment to his own faith to better promote his ideas. Montini's mentor Maritain reportedly entertained a 30-year friendship with Alinsky, whom Maritain later introduced to Montini. According to an article from one Traditionalist website, [65] Montini, while a cardinal, spent a week in the cardinal's quarters closeted with Maritain and Alinsky. They then hobnobbed with Italian union-affiliated communists, determining how best to apply Alinsky's principles to leadership training for the Catholic social justice movement (as reported in Alinsky's biography by Marion Sanders). Montini emerged as a fan of Alinsky's, later styling him as "one of the few really great men of our century." [66] If this is not favoring and endorsing Communists, then the papal condemnation for this heresy loses all meaning.

According to best-selling author and award-winning journalist Richard Poe (quoted from the website www.discoverthenetworks.org):

> When President Johnson launched his War on Poverty in 1964, Alinsky allies infiltrated the program, steering federal money into Alinsky projects. In 1966, Senator Robert Kennedy allied himself with union leader Cesar Chavez, an Alinsky disciple. Chavez had worked ten years for Alinsky, beginning in 1952. Kennedy soon drifted into Alinsky's circle. After race riots shook Rochester, New York, Alinsky descended on the city and began pressuring Eastman-Kodak to hire more blacks. Kennedy supported Alinsky's shakedown. [67]

No doubt Kennedy, a devout Opus Dei member, was only following his pontiff's lead. The website further explains Alinsky's *modus operandi*, quoting again from Poe: "Alinsky scolded the Sixties Left for scaring off potential converts in Middle America. True revolutionaries do not flaunt their radicalism, Alinsky taught.

They cut their hair, put on suits *and infiltrate the system from within."* Paul 6 knew all about this strategy, having implemented it to work his way to the top of the dogpile and assume his role as King of Rome. No wonder he and Alinsky had so much in common. For those unfamiliar with them, Alinsky's *Rules for Radicals* [68] explain everything that happened within the Church following Paul 6's election as a false pope and all that has happened in the U.S politically in the last several decades. This work is readily available on the Internet.

After reading Alinsky's book, two Columbia University sociologists Richard Andrew Cloward and Frances Fox Piven formulated rules to implement socialism, known as the "Cloward-Piven Strategy." The plan is to use these rules to pursue the fall of capitalism by inundating the government bureaucracy with a series of unreasonable and incapacitating demands, thereby precipitating social crises and economic collapse. This strategy runs as follows:

1) Healthcare – Control healthcare and you control the people.
2) Poverty – Increase the poverty level as high as possible. Poor people are easier to control and will not fight back if you are providing everything for them to live.
3) Debt – Increase the debt to an unsustainable level. That way you are able to increase taxes, and this will produce more poverty.
4) Gun Control – Remove people's ability to defend themselves from the government. That way you are able to create a police state.
5) Welfare – Take control of every aspect of their lives (food, housing, and income).
6) Education – Take control of what people read and listen to – take control of what children learn in school.
7) Religion – Remove the belief in God from government and schools.
8) Class Warfare – Divide the people into the wealthy and the poor. This will cause more discontent and it will be easier to

Tragically, all these goals have either already been accomplished or are well within the reach of the Progressives. As the Fatima seer Lucia dos Santos told Father Fuentes during her interview with him in 1957, Communism would prevail in all countries, even the United States. It was Poe and author David Horowitz who first alerted Americans to the fact in 2008 that both Hillary Clinton and Barack Obama were disciples of violent radical William "Bill" Ayers, a Saul Alinsky fan. Alinsky taught that *"Change is brought about through relentless agitation and 'trouble making' of a kind that radically disrupts society as it is,"* and Ayers took this to its ultimate extreme in order to publicize and politicize his cause. We see this principle realized in the chaos prevailing today. Ayers headed a nationwide group of terrorists who were murdering policemen and FBI agents during the 1960s and 1970s, long before the "domestic terrorism" and police killings making headlines today. Paul 6's legacy has come home to roost in America, then, and it remains to be seen whether there is any hope of reversing the damage that has already been done.

Other heresies
Theologians generally agree that Antichrist will deny the Incarnation. Henry Cardinal Manning describes "those who have lost faith in the Incarnation as *humanitarians*, rationalists and pantheists." [69] But an out and out denial would have been too obvious, and might have alerted some of the faithful. So instead Montini did all in his power to elevate man to the level of God, even above God, and demote God to a mere man, the "brother" of the faithful. "All men" became equals to God. In his *Dialogues* (Monsignor John Clancy editor), Archbishop Montini wrote: "Sin is an offense against man before it is an offense against God...Are you looking for God? You will find him in man." Montini tore down the beautiful Churches built to honor Our Lord and replaced them with modern monstrosities pleasing to man. He placed tables in front of the beautiful main altar on which to celebrate the NOM in the language of the people that man might be honored, when before the priests had raised the Host and Chalice to Heaven, honoring God alone in the Latin tongue. He instituted totally secular rites and ceremonies, even those provocative

and scurrilous in nature, to be celebrated in the House of God. He replaced the Gregorian Chant and cherished Catholic hymns with modern music and Protestant hymns. Montini never said that Christ was not God, only a man; he didn't have to. Everything he did while usurping the papal throne screamed it.

Goffine's commentary on the Gospel and Epistle for the fourth Sunday in Lent teaches that in denying the divinity of Christ, the Jews and Gentiles alike in Christ's time denied the reality of the Holy Trinity — God the Father, God the Son, and God the Holy Ghost — by denying the divinity of one of its members. This can be done implicitly by rejecting the teachings of the continual magisterium and accepting instead the teachings and presumptions of mere men, not even in communion with the Roman Pontiff. Those believing themselves to be the Catholic remnant follow such men, who have not truly "received the Holy Ghost" in valid and licit consecration as bishops, and who, as usurpers, were never duly endowed with Divine jurisdiction, the guarantee of infallibility imparted by the Holy Ghost. Therefore, these misguided souls essentially deny the need for and the existence of the Third Person of the Blessed Trinity, and thereby deny the Incarnation.

According to Canon 1325, heresy can be committed by silence, subterfuge, or *manner of acting*. Montini was a heretic pre-election on the following counts:

- As an archbishop and Vatican pro-secretary, he collaborated with the Communists and failed to advise Pope Pius XII of the true state of affairs regarding the bishops in China.
- He *publicly* cooperated in heretical acts with false pope John 23.
- He *publicly* praised the works of Communist agitator Saul Alinsky
- prior to his "election," one of the types of cooperation (see Canon 2209 § 7).
- He was "elected" by a majority of cardinals invalidly appointed by a false pope and any remaining cardinals from Pope Pius XII's time, who accepted Roncalli as a true pope. Therefore, he never received the required number of votes to validly become pope,

per Pope Pius XII's *Vacantis Apostolicae Sedis*, which required two-thirds plus one for validity.

- He *publicly and notoriously*, prior to his "election," gave the addresses mentioned above, committing these heresies in more than one place and on more than one occasion. These were later printed and circulated *universally*.
- As secular king and false pope both, he wore the ephod and teraphim symbolic of the apostate Jewish religion *publicly*, completing his defection from the faith by becoming an apostate.
- He instituted the Novus Ordo Missae as an official act of his "papacy" with its heretical canon containing "for all" versus "for many."

Once again, *one* heresy is enough to sever anyone from membership in the Church, according to Canon Law. Montini was guilty of numerous pre-election heresies, and only a few of these are listed here. Giovanni Battista Montini was not a Catholic and therefore could never have become pope.

Conclusion

It is difficult if not impossible to see how, if one adheres to the spiritual interpretation of who and what the Church expected Antichrist to be, he could be anything other than Montini. A worldwide political ruler claiming to be Christ Himself would have no basis for his claim, no perfect opposition to Christ emanating from long centuries of Tradition. Decades of horror films have desensitized Catholics to the point they can no longer perceive the loss of the Church, the hierarchy, Mass, Sacraments and Catholic institutions as the most horrific loss imaginable. Everything has been reduced to the material and the physical; the spiritual no longer has any meaning or value. Roncalli and Montini worked together as two men of one mind to bring this about. Only blood, guts and gore, horns and sulphurous fumes impress anymore. Had these two men presented as anything other than what they were, they would have been unable to accomplish what they did. Few among the faithful and clergy realized they had secretly been working together for years prior to Roncalli's "election." As Canon 2209 states: "Persons who conspire to commit an offense and also physically concur in the execution of the same are all guilty in the same degree...." Roncalli and Montini were joint Antichrists, so to speak. But only Montini himself was *the* Man of Sin, because only Montini brought to a close the false Vatican 2 council, the cessation of the Holy Sacrifice, the alteration of the form of the Sacraments, and the overall destruction of doctrine. Roncalli's reign was too brief for all these things, although he was successful in providing everything Montini would need to be "elected." The juridic Church ended the day Pope Pius XII died, and the anti-Church was born. It was up to the abandoned remnant to decide how they should proceed, and they were deliberately rounded up and led in the wrong direction. What follows shows where they should have headed and why.

Chapter XI Endnotes

[1] Giovanni Battista Montini, *The Church*, Helicon Press, Inc., Baltimore, Md.,1964; a series of addresses written by Montini between 1957-1962, 54-57, 127.
[2] http://newmanreader.org/works/arguments/antichrist/lecture1.html
[3] Dom Prosper Gueranger's *Liturgical Year,* Vol. III, Briton's Catholic Library, London, 1983 (reprint; imprimatur by Henry Cardinal Manning, 1867), 257-58
[4] William Strojie, *Letters*, Letter no. 37, Feb. 14, 1979
[5] www.newadvent.org
[6] Herman B. (Bernard) Kramer *The Book of Destiny,* Apostolate of Christian Action, Fresno, Calif., 1972
[7] Rev. R. Gerald Culleton, *The Reign of Antichrist*, TAN Books and Publishers, Rockford, Ill., 1974, 79-80 (quoted from St. Iranaeus' *Adversus Haereses*, Book V, Chapter 5, Verse 1)
[8] Douay-Rheims edition of Holy Scripture, Apoc. 13:18
[9] Ibid.
[10] 1989 edition
[11] https://w2.vatican.va/content/pius-x/en/encyclicals/documents/hf_p-x_enc_04101903_e-supremi.html

¹² WARNING: The reference to this document is for purposes of illustration only. While it accurately provides a summary of Paul 6's teaching on man, his abandonment of the tiara and other topics, it advises readers to attend Traditional and/or Byzantine masses as a solution to the absence of a true pope in Rome. It focuses only on the illegitimacy of Montini and does not examine the "election" of John 23 and the events which preceded it, nor does it reference papal or conciliar documents which infallibly teach that the Church cannot exist without a canonically elected pope. It gives readers the impression, therefore, that contrary to the teachings of the (only) Vatican Council, a validly elected pope can *become* a heretic, (versus the Church's true teaching that he must *have already been* a heretic pre-election). Furthermore, the author of this work does not identify him/herself, which is never a sign of good faith. In reality, Montini never was and never could have been validly elected, nor for that matter was John 23 validly elected as proven in documents presented in the previous Chapter on Roncalli.
http://romancatholicfaith.weebly.com/uploads/2/9/4/7/29473625/the_scandals_and_heresies_of_antipope_paul_vi.pdf

¹³ Douay-Rheims edition of Holy Scripture, Dan. Ch. 7:25

¹⁴ Ibid., Dan. Ch. 8:25

¹⁵ Ibid., Dan., Chapters 7:25, 8:24; Apoc., Ch. 13:7

¹⁶ Douay-Rheims edition of Holy Scripture, 2 Thess. 2: 3

¹⁷ Ibid., 2 Thess. 2:4

¹⁸ Rev. Maurice De La Taille, *The Mystery of Faith*, Bk. 1, Sheed and Ward, New York, N.Y. and London, 1940, 228

¹⁹ http://www.newadvent.org/cathen/01559a.htm

²⁰ Henry Cardinal Manning, *Temporal Power of the Vicar of Jesus Christ*, Burns and Lambert, 1862, London, reprinted by Refuge of Sinners Publishing, Inc., Pekin, In., 117-127

²¹ "Cardinal" Giovanni Battista Montini, *The Church*, by Helicon Press, Baltimore, Md., 1964; a series of addresses written by Montini between 1957-1962, 54-57; 185, 218

²² Ibid., 127

²³ http://www.katolikus.hu/hist_ang.html

²⁴ Henry Denzinger, *The Sources of Catholic Dogma*, 30ᵗʰ Edition, Marian House, Powers Lake, N.D., 1957, DZ 1831

²⁵ Douay-Rheims edition of Holy Scripture, Kings 3:24, 32, 38

[26] Anne Roch Muggeridge, *The Desolate City*, Harper and Rowe, San Francisco, Calif., 1986, 62-64

[27] Sir James Frazer, *The Golden Bough*, McMillan Co., New York, N.Y., 1951, 173

[28] Grand Master Albert Pike's *Morals and Dogma*, printed at the behest of the Ancient and Accepted Scottish Rite Southern Jurisdiction, Charleston, W. H. Jenkins, Richmond, Va., 1871, 202

[29] J.R. Church, *Guardians of the Grail*, Prophecy Publications, Oklahoma City, Okla., 1989, 163-65

[30] Piers Compton, *The Broken Cross: The Hidden Hand in the Vatican*, Veritas Publishing Co., Party LTD, Australia, 1984, 12

[31] Douay-Rheims edition of Holy Scripture, Dan. 11:45

[32] Sir James Frazer, *The Golden Bough*, McMillan Co., New York, N.Y., 1951, 173

[33] This is a mere opinion on the part of the author, constructed from various English dictionaries. Rev. Bernard O'Reilly's *Catholic Bible Dictionary*, reprinted from the original 1881 edition by Catholic Treasures, Monrovia Calif., 1991, calls this place name "a word of disputed meaning."

[34] Douay-Rheims edition of Holy Scripture, Apoc. 13:15

[35] Rev. P. Huchede, *History of Antichrist*, first printed in 1884 and republished by TAN Books 1968, 15

[36] Rev. Denis Fahey, *The Kingship of Christ and the Conversion of the Jewish Nation*, The Christian Book Club, Hawthorne, Calif, first printed in 1953 and reprinted in 1987, 49

[37] Father Joaquin Saenz y Arriaga, *The New Montinian Church*, translated by Edgar A. Lucidi M.D. from the Spanish, La Habra, Calif., 1985, 391

[38] Maurice Pinay (Anacleto Gonzalez-Flores and Joaquin Saenz y Arriaga), *The Plot Against the Church*, St. Anthony Press, Calif., 1967, 509

[39] Douay-Rheims edition of Holy Scripture, Zach. 13:6

[40] Father Joaquin Saenz y Arriaga, *The New Montinian Church*, translated by Edgar A. Lucidi M.D. from the Spanish, La Habra, Calif., 1985, 389

[41] Montini's signature can be found on the last page of the document listed at the end of this footnote. WARNING: The reference to this document is for purposes of illustration only. While it accurately provides a summary of Paul 6's teaching on man, his abandonment of the tiara and other topics, it advises readers to attend Traditional and/or Byzantine masses as a solution to the absence of a true pope in Rome. It focuses only on the illegitimacy of Montini and does not examine the "election" of John 23 and the events

which preceded it, nor does it reference papal or conciliar documents which
infallibly teach that the Church cannot exist without a canonically elected
pope. It gives readers the impression, therefore, that contrary to the
teachings of the (only) Vatican Council, a validly elected pope can *become*
a heretic, (versus the Church's true teaching that he must *have already been*
a heretic pre-election). Furthermore, the author of this work does not
identify him/herself, which is never a sign of good faith. In reality, Montini
never was and never could have been validly elected, nor for that matter
was John 23 validly elected as proven in documents presented in the
previous Chapter on Roncalli.
http://romancatholicfaith.weebly.com/uploads/2/9/4/7/29473625/the_scand
als_and_heresies_of_antipope_paul_vi.pdf

[42] Robert Macoy, 33rd Degree Mason, *Illustrated History and Cyclopedia of Freemasonry*, Macoy Publishing and Supply, New York, N.Y., 1908
[43] Robert Bergin, *Prophecy for Today*, Fatima International, Hamilton, Ontario, Canada, 1970, 83
[44] Andre Fabert, *Pope Paul VI,* Monarch Books, Derby, Conn., 1963, 129
[45] Revs. Stanislaus Woywod and Callistus Smith, *A Practical Commentary on the Code of Canon Law*, Joseph F. Wagner, Inc., New York, N.Y. and London, 1957
[46] Ibid.
[47] Peter Cardinal Gasparri, *Codex Iuris Canonici*, Newman Press, Westminster, Md.,1957
[48] Rev. Amleto Cicognani, *Canon Law*, Dolphin Press, Philadelphia, Penn., 1935
[49] Revs. Stanislaus Woywod and Callistus Smith, *A Practical Commentary on the Code of Canon Law*, Joseph F. Wagner, Inc., New York and London, 1957, Can. 232
[50] Douay-Rheims edition of Holy Scripture, John 8:44
[51] Ibid., Jude 1:4, 8
[52] Ibid., 2 Thess. 2: 6-9
[53] Rev. P. Huchede, *History of Antichrist*, reprint of the 1884 edition, TAN Books and Publishing, Rockford, Ill., 19
[54] St. Thomas Aquinas, *Summa I*, Q. 114, Art. 4, Pt.1, Benziger Brothers Inc., New York, N.Y., Cincinnati, Ohio, Chicago, Ill., 1947
[55] Nesta H. Webster, *Secret Societies*, Christian Book Club of America, Hawthorne, Calif., 1924, 92
[56] Douay-Rheims edition of Holy Scripture

[57] http://www.betrayedcatholics.com/free-content/reference-links/1-what-constitutes-the-papacy/apostolic-constitution-vacantis-apostolicae-sedis/
[58] http://www.papalencyclicals.net/Councils/ecum11.htm
[59] Andre Fabert, *Pope Paul VI*, Monarch Books, Inc., Derby, Conn., 1963, 68
[60] William Barrett, *Shepherd of Mankind,* Doubleday and Company, Inc., Garden City, N.Y., 1964, p. 265-66
[61] William F. Strojie, *The Last Days of the Catholic Church*, 1978, 17
[62] "Cardinal" Giovanni Battista Montini, *The Church*, by Helicon Press, Baltimore, Md.; a series of addresses written by Montini between 1957-1962, 54-57; 185, 218
[63] Melton S. Davis, *All Rome Trembled,* G.P. Putnam's Sons, New York, N.Y., 1957, 95
[64] http://svfonline.org/wp-content/uploads/2016/08/06-Grand-Convergence.pdf (taken from Ch. XI of *Fatima in Twilight*, by Mark Fellows)
[65] www.traditioninaction.com (No endorsement of this site is intended here; it is cited only for purposes of attribution.)
[66] https://townhall.com/columnists/ralphbenko/2012/01/29/dear-president-obama-youre-no-saul-alinsky-n1320398
[67] http://www.discoverthenetworks.org/individualProfile.asp?indid=2314
[68] https://archive.org/stream/RulesForRadicals/RulesForRadicals_djvu.txt
[69] Abp. Henry Edward Manning (later Cardinal Manning), *Temporal Power of the Vicar of Jesus Christ*, Burns and Lambert, 1862, London, reprinted by Refuge of Sinners Publishing, Inc., Pekin, In., 109

Chapter XII —False Shepherds and Hirelings
Unlawful pastors are "thieves and robbers" (Trent)

A. Without the Pope there *IS* no Church

Not only do Traditionalists and the church in Rome falsely style themselves as Catholic, but they also pretend that the Church can exist and function without Her Supreme Head for an extended period of time. *While Christ is the true Head of the Mystical Body*, the Supreme Pontiff is its visible head on earth. The testimony of the theologians tells us that without the Pope, the *juridical* Church cannot exist.

St. Thomas Aquinas writes: "Therefore the unity of the Church demands that there be one who is at the head of the entire Church." [1] This is easily proven when the teaching of the Church Herself on this topic is understood. As Reverends Devivier and Sasia, [2] whose work was personally endorsed by Pope St. Pius X, taught,

> "This unity is twofold, (1) Unity of *doctrine and Faith*, which consists in the common accord of all the Faithful in admitting and believe all that the teaching Church proposes to them as revealed or confirmed by Jesus Christ. (2) Unity of *government*, which produces unity of *communion*, and which consists in the submission of all the faithful to their respective Bishops, and in particular to the Roman Pontiff, Supreme Head of the Church."

One breaks unity of Faith by rejecting only one point of doctrine; unity of government by rejecting the authority of the *legitimate heads*, the authors continue. How can there possibly be unity of the type intended by Christ for His Church when nearly all those calling themselves Catholics have rejected all doctrine and its very source, the continual magisterium that taught it? There are those today who still hold the truths of Faith as one body and constitute a communion of the faithful who accept all the teachings of that magisterium. But because of the infernal doctrinal confusion spread by the legions of Antichrist, Our Lord is the only one who knows who may be included in that unity. In an allocution to the Roman Curia given December 4, 1943, Pope Pius XII reminded Catholics that it is true that "the Church's indefectibility is visible, inasmuch as it is demonstrable" and that this indefectibility evidenced from the past is "the gauge of Her future." Nevertheless, he cautions,

> But if this indefectibility is a matter of experience, it remains, nonetheless, a *mystery* (emph. the Pope's); for it cannot be explained naturally, but only by reason of the fact, which is known to us by divine revelation, that Christ who founded the Church is with Her in every trial until the end of the world. [3]

The Church, therefore, will continue to exist in a mysterious manner, united to Christ's Mystical Body, for He is Her true Head. Nor is that Church invisible, inasmuch as every true Catholic professes his Faith whenever Catholic truth is defiled. But it does not now exist in the manner in which Christ established His Church; nor does it any longer possess that government which is essential to the constitution of the mark of unity by guaranteeing the authenticity of faith. In matters of divine Faith, we must have certitude. No one can ascribe certain unity to a body that is in itself not certainly known and positively identifiable, and a Church without the infallible head assigned to it by Christ. Therefore, the Church today lacks the intended external *mark* of unity, but yet posseses unity in and of itself, albeit in a mysterious manner. Catholics have become confused in this respect because they were taught that the Church "will last until the end of the world ever unchangeable and unchanged in its constitution." [4] But this statement was taken from a first draft of the Vatican Council's constitution on the Church, written in 1870, but never voted upon and included in the official council documents. Those reading histories of the council know that the drafts and statements therein can change many times over the course of the discussions before a vote makes the statement an official Church document. And Pope Pius XII's description of this indefectibility above as a "mystery" adds a new dimension to the Church's teaching on this subject.

That draft never became an official document, and the editors of the work quoted explain that the draft "contains no official teaching on the part of the Church...[although] the draft may be said to reflect the mind of the teaching Church *at that time*." [5] Still, without approval by the pope as a final Church document, it cannot be taken as the last word on the Church's constitution, and indeed the statement of its unchangeableness until the very end is contradicted by Cardinals Manning and Pie, among other theologians. Once again, the Church's persecution and the extent of that persecution in the end times is a *mystery*, and with the exception of the La Salette and Fatima warnings and those of other saints and holy people, Catholics had little inkling of just how ravaged their Church would be during the reign of Antichrist and his system.

The Catechism of the Council of Trent teaches: "*It is the unanimous teaching of the Fathers that this visible head is necessary to establish and preserve unity in the Church*," and this from Christ's guarantees to St. Peter found in Holy Scripture. [6]

The Vatican Council documents teach concerning Christ's promise to St. Peter: "No one is permitted to interpret Sacred Scripture itself...contrary to *the unanimous agreement of the Fathers*" (DZ 1788).

Pope Pius IX taught concerning the mark of unity in the Church: "The true Church of Jesus Christ was established by divine authority and is known by a fourfold mark, which we assert in the Creed must be believed; *and each one of these marks so clings to the others that it cannot be separated from them; hence it happens that the Church which truly is, and is called Catholic should at the same time shine with the prerogatives of unity, sanctity and apostolic succession*." [7]

Reverend E. Sylvester Berry, regarded as one of the most reliable and leading authors on the Church from the (early) 20th century, emphasizes the necessity of doctrinal unity among Catholics, which is impossible without a pope. Berry gives a very thorough and enlightening explanation of unity of doctrine in his work. He teaches that according to Matt. 28: 19-20,

> The Church must teach *all* the doctrines committed to Her; She must teach them to *all* nations, at *all* times, *even to the consummation of the world*....The Church enjoys the most perfect unity; Her doctrines are the same at all times and in all places....She must teach *all* truths at *all* times and in *all* places....*Unity in profession of faith is a natural consequence of the unity of doctrine.* Members of a society must accept its principles, because he who rejects the very principles of a society by word or act thereby rejects the society itself and ceases to be a member. Therefore, every member of the Church must accept its teachings, i.e., *he must make at least an outward profession of faith, 'for with the heart we believe unto justice, but with the mouth, confession is made unto salvation.'* (All emphasis here is Berry's.) [...] The Church has always demanded the strictest unity in the profession of faith; those who refused to profess even a single doctrine were condemned as heretics *who had already ceased to be members.* [8]

And no one can deny that *all* these doctrines of faith prescribed by the Church have *not* been taught and believed (far less professed) by Traditionalists. For Traditionalists teach only those doctrines they have attenuated themselves in order to prop up the validity of their false clergy. They can pretend all they like that they possess the four marks of the Church, but this is a fantasy. For without a canonically elected pope, without apostolicity of succession and its accompanying apostolicity of doctrine, they have nothing.

The Church established by Jesus Christ teaches precisely as Pope St. Pius X, in his Oath Against Modernism, wrote:

> I accept sincerely the doctrine of faith transmitted from the apostles through the orthodox fathers, *always in the same sense and interpretation, even to us*; and so I reject that

heretical invention of the evolution of dogmas, passing from one meaning to another, different from that which the Church first had....

All must hold as binding papal documents recorded in the *Acta Apostolica Sedis,* even those expressing only opinions. Because if this is not the case, they are not members of *the one, true Church on earth, as Jesus Christ constituted it,* which holds as inviolable the belief that the Roman Pontiff alone possesses the supremacy of jurisdiction and apostolic primacy over the entire Church. Unity of profession of faith is always possible but is not in evidence today because only a canonically elected pope can be the guarantor of that unity. This is probably some of the best evidence available that the Apostolic See is vacant.

Revs. Devivier and Sasia wrote the following:

> As it is to the character of the foundation that a building owes its solidarity, the close union of its parts, and even its very existence, it is likewise from the authority of Peter that the Church derives Her unity, her stability, and even Her existence Herself. The Church, therefore, cannot exist without Peter. [9]

Pope Pius IX teaches this fact from his own mouth: "May God give you the grace necessary to defend the rights of the Sovereign Pontiff and the Holy See; *for without the Pope there is no Church, and there is no Catholic Society without the Holy See.*" [10]

Pope Pius XII confirmed this truth for our times in *Vacantis Apostolicae Sedis*, when he wrote infallibly that:

> We declare invalid and void any power or jurisdiction pertaining to the Roman Pontiff in his lifetime, which the assembly of Cardinals might decide to exercise (while the Church is without a Pope)... If anything contrary to this prescript occurs or is by chance attempted, we declare it by Our Supreme authority to be null and void. [11]

And if the cardinals are forbidden to exercise such rights, then certainly lesser clerics would not have any such right. What acts of papal jurisdiction have Traditionalists attempted to exercise?

1. Assumption of supplied jurisdiction, which only the pope can provide and has historically provided over the centuries, being the supreme source of all jurisdiction. No jurisdiction can be supplied during an interregnum, for Pope Pius XII says all is to be left to the future pope.
2. They have attempted — but have been unable to supply — the papal mandate in all Traditional "consecrations" of bishops, essential to granting an office and valid orders to said bishop.
3. Exercise of orders and participation in sacred functions, without the dispensation from infamy of law, available only from the pope (Canon 2295).

The message to be taken away from the allocution to the Roman Curia by Pope Pius XII above is that the Church's indefectibility is a *mystery*, and mysteries are to be accepted on faith even if they are not completely understood. Isn't the Pope telling us in this quote, then, that past experience of this "mystery" is not able to be precisely defined and used as a gauge for future reference? And if indefectibility is a *mystery*, doesn't this leave some room for its interpretation that we mere mortals cannot fathom?!

Reverend Berry states that indefectibility is really promised only to the Roman Pontiff, which explains precisely why the Church cannot exist without Her head. In his already cited work above, he wrote: *"The Apostolic See of Rome is the only PARTICULAR Church to which the promise of indefectibility has been made."* [12] Emphasis here is on "particular" because those quoting this and similar texts concerning the constitution of the Church tend to interpret it as the Church spread throughout the world, to include all the bishops and cardinals. This could not be said without injuring the dogma that the bishops teach infallibly only in union with the Roman Pontiff. Henry

Cardinal Manning, writing prior to Berry's work, is quoted to this effect in Chapter VII, section B above.

Next, Berry repeats what other theologians and St. Robert Bellarmine teach, that the Church cannot do much of anything during an interregnum. Then he says:

> The Apostolic succession cannot fail in the Apostolic See *so long as the Church Herself continues to exist,* for although the see be vacant for many years, the Church always retains the right to elect a legitimate successor, who then obtains supreme authority according to the institution of Christ. [13]

In this Berry agrees with the oft-cited quote from Reverend Edmund O'Reilly:

> The Great Schism of the West [14th-century] suggests to me a reflection which I take the liberty of expressing here. If this schism had not occurred, the hypothesis of such a thing happening would appear to many chimerical. They would say it could not be; God would not permit the Church to come into so unhappy a situation. Heresies might spring up and spread and last painfully long, through the fault and to the perdition of their authors and abettors, to the great distress too of the faithful, increased by actual persecution in many places where the heretics were dominant. But that Catholics should be divided on the question of who is Pontiff, that the true Church should remain between thirty and forty years without a thoroughly ascertained Head, and representative of Christ on earth, this would not be. Yet it has been; and we have no guarantee that it will NOT be again, though we may fervently hope otherwise.
>
> What I would infer is, that we must *not* be too ready to pronounce on what God *may* permit. We know with absolute certainty that He will fulfill His promises; not allow anything to occur at variance with them; that He will sustain His Church and enable her to triumph over all enemies and difficulties; that He will give to each of the

faithful those graces which are needed for each one's service of Him and attainment of salvation, as He did during the great schism we have been considering, and in all the sufferings and trials which the Church has passed through from the beginning. We may also trust He will do a great deal more than what He has bound Himself to by His promises. We may look forward with a cheering probability to exemption for the future from some of the troubles and misfortunes that have befallen in the past.

But we, or our successors in future generations of Christians, shall perhaps see stranger evils than have yet been experienced, even before the immediate approach of that great winding up of all things on earth that will precede the day of judgment. I am not setting up for a prophet, nor pretending to see unhappy wonders, of which I have no knowledge whatever. All I mean to convey is that contingencies regarding the Church, *not* excluded by the Divine promises, *cannot* be regarded as practically impossible, just because they would be terrible and distressing in a very high degree. [14]

As Henry Cardinal Manning wrote concerning "he who withholdeth," the saints can be overcome and Antichrist can triumph only when *the pope* is taken out of the way.

Pope Leo XIII taught in *Satis Cognitum*:
But it is opposed to the truth, and in evident contradiction with the divine constitution of the Church to hold that while each bishop is individually bound to obey the authority of the Roman Pontiffs, taken *collectively* the bishops are not so bound. For it is the nature and object of a foundation to support the unity of the whole edifice and to give stability to it rather than to *each component part*; and in the present case this is much more applicable since Christ the Lord wished that by the strength and solidity of the foundation the gates of hell should be prevented from prevailing against the Church. All are agreed that the divine promise must be understood of the Church as a whole, and not of any certain portions of it. *These can*

> *indeed be overcome by the assaults of the powers of hell,*
> *as in point of fact has befallen some of them.* [15]

That it should seem for a time that the gates of hell had indeed prevailed is foretold in Holy Scripture, for Antichrist will crush the saints and remove their Sacrifice. That this interruption is only temporary is also foretold, for perpetuity, as defined, can survive a temporary break and resume, while yet retaining the integrity of its definition. Yet even if the See of Rome is vacant for many years, a pope can always be elected, although it may require a miracle from Christ Himself. This is true because without the hierarchy it is impossible for an election to be held. But if it is God's will that another pope is elected, either He will provide the means for election miraculously or bishops and priests will be found yet surviving somewhere on earth. When the bishops all abandoned Pius XII and embraced Modernism and ecumenism, then was the foundation weakened and the shepherd struck. And in the absence of a true pope, so-called Traditionalist clergy can neither establish unity nor rule the faithful.

Christ's promise to St. Peter

It is necessary to explore the source of the confusion on the power of the bishops. First, many do not understand that Christ *promised* the power of the papacy to St. Peter when He said: "Thou art Peter…," but that the actual grant of this power would not come until after His Resurrection, when the Ascension was near. The Church could not have two heads; Peter could become head only after Christ's death, because He was yet with His Apostles in glorified form. Christ predicted that Peter would fall from this promised dignity by denying Him three times (Luke 22: 31-32) and also predicted his restoration. The verse reads: "And the Lord said: 'Simon, Simon, behold Satan hath desired to have you, that he might sift you as wheat. But I have prayed for thee, that thy faith fail not; and thou being once converted, confirm they brethren.'" Reverend Leo Haydock comments on this verse in the New Testament: "That the disciple might not lose courage, He promises him pardon before he has committed the crime, *and restores him again to his apostolic dignity*, saying 'confirm thy brethren.'" [16]

As St. Thomas Aquinas teaches in his catechism, what Christ prays for is always granted; Christ's promise to Peter alone, that his faith would never fail, must ever be seen as unfailing itself. [17] By virtue of this promise and pardon, when he received the keys following the Resurrection, Peter then was to confirm his brethren, the Apostles. He was to grant them a share in the jurisdiction imparted to him by Christ. Thus must the very words of Christ be seen to confirm Pope Pius XII's decision on the bishops, that:

> ...As far as his own diocese is concerned, each one as a true Shepherd feeds the flock entrusted to him and rules it in the name of Christ. Yet in exercising this office they are not altogether independent, but are subordinate to the lawful authority of the Roman Pontiff, although enjoying the ordinary power of jurisdiction which they receive directly from the same Supreme Pontiff. [18]

Traditionalists are saying, by the very fact that they maintain it to be so, that the Church can indeed exist as promised without Peter, but in this they deny the very faith they pretend to profess. In saying that the governing body of the Church could never cease to exist, they exclude the pope when it is Catholic doctrine that the visible (juridical) Church cannot exist without *the Roman Pontiff*, not the bishops. Cardinal Manning wrote:

> The Vicar of Jesus Christ...being the special representative of the Divine Head, bears all his communicable powers in the government of the Church alone. The other bishops and pastors, who are united with him, and act in subordination to him, *cannot act without him.* [19]

Whatever bishops exist cannot possess any authority unless they are in union with the pope and were created in union with him. What Traditionalists must realize, especially Sedevacantists, is that by claiming the See is vacant they are admitting that at present the

398

Church cannot function hierarchically. They hesitate to mention the arrival of Antichrist, even though clearly the Antichrist has almost certainly come and gone in Paul 6, who inaugurated the system of the beast which remains to this day. Although the end of the world has not yet arrived, Holy Scripture tells us that there will definitely be a disastrous disruption in the Church at the time of Antichrist.

Antichrist will crush the saints

Henry Cardinal Manning continues:

> The event may come to pass that as our Divine Lord, after His three years of public ministry were ended, delivered Himself of His own free will into the hands of men, and thereby permitted them to do that which before was impossible, so in His inscrutable wisdom He may deliver over His Vicar upon earth, as He delivered Himself, and that the providential support of the temporal power of the Holy See may be withdrawn when its work is done...when the whole number of those whom He hath chosen to eternal life is filled up. It may be that when that is done, and when the times of Antichrist are come, that He will give over His Vicar upon earth, and His Mystical Body at large, [for a time]... *The Church would, as in the beginning, again be made up of members voluntarily uniting themselves together throughout the whole world, having indeed a legal recognition here and there, but wandering up and down the earth, without any contact with the nations of the world as such.* The state of the world before Constantine would be reproduced; the Church would descend again, if I may say so, *into the Catacombs,* and would be hidden from society; it would cease to take its place with the powers of the world, having an existence beside and above them. It would cease to be seen in the council of princes, in the legislatures of states, to have a status in the world; it would have no place in the public legislature except to be prohibited. [20]

This only reinforces comments above regarding the unity of the Church. That unity will not be recognized legally or constitute the visible unity the Church once enjoyed. The Church will be hidden once again in the Catacombs, which indeed it is.

Attempts to reduce the Church to this state were already afoot in St. Paul's time, for the Gnostic Simon Magus had attempted to purchase the episcopal power from the Apostles; for this he was sharply rebuked by St. Peter. Magus would later proclaim himself "the principal emanation of the Deity and the Redeemer." [21] The early Fathers identified him as "the first heretic." [22] By resisting Magus, St. Peter was "holding fast to the faith which he had received." [23]

"For the mystery of iniquity already worketh; only that he who now holdeth do hold until he be taken out of the way." [24] This restraining power, Manning says — this "he who withholdeth" — is none other than: *"Christendom and its head; the Vicar of Jesus Christ."* For in that twofold authority, temporal and spiritual, the Supreme Pontiff:

> *"is the direct antagonist to the principle of disorder ...It was the will of God; it was the concession of the Father that Pilate had power over His Incarnate Son... In like manner with His Church. Until the hour has come when the barrier, by the Divine will, be taken out of the way, no one has power to lay a hand upon it.* The gates of Hell may war against [the Church]; they may strive and wrestle, as they struggle now, with the Vicar of Our Lord; but no one has the power to move Him one step until the hour shall come when the Son of God shall permit, *for a time, the powers of evil to prevail. That He will permit it for a time stands in the book of prophecy. But the imperishable Church of God...will live on still through the fires of the times of Antichrist...."* [25]

Louis-Edouard Cardinal Pie of Poitiers, a contemporary of Cardinal Manning's and a drafter of the Vatican Council proclamation on infallibility, wrote:

The Church, though of course still a visible society, *will be increasingly reduced to individual and domestic proportions.* She who in Her young days cried out: 'the place is strait: give me room wherein to dwell,' will see every inch of Her territory under attack. Surrounded on all sides, as the other centuries have made Her great, so the last will strive to crush Her. *And finally the Church on earth will undergo a true defeat: '...and it was given unto him to make war with the saints and to overcome them,'* (Apocalypse 13:7). The insolence of evil will be at its peak. [26]

Hilaire Belloc says the same in his *The Great Heresies:*

The Church will not disappear, for the Church is not of mortal stuff; it is the only institution among men not subject to the universal law of mortality. Therefore we say, not that the Church may be wiped out, but that it may be reduced to a small band almost forgotten amid the vast numbers of its opponents and their contempt of the defeated thing. One of the most intelligent of French Catholics, a converted Jew, has written a work to prove (or suggest) that the first of these two possible issues will be our fate. He envisages the last years of the Church on this earth as lived apart. He sees a Church of the future reduced to very few in numbers and left on one side in the general current of the new Paganism. [Pope Pius XII calls this resurgence of former errors "the current of Black Paganism" – Ed.] He sees a Church of the future within which there will be intensity of devotion, indeed, but that devotion practised *by one small body, isolated and forgotten in the midst of its fellowmen.* [27]

Even Pope Pius XII taught, "History gives clear evidence of one thing: the gates of Hell will not prevail (Matt. 16: 18). But there is some evidence on the other side too; *the gates of hell have had partial successes.*" [28] To understand that the gates of hell will not "prevail" we must understand that prevail itself means to defeat, conquer, or triumph over; that will never happen. But to temporarily *appear* to do so is another thing entirely. Manning sets that period aside from the prophecies concerning the gates of hell *because the exception is part of divine revelation, which cannot be contradicted.* Prior to Christ's death on the cross, Manning explains, the Devil believed that in slaying our Lord he could scatter the flock forever. But following the redemption, and the substitution of Christ's Vicar for his Son, "the flock can be scattered no more." It can be dispersed, perhaps, in the sense that it survives as those above describe it; but it cannot be wiped out entirely.

"And so it shall be to the end," as Christ promised, Manning concludes. This is the fulfillment of the promise that the Church shall last until the consummation, for in the end the papacy will most likely be restored. Pope Pius XII explains in *Mystici Corporis* that we will never be able to understand entirely the mystery of the Mystical Body, but we know that Christ is its Head, we desire with all our hearts to be its members, and we believe as an undeniable truth expressed in the Act of Faith that He is ever true to His promises. *There is nothing more…*

B. Tracing Traditionalism to its Masonic origins

The length and breadth of this topic requires an entirely separate work of its own, provided at www.betrayedcatholics.com. [29] Needless to say, no Catholic worthy of the name could even consider cooperating with an organization even when a tie to Freemasonry is merely suspected. The Knights of Malta/Order of St. John (OSJ) connection was illustrated earlier in this work, and this same connection leads straight into Traditionalism. The priests James Wathen, Joaquin Saenz-Arriaga, Gommar De Pauw, Paul Wickens (for a time), and others were all members of either the (Russian) orthodox branch of the Order of St. John Hopsitallers, the Shickshinny Knights, or other offshoots (not to be confused with the Knights of Malta/OSJ, which was at one time a Catholic lay group before its infiltration). Below is a summary of what early Traditionalists thought about "priests" operating in the post-Vatican 2 period, and why they advised Catholics not to associate with them. They may not have known their actual Masonic orientation, but their

Catholic instincts place them on guard against the thieves and hirelings warned about by Our Lord.

Mary Lejeune

When faithful Catholics left the Church in the late 1960s and began referring to themselves as "Traditionalists," they fell under the spell of priests who appeared to be orthodox but who secretly and carefully were prepared to intercept those exiting the NO church. In her *Sword of Truth* published in the 1970s, that champion of the Catholic faith Mary Lejeune traces these "priests" to their true source:

> Awhile back, I received a booklet from a reader. It is entitled, *Brotherhood of the Illuminati* and it is written by the Freemasons themselves. It is published in London, England and within the pages we read all about the so-called "Pre-Nicene Church" (Arianism) which these Freemasons set up in October 1953 while we Catholics were praying and acting like Catholics, unaware of the fact that a Masonic revolution was about to come down upon our unsuspecting heads. Let me quote, please: 'This Church was formed in October 1953, with the object of carrying on the true Catholic Tradition and the original *Mysteries of Jesus* and the Gnosis of the Soul. Candidates for the Priesthood (which would maintain the traditions) must have completed three years' probation in the Brotherhood of the Illuminati; they are required to have a thorough knowledge and understanding of the Gnostic Church for the first three centuries of the Christian Era. *Private chapels will be established as and when the need arises.* [30]

Former Communist and Catholic convert Bella Dodd also warned of such an infiltration that began at an even earlier date. In an article written from a speech given in the 1950s, Dodd revealed that prior to World War II, Communist leaders issued a directive throughout the world that the Catholic Church must be infiltrated. "In the 1930s we put eleven hundred men into the priesthood in order to destroy the Church from within," she told her audience. Dodd warned that these men "now...are in the highest places in the Church." In her book, *School of Darkness*, Dodd explains exactly how the political side of Communism would be introduced to Americans: "Trachtenberg once said to me that when communism came to America it would come, 'in labels acceptable to the American people...' and one of those labels, he added, would be that of '*progressive democracy*.'" [31]

Senator Joseph McCarthy's Communist "witch hunt" was well timed, then; but the infiltration was far too advanced to be contained. For already it had risen, as Dodd noted, to the highest places in the Church. As Mary Lejeune rightly noted, she herself and others, McCarthy included, valiantly fought to save this country, but they lacked the support of their bishops. "America is doomed — not because good people didn't fight to save her. America is doomed because the Catholic Hierarchy (made up of enemies and cowards) robbed the American people (both Catholics and Protestants) of a strong, spiritual leadership." [32] In her later years, European Catholic Traditionalist Countess Elizabeth Gertsner would come to the same conclusions.

Similar to the effort to raise consciousness concerning the threats of Socialism and Communism in conservative circles today, the John Birch Society began its organization on a conservative, patriotic basis in the 1950s, contributing to the doctrinal warfare effort. The group especially zeroed in on those recently estranged from the NO church, who believed Communism was the undisputed enemy. But as Lejeune noted,

> Mr. Welch is not very interested in having Catholics (the strong ones) join his Society. I quote from the *Blue Book* (page 135) as follows: "For those who already have such a bedrock of faith and stand by it, I can offer nothing. But for those who are no longer sure exactly where they do stand, on what rocks or how firmly, I want to try to show them." Mr. Welch believes in evolution (some Christian!) as anyone turning to page 140 of his *Blue Book* can clearly

see. On page 155 of the same book we find that the Society
is both '*a religion and a revolution...* [33]

And as such Catholics were forbidden under Canon 1258 and
1325 to participate in whatever might pass as the "services" of such a
religion under penalty of excommunication. Hearing these words,
Catholics must remember that especially today, Freemasonry wears
many masks, hides itself among the seemingly most respectable
enterprises and constantly adapts itself to the circumstances and
needs of the times. While it wore the face of conservatism and was
even embraced by many of the laity and "Traditional" clergy, who
thought nothing of preaching their philosophy from the pulpit,
Welch's organization simply was not Catholic.

In short, the aims and philosophy of the JBS are not unlike those
of the Masonic sects themselves (although most would agree that the
JBS is not *overtly* Masonic). And those offering their own solutions
to the problem may only be well placed but clueless plants, no matter
how sincerely they may believe in their cause. This is especially true
since so many sounding the alarm today seem intent on omitting the
fact that Socialism and Communism were spiritual dangers long ago
condemned by the Church, dangers arising *from* Freemasonry and
not to be disassociated from it. As Pope Leo XIII taught in *Humanum
Genus* in 1888, it is clear that although these sects all took great pains
to appear unrelated, they "are identical to Freemasonry, which is the
central point from which they proceed and toward which they
converge." [34] In 1902, he also described Freemasonry as "the
permanent personification of the Revolution. It constitutes a sort of
society in reverse whose aim is to exercise an occult overlordship
upon society as we know it, and whose sole *raison d' etre* consists in
waging war against God and His Church." [35] In 1849, Pope Pius IX
threatened the faithful with Divine vengeance if they cooperated in
the schemes of Socialism and Communism, warning, "There will
come from these *conspiracies* an increase in miseries and
calamities." [36] And despite the efforts of so many Catholics who truly
love their country and have struggled to save her from these evils,
these miseries and calamities have arrived.

William Strojie

Catholic writer William J. Strojie, who wrote books and periodic newsletters from the early 1970s until his death in the late 1980s, also was convinced that Gnostics had taken over the Church. Speaking of those who began acting as priests following Vatican 2, Strojie cites the cases of several men with shady backgrounds and questionable credentials. Of "Father A," the tape priest, Strojie wrote in his book:

> These men have no authority for their Mass centers; they lack the necessary delegated jurisdiction to absolve sin in the confessional....The tie-in of Traditionalists with the schismatic old Catholics and bishops of the "ecclesiastical underworld," as the thorough investigator Peter Anson called it [in his *Bishops At Large*, 1964], surely explains Father A's graveside emergence as a bishop. We had a priest on our mailing list who, as we were informed at the time of his death, was also buried as a bishop....
>
> The Traditional door is wide open to all priests who come speaking their opposition to Vatican Two, and who promise Mass and Sacraments to Catholics opposed to Vatican Two... I might seem to have deliberately chosen mostly bad examples of Traditional priests. Not at all. I have painted a dark picture lightly. When the door is open to any priest who calls himself Traditionalist, and who is therefore accepted by laymen uninformed in these matters, (many are misinformed and self-deceived), the house, wide open to every kind of opportunist, is sure to be crowded... *I myself know of several hundred families who simply say their prayers at home.* They decline both the new religion and offers of Traditionalist priests to act for them in the place of their Church... Before Vatican Two Catholics cared enough about their Protestant friends and neighbors to want them to have the fullness of Catholic faith and practice... Now our reformed clergy wallow in the added confusion of the Second Vatican Council. *Catholics and*

> *others are invited to join them in their renewal of the ancient Gnosticism.* [37]

Peter Anson

So where exactly did these Gnostic priests and bishops come from? In *Bishops at Large* [38] (quoted by Strojie above), author Peter Anson traced the origins of these schismatic groups through countless transformations and factionalizations. When the Stuart Jacobists fled from England to France in the late 1700s, they were able to take advantage of political conditions there, already stirred up by Illuminist Adam Weishaupt, to further their own "spiritual" aims. After the French Constitutional Church was founded in 1790, Pope Pius VI forbade Catholic clergy to take an oath upholding this unlawful seizure of the monarchy. Initially, nearly the entire body of the clergy refused to take the oath and went into exile. Left with only four bishops brazen enough to defy the Pope's commands, the state church eventually recruited other schismatic Catholic priests and bishops who gained adherents for the new church.

When this situation was remedied under Napoleon and the dissenting bishops submitted to Pius VII, others faithful to the state church remained with schismatic clergy who refused to submit to the Pope. Thus was one schismatic body created. The second schism arising from the French Revolution came when Pius VII ordered all the priests in exile to return to their dioceses. Certain of these priests refused to accept any agreement between the Pope and the new French government, maintaining that no such agreement could be made from a "Catholic" point of view. Many lay people faithful to these pastors followed them into schism to become the *"petite eglise"* (little church), joining forces with some of the Jansenists. The clergy in these two groups provided the anti-papal clerical pool from which the Old Catholics and their offshoots would later emerge. And as theosophical (known today as New Age) influence increased, these groups gradually regressed to their Gnostic origins.

Anson tracked this Gnostic resurgence to the Martinists, who were said to have secretly kept a (non-Catholic and entirely gnostic) group of Knights Templar alive in France. (The Templars were originally a commendable group of Catholic knights who valiantly fought in the Crusades but were later disbanded by one of the Avignon popes for the degenerate and blasphemous practices of a few of its members.) This occurred following the "Little Resurrection" of the Templars in 1804. Some of them, Anson says, had been initiated into the Memphis-Mizraim rites, reportedly introduced in Europe in the first century A.D by the Egyptian priest Ormus. Thus Priory of Zion influence, discredited by some but known as "Catholic" Masonry to others, surfaced in the early appearance of neo-Gnosticism, first founded by Jules Doinel in 1890. Doinel's example was soon followed by the ex-Catholic Jean Bricaud, Recteur de la Rose-Croix, who founded his own Gnostic sect.

"Gnosticism was very much in the air," Anson writes. "All over France, especially in the South and West, little groups of neo-Gnostics flourished. Most of them had their own priests and bishops...." [39]

It is no wonder that Giovanni Papini calls France 'Satan's Promised Land.'" [40] Melanie Calvat, the seer of La Salette, knew well the extent of perversion in her native land, having experienced firsthand the resistance of Gallicanist-minded priests and bishops to the release of Our Lady's warning. *L'Osservatore Romano*, in its Christmas 1904 edition, admitted that Melanie knew her crusade to reveal the secret would incur the wrath of French Freemasonry. [41] Horribly maligned by her enemies, forced to relocate repeatedly, suffering from ill health, she refused to give the enemy any quarter. The Secret was published twice during Melanie's lifetime, in 1878 and 1904, even though it has been discredited and suppressed for over 100 years. One author relates that Reverend Garrigou-LaGrange wrote to him on September 1, 1957: "I am inclined to believe that Melanie remained faithful to her mission right up to her death," adding that he also believed her order was the fulfillment of St. Louis Grignon de Montfort's Apostles of the Last Times. [42]

Gnostics fit in well with the hodgepodge of Old Catholic believers, Rosicrucians, Theosophists, Freethinkers, Spiritists, and others. Regardless of their variations, however, Anson described all these groups as embracing the Gallican premise that championed bishops and faithful over the authority of the pope. He reported that it was Gnosticism that fueled reunionist activities (the attempts by the Anglicans in the 1800s to induce Rome to soften Her teachings and accept them back), noting that French Gnostics celebrated one of the first Roman Rite masses in the vernacular. Later, former Old Catholic bishops turned Liberal Catholic would celebrate a "magical" edition of mass in the vernacular (Sydney, Australia, 1917). These developments demonstrate that the Novus Ordo Missae wasn't nearly as new as its creators pretended and in fact already was in the process of adaptation shortly after its appearance among quasi-catholic sects. These are the very Old Catholics who left the Church following the definition of infallibility at the Vatican Council. Henry Cardinal Manning tells us that, like the French Constitutionalist church, this schism was a well-orchestrated conspiracy conceived between the dissident bishops and the German state before the council ever convened. The ultimate goal was to use the Old Catholics as the basis for a national German Church, a plan that succeeded only temporarily. [43]

Hugo Maria Kellner

It was Hugo Maria Kellner who in the 1970s first exposed the Masonic affiliation of Achille Lienart, who both ordained and consecrated Society of St. Pius X (SSPX) founder Marcel Lefebvre. Kellner held Lefebvre as invalidly ordained and consecrated, a claim the St. Pius X Society vehemently denies to this day. Lienart's Masonic affiliations were documented by Andre Henri Jean Marquis de la Franquerie, a papal Secret Chamberlain who lived in Lucon, Vendee, France, "a recognized, learned historian with special knowledge in the field of the penetration of the Catholic hierarchy by Freemasonry in France and of the Freemasonic activities of Cardinal Rampolla." These proofs are found on pages 80 and 81 of Franquerie's book, *L' Infallibilite Pontificale* [Papal Infallibility]. Kellner notes that Lefebvre admits he knew Lienart was a Freemason in his *The Final Unmasking of "Archbishop" Lefebvre's Satan*

Inspired "Traditionalist" Imposture by the Detection of the Invalidity of His Own Orders. [44]

Now, two months ago, in Rome, the traditionalist periodical *Chiesa Viva* [Living Church] published — I have seen it in Rome with my own eyes — on the back side of the cover, the photograph of Cardinal Lienart with all his Masonic paraphernalia, the day of the date of his inscription in Masonry... then the date at which he rose to the 20th, then to the 30th degree of Masonry, attached to this lodge, to that lodge — at this place, at that place. Meanwhile, about two or three months after this publication was made, I heard nothing about any reaction, or any contradiction. […]

The dates important for the judgment of the validity of the own Orders of Achille Lienart and Marcel Lefebvre are...

- Cardinal Achille Lienart, born in Lille, France February 7, 1884, ordained June 29, 1907
- Entered Masonic lodge at Cambrai 1912, "Visitor" in Masonry - 18th degree 1919, arrived at 30th degree 1924
- Was, before his consecration, professor in the priest seminary in Lille
- Consecrated bishop December 8, 1928
- Created cardinal by Pope Pius XI June 30, 1930
- [Marcel] Lefebvre, born in Tourcoing, Diocese of Lille, France November 29, 1905
- Attended the priest seminary in Lille in which Achille Lienart was professor
- Ordained by Bishop Lienart September 21, 1929
- Consecrated a bishop by Cardinal Lienart September 18, 1947

Dogmatic-canonical reasons for the invalidity of the consecration of Achille Lienart

One of the reasons why Marcel Lefebvre has to be regarded as an invalidly ordained priest and an invalidly consecrated bishop is the fact that the man who ordained and consecrated him, i.e., Achille Lienart, was himself an invalidly consecrated bishop. As is evident from the preceding table, Lienart was consecrated a bishop in 1928 at a time when he, after a 16-year membership in Freemasonry, had reached the thirtieth degree.

Here Kellner cites Canon Law, but misses many of its applications. First of all, given this information on his Masonic membership and its publication in various places without any refutation, Lienart would at least be a material heretic and outside the Church:

> Apostates, heretics and schismatics incur, on the ordinary conditions of full guilt, knowledge, etc., an excommunication specially reserved to the Holy See...All theologians teach that *publicly known heretics, that those who belong to a heterodox sect through public profession, or those who refuse the infallible teaching of the authority of the Church*, are excluded from the body of the Church, *even if their heresy is only material heresy.* [45]

Because only a bishop can create a priest — and as a Mason Lienart did not and could not possess the proper intention to be consecrated — he can be assumed to have never become a bishop. Ergo, Lefebvre never became a priest, either, far less a bishop. Did Lienart's status as a cardinal grant him immunity from censure in this matter? Since he was already a Freemason when created a cardinal, and guilty of a canonical irregularity (Canon 985),[46] the answer is "no." Canon 232 says such a person is barred from receiving the dignity of the cardinalate. And under Canon 188 §4, a cleric who has publicly lapsed from the Catholic faith *ipso facto* resigns his office. Lienart lapsed from the Catholic faith the minute he became a Mason, of whatever degree. Was his lapse public? Even if his Masonic initiation was not public, his acceptance of John 23, a false pope, certainly was. At any rate, since there is doubt in this matter, neither Lienart nor Lefebvre could ever be approached for the Sacraments (see below). And given such doubt, one must return to the old law that says anytime it is becomes clear that such a man is an apostate or heretic, all his acts performed while in office are null and void (*Cum ex Apostolatus Officio*, the old law cited under Canon 188 §4). Pope Pius IX says much the same in *Etsi Multa*, [47] quoted under disciplinary laws above. All the cardinals, in electing John 23, lost their offices once they subsequently accepted him.

Despite the SSPX's fierce denial of Lienart's inability to consecrate Lefebvre, or validly ordain him for that matter, the laws of the Church and papal decrees on this topic are clear. As noted above, it is no surprise that the SSPX spearheaded the attack on *Cum ex Apostolatus Officio* and has continued to oppose it for decades. Indeed, as Argentinian Professor Carlos Disandro reported in the 1970s, the SSPX even attempted to suppress it when he first printed the bull in 1978, rightly perceiving that the bull posed a grave threat to the validity of their sainted archbishop.

Kellner also, early on in the crisis in the Church, realized how Traditionalists intended to ambush the faithful, writing in this same letter:

> As I have proved in my article No. 70 of January 15, 1976, the apostasy of the almost complete Catholic Church 'organization' from true God-centeredness and God-centered morality following Vatican II was the concluding stage of the apostasy of mankind. This apostasy started on a worldwide basis with the Protestant 'Reformation' in the sixteenth century and will end according to the prophecies of Holy Scripture, with the annihilation of mankind. This annihilation is already ominously heralded by the nuclear weapons which are stocked by the military superpowers in quantities sufficient to destroy mankind hundreds of times over at any time.

> The 'traditionalists' in the apostate 'Catholic' church organization recognize correctly the falling away from the faith in the teachings of Vatican II, it is true, and they see correctly in the replacement of the Tridentine Mass by the Protestant 'Novus Ordo Missae' the liturgical expression of the falling away from the faith introduced by the Council.

But what they do not see in their incredible blindness agreeing with the blindness Scripturally predicted (St. Paul in 2 Thess. 2:10-12) is the apostatic character of this falling away from the faith which, according to Catholic doctrine, is irreversible (see, e.g., St. Paul in Hebr. 6:4-6) and is confirmed, e.g., by the fact that not one of the apostate Protestant sects has ever returned as a sect to the Catholic Church. They do not see the eschatological significance of this apostasy in the history of mankind. *They do not see or do not want to see, not even their theologically educated leaders, that this apostasy is the concluding stage of the revolt of mankind against God and His commandments predicted in Holy Scripture which started with the Protestant 'Reformation' in the sixteenth century and now will lead to the Scripturally predicted, punitive annihilation of mankind.* They are blind to the scientific fact known for several decades and, in recent years, discussed almost daily in the popular press, that this annihilation is unmistakably announced by the stockpiling of nuclear weapons by the military powers in quantities able to destroy mankind hundreds of times over, at any time.

The recognition of Paul VI as the legitimate pope of the Catholic Church by Lefebvre has a specific significance insofar as Paul VI is not any of the numerous devious 'popes' in Church history, but the illegitimate pope who brought the apostasy of mankind from God-centeredness and God-centered morality, which had started in the Protestant "Reformation" and then spread all over the earth, to a conclusion by causing, by his diabolic activities at Vatican II and in the post-conciliar time, the almost complete apostasy of Christ's Church, the last large, though already punctured bulwark of genuine devotion to God. In so doing, he introduced the eschatological time of the history of mankind (see St. Paul in 2 Thess.) whose reality is underlined by the terrible nuclear threat to humanity developed in the last decades. In the face of the unique role which Paul VI played in this unique situation of mankind and [the role his "successor"] still plays, *one hardly goes wrong by assuming that he is the Antichrist predicted in Holy Scripture. Lefebvre's recognition of Paul VI as the legitimate pope of the Catholic Church and the invalidity of his ordinations caused by it give to his activities a particularly ominous character in the eschatological history of the Church, as was already mentioned in the preamble to this article.*

...The standstill in the functioning of the Catholic Church predicted for the eschatological time of the history of mankind in the apocalyptic prophecy on the two 'witnesses' [Kellner identifies them as Pope Pius IX and Pope St. Pius X] is drawing to its end. This standstill started when, in agreement with the above-discussed apocalyptic prophecy, as a consequence of the Modernist apostasy of the whole Catholic Church organization after Vatican II, the main task of the Catholic Church, to act as the distributor of the redeeming graces of Christ, had ceased. This was mainly brought about by changes in the matter, form, and intention which are necessary for the performance of valid sacraments. The most important change consisted in the replacement of the Latin-Tridentine Mass by the sacramentally invalid 'Novus Ordo Missae.'

Satan's intentions to retain the non-apostatized Catholics in the apostate 'Catholic' church organization by the machinations of the 'traditionalist' leaders and, in so doing, *to prevent the organization of the Remnant Catholic Church* can obviously not be successful much longer. For, the apocalyptic prophecy on the two 'witnesses' to be identified with the popes Pius IX and Saint Pius X indicates that their teachings will, after their extinction by the vast eschatological apostasy from the faith, soon be revived and that, therefore, the functions of the Catholic Church after their temporary shutdown by the vast defection from the faith, will again be at the disposal of the remaining faithful Catholics in the Remnant Catholic

Church. This means that, in the near future, the collapse of [the] 'traditionalist' church has to be expected.

"The gates of hell shall not prevail against it."

But, because of the eschatological state of universal apostasy of mankind, the revived Catholic Church will be only an extremely small organization serving the few remaining true Catholics. For, only such a dwarf-like Church fits the words of Luke 18:8: "Yet when the Son of Man comes, will he find, do you think, faith on earth?" [48]

Lefebvre and his organization, however, was only the culmination of the successful campaign to subvert the Church, in motion for over 100 years. And as Craig Heimbichner observes below, Traditionalists were very much on the Masonic radar.

Craig Heimbichner

In his *Blood on the Altar*, [49] Craig Heimbichner agrees with Lejeune, writing the following concerning the infiltration of Freemasonry's Order of Oriental Templars (OTO) into Traditionalist ranks:

[The OTO] planted the seeds of destruction both on Christianity's Left wing (the 'ecumenists' and 'conciliarists') *as well as on its right wing,* (the 'traditionalists'), in a process known in alchemy as *coincidentia oppositorum,* ('coincidences of opposites'). Much has been written about occult infiltration coming from the Left; but most analysts have failed to investigate and expose subversion playing on right-wing tastes and affinities. Yet secret societies have a record of manipulating both sides of the human psyche and persona, shepherding those who crave egalitarianism and anarchy, as well as those who seek elite standards and authority. [50]

Heimbichner describes a book written by OTO author James Wasserman as "the opening of a new and daring public appeal to the American Right Wing." He notes that Wasserman openly praises the John Birch Society (JBS), although admitting he is not a member "for personal reasons," while endorsing its condemnation of Islamo-fascism. Like the JBS, Heimbichner explains, Wasserman seeks to focus the spotlight on organizations such as the UN, directing the reader's attention away from Freemasonry and the (more radical) elements of Judaism. Heimbichner concludes: "The OTO believes that the [JBS] is a highly useful tool for distracting attention away from Judaism to Islam, and away from Masonry to the United Nations." [51]

Heimbichner identifies many of those initially singing the praises of the Latin Tridentine Mass in the late 1960s and early 1970s as practicing theosophists, who succeeded in luring would-be traditionalists into "Latin Mass" groups. He links the awe for the old Mass to C.W. Leadbetter, founder of the Liberal Catholic (Theosophical) church in Sydney, Australia in 1917, citing several quotes proving that theosophic occultism later was introduced into Traditional circles. He quotes Wasserman as stating:

> Persons of Gnostic-hermetic interests have more in common with traditionalist Catholics than with either modernist Vatican II Catholics or with Protestants....The Right-wing exploits a superstition among some Catholics who hold to a kind of unspoken "magic sacramentalism," [condemned by Pope St. Pius X in his encyclical *Pascendi Domenici Gregis* against Modernism], i.e., the notion that being present at the Holy Mass itself, with its awe-inspiring solemnity and its bells, incense and candles, and not one's state of grace, fidelity to the Commandments of God or relationship with Jesus Christ — becomes the individual's guarantor of sanctity. [52]

Heimbichner calls this *a "Satanic perversion" of Catholicism,* mixing pagan elements with the true, much as is done in the Satanic rituals connected to Voodoo and Santeria. In a footnote to his work, Heimbichner notes:

> This writer and other investigators have compiled evidence of occult agents making inroads into the Traditional Mass movement in the U.S. in the past 12 years. [His work was

written in 2005; Lejeune, in her newsletter, *Sword of Truth*, and Comte Leon de Poncins had detected this trend much earlier written in the 1960s-80s.] It should be noted, however that many Traditional Catholics have — thus far — remained free of these connections and would be horrified if they were to learn of them. A similar struggle occurred in the Church centuries ago between advocates of the Council of Trent, from which the name 'Tridentine' is derived, and Renaissance-humanist advocates of a "Christian Kabbalah." [53]

(The popes, however, at least according to one source, never denied the existence of a benign Mosaic Kabbalah, which offered a correct perception of God-centered astronomy as it related to the Israelitic faith. It was the perversion of this astronomy and other Kabalistic teachings that Freemasonry would later appeal to in its use of the *false* Kabbalah.)

This perverse process of high level, alchemic Masonry is constructed so that the Left creates the crisis, the Right reacts, and the clean-up crew rushes in to "rescue" the survivors. Always the clean-up crew, then and now, was patiently waiting in the wings: the very ones riding to the rescue had anticipated the crisis all along. Moreover, they were trained to deal with it, to head it in a specific direction; and in reality, they are a hidden extension of the same people and organizations that the survivors ran from in the first place. It happened to the Church, and it is happening today. The first clean-up crew promoted religious conservatism with a political bent (Traditionalism) and the second, political conservatism with a "spiritual" outlook (as promoted by some Tea Party and patriot groups today). But Lejeune and others knew more than 30 years ago that the fight does not lie in the political ring.

Today, dear readers, we are in a spiritual battle, a death-struggle between the real Catholic Church and Satan himself and there isn't a political organization in existence today which can save the world — especially this country. The morals in this country today are so decadent that only the great chastisement from the hand of God can purify it…The chief cause of the immorality in our country today is that Catholics, among its citizenry, lost their way and adopted the secular ideas of the world. They have not listened to Our Lady of Fatima (she, who is the great foe of communism) when she pleaded for prayers, sacrifice and reparation for the sins of the world. [54]

Lejeune died in the 1980s. Thank God, she was spared witnessing the horrors of these past 35 plus years and has escaped the full fury of the Evil One, now ferociously venting the last vestiges of his vengeance on the world. The information that should have convinced Catholics early on that they indeed were witnessing the dreaded arrival of the Antichrist was readily available, but those who should have seen the truth were craftily rechanneled by neo-Modernists into believing that there was no real way to arrive at certainty concerning their true identity and the seriousness of the times in which they lived. Instead they were coerced into ignoring their best instincts and denying the necessity of the papacy and the apostolic authority structure of the Church as taught by Christ. In this William Strojie serves as a prophet, for as he predicted, indeed the lengths that Satan's henchmen would go to in order to seduce the remnant went far beyond anything those exiting the NO could anticipate or comprehend. And, as he also noted, while many Traditionalists believe that they embrace all the Catholic Church believes and teaches, they "do not long for Christ's return in this time of general apostasy but only for a return of the old parish." [55] Sadly, they forget that this world is not their true home, and Heaven is far preferable even to any restoration of the Church on earth.

C. The safer course: only the pope is infallible

St. Paul refers to Antichrist as "the lawless one." [56] Surely those who refuse to obey the laws of God and His Church are exhibiting the spirit of Antichrist. It may surprise those who believe themselves to be Catholic, but one of the requirements for Church membership as taught infallibly by Pope Pius XII is precisely such obedience to the law. This pope taught in the encyclical *Mystici Corporis*:

> Now since its Founder willed this social body of Christ to be visible, the cooperation of all its members must also be externally manifest through their profession of the same faith and their sharing the same sacred rites, through participation in the same Sacrifice, *and the practical observance of the same laws.* Above all, it is absolutely necessary that the Supreme Head, that is, the Vicar of Jesus Christ on earth, be visible to the eyes of all, since it is He who gives effective direction to the work which all do in common in a mutually helpful way towards the attainment of the proposed end. [57]

But as is clearly demonstrable, Traditionalists do not believe they are bound by many of the Canon Laws in the 1917 Code of Canon Law, or at least bound in the manner intended by the Church prior to Pope Pius XII's death. Their "clergy" continue to flaunt these laws and refuse to examine irrefutable proofs they are acting outside of what the popes often have referred to as "the Sacred Canons." As pointed out from many pre-1959 approved sources, most of Canon Law is founded on those laws emanating from papal documents and the teachings of the ecumenical councils, particularly the Council of Trent. This disregard for the law began long before the death of Pope Pius XII, as evidenced by the controversies addressed in periodicals such as the *American Ecclesiastical Review* and *Homiletic and Pastoral Review*, among others. So when even those who contested the ages-old application of the law in the 1950s agree that it most certainly binds where a doubt of law is concerned, this is especially compelling proof that in the case under discussion here, it does indeed bind as a matter of faith. Reverend Dominic Prummer, O.P., writes in his *Handbook of Moral Theology*:

> A doubtful law has no binding force whenever the doubt concerns the *lawfulness* of an act and not its *validity*. Whatever may be said about the truth of this principle, which is fiercely attacked by some theologians, *all modern theologians are agreed* that it cannot be applied in the following cases:
>
> a) When the doubt concerns *the validity of the Sacraments*;

b) When the doubt concerns something which is absolutely
necessary for salvation; so, for example, *when there is a risk of
losing eternal life, the safer opinion must be followed*;
c) When the question involves the established right of a third party.
Thus, for example, a judge would not be justified in giving
judgment on the basis of a probable opinion while refusing to
follow what is certainly the more probable opinion. [58]

Reverend Amleto Cicognani discusses the canon law that most
Traditionalists cite to justify dismissing a doubtful law as non-
binding:

> All laws, including invalidating and disqualifying laws,
> lose their force in a case of [a doubtful law or fact] ...
> Doubt may exist with respect to the law or the fact. It is a
> doubt of law when it concerns the existence, the force, the
> extent, or the cessation of the law. It is a doubt of fact
> when aware of the existence of the law, I hesitate
> concerning some circumstance or fact thereof.... Doubt is
> positive when there are reasons now for affirming and
> again for denying, but the intellect can form no judgment
> since the reasons more or less mutually destroy their initial
> force. Doubt is objective...when there is something in the
> nature of things to respond to the doubt existing in the
> mind.... This canon is concerned with positive and
> objective doubt either of the law or of the fact, and not with
> negative doubt [when no reason can be found to support
> either proposition], or subjective doubt [when neither a
> doubtful law or fact exists, i.e., ignorance]. [59]

Here Cicognani refers the reader to Canon 16 on ignorance. He
continues:

> The present canon is not concerned with doubts about the
> Divine law or those regarding the matter and form of the
> Sacraments. These points we leave to Moral Theology
> [and]... Probabilism...The inscription of this title of the
> Code is *Ecclesiastical Laws,* and of these, alone therefore,
> do we speak. [60]

Cicognani then goes on to cite what Prummer states in his *Handbook of Moral Theology* quoted above. So Traditionalists cannot pretend that Canon 15 can be invoked to excuse them. Certainly the laws exist, and as seen above from St. Alphonsus Liguori, are presumed to continue.

In *Tuas Libentur* (December 21, 1863; DZ 1683) Pope Pius IX teaches that faith and obedience

> must not be limited to those matters which have been defined by express decrees of the ecumenical Councils, or of the Roman Pontiffs of this See, but would have to be extended also to those matters which are handed down as divinely revealed by the ordinary teaching power of the whole Church spread throughout the world, and therefore, by universal and common consent, are held by Catholic theologians to belong to faith. [61]

And the very validity of the Sacraments, instituted by Christ, most definitely belongs to the faith. Monsignor J. C. Fenton writes:

> "When the entire body of scholastic theologians asserts that some thesis is of Catholic faith, their testimony is absolutely reliable. Because of the particular function of the scholastics, if all of them should be in error on a point of this kind, then the Catholic Church would be deceived.... Their unanimous testimony to the effect that a definite doctrine is to be accepted by all with the assent of divine faith mirrors the teaching of the Church itself. [It] must be reckoned in the same way as that of the Church Fathers." [62]

Pope Pius XII would later infallibly reiterate this same teaching in *Humani Generis*.

Moreover, a decree of the Holy Office issued March 4, 1679 under Blessed Pope Innocent XI condemned the proposition: "It is not illicit in conferring Sacraments to follow a probable opinion, regarding the value of the Sacrament, the safer opinion being abandoned...." [63] This teaching was later sanctioned outright by Pope Benedict XIV in his bull, *Solicita et Provide.* [64]

Returning to the citation from Prummer above, in reference to a), the Church already has condemned the use of a probable opinion regarding the validity of the Sacraments and her theologians reflect that condemnation in their unanimous and common consent.

Regarding b), Catholics must revert to the decree of Boniface VIII: "We declare, say, define and proclaim *to every human creature* that by *necessity for salvation* they are *entirely subject* to the Roman Pontiff." [65] Being *entirely* subject to the Roman Pontiff means obeying all the popes have taught in these matters, not only in those things strictly of faith or morals but also the following:

> Since it is not sufficient to shun heretical iniquity unless these errors also are shunned which come more or less close to it, we remind all of the duty of observing also the constitutions and decrees by which base opinions of this sort, which are not enumerated explicitly here have been proscribed and prohibited by this Holy See. [66]

This was reiterated in Pope Pius XII's *Humani Generis.* So if anyone doubts that we are required to obey the popes even when they define something only to be held as an opinion, or as certain, then that doubt is resolved by Boniface VIII's decree above: "by necessity for salvation." Monsignor Fenton notes this in his own works as well. We are to follow the safer opinion if we wish to be saved. For it is safer in these circumstances to take ALL the popes say as binding until further notice and follow it than to play pick and choose with the opinions of the "new" theologians of the late 1950s and Traditional "clerics." To safeguard the deposit of faith and the rights of the Church, Pope Pius XII infallibly <u>commands</u> us to admit nothing that violates Church law or usurps papal jurisdiction during an interregnum, (*Vacantis Apostolicae Sedis*).

Regarding the established rights of third parties mentioned by Prummer under (c) in the above quotation, some explanation is required.

Doesn't Canon Law say we have a *right* to request Mass and Sacraments?

Traditionalists maintain that they have a right to the spiritual goods of the Church; but in fact, only those who are certain that they were validly baptized Catholic have the right to such a request. Any doubt concerning valid baptism voids that right, and those baptized in the Novus Ordo or by Traditionalists have every right to question the validity of their baptisms, which were illicit at best (Canon 87). For we must and we do demand here a definition of exactly *what* church those being baptized were indeed baptized into, and how such a church could possibly be Catholic when neither were headed by a true pope or valid and licit hierarchy. A baptism is valid only if the intent is to baptize that person into the Catholic Church as she was understood to exist up until the death of Pope Pope Pius XII. And how many Traditional and NO "priests" (*very* few) believed Pope Pius XII was the last true pope? How many of them understand the true teachings of that Church as the Church Herself taught and understood them?!

At the very least there would be a question as to whether the one baptizing truly understood the Church in this way, making it necessary for those not certainly baptized to be conditionally baptized.[67] Regarding the rights of the validly baptized faithful to the Sacraments, according to Canon 467, the people can ask only a *lawful* minister for the Sacraments, and only then if they themselves (lay persons requesting the sacraments) have not incurred a censure of excommunication. (Canon 682 says these rights are operable only "according to the rules of ecclesiastical discipline." See also DZ 960 and 967,[68] repeated in Canon 109 and appended by Pope Pius XII to Canon 147, with a *speciali modo* excommunication attached). The law is clear about those who "come from a different source"[69] and do not hold an office by "canonical appointment" (Canon 147).[70] It is lawfulness that is important in this particular case, the Council of Trent teaches, NOT validity.

In order to operate *lawfully*, even a validly ordained priest must be able to produce proofs of current, verifiable jurisdiction (Canon 200) and proof of an assignment to a diocese and parish by "competent ecclesiastical authority" (Canon 147). He must hold an office to receive delegated jurisdiction from a validly consecrated bishop, which expires and must be renewed every few years or so. Canon Law, as prescribed by Pope Innocent III and two ecumenical councils, teaches that without an office he can say Mass *only privately* (Canon 804).

> The Council of Trent again made the rule *absolute* — as the Council of Chalcedon had it — that no priest should be permitted to celebrate Mass and administer the Sacraments without letters of recommendation *from his own bishop*.... Pope Innocent III issued the same prohibition, but said that the priest who did not have his letters of recommendation might be admitted to celebrate Mass if he desired to do so out of devotion: *he might not, however, say Mass before the people, but privately.* [71]

This should answer all the questions and any objections Catholics might have concerning who holds lawful authority over them and how it is held. It is a demonstration of that very theological reasoning demanded by the popes throughout the ages regarding the scholastic method of St. Thomas Aquinas, as echoed here by Monsignor Fenton. The Popes alone have the right to specify and decide what we are to believe, not wandering priests or bishops not in communion with the true pontiff. As Pope Pius IX taught in *Noscitis et Nobiscum* paragraph 17:

> Indeed, one simple way to keep men professing Catholic truth is to maintain their communion with and obedience to the Roman Pontiff. For it is impossible for a man ever to reject any portion of the Catholic faith without abandoning the authority of the Roman Church. In this authority, the unalterable teaching office of this faith lives on. [72]

The teaching of these vicars appointed by Christ is eternal, which is why we call the papacy throughout the ages the continual magisterium. The teaching of theologians is trustworthy only if they adhere to the scholastic method, are approved by the Holy See, and echo the teachings of the magisterium. Prior to the "election" of the false pope John 23, the administrative machinery existed in the Church to determine if this was the case; today it does not. This is why the wealth of teaching found in papal documents, readily available on the Internet, are the faithful's surest guarantee of salvation and the only real recourse Catholics have today.

But the Council of Trent Catechism says
we will always have the Mass

The Catechism of the Council of Trent cannot contradict Holy Scripture. The following is often erroneously quoted to prove that the Mass will never cease and that those who believe it has ceased are wrong.

> This mystery, therefore, the pastor will carefully explain to the people, that when assembled at its celebration, they may learn to make it the subject of attentive and devout meditation. He will teach, in the first place, that the Eucharist was instituted by our Lord for two great purposes, to be the celestial food of the soul, preserving and supporting spiritual life, and to give to the Church a perpetual sacrifice, by which sin may be expiated, and our heavenly Father, whom our crimes have often grievously offended, be turned from wrath to mercy, from the severity of just vengeance to the exercise of benignant clemency. Of this the paschal lamb, which was offered and eaten by the Israelites as a sacrament and sacrifice, was a lively figure. Nor could our divine Lord, when about to offer himself to his eternal Father on the altar of the cross, have given a more illustrious proof of his unbounded love for us, than by bequeathing to us a visible sacrifice, by which the bloody sacrifice, which, a little after, was to be offered once on the cross, was to be renewed, and its memory celebrated daily throughout the universal Church even to the consummation of time, to the great advantage of her children. [73]

This does not say that the Mass could not cease for a time (the time of Antichrist) then resume when/if the Church is restored. Most stay-at-home Catholics believe that they are living in the end times and Antichrist already has come. Cardinal Manning teaches in his lectures on Antichrist that it is the unanimous opinion of the Fathers, hence infallible, [74] that the Holy Sacrifice will cease during the reign of Antichrist. St. Alphonsus teaches that in reality the Mass and priesthood will never cease, since, "the Son of God, Eternal Priest, will always continue to offer Himself to God, the Father, in Heaven as an Eternal Sacrifice." [75] Most Traditionalists place Antichrist and the cessation of the Sacrifice in the remote future, or hold that the Mass will only cease publicly, not privately, (as if their masses, held in public places of worship and advertised in newspapers and periodicals are not public). They condemn those they denigrate as "homealoners" for obeying the command to follow the Fathers and St. Thomas Aquinas and for refusing to accept clergy sent by the people and their representatives, not the Pope — another clear teaching of Trent.

Those who refuse to join Traditionalists in false worship are castigated for uniting their prayers with that Heavenly altar described by St. Alphonsus; something the ancient Fathers also recommended when unable to participate in the Holy Sacrifice. Reverend Maurice de la Taille explains St. Alphonsus' statement by reminding us that in Heaven, the Sacrifice is not renewed, for there the resurrected Christ stands as Altar, Victim and Priest. "The altar of Holocausts is the Body of Christ...The Lord says to Moses (Lev. 6:13): 'This is the perpetual fire which shall never go out on the altar. For God is a spirit, and they that adore Him must adore Him in spirit and in truth.'" [76]

St. Gregory Nazianzus, after being expelled unjustly from his office of bishop, bids us to approach this divine altar. He writes in the fourth century:

> I know of another altar.... All activities about that altar are spiritual and one ascends to it by contemplation. At this altar I will stand, upon it I shall make immolations to God

— sacrifices, oblations and holocausts *better than are offered now,* just as truth is better than the shadow of truth.... Let us immolate ourselves to God in every action of ours, every day of our lives. Let us accept all things for the sake of the Word. Let us eagerly ascend to the Cross itself. [77]

(And this from a bishop who made many converts and regularly offered the Holy Sacrifice, but understood the inestimable value of the contemplative life.)

Likewise, St. Cyprian wrote in the early centuries, commenting on the condition of those condemned to the mines:

Neither in this can any loss of religion or of faith be sustained, that amongst you liberty is not now granted to the priests of God to offer and celebrate the Divine sacrifice. Yea, do ye celebrate and offer to God both precious and glorious, and which will avail you exceedingly towards obtaining the recompense of the heavenly rewards, seeing that...Scripture declares, '*A sacrifice to God is an afflicted spirit; a contrite and humble heart God will not despise.*'"

Reverend de la Taille queries,

Who is that sinless priest, offerer of a sinless Victim, but the man who firmly professes his faith and attains to a perfect martyrdom? For by martyrdom we are brothers and kinsfolk of the Lamb St. John saw lying on the altar. We are worthy in consequence to stand thereat... The holy martyrs who shed their blood are, with good reason, seen by John standing at the celestial altar. For there, under the altar of God, the souls of the martyrs are said to abide... In this abode they assist at the Divine sacrifices. [78]

Those who call themselves catacomb or stay-at-home Catholics recite the Mass prayers or the Consecration prayers (St. John's Mass, as promoted by Reverend Mateo Crawley-Boevey in *Jesus King of*

Love and also by Reverend Leo McNamara, who died in 1973); they say their Perfect Act of Contrition in place of confession and make frequent acts of Spiritual Communion. They unite themselves to any and all valid masses now being offered privately throughout the world. They are faithful to their Rosary and make use of all the many prayers left to them by the Church. They offer themselves and their inability to attend Mass and receive the Sacraments as a perpetual holocaust to God and in willing obedience to His holy will for these times. They do this out of their love for God and His laws and to avoid all that could possibly involve them in sacrilege or communication with non-Catholics, which results in loss of Church membership. The lives they lead and the prayers they offer have every hallmark of a "memory celebrated daily" that is mentioned in *The Catechism of the Council of Trent* quote above. And this is not the only time in history God's people have been without true clergy who could avail them of their services and teach them the truth.

Stay-at-home (Catacomb) Catholics

Has the flock ever appeared to be abandoned before in the history of Scripture, outside the three days that followed Christ's death on the Cross? Yes it has, in the time prior to Christ's birth. Does anyone ever wonder how the faithful Jews survived their captivity during the Babylonian exile without the Temple and the Ark? How did they keep their faith? Was their priesthood destroyed? As we read from Scripture: "You are in error because you know neither the Scriptures nor the power of God." [79]

The Old Testament prefigured our own time. The historian Reverend Henri Daniel-Rops ably demonstrates this, relating:

> The Chosen People accomplished, during their exile, a remarkable effort of fidelity. The rites proper to Jahweh's worship were strictly observed: Circumcision, rest on the Sabbath, commemoration of the Passover. The priests, who had no longer a Temple, as their cult could only be practiced on holy ground, were held in high respect. The faithful grouped themselves about them and their places of meeting became synagogues. [80]

> A veritable caste of jurists and scribes was constituted, for the purpose of tending the law — arduous upholders of the more rigorous observance... In their exile the Chosen People had recognized the punishment of their faults and resolved to expiate them. *The 'return' so greatly desired was in the first place a return to God.* [81]

It was under Cyrus, the Great King, that the Babylonian Jews finally returned to Palestine from their exile; and it was Cyrus whom God told to rebuild the Temple (Isaias 44:28 and 45:1). Daniel-Rops writes:

> To rebuild the Temple — what did that mean? In the religious conception that the Prophets had introduced, the real Temple of God is interior; its sanctuary is situated in the hearts of the saints... 'This is the one whom I approve: the lowly and afflicted man who trembles at my word' (Isaias 66: 1-2). [82]

Christ would later tell His apostles: "The kingdom of God is within you." Could Daniel-Rops say of Traditionalists today what he said of the Jews — that they "Accomplished...a remarkable effort of fidelity"? That they are "arduous upholders" of the Law? That they have "recognized our faults" and expiated them? Yes, the Jews had their priests; no analogy or prefiguration is perfect. But notice what those ancient priests did: They taught the people in the synagogues; they did not dare offer sacrifices. They observed the Law. And it is certain that these priests were descended from the Levitic line, so carefully documented and preserved.

After Vatican 2, those validly ordained priests who never celebrated the Novus Ordo could have done the very same — they could have offered Mass alone privately and taught and prayed with the people publicly. A scarce few who were "granted permission" to say the Latin Mass when the Novus Ordo Missae was introduced did say it privately, in their monasteries or in hiding. But the rest of their fellow priests chose to contravene the Law; they failed to recognize the "signs of the times" — the advent of Antichrist — and they neglected to implore the faithful to expiate their sins and make reparation like the prophets of old. While it may gall Catholics to hear it, the Israelites were more faithful to God by far in their day of trial than Traditionalists are today.

How Catholics kept their Faith without clergy

The first mention of "house churches" is found in Acts and mention of them is made throughout the epistles. [83] It is suspected there were many others beside those that are actually mentioned. So given this precedent, why is it that Traditionalists have such disdain for this practice? What they should fear is the penalty for associating with non-Catholics, that is, Traditionalist "clerics." This sin (*communicatio in sacris*, i.e., communication with heretics or schismatics in divine worship, prayers, services) has been punished with excommunication and infamy of law since the earliest ages of the Church. [84] While some seem to believe that their allegiance to Traditionalist clergy somehow does not fall under this classification, what is explained below will demonstrate that it is no different than any other deviation from the faith found in former ages, and in actuality is remarkably akin to all previous deviations.

Because the Church never changes, Traditionalists reading these pages should ask themselves: How do our actions today differ from what Catholics refused to do 1,500, 500, 400, 200 or 75 years ago?! And since this is the common practice of the Church, what possible excuse could anyone have for deviating from it? Whether in England in the 1500s, Japan in the 1600s, France in the 1700s, or Communist Russia in the last century, those faced with returning to paganism, Protestantism, or the Orthodox church chose persecution and death rather than compromise their faith. Their fidelity and heroism are absent today.

Some object they cannot "judge" those men heretics for functioning as priests and bishops after having celebrated the NO and/or being involved in other Traditionalist groups. But there is no judgment involved; the censures for *communicatio in sacris* and heresy/schism are *latae sententiae* — *ipso facto* — meaning that the Church already has judged these men. Does a declaration need to be issued for the censure to bind? Not in the case of notorious heresy or schism, Reverends Ayrinhac and Woywod-Smith aver, for the law itself imposes the censures, binding the offender from the moment the crime is committed. [85] Are there excusing factors? Canon 2200 states that culpability is presumed in the external forum until the competent ecclesiastical authorities determine otherwise, and unfortunately none of these authorities exist. The gravity of the offense is judged by the external act itself, and the sacrilegious administration of sacraments is unquestionably a very serious violation, involving contempt of faith. "An ecclesiastical office cannot be validly obtained without canonical appointment. By canonical appointment is understood the conferring of an ecclesiastical office by the competent ecclesiastical authority in harmony with the sacred canons." [86] In accepting John 23 as a true pope and participating in the false V2 council, all the bishops following him tacitly resigned their offices for publicly lapsing from the Catholic faith. [87] Having so resigned, they lost all jurisdiction. None of these "bishops" ever formally abandoned the Novus Ordo nor their Traditionalist positions, renounced their errors and made reparation. Therefore, they are considered obstinate in their errors and guilty of the censures incurred.

Those attending Traditional services today need to consider the following: the entire state of affairs in the Church since the death of Pope Pius XII has left many in doubt about numerous Church laws and teachings. Without a true pope, there is no possible way to determine the answers to many things; we remain in doubt, although generally we can arrive at the certitude sufficient to reason out our faith and function in our daily lives. So what is the rule about doubt taught in moral theology? One cannot act when in a state of doubt until the doubt is resolved; Reverend Cicognani explains this above. The notion that one may ignore such doubts before proceeding to act was condemned by Pope Innocent XI as heretical. [88] While certitude can be arrived at in most cases, this is not true concerning the Sacraments, as seen in the preceding section. The entire purpose of this work has been to dispel those doubts and to demonstrate that Catholics must realize that without a pope there IS no visible or juridical Church; and the only time this will happen is during the reign of Antichrist. Unless the integral teachings of the continual magisterium throughout the centuries are followed, then we cannot claim to be Catholic. There are specific practices set out for Catholics who determine they must keep the faith at home, and these will be detailed in a soon-to-be released work.

Traditionalists claim that the Perfect Act of Contrition will not suffice for the forgiveness of sins, but then neither will their sins be forgiven by "priests" lacking supplied or any other type of jurisdiction. Pope Pius XII teaches in *Humani Generis* that we can believe the constant teaching of the theologians in catechisms and other theological works on these matters, and they all affirm that both a Perfect Act of Contrition and Spiritual Communion are sufficient for salvation when the Sacraments are not available. Nor do we need to give any credence to the accusations that Catacomb Catholics deny the indefectibility and perpetuity of the Church as it was constituted by Christ in saying there currently are no perceptible bishops. Bishops exist somewhere, even if hidden or unknown to anyone but God Himself. In fact, some believe these bishops could even be Enoch and Elias, described as the two candlesticks standing before the Lord (a term used to refer to bishops) in St. John's Apocalypse, according to St. Augustine. [89] Those keeping their faith at home firmly and without reservation believe that Christ will be true to His promises that the gates of Hell will not prevail, and the Church will last unto the consummation. Most believe the Church, as predicted by Our Lady at Fatima, will enjoy a brief period of peace and complete restoration prior to the Final Judgment. They simply do not pretend to know exactly how Our Lord will accomplish this. For more on this topic, see Chapter XIII below.

Finally, had validly ordained priests offered Mass privately and focused on teaching and training Catholics to function in such lay positions following Vatican 2, instructing them on how to remain Catholic without Mass and Sacraments, they could have provided the Church with a way to survive this crisis. Had they done so, those exiting the Novus Ordo church would never have fallen for Traditionalism. But that was never the plan.

Pope St. Pius X taught:

> All those who are pastors of souls...are certainly obliged by the precept of Christ to know and nourish the sheep confided to them; now to *nourish* is first of all to *teach*.... And so the Apostle said, "Christ sent me *not to baptize, but to preach the Gospel*," indicating thus that the first office of those who are set up in any way for the government of the Church is to *instruct in sacred doctrine.* [90]

This is yet another *rare, papal definition of Holy Scripture,* which condemns the false Traditionalist interpretation and application of "the means necessary for salvation," i.e. for them the Mass and Sacraments only. As Reverend Louis Billot teaches in his *De Ecclesia Christi, "Theological faith* is more necessary still than the Sacraments, since nothing can replace it, whereas those who possess it already possess the Sacraments as by desire, *voto.*" And Monsignor Fenton described Billot as one of the Church's most prestigious theologians.

As painful as it is for Traditionalists, they must admit that their leaders are pseudo-priests and bishops. In any prayer book or catechism, Catholics may find the form of valid Baptism and the injunction of the Church that in an emergency, when no clergy are available, any man, woman, or child can and should baptize those in danger of death. We also have substitute Sacraments — the Perfect Act of Contrition and Spiritual Communion, to replace Confession and the reception of the Holy Eucharist; also the emergency laws for marriage enacted by Pope Pius XI and Pius XII remove all need for dispensations and the presence of a priest (although no one knew until only the last decade that these laws could be invoked in the present situation). All the other Sacraments are not, strictly speaking, necessary for salvation. So why didn't Catholics know about the marriage laws and the substitutes for the other Sacraments? Because Traditional "shepherds" did not teach them. Although they pass themselves off as genuine theologians, the truth is they probably didn't know many of these things themselves. They kept insisting Catholics must come to *them* for the Sacraments, that without them they would lose their souls. Funny that they never mentioned Catholics losing their souls for lack of instruction in the faith and obedience and subjection to the Roman Pontiff!

Those maintaining their faith at home are lonely, afraid, tired, discouraged, and at their wits end much of the time. Many feel abandoned and are burdened with illnesses, financial problems, marital problems, problems with their children, and other woes. All of them have unique crosses to bear and the only way to bear them is to look to Calvary. But they are not without help. The popes continue to guide them, rule them, and assist them with their infallible teachings; and as one stay-at-home Catholic observed, in this way the reign of Pope Pius XII is extended indefinitely, since it is he himself who contributed so generously to Catholics' knowledge base of the faith. It is for Catholics today to put this legacy to use and to do all in their power to preserve what remains until the chastisement, the sudden restoration of the Church, or the coming of the Lord. Papal teaching is eternal; its source is Christ himself. That is the sum total of all that has been said above. As long as those teachings are read and understood; as long as Catholics believe that the papacy will one day be restored, or barring that, that Christ Himself must come to judge the living and the dead because His Church has ceased to exist, then the Church has existed and will continue to exist until the end of time.

D. The call to Catholic Action

There is a reason why the Church on earth is called the Church Militant. The word militia is derived from militant, which Webster's Seventh Collegiate Dictionary, 1941, defines as "engaged in warfare; aggressively active." So where might we find this "aggressively active" Church today? Certainly not among the ranks of Traditionalists; and sadly, not even among those who claim allegiance to the Pope with their lips yet deny it by their actions, or more specifically their entrenched *inaction*. Today the Church could be classified as the Church Milquetoast, but not the Church Militant. This is a sad commentary on the failure of Catholics to live up to the expectations set for them by the popes who repeatedly urged the faithful to engage in Catholic Action.

Before he was elected pope, Pope St. Pius X (then Giuseppe Cardinal Sarto) delivered the following speech to Italian youth in the late 1800s:

> Catholic Action is directed toward the defense of and revindication of the rights of the Roman Pontiff, who is to the Church of Jesus Christ what the head is to the body, what the foundation is to the building, for where the Pope is there is the Church. *The more open the war against the Pope is the more active, the more resolute should Catholic Action be in defending and maintaining the inviolable rights of the Sovereign Pontiff....* Catholic Action is properly lay in character for another reason also, which is obvious even to the most undiscerning, but which must not be forgotten. At one time the rights of Jesus Christ, of the Church and of the Pope entered into the legislation of all Christian states, and no one dared to deny to the hierarchy, the Church and the Pope those immunities and those privileges which they received from Christ, recognized by so many centuries of State law.

> Now it is no longer so. The Church, the Pope are no longer recognized as such and no longer form part of the social organism; they are relegated to the sphere of common rights; nay, they are even considered as enemies; they are ranked with evildoers. Since these things are so, who is it that must bestir himself to defend the violated rights and insulted dignity of the Pope, the Bishops and the Church? In other times, it was the Pope and Bishops who intervened in the defense of their children, threatened by the savage invasions of the barbarians; today it must be the children who will rise up in defense of their Father, the laity in defense of the Hierarchy.... *Catholic Action has been commanded by the Pope*, who has signified his mind in so many ways, and that is enough for us to be sure that it is the will of God also. One would need, then, a pretty dose of temerity and pride to say that a work which has been

commanded by the Pope and is the will of God is useless
and of no avail..." [91]

Catholics, then, are not encouraged, but rather are *commanded* by the
popes to engage in some form of Catholic Action. Many examples of
commands issued by the popes have been recorded here, and now
such commands cannot be ignored. Pope Benedict XV reminded
Catholics: "Hence, therefore, whenever *legitimate authority* has once
given a *clear command*, let no one transgress that command, because
it does not happen to commend itself to him" [92] (see also Canon
2331). And not only did the Vatican Council, Pope Pius IX, Pope
Leo XIII, and Pope St. Pius X command Catholic Action, but so also
did all the popes of the 20th century.

Catholic Action as enjoined by the Church

Pope Pius XII defined Catholic Action as "the first and essential
duty of personal sanctification combined with an intense apostolic
activity." And today, how many have barely begun this task of
personal sanctification, or begun it at all? How far down the road of
their life's journey have they traveled without beginning or
accelerating this most essential task? And, this being the case, is it
even possible that they will be fit to participate in Catholic Action
before they appear before God for their Private Judgment? This is
especially true of older Catholics no longer strictly bound by duties
to family and home. How they spend their remaining years most
certainly will determine their eternal destination. Yet how few seem
to realize that neglect of this "intense apostolic activity" commanded
by the popes could result in the loss of their souls?

The Apostolic Nuncio to Australia, Monsignor Romolo Carboni,
directed by and answerable only to Pope Pius XII, has commented
further on the formation necessary to commence Catholic Action.

> Prayer and adequate intellectual formation are
> indispensable requisites to any efficacious apostolate....
> There are, unfortunately, many who fritter away their
> leisure time in a round of sports or social life, in pleasure,
> laziness and ease, while the world is crashing about our

ears. (Catholics) are called by their Baptism to be apostles. This is a basic and universal duty insisted on by the Popes. [93]

Carboni goes onto explain that the immediate aim of Catholic Action is "the education of minds and formation of conscience… (this group must be) intimately acquainted with the doctrine of the Church." And according to Pope Pius XI, such groups "will assuredly be served by study circles, conferences, and lecture courses." While Carboni admits that not all have the aptitude to be "intensely" active lay apostles, he does not excuse even busy wives and mothers or working fathers of families from contributing to Catholic Action in some routine and meaningful way. This is consistent with the teachings of Pope Pius XI on this topic, who declared: "Catholic Action is almost as indispensable as the priestly ministry: all should contribute to it at least a minimum" (December 4, 1924). Pope Pius XII urged wives and mothers of families to promote Catholic Action in general, not only in the family circle, stating:

> The Apostolic See simply does not tolerate your action: it enjoins you to exercise the apostolate, to devote your efforts to fulfilling the Christian's great missionary duty, that all the lost sheep may be assembled in one fold… Individual initiative has its place along with action that is organized and applied through various associations. This initiative of the lay apostolate is perfectly justified even without a prior explicit 'mission' from the hierarchy… You must reject every attitude of passive acceptance or indifference, every form of apathetic quietism… Especially in countries where contacts with the hierarchy are difficult or practically impossible, the Christians upon whom this task falls, must with God's grace, assume all their responsibilities [the hierarchy's]…. Even so, nothing can be undertaken against the explicit and implicit will of the Church, or contrary in any way to the rules of *faith and morals or to ecclesiastical discipline.* [94]

In a speech to Australian Third Order Members in 1955, Monsignor Carboni further addressed the apathetic quietism that affected so many Catholics even prior to Vatican 2, imploring them as follows:

> I beg you, I pray of you, to become true leaders of a great reawakening to the demands of our Christian vocation. Awaken your fellows from their unchristian apathy; stir them from their lifeless indolence, their anemic inertness, and their terrifying passiveness. Awaken them from their 'fatal lethargy,' as Pope Pius XII has described it, lest that lethargy should become the death to freedom and to faith.[95]

Pope Pius XI prophetically described what would happen if such lethargy were not overcome. "All who do not want anarchy and *terrorism* to replace decent civilization should line up with the forces of Catholic Action." We have merited both plagues today because the popes' commands have been ignored. Pope Pius XI also taught that the omission of this vital duty of Catholic Action could bind under pain of serious sin. He wrote: "All are bound to collaborate in spreading the Kingship of Christ, since all are the favored subjects of this tender King.... To exempt oneself is a *sin of omission,* which, in certain cases, could be *serious.*" And elsewhere, "Catholic Action is nothing else than the exercise of Christian charity, which is obligatory upon all men," (Discourse of September 29, 1927). It should then come as no surprise that Pope Pius XII's address above to Catholic women is a binding document, for it is listed in the *Acta Apostolica Sedis*, 49: 906-922, November 22, 1957. As stated above, this indicates the address was intended by the pope to be part of his authoritative teaching, delivered in the ordinary magisterium. Catholics know this from the infallible encyclical *Humani Generis*, which clearly indicates what constitutes "normative" pronouncements of the Roman Pontiff. It may be only an address, it may seem innocuous enough, but Pius XII was telling us something important here, and its inclusion in the *Acta* is proof of this.

Conclusion

Remnant Catholics held the tools in their hands but failed to use them to rebuild the Church. They let others — "priests," "bishops" and misinformed lay leaders — convince them they could not act because Church law forbids it. True, they were deluded and deceived. But had they better studied their faith, they would have known the mind and intention of the Roman Pontiffs, especially the intention of the last true pontiff expressed so clearly in the above addresses. These priceless instructions gave them the mandate they needed to continue practicing their faith, to defend it and propagate it. Staying at home is not enough; obedience to *all* papal decrees as well as Canon Law — which only reflects the mind of the Papacy — is required of Catholics if they wish to remain members of the Church. And as Pope Pius XI points out, we are bound under the laws of Catholic charity to exercise this apostolate. True Catholics could still choose to do so, and if they do not at least begin upon such a course immediately, they may see even the last vestiges of faith slip from their hands. There are many ways open to the faithful to perpetuate the teachings of the Popes and Councils; they have only to search them out and devise a way to apply them. But unless the Church Militant becomes the army it was intended to be, not only the Church, but the country as well will fall. For as Cardinal Pie so wisely said, "Everything must crumble that is not grounded on the one cornerstone which is Christ Jesus."

We seem to exist in that time period between the death of Antichrist and the Final Judgment. No one knows for an absolute certainty whether Christ will somehow miraculously restore his Church on earth or simply bring an abrupt end to this world, saturated with the spirit of impurity, given over to Satanic pride, and careening toward a violent and sudden demise. When Our Lord comes, our lamps must remain lit in this chaotic darkness to greet Him; we cannot succumb to the quietistic impassivity Pope Pius XII warns against. No one knows the day nor the hour, but saints and holy people have left a wealth of indicators regarding what we may expect and what might happen in the meantime. While private prophecy is never to be trusted over dogma, so many prophecies predicting the same outcome cannot be ignored either. The final chapter of this work will explore what may lie ahead and what we can reasonably expect.

Chapter XII Endnotes

[1] St. Thomas Aquinas, *Summa Contra Gentilis*, Vol. IV, Salvation, Image Books, a division of Doubleday and Co., Garden City, New York, 1957, Ch. 76 (3)

[2] Rev. W. Devivier, S.J., Rev. Joseph C. Sasia, S.J., *Christian Apologetics*, Vol. II, Joseph Wagner, Inc., New York, N.Y., and London, 1924, 17-24

[3] *Papal Teachings: The Church*, by the Monks of Solesmes, translated by Mother E. O'Gorman, St. Paul Editions, 1962; no. 1115, 581-82

[4] Editors and translators John F. Clark, S.J., John H. Edwards, S.J., William Kelly, S.J., and John J. Welch, S.J., *The Church Teaches, Documents of the Church in English Translation*, St. Mary's College, St. Marys, Kan., reprinted by TAN Books and Publishers, Rockford Ill., 1973, 92

[5] Ibid., 86-87

[6] (Revs. McHugh and Callan edition, 104)

[7] Henry Denzinger, *The Sources of Catholic Dogma*, 30th Edition, Marian House, Powers Lake, N.D., 1957, DZ 1686

[8] Rev. E. Sylvester Berry, *The Church of Christ*, B. Herder Book Co., London and New York, N.Y., 1927, 95

[9] Rev. W. Devivier, S.J., Rev. Joseph C. Sasia, S.J., *Christian Apologetics*, Vol. II, Joseph Wagner, Inc., New York, N.Y., and London, 1924, 111

[10] Allocution to religious superiors, June 24, 1872; *Papal Teachings: The Church*, by the Monks of Solesmes, translated by Mother E. O'Gorman, St. Paul Editions, 1962; no. 391, p. 226

[11] http://www.betrayedcatholics.com/free-content/reference-links/1-what-constitutes-the-papacy/apostolic-constitution-vacantis-apostolicae-sedis/

[12] Rev. E. Sylvester Berry, *The Church of Christ*, B. Herder Book Co., London and New York, N.Y., 1927, 57

[13] Ibid.

[14] Rev. Edmund James O'Reilly, S.J., *The Relations of the Church to Society — Theological Essays*, John Hodges, London, 1892, from the chapter "The Pastoral Office of the Church," (all emphasis by Rev.

O'Reilly in the original). Rev. O'Reilly was the theologian of choice in Ireland for local Irish Councils and Synods, was a professor of theology at the Catholic University of Dublin and was at one time considered as a candidate for a professorship at the prestigious Roman College by his Jesuit superior.

[15] *Satis Cognitum,* http://www.papalencyclicals.net/Leo13/l13satis.htm

[16] Rev. George Leo Haydock, Comprehensive Catholic Commentary on Douay-Rheims edition of Holy Scripture, original printed in 1859, reprinted in 1991 by Catholic Treasures, Monrovia, Calif.

[17] St. Thomas Aquinas, *Catechism of the Summa Theologica*, Rev. Thomas Pegues, O.P., first printed in 1921; reprinted by Roman Catholic Books, Harrison, N.Y., (b) 232

[18] Mystici Corporis Christi (June 29, 1943) | PIUS XII

[19] Henry Cardinal Manning, *The Temporal Power of the Vicar of Jesus Christ*, Burns and Lambert, 1862, London, reprinted by Refuge of Sinners Publishing, Inc., Pekin, In., 142

[20] Ibid., 55-57

[21] (*Catholic Encyclopedia*, under Simon Magus).

[22] (Ibid.).

[23] Douay-Rheims edition of Holy Scripture, 2 Thess. 2:14

[24] Douay-Rheims edition of Holy Scripture, 2 Thess. 2:7

[25] Henry Cardinal Manning, *The Temporal Power of the Vicar of Jesus Christ*, Burns and Lambert, 1862, London, reprinted by Refuge of Sinners Publishing, Inc., Pekin, In., 139-143

[26] http://jonahintheheartofnineveh.blogspot.com/2014/08/

[27] Hilaire Belloc, *The Great Heresies,* first published in 1938; reprinted by TAN Books and Publishers, Rockford Ill. in 1991; 156

[28] *The Pope Speaks*, "Preaching the Word of God," address given during the Sixth National Week on New Pastoral Methods, Sept. 14, 1956

[29] Free Content page, no. 7, recent articles, *Tracing Traditionalism to Its Masonic Origins*

[30] Mary Lejeune, *Sword of Truth,* May-June 1977 issue

[31] *Christian Order* magazine, November 2000 issue

[32] Mary Lejeune, *Sword of Truth,* September-October 1976 issue

[33] Ibid.

[34] http://w2.vatican.va/content/leo-xiii/en/encyclicals/documents/hf_l-xiii_enc_18840420_humanum-genus.html

[35] Vicomte Leon de Poncins, *Freemasonry and the Vatican*, Omni Publications, Palmdale, Calif., 1968, 34

[36] http://www.papalencyclicals.net/Pius09/p9nostis.htm

[37] Letter No. 84, April 15, 1986

[38] Peter Faber Anson, *Bishops at Large*, October House, Inc., New York, N.Y., 1964

[39] Ibid., 309

[40] Msgr. L. Cristiani, *Satanism in the Modern World*, Barrie and Rockliff, London, 1959, 164

[41] Fr. Paul Gouin, *Sister Mary of the Cross, Shepherdess of La Salette*, 101 Publications, Asbury N.J., 1981, title page

[42] Ibid., 9

[43] Henry Cardinal Manning, *The Vatican Decrees in Their Bearing on Civil Allegiance*, The Catholic Publication Society, New York, N.Y., 1875, 111, 115-116

[44] Letter no. 72, July 1977

[45] Rev. Adolphe Tanquerey, *Manual of Dogmatic Theology*, Vol. I, translated by Rt. Rev. Msgr. John J. Byrnes, Desclee Co., New York, Tournai, Paris Rome, 1959, 160

[46] All Canon Law quotes taken from Revs. Stanislaus Woywod and Callistus Smith, *A Practical Commentary on the Code of Canon Law*, Joseph F. Wagner, Inc., New York and London, 1957

[47] http://www.papalencyclicals.net/Pius09/p9etsimu.htm

[48] Letter no. 72, July 1977

[49] Craig Heimbichner, *Blood on the Altar*, Independent History and Research, 2005

[50] Ibid., 33

[51] Ibid., 37

[52] Ibid., 41

[53] Ibid., 44

[54] Mary Lejeune, *Sword of Truth,* September-October 1976

[55] Strojie Letter 84, April 15, 1986

[56] Douay-Rheims edition of Holy Scripture, 2 Thess. 2:9

[57] Mystici Corporis Christi (June 29, 1943) | PIUS XII

[58] Rev. Dominic Prummer, O.P., *Handbook of Moral Theology*, Newman Press, 1957, 64; Can. 15, *A Practical Commentary on the Code of Canon Law*, Revs. Woywod-Smith. 1957

[59] Rev. Amleto Cicognani, *Canon Law,* Dolphin Press, Philadelphia, Penn., 1935, Can. 15 and commentary

[60] Ibid., 585-86

[61] *Papal Teachings: The Church,* by the Monks of Solesmes, translated by Mother E. O'Gorman, St. Paul Editions, 1962, Obedience to the Teaching Power, 171

[62] Msgr. Joseph C. Fenton, *The Concept of Sacred Theology*, Bruce Publishing Co., Milwaukee, Wis., 1941, 140

[63] Henry Denzinger, *The Sources of Catholic Dogma*, 30th Edition, Marian House, Powers Lake, N.D., 1957, DZ 1151

[64] Ibid; see footnote to DZ 1151

[65] Ibid., DZ 469

[66] Ibid., Vatican Council, DZ 1820

[67] See *The Catechism of the Council of Trent,* translated by Rev. J. Donavan, Professor and c..., Royal College, Maynooth, 1829; Catholic Book Publishing Co, New York under "Baptism."

[68] Henry Denzinger, *The Sources of Catholic Dogma*, 30th Edition, Marian House, Powers Lake, N.D., 1957

[69] Ibid., DZ 967

[70] All canons in this section taken from Revs. Stanislaus Woywod and Callistus Smith, *A Practical Commentary on the Code of Canon Law*, Joseph F. Wagner, Inc., New York and London, 1957

[71] Ibid. Can. 804

[72] http://www.papalencyclicals.net/Pius09/p9nostis.htm

[73] *Catechism of the Council of Trent*, translated by Rev. J. Donavan, Professor and c..., Royal College, Maynooth, 1829; Catholic Book Publishing Co, New York, 172

[74] Henry Denzinger, *The Sources of Catholic Dogma*, 30th Edition, Marian House, Powers Lake, N.D., 1957, DZ 1788 (Vatican Council)

[75] St. Alphonsus Liguori, *The Holy Eucharist*, Edited by Rev. Eugene Grimm, Redemptorist Fathers, St. Louis, Mo., Brooklyn, N.Y., Toronto, Canada, 1934, 22

[76] Rev. Maurice de la Taille, *The Mystery of Faith,* Bk. I, Sheed and Ward, New York, N.Y., and London, 1940, 225

[77] Ibid., 225, footnote

[78] Ibid., 223-24

[79] Douay-Rheims edition of Holy Scripture, Matt. 22:29

[80] This principle was not in opposition to the Temple. There was, however, no cult in the synagogues; they *merely read the Law and the Prophets.* Henri Daniel-Rops, *Israel and the Ancient World*, Image Books, a division of Doubleday and Co., Garden City, New York, 1964 translation, 365
[81] Ibid., 285-86
[82] Ibid., 310
[83] Douay-Rheims edition of Holy Scripture: Acts 12:12; Mary the mother of John, also known as Mark; Acts 16:40, the house of Lydia; Romans 16:3, 5, Prisca and Aquila; Colossians 4:15, house church of Nympha; Philemon verses 1-2, Philemon and Apphia.
[84] From William DeTucci's *Rome Has Spoken*, available on the Internet. Although DeTucci is reportedly a Feeneyite, many good quotes can be found in his work.
[85] Stanislaus Woywod and Callistus Smith, *A Practical Commentary on the Code of Canon Law*, Joseph F. Wagner, Inc., New York and London, 1957, Canons 188 no. 4 and 2242 §2).
[86] Ibid., Can. 147
[87] Ibid., Can. 188 no. 4
[88] Henry Denzinger, *The Sources of Catholic Dogma*, 30th Edition, Marian House, Powers Lake, N.D., 1957, DZ 1231
[89] Rev. James Meagher, *How Christ Said the First Mass*, Christian Press Association Publishing Co., New York, N.Y., 1906, 27-28
[90] *Acerbo Nimis*, http://www.papalencyclicals.net/Pius10/p10chdoc.htm
[91] John Fitzsimons and Paul McGuire, *Restoring All Things in Christ: A Guide to Catholic Action*, Sheed and Ward, New York, N.Y., and London,1938, 107-109
[92] Pope Benedict XV, encyclical letter *Ad Beatissimi,* Nov. 1, 1914, http://w2.vatican.va/content/benedict-xv/en/encyclicals/documents/hf_ben-xv_enc_01111914_ad-beatissimi-apostolorum.html
[93] Romolo Carboni, *An Apostolic Delegate Speaks*, St. Anthony's Guild, Paterson N.J., 1961, 222
[94] *The Pope Speaks*, Vol. IV, Summer 1957, "The Mission of the Catholic Woman," an address of Pope Pius XII to the 14th Congress of the World Union of Catholic Women's Organizations, Sept. 29, 1957
[95] Romolo Carboni, *An Apostolic Delegate Speaks*, St. Anthony's Guild, Paterson N.J., 1961, 274

Chapter XIII — Will We See the Peace Promised by Our Lady?

No one knows the day nor the hour

A. Our Lady's promise

Fatima, La Salette and Marian apparitions as a whole point to decisive events that will remove all doubt concerning the real enemies of religion. For many centuries prior to the death of Pope Pius XII, the popes taught that it would be Our Lady who would one day win this long-awaited victory over all heresies in the Church. This is not merely something that we can choose to believe in or reject, for it is not a matter of human faith. This doctrine is the constant teaching of the popes in their ordinary magisterium, Christ speaking directly to us through His Vicars on earth. The prophecy on which the Popes base their teaching is found in Genesis, where from the beginning God predicts that the Blessed Virgin will crush Satan's proud head. She promised this triumph to St. Dominic, who with St. Anthony of Padua worked to convert the Cathars, when she told Dominic: "One day, through the Rosary and the Scapular *she will save the world.*" [1]

Sadly, those "patriots" who wave the flag with the segmented snake eating its tail today bearing the words "Don't tread on me" obviously are unaware that they are begging Satan to allow his reign on earth to continue and to delay the triumph of Our Lady and her Son. Clearly this great victory has not yet occurred, and just as clearly it was solemnly taught by Christ's Vicars that it would definitely take place. Proof of this is found in the work *Papal Documents on Mary.* [2] These Marian documents from Pope Pius IX through Pope Pius XII tell us that Our Lady:

- will dissipate all errors
- is the vanquisher of all heresies
- is the crown of all miracles
- possesses all but unlimited power
- is an eternal pledge of the restoration of peace and salvation

445

- holds the treasury of mercy
- is Mediatrix and Reparatrix
- is a rainbow of peace and unity, as St. Alphonsus describes her
- will hear our prayers
- will see that the gates of hell will not prevail
- will obtain from Our Lord whatever she petitions.

The best summary of these teachings is offered as follows by Pope Pius IX:

> We expect that the Immaculate Virgin and Mother of God, Mary, through her most powerful intercession, will bring it about that Our Holy Mother the Catholic Church, after removal of all obstacles and overcoming of all errors, will gain an influence from day to day among all nations and in all places, prosper and rule from ocean to ocean, from the great stream to the ends of the earth, that she will enjoy peace and liberty…that all erring souls will return to the paths of truth and justice after the darkness of their minds has been dispelled and that there will be then one fold and one shepherd… [3]

Pope Pius IX also said that the Church "would suffer exceedingly," but that there would come "a great wonder that will fill the world with astonishment." [4]

Many insist that not all the signs necessary to identify Antichrist and be certain of his coming have transpired. They especially point to the fact that Enoch and Elias have not come and no one fitting Antichrist's description has outright proclaimed himself to be God. In his *History of Antichrist,* [5] Reverend P. Huchede says that Enoch and Elias will "very probably appear simultaneously" with Antichrist; and although he cites Holy Scripture, Tradition and the Fathers, it is not known if this is the unanimous opinion of the Fathers. One would suspect it is not, or he would have mentioned this and would not have said "very probably." A unanimous opinion is binding in belief per the Councils of Trent and the Vatican, not "in physical matters," but only in those matters "which really pertain to faith and is intimately connected with it." No one would dismiss the coming of Enoch and Elias since it is verified in Holy Scripture, but the timing of their coming is not certain.

St. Bellarmine says that it is the common (not the unanimous) opinion of the early Fathers that Antichrist's reign will last only 1,290 days or three and a half years and that Enoch and Elias' appearance will happen at the same time of Antichrist's reign. [6] Others suggest these two witnesses will appear at the very end, when Satan encircles the camp of the saints. This is said to coincide with the conversion of the Jews, and seems to be supported by a statement in the Breviary for the Third Sunday in Advent, where Elias is said to be "the forerunner of Christ the Judge." This would place him (and Enoch?) right before the Last Judgment. But St. Bellarmine wrote prior to Pope Leo XIII, who settled many things regarding the individual opinions of the early Fathers and their interpreters.

In *Providentissimus Deus* Pope Leo writes that the Fathers, in interpreting passages where physical matters are concerned, *have made judgments according to the opinions of the age and this not always according to truth,* so that they have made statements which today are not approved. He quotes St. Thomas Aquinas to explain: "In those matters which are not under the obligation of Faith, the saints were free to have different opinions, just as we are." Furthermore, Pope Leo continues, Scripture commentators

> "must not on that account consider that it is forbidden, *when just cause exists,* to push inquiry and exposition beyond what the Fathers have done; provided he carefully observes the rule so wisely laid down by St. Augustine — not to depart from the literal and obvious sense, *except only where reason makes it untenable or necessity requires*; a rule to which it is the more necessary to adhere strictly in these times, when the thirst for novelty and unrestrained freedom of thought make the danger of error most real and proximate. [7]

Henry Cardinal Manning also writes on the interpretation of Sacred Scripture:

> The Council of Trent (Sess. IV) declares that to the Church it belongs to judge of the true sense and interpretation of Holy Scripture. Now the sense of the Holy Scripture is two-fold; namely, the literal and grammatical, or, as it is called, the *sensus quis*; and the theological and doctrinal, or the *sensus qualis*. The Church judges infallibly of both. It judges of the question that such and such words or texts have such and such literal and grammatical meaning. It judges also of the conformity of such meaning with the rule of faith, or of its contradiction to the same. The former is a question of fact, the latter of dogma. That the latter falls within the infallible judgment of the Church has been denied by none but heretics. [8]

Pope Leo XIII's encyclical definitely deals with interpretation, which falls under dogma. One can scarcely deny what has transpired in the Church for more than six decades, for as Pope Leo teaches, this would violate all reason. Necessity requires Catholics to oppose the errors that engulf them and depart from those who perpetrate them. One cannot fail to profess the Catholic faith simply because some Fathers' opinions seem to trend in a different direction. It is the popes we must follow.

But Traditionalists cannot and will not accept this as a rule of faith. They prefer the opinions of those theologians who support their own views or bolster the Traditionalist case. One of their most besetting sins is to dredge up some writings antecedent to the more recent teachings of the Roman Pontiffs and use these to justify their beliefs. This is precisely what has been done with the excommunication question (NOT settled by Pope Martin V's *Ad Evitanda*, as St. Robert Bellarmine himself observes) and the necessity of the Apostolic Mandate, (as defined by Pope Pius XII in both *Ad Apostolorum Principis* and *Mediator Dei*). Only the Roman Pontiffs — not the College of Cardinals, not the bishops as a moral body unless united to the Roman Pontiff, or the Fathers, or even the theologians when not pronouncing unanimously — can bind Catholics to belief. Demonstrating this truth is the entire purpose of this work.

Here's your sign

As St. Hippolytus teaches, "When he [Antichrist] appears, the blessed one will show us what we seek to know." Reverend Gerald Culleton writes in *The Reign of Antichrist*:

> This last book by the Apostle St. John [the Apocalypse] …
> spoke to generations yet unborn just as had the great Isaias,
> Jeremias and Daniel. When the generations for whom it
> was chiefly intended would come into being the true author
> of all prophecy, the Holy Ghost, would in his own way
> allow his elect to take from the text the knowledge that had
> from the beginning been concealed therein. In this then is
> to be found the reason why the *magisterium* of the Church
> (emphasis Culleton's), which is based directly on tradition
> in all matters of doctrine and morals, *must depend largely
> on experience and the interpretation of signs when there is
> a question of unfulfilled or only partially fulfilled
> prophecy.* [9]

The faithful who are left must do their best to interpret these signs. But in doing so they must, as far as is possible, rely only on the popes and those approved Scripture commentators and theologians writing before the death of Pope Pius XI, who addressed the things which have come to pass in these times. So what are the primary signs of Antichrist's reign?

St. Paul teaches [10] that first will come an apostasy and revolt; it is at that time Antichrist will appear. Once "he who withholdeth" is taken out of the way, then the Man of Sin will enthrone himself in the temple, which more modern commentators believe to be re-paganized Rome. The apostasy and revolt began with the Protestant Reformation. And who can deny that today paganism reigns once again? Today we have the gods of sports, the gods of Hollywood, the gods of popular music, money gods, political gods, and even the gods of psychological and religious sects. In fact, Francis, just as his predecessors, is a sort of pop culture god in his own right.

According to Henry Cardinal Manning, it is the unanimous opinion of the Fathers that the Sacrifice will indeed fail, [11] a teaching so interconnected with dogmas of faith it must be believed. But one can scarcely say, as some modern prophets have ventured, that all the above can be satisfied in way of fulfillment then abandoned simply because the two prophets, Enoch and Elias, have not yet come; or that the desolation of the churches accompanying the abomination has lasted longer than the three-and-a-half years, so the fulfillment must not apply. The Church has never defined these things as matters of Divine revelation.

In *The Present Crisis of the Holy See Tested by Prophecy,* Cardinal Manning lists three marks of persecution which will be evident in the last days. They are the abomination of desolation making the sanctuary desolate, the cessation of the Continual Sacrifice, and the casting down of the "Prince of strength" and the "stars" prophesied in the Apocalypse. [12] The cessation of the Sacrifice, he says, has already been partially fulfilled in type with the destruction of Jerusalem. Then came the Eastern Schism followed 500 years later by the Reformation. It was with the Reformers' hatred of the Mass and with their sacrilegious substitutes for it, he explains, that the slow slipping away of the unbloody re-presentation of Christ's Passion began.

> What is the great flood of infidelity, revolution and anarchy which is now sapping the foundations of Christian society...and encompassing Rome, the centre and sanctuary of the Catholic Church, but the abomination which desolates the sanctuary [culminating in Antichrist proper and his system] and takes away the continual sacrifice? The secret societies have long ago undermined and honeycombed the Christian society of Europe and are at this moment struggling onwards toward Rome, the centre of all Christian order in the world. [13]

Regarding the prince of strength and the stars, Manning tells his readers that this prince symbolizes Christ's Vicar and his authority. "The dethronement of the Vicar of Christ is the dethronement of the hierarchy of the universal Church and the public rejection of the presence and reign of Jesus." This is borne out by the texts of the book of Apocalypse, where St. John refers to the bishops of the seven Churches as "stars." [14] Reverend Leo Haydock in his commentary says: "These are the bishops of the seven churches," and represent all the churches, as Haydock also notes in his comments on verse 1:16. [15] In Apoc. 6:13, the stars of heaven "fell upon the earth." Reverend E. Sylvester Berry in his *The Apocalypse of St. John* comments: "The seven stars represent all the bishops of Asia and through them all the bishops of the Church." [16] Commenting on Apoc. 6: 13, Berry writes:

> In various passages of Scripture, stars represent the faithful. In the first chapter of the Apocalypse, the bishops of the Church are symbolized by stars. The falling stars predict the defection of large numbers of bishops, priests and faithful from the true Faith. History shows how these words were verified in the Arian heresy, the Greek schism and the so-called Reformation. The stars fall thick and fast like winter figs from a tree shaken by a strong wind. Discord and laxity in Church discipline prepare the way for great defections in time of trial and persecution. [17]

Concerning the prince of strength, the prophet Daniel says the continual sacrifice will be taken away from him, and his sanctuary cast down. Haydock explains that this is what happened to the high priest Onias during the time of the Jewish antichrist Antiochus. Onias was deceived by "ambitious pontiffs, the king and his officers," and was drawn out and slain (Dan. 8:12). Before this "Many priests gave way to idolatry...the sacrifices were neglected and then Antiochus prevailed." [18]

And this is true also today. Catholics could have known this was the situation they likely faced as early as 1970, when a work by Fatima International quoted Cardinal Manning on this subject as follows: "Some interpret the reference in 2 Thessalonians —

Antichrist showing himself in the temple of God as though he were God — to mean Antichrist will seize St. Peter's and usurp the papal see." The work then quotes Cardinal Manning's *The Present Crisis of the Holy See*:

> The Holy Fathers who have written upon the subject of Antichrist and the prophecies of Daniel — all of them unanimously — say that in the latter end of the world, during the reign of Antichrist, the Holy Sacrifice of the altar will cease. [19]

Despite Pope Pius XII's attempts in *Mediator Dei* and other encyclicals to stem the tide of liturgical renewal and neo-Modernism, Roncalli and Montini were working behind the scenes to take the Sacrifice away and place the papacy in their own hands. That his sanctuary was taken from him could allude to the fact that Pope Pius XII did not die a natural death, but was poisoned, as some have ventured. In her conversation with Father Fuentes, Fatima seer Lucia dos Santos told the faithful not to wait on the pope or the bishops to do anything. She informed those still listening that the Third Secret is contained in the Apocalypse, examined further below.

B. A brief peace or the final conflagration?

Reverend Hugh Pope, O.P, S.T.M, D.S.S.cr (a one-time professor of New Testament exegesis at the Collegio Angelico in Rome and a member of the Biblical Commission) made some very astute observations on the various methods used by commentators to interpret the Apocalypse. He wrote:

> The Apocalypse must be judged from the standpoint of prophecy...The interpretation, then, of the Apocalypse must be governed by the rules which hold good in the interpretation of all prophecy. For the original hearers...of the prophecies of Isaias or Jeremias, only one thing was certain, namely that, being divinely inspired prophecies, *the things foretold would infallibly come to pass....* Since, then, the ultimate goal of the Apocalypse is the last things;

full light will not be thrown on this prophetic book till those last things have received their ultimate fulfillment."[20]

Pope explained that the attitude of commentators, "has led to much harmful interpretation of the Apocalypse." Some of these commentators believed, for example that contemporaries of St. John [the Apostle] possessed

> "a key to its [the Apocalypse's] interpretation... Yet why should [they] have had an 'open sesame' to the Apocalypse any more than Isaias' contemporaries had a key to the full understanding of *his* prophecies? [...] As the centuries before Christ rolled on, the teaching of Isaias spoke ever more clearly for those who had ears to hear. It is the same with the Apocalypse. Compared with St. John's earliest readers, [we] stand at the threshold of those last things [and] can see that many of the things which he therein describes touching the conflicts which the Church will have to endure have already been fulfilled. [21]

And so, Pope continues, there are two types of false interpretations.

1) When so-called *preterist* interpreters of the Apocalypse maintain that St. John is speaking of events already past in his own day, that he depicts Nero as Antichrist, etc., we feel that such interpreters have wholly failed to grasp the idea of prophecy. And if it is urged that the seer clearly had Nero in his mind, and that consequently this tyrant serves as the key and the pivot on which the whole turns, we agree that it would have been impossible for St. John *not* to have had Nero in his mind, since his repellent figure must needs have loomed large as a persecutor of the Church. But that fact does not preclude St. John from using Nero as a type and symbol of all persecutors who were ever to afflict the Church. Similarly, when so called *futurist* interpreters insist that the entire prophecy is concerned with the remote future, with those last things which bulk so largely in the closing scenes, such a statement

is clearly contrary to facts, since the merits and demerits of the bishops of the Seven Churches were contemporary historical facts; just as Nero served for a symbol for all persecutors, so too did those Churches with their Bishops stand for the Collective Church of all ages.

2) The same misconceptions prevail in the *continuous history* school of interpretation, which regards the Apocalypse as the history of the Church till the end of time, opening with the contemporary history depicted in the letters to the Seven Churches, passing on to sketch the various persecutors and concluding with the scenes of the final judgment. But then who are the various persecutors and who is to distinguish them? What note of time have we?

Whenever a great world crisis has arisen, men have come forward with the Apocalypse and have endeavored to show — often with great reason — that it exactly fits the present situation. But the crisis passes and the final denouement — the last Judgment — does not come. Another crisis arises and again comes the cry: 'The end of the world is at hand!' Such interpreters are not mistaken. For this seems to be the precise function of this awe-inspiring book...So it is in the history of the world, of nations, and of the Church. Men say, 'Now is the end!' Yet the end comes not and a fresh start is made. Nonetheless, the end had come for those individual nations and people [the end of an age]... Is not this the real purport of the Apocalypse? Is not its message, "Watch, for you know not the day, nor the hour?" [22]

Pope says that two things concerning the Apocalypse are certain according to the Fathers:

- The universal Church is signified by the seven Churches.
- The book is replete with mystery; it is itself the sealed book of Apocalypse 5. St. Jerome says: "John's Apocalypse contains as many mysteries as words...in every single word lie hid many meanings." And St. Augustine said:

"In…Apocalypse, many things are said in obscure fashion for the exercising of the reader's mind. There are but few points in it, but their investigation opens up a laborious understanding of other points…"

Pope comments:

Here we have the keynote to the Apocalypse: St. John is not writing a continuous exposition of the Church's future history in chronological order; he is setting before us various phases of that history through the medium of different symbolical visions. There is no succession of time but solely of the symbols which represent that one thing which is synchronous with all time, the trials of the Church of God…

Agreeing with Pope, Reverend H. B. Kramer comments on another problem common in our day: "Rationalistic and Modernistic scripturists have put up the principle that prophecies are always general in terms, never specific and always vague in their applications. This false principle is tantamount to denying all prophecy." [23] This is precisely why Traditionalists, unknowingly reared as Modernists but believing themselves to be Catholic, never tumbled to the fact that they were living in the time of Antichrist.

There has been much speculation on the interpretation of the Apocalypse and in the final analysis, it comes down to conflicting opinions and the false interpretations that Pope describes. Some commentators believe that there will be no peace of any kind before the consummation, which they place at the end of Antichrist's reign. St. Bellarmine is among them. Others describe the peace in great detail and many private prophecies also predict the peace. Reverend Charles-Marie-Antoine Arminjon, [24] Reverend E. Sylvester Berry, and Reverend H.B. Kramer believe that the peace will follow the death of Antichrist. Reverend William G. Heidt is not certain whether there will be a "millennium" of sorts or not. [25] Reverend Wilfred Harrington, O.P., says that some believe that after the end of Antichrist's persecution of Rome, *the "resurrection of the martyrs" refers to the renewal of the Church.* This he relates to Ezekiel's vision of the "dry bones" (Ezek. 37) and the "metaphorical resurrection of the people of God, which immediately precedes the attack on the Holy Land by Gog, King of Magog (Ezek. 38-39)." [26]

Harrington himself, however, expresses a different interpretation of these verses (but since his work was published in 1969, this interpretation is not approved by the Church). What is interesting is that he points out that the Battle of Armageddon is not a physical battle if the Apocalypse is to be taken in a spiritual sense. Rather it is the fierce spiritual combat waged by remaining Catholics until the destruction of Rome and with it, Antichrist. Huchede believes many of the elect will survive the chastisement, but he does not specify how long they will remain on earth before the final judgment. [27] Although Reverend Bernard LeFrois sees "only a spiritual millennium" in Apoc. 20: 4-6, he does not elaborate on what this might be. [28]

Abbe Constant Fouard says that following the loosing of the seventh seal, "'All those who have defiled the earth are exterminated.' This supreme execution is accomplished amid unheard of ravages, in the convulsion and crumbling to pieces of nature." When the Lamb looses the seventh seal, Fouard writes:

> There is silence in Heaven about the space of half an hour. As all was consummated on earth, the opening of this last Seal could be naught else save a vision of Heaven. [This could mean either Heaven itself or a brief taste of Heaven in a spiritual sense on earth prior to the Last Judgment.] Nevertheless, the endless hour of eternal blessedness was not discovered in its full glory to the seer's eyes. All that Jesus, in this first apparition, reveals thereof, is that a silence, an unspeakable peace, shall succeed the world's troubles. [29]

Quoting Bossuet, Fouard tells us: "When speaking of the peacefulness of the age to come, St. John says there shall be no more sea." And the Abbe writes concerning the meaning of earth and sea in the Apocalypse:

> By the words earth and sea…he means us to understand all
> such souls as, not being consecrated by Baptism and Faith
> in the Christ, remain outside of the Fold guarded by the
> Angels. Woe to this world of unbelievers, for over them
> Satan retains all the superiority belonging to him by
> angelic birthright. [30]

A number of the Scriptural commentators hold and many holy
people predict that a reign of peace following the death of Antichrist
would be preceded by a physical chastisement that would destroy
two-thirds to three-fourths of the earth's population, primarily the
wicked. Henry Cardinal Manning said in 1875:

> Invasions of the spiritual domain ever have been from the
> attempts of Governments to subject the Church to their
> own jurisdiction; and now more than ever, from a universal
> and simultaneous conspiracy against it. A leader of this
> conspiracy said the other day, 'The net is now drawn to
> close about the Church of Rome that if it will escape this
> time, I will believe it to be divine.' […] That the Church of
> Rome will escape out of the net is certain, and that for two
> reasons: First, for the same reason why its Divine Head
> rose from the grave — 'it was not possible that He should
> be holden by it.' And next, because the civil governments
> that are now conspiring against it are preparing for their
> own dissolution. [31]

Kramer believes that after the "mystery of iniquity" is fulfilled
in the breaking of the seventh seal and God's enemies are
exterminated, the "conversion of all nations" will occur and an
unending peace…a golden age for the Church" will dawn. [32] When
Berry treats of the same passage, he directly links it to earthquakes
and volcanoes and unparalleled persecutions. He then comments:

> The prophecies therein revealed to St. John…shall be
> understood in due time according to the needs of the
> Church. [The phrase, "Time shall be no more" means that]
> the time for judgment against obstinate sinners and

persecutors has arrived... After the destruction of Antichrist and his kingdom all peoples shall accept the Gospel and the Church of Christ shall reign peacefully over all nations. [33]

When he reaches Chapter 20 in his *Apocalypse of St. John*, Berry writes:

> A careful reading of the Apocalypse shows clearly that Antichrist will appear long centuries before the last judgment and the end of the world. In fact, his reign will be but the final attempt of Satan to prevent the universal reign of Christ in the world... After the defeat of Antichrist, the Gentile nations will return to the Church and the Jews will enter her fold. Then shall be fulfilled the words of Christ: 'There shall be one fold and one shepherd' (John 10:16). Unfortunately sin and evil will not have entirely disappeared; the good and the bad will still be mingled in the Church although the good shall predominate. After many centuries, symbolized by 1,000 years...Satan [will be] unchained for a short time, [persecute the faithful once again, and the end proper shall arrive, culminating in the final judgment]. [...] The establishment of the Church over all nations is foretold on almost every page of Holy Scripture.... *Can it be supposed that these prophecies are fulfilled by the conversion of a few thousand souls in the various pagan countries of the world? Can we admit that a world steeped in paganism and torn with schism and heresy is the only result of Christ's death on the Cross?*[34]

There is no single more powerful argument than this to convince Catholics that the peace of Fatima will be fulfilled and Fatima is indeed worthy of belief. The world today is so wicked, however, and the Church so completely reduced to rubble that faithful Catholics are hard-pressed to see how a victory could now be wrung from the current situation. But then they are looking at things from an entirely human perspective. By our own feeble efforts, we cannot resurrect the Church or accomplish the overthrow of the current usurpers in Rome because we have no valid and licit means to re-establish the papacy, and this is the only way the Church could be restored. Only Jesus and Mary can resolve this situation, and as some authors have commented, this actually will be the case to show the world that God is all-powerful and all-just and that He alone is in charge. But to say this means that the resolution of the current world crisis will take a miracle, and even those who believe in miracles find it difficult to wrap their minds around this probability. So perhaps it will help to demonstrate this likelihood from Holy Scripture, as perceived by at least some commentators, who clearly state that such a miracle may well be predicted for these times.

The most compelling Scriptural evidence for an end-times miracle is found in the book of Daniel, which commentators agree applies to 1) the Jewish Antichrist and 2) to the Antichrist predicted for our own time. Daniel 12:7 states: "When the scattering of the band of holy people shall be accomplished, all these things shall be finished." This is in reference to the time when Michael shall stand for the people and when the learned "shall shine as the brightness of the firmament." [35] Reverend George Leo Haydock writes: "When the people shall be destitute of strength, God will miraculously deliver them." [36] Berry refers to Dan. 12:4 in his commentary on Apoc. 10:3-4, where St. John is told not to write down what the seven thunders say. [37]

In his commentary on Apoc. 16:8, Berry says that during the manifestation of the seven plagues God "will manifest his power in a special way to protect the Church against the onslaughts of her enemies." [38] Also, in the commentary compiled by several contributors headed by Dom Bernard Orchard, the authors say that Dan. 12:7 refers either to "[t]he persecution of Antiochus or the persecution of the last days. Persecution will cease when the holy people seems to be annihilated...when [Antichrist] is dead." [39] In the next verse, Daniel presses the angel for more details, but the angel refuses to relay them, sealing up the prophecy. The miracle is implied, but the sense remains.

In his 1953 work, Reverend Bernard Le Frois describes how God sends the woman (Mary and the Church) "eagle's wings, which point to the extraordinary [that is] through special angelic assistance and she is kept [miraculously] from harm and destruction." [40] While being sheltered in the wilderness with Our Lady, which Le Frois refers to several times, the faithful are miraculously protected. And although he explains it in a different way, Kramer also intimates this miraculous intervention, commenting on Apoc. 10:7, which he interprets as assuring "the preservation of the faithful and the triumphant ascendancy of the Church above the smoke of the great conflagration." [41]

Similar prophecies abound in approved private revelation, as seen in the summary offered by Gaudentius Rossi, a missionary priest writing with his superior's permission. In his work, Rossi explains that God may permit the evils so widespread today, but especially the schism that now exists, for the trial and purification of His holy Church before rewarding her fidelity with the most splendid universal triumph over all of her visible enemies upon Earth. Such trial and purification are so often and so emphatically foretold as fast approaching by almost every remarkable prophetical seer of ancient and modern times that it is hard to believe it is not what God has planned. Rossi writes:

> The pious and learned author, Father Edward Healy Thompson, says: 'In respect to the great calamities which Anna Maria Taigi announced as impending over mankind, as well as the splendid triumph which will follow for the Pope and the Church, together with the renovation of the entire world, one may say that such is the general object and the common end of all the prophecies, whether ancient or modern, which bear upon these latter times.' [42]

Anna Maria Taigi also prophesied that, "After many and varied trials and humiliations the Church shall achieve, before the eyes of the world, such a glorious triumph that men will stand in silent awe and admiration." [43]

Rossi's quotation of Reverend Thompson continues:

Each seer, it is true, has added or dwelt more at large on some special circumstances, but they all agree in two leading features.

I. First, they all point to some terrible convulsion, to a revolution springing from most deep-rooted impiety, consisting in a formal opposition to God and His truth, and resulting in the most formidable persecution to which the Church has ever been subject.

II. Secondly, they all promise for the same Church a victory more splendid and complete than she has ever achieved here below.

III. We may add another point in which there is a remarkable agreement in the catena of modern prophecies, and that is the peculiar connection between the fortunes of France and those of the Church and Holy See, and also the large part which that country has still to play in the history of the Church and of the world, and will continue to play to the end of time. [44]

In his *The Church of Christ,* Berry states: "It is generally held by Catholic theologians that the Church will be completely Catholic after the days of Antichrist." [45] Cardinal Manning, who elsewhere teaches the Church can never be separated from Her head and the head from the episcopacy, also teaches that just as Her Master suffered and died, so too will the Church suffer and appear to die, but shall rise more glorious than before.

As the wicked did not prevail against Him...even so it will be with His Church: though for a time persecuted, and, to the eyes of man overthrown, trampled on, dethroned, despoiled, mocked and crushed, yet in that high time of triumph the gates of hell shall not prevail. There is in store for the Church of God a resurrection and an ascension, a royalty and a dominion, a recompense of glory for all it has endured. Like Jesus, it needs must suffer on the way to its crown; yet crowned it shall be with Him eternally. [46]

But isn't this Millenarianism?

It is true that nearly all but Le Frois wrote prior to the decision of the Holy Office regarding the dangers of even mitigated Millenarianism. That decision stated:

> In recent times on several occasions this Supreme Sacred Congregation of the Holy Office has been asked what must be thought of the system of mitigated Millenarianism, which teaches, for example, that Christ the Lord before the final judgment, whether or not preceded by the resurrection of the many just, will come visibly to rule over this world. The answer is: The system of mitigated Millenarianism cannot be taught safely." [47]

According to the *Catholic Encyclopedia*, the points pertinent to Millenarist beliefs include the following:

- the early return of Christ in all His power and glory,
- the establishment of an earthly kingdom with the just,
- the resuscitation of the deceased saints and their participation in the glorious reign,
- the destruction of the powers hostile to God, and,
- at the end of the kingdom, the universal resurrection with the final judgment, after which the just will enter heaven, while the wicked will be consigned to the eternal fire of hell.

The article goes onto explain:

> The Middle Ages were never tainted with millenarianism; it was foreign both to the theology of that period and to the religious ideas of the people. The fantastic views of the apocalyptic writers (Joachim of Floris, the Franciscan-Spirituals, the Apostolici), *referred only to a particular form of spiritual renovation of the Church*, but did not include a second advent of Christ. The 'emperor myths,' which prophesied the establishment of a happy, universal kingdom by the great emperor of the future, contain indeed

descriptions that remind one of the ancient Sybilline and millenarian writings, but an essential trait is again missing, the return of Christ and the connection of the blissful reign with the resurrection of the just. Hence the millennium proper is unknown to them. [48]

There is no attempt here to even imply that Christ Himself will return to rule on earth with his "saints," whether alive or brought back to life. That He might briefly appear in the clouds should He visit the earth at the time of a physical chastisement is suggested in the manifestations accompanying the Miracle of the Sun on October 13, 1917; but this is not a teaching of the Church. Nor does any Catholic believe that He will establish a visible, earthly kingdom prior to the final judgment; that it will last many centuries; that there will be peace, abundance, and the total destruction of the wicked; or that a Great Monarch will ride in on a white horse and save the day. The prophecies tell us that some type of physical chastisement may destroy many of the wicked; and Holy Scripture and other prophecies predict that Rome will be physically destroyed, but still there will be remnants of Antichrist's system (which will eventually return). Scripture commentators suggest the Church will be miraculously re-established at this time, and when a true pope is placed on the throne he will be aided by a holy governmental leader of some sort to restore order to the world. Some believe that Enoch and Elias will be the angelic pastors, a pope and perhaps a great missionary saint, sent to convert the Jews. The peace will not be long, but brief. It will culminate in the death of the two witnesses, the universal resurrection and the Final Judgment, followed by the destruction of the earth by fire.

Certain biblical commentators agree that what has come to be known as "the peace of Fatima" will be granted to the Church. Long before Fatima occurred, saints, holy people, and theologians predicted a period of peace as well; and the popes have assured us of Our Lady's victory, which implies peace. But one question remains unanswered: Our Lady predicated her promise on whether enough Catholics offered sacrifices, prayed the Rosary, and did penance. Can we trust the opinion of those writers who pretend that this promise was absolute rather than contingent upon the devotion manifested by faithful? Not given what we know today regarding their orthodoxy. So it is still possible that Our Lord could simply come suddenly to judge the world without first granting it peace? Given the extent of evil today, the world does not deserve to see the Church restored. Yet it seems contrary to all that has been said here to ignore what the popes have taught concerning Mary's triumph and the future of the Church.

It is true that we may have forfeited such a restoration by our wickedness. But what Berry said above is also true: it better reflects Christ's glory and the perpetuity of His Church that She be restored rather than have it appear that the Church no longer existed when the world came to an end. It is difficult to believe that those who have for so long labored under the deceits of Antichrist do not owe the Church their fervent assistance via Catholic Action to at least attempt to organize and educate the remaining faithful and in this way make amends for years of disbelief and communication with non-Catholics. Nineveh and Tyre were spared destruction for performing penance, and it is the condition upon which Our Lady's promise was contingent. To satisfy the conditions necessary for the fulfillment of the Blessed Virgin's promise will no doubt require a valiant effort now from the laity to right the wrongs of more than 70 years. It remains to be seen, however, whether Catholics love their faith enough to rise to the occasion. Whichever end may come, may all those who truly love Our Lord and His Church find themselves in His grace, awaiting Him with their lamps glowing brightly. Even then: Come Lord Jesus!

Chapter XIII Endnotes

[1] John Haffert, *The Sign of Her Heart*, (a prophecy Haffert says was made by St. Dominic and recorded in an ancient historical work; see http://catholictradition.org/Mary/dominics-prophecy.htm)

[2] Msgr. William J. Doheny C.S.C, J.U.D and Rev. Joseph P. Kelly, S.T.D, editors; 1954, *Papal Documents on Mary*, Bruce Publishing Co., Milwaukee, Wis., 1954, 26-27, 59, 105

[3] Edward Connor, *Prophecy for Today*, Academy Library Guild, 1956; reprinted by TAN Books and Publishers, Rockford, Ill., 1984, 50

[4] Ibid.

[5] Rev. P. Huchede, *History of Antichrist*, first printed in 1884 by Nicholas Bray, New York, N.Y.; later reprinted by TAN Books and Publishers, Rockford, Ill, 1976, 34

[6] *Antichrist*, in a recent partial translation by Ryan Grant of St. Robert Bellarmine's *de Romano Pontifice,* (1590), Mediatrix Press, 2015, Ch. VI

[7] *Providentissimus Deus*, http://www.papalencyclicals.net/Leo13/l13provi.htm (Also see the article at http://www.betrayedcatholics.com/10-14-how-long-will-antichrists-reign-last/).

[8] Henry Cardinal Manning, *The Vatican Council and Its Definitions: A Pastoral Letter to the Clergy*, D. and J. Sadlier New York, N.Y., 1887, 75

[9] Rev. R. Gerald Culleton, *The Reign of Antichrist*, TAN Books and Publishers, Rockford, Ill., 1974, 40

[10] Douay-Rheims edition of Holy Scripture, 2 Thess. 2: 1-11

[11] Henry Cardinal Manning, *The Present Crisis of the Holy See Tested by Prophecy*, Burns and Lambert, London, 1861, 78-81 (Google free download)

[12] Ibid., 69-81

[13] Ibid.

[14] Douay-Rheims edition of Holy Scripture, Apoc. 1:16, 20

[15] Douay-Rheims version of Holy Scripture, Matt. 12: 33; commentary compiled by Rev. George Leo Haydock, reprint 1859, (Monrovia Calif.: Catholic Treasures, 1991).

[16] Rev. E. Sylvester Berry, *The Apocalypse of St. John,* John W. Winterich, Columbus, Ohio, 1921, commentary on Apoc. Ch. 6:13, 76

[17] Ibid., Apoc. 1:16, 30

[18] Douay-Rheims edition of Holy Scripture, Dan. 8:10, 12

[19] Robert Bergin, *Prophecy for Today*, Fatima International, Hamilton, Ontario, Canada, 1970, 23

[20] Rev. Hugh Pope, O.P., S.T.M, D.S.S.cr, *The Catholic Student's Aids to the Bible*. Vol. V, Burns, Oates and Washbourne, 1926, 348-350

[21] Rev. Hugh Pope, O.P., S.T.M, D.S.S.cr, *The Catholic Student's Aids to the Bible*. Vol. V, Burns, Oates and Washbourne, 1926, 348-350

[22] Ibid., 350-352

[23] Rev. Herman Bernard Kramer, *The Book of Destiny,* Apostolate of Christian Action, Fresno, Calif., 1972, commentary on Apoc. 11:13

[24] Rev. Charles-Marie-Antoine Arminjon, (translation from the 1881 French edition by Peter McEnerny), *The End of the Present World and Mysteries of the Future Life*, Briton's Catholic Library, 1985, 36 (This author is said to have been a favorite of St. Therese of Liseux.)

[25] Rev. William G. Heidt, O.S.B. *The Book of the Apocalypse*, Liturgical Press, Collegeville, Minn., 1962, 117

[26] Rev. Wilfred Harrington O.P., *Understanding the Apocalypse,* Corpus Books, Washington, D.C., Cleveland, Ohio, 1969, 239-240

[27] Rev. P. Huchede, *The History of Antichrist*, first printed in 1884 and republished by TAN Books 1968, 41

[28] Rev. Gerald Culleton, *The Reign of Antichrist*, TAN Books and Publishers, Rockford, Ill., 1974, 9

[29] Abbe Constant Fouard, *St. John and the Close of the Apostolic Age*, Longmans. Green and Co., 1905, 102, 110

[30] Ibid., 110-11

[31] Henry Cardinal Manning, *The Vatican Decrees in Their Bearing on Civil Allegiance*, Catholic Publication Society, New York, N.Y., 1875, 111, 115-16

[32] Rev. Herman B. (Herman Bernard) Kramer, *The Book of Destiny,* Apostolate of Christian Action, Fresno, Calif., 1972, commentary on Apoc. 10: 7

[33] Rev. E. Sylvester Berry, *The Apocalypse of St. John*, John W. Winterich, Columbus, Ohio, 1921, commentary on Apoc. Ch. X, vs. 2-7

[34] Ibid., Ch. XX commentary

[35] Douay-Rheims edition of Holy Scripture, Dan. 12:1, 12:3

[36] Ibid., Haydock commentary on Dan. 12:7

[37] Rev. E. Sylvester Berry, *The Apocalypse of St. John*, John W. Winterich, Columbus, Ohio, 1921

[38] Ibid.

[39] Dom Bernard Orchard and various editors, *A Catholic Commentary on Holy Scripture*,

[40] Rev. Bernard LeFrois S.V.D, *The Woman Clothed With the Sun*, a commentary on Apocalypse XII, Orbis Catholicus, Rome, Italy, 1954, 188, 268

[41] Rev. Herman B. (Herman Bernard) Kramer, *The Book of Destiny,* Apostolate of Christian Action, Fresno, Calif., 1972

[42] Pellegrino (Gaudentius Rossi), *The Christian Trumpet*, Thomas A. Noonan and Co., Boston, Mass., 1878, xii, third edition preamble

[43] Rev. Richard Brennan, A. M., *Life of Pope Pius IX*, Benziger Bros., New York, N.Y.,1878, 73

[44] Pellegrino (Gaudentius Rossi), *The Christian Trumpet*, Thomas A. Noonan and Co., Boston, Mass., 1878, xii preamble to third edition

[45] Rev. E. Sylvester Berry, *The Apocalypse of St. John*, John W. Winterich, Columbus, Ohio, 1921, 138

[46] Abp. Henry Edward Manning (later Cardinal Manning), *Temporal Power of the Vicar of Jesus Christ*, Burns and Lambert, 1862, London, reprinted by Refuge of Sinners Publishing, Inc., Pekin, In., 147-48

[47] Henry Denzinger, *The Sources of Catholic Dogma*, 30th Edition, Marian House, Powers Lake, N.D., 1957, DZ 2296

[48] *The Catholic Encyclopedia*, 1911, http://www.newadvent.org/cathen/10307a.htm

CONCLUSION

The profound influence of the Catholic Church on world culture and civilization for nearly 2,000 years cannot be disputed. Next to the Jewish faith, which was never worldwide, it is the only major religion that has shaped the entire universe and man's social and religious course throughout the ages. Regardless of what people think or believe regarding the Church, a brief review of history will show Her magnanimous contributions far exceed any perceived wrongs that Rome continually has been

falsely accused of perpetrating. Despite countless examples of good will toward all men, She has been hated and hunted for centuries by Her enemies and finally run to ground.

There is no reason save envy and hatred of her doctrines that would prompt those who pursued Her to commit this act. The Church's own teachings forbid Her to force conversion on anyone, and She has taught this since the early centuries. In many different documents, She has consistently denied and demonstrated that while She will never lay aside Her claim to temporal power, She has no power over heads of state who are not Catholic and do not happen to lead nations that are predominantly Catholic, or willing to declare Catholicism the religion of the land. The official teaching of the Catholic Church regarding nations such as America is that Catholics can live among their non-Catholic brethren in a spirit of toleration precisely because no one is allowed to force others to become Catholic.

In an official interpretation of Canon 2314 on the toleration Catholics are allowed to show non-Catholics in a civil setting, Pope Pius XII writes that many rulers:

> ...violate consciences and... impose on the Catholic part of the population a yoke of oppression, especially in regard to the rights of parents in the education of their children.... The ever-increasing frequency of contacts and the promiscuity of the various religious confessions within the same country have led the civil tribunals to follow the

principles of 'tolerance and freedom of conscience.' *And indeed there is a tolerance — political, civil, and social, toward the adherents of other faiths — which is, under these circumstances, a moral obligation also for Catholics.* The Church Herself, in Canon 1351 of the Code of Canon Law, has given the force of law to the maxim: No one is to be forced to embrace the Catholic faith against his will... [But] We must add that the ecclesiastical tribunal in the exercise of its jurisdiction cannot adopt the same norm which is followed by civil tribunals. The Catholic Church...is a perfect society which has for its foundation the truth of the faith infallibly revealed by God. Whatever is opposed to this truth is necessarily error, and *error cannot be objectively entitled to the same rights as the truth.* And so freedom of thought and freedom of conscience have their essential limitations in the veracity of God, the author of revelation. [1]

Pius XII goes on to emphasize that the Church has the inherent right to punish those members guilty of heresy, apostasy or schism by excluding them from the community of the faithful and acts strictly within the bounds of Her competency and "domestic right" in imposing such punishment. Having once confessed the true faith, no Catholic is ever free to defect from that faith on the pretext of freedom of conscience; this error was condemned at the Vatican Council. The Church here is marking Her boundaries and declaring that She, not civil governments, has jurisdiction over Catholics and the right to determine if they have renounced their faith. Any Catholic who would read Pope Leo XIII's *Testem Benevolentiae* on Americanism would quickly realize that what was done by the C.I.A. regarding its diabolical doctrinal warfare accomplished precisely what Pope Leo condemned in his infallible letter. For he specifically forbade:

The new opinion [that]...the Church should come closer to the civilization of this advanced age and relaxing its old severity, show indulgence to those opinions and theories of the people which have been recently introduced...even in regard to the doctrines in which the deposit of faith is contained. For they contend that it is opportune to win over those who are in disagreement if certain topics of doctrine are passed over [doctrinal minimism] as of lesser importance, or are so softened that they do not retain the same sense as the Church has always held... Now the history of all past ages is witness that this Apostolic See, to which not only the office of teaching but also the supreme government of the whole Church were assigned, has indeed continually adhered 'to the same doctrine, in the same sense and in the same mind.' (Vatican Council) [2]

Subversive forces acting in the late 1940s and throughout the 1960s convinced Catholics they no longer needed to believe one must belong to the one, true Church to be saved; in short, they made ecumenism the order of the day and defined its parameters contrary to the constant teachings of the continual magisterium. The Church posed no political threat to this country; Pope Pius XII had gone out of his way to make it clear that Catholics must show political, civil, and social tolerance; but strictly religious toleration, never. This false teaching follows directly from complete religious liberty and unrestricted freedom to believe as one wishes which deluded Catholics accepted, contrary to faith. This advanced the odious idea that others are completely free to choose even a pagan religion or no religion, including baptized non-Catholics or those who once professed the Catholic faith. And moreover, Catholics are obliged to support and commend them for this decision. Taught as it was by Roncalli and Paul 6 in *Pacem in terris* and later at the false Vatican 2 council, those suffering under the operation of error accepted it as true. Moreover, the false Vatican 2 council gave the impression in *Dignitatis humanae* that a truly Catholic state is not possible in today's world. This effectively forbade any one group of Catholics opposing — as they were bound to do — the dictates of the state and the false church that commanded them to accept a lie for the truth. It potentially struck down any attempt by faithful cardinals to elect a true pope and create a Catholic state in opposition to the usurpers in

Rome (although this has never been pointed out as a natural consequence of this teaching to the best of this author's knowledge).

Those reading this today who might doubt the present attitude of Rome regarding anyone who would openly oppose liberalism and progressivism and adhere to the past teachings of the one, true Church should study a July 2017 missive issued by the Vatican. In *Evangelical Fundamentalism and Catholic Integralism: A Surprising Ecumenism,* "Pope Francis'" ghost writer, Antonio Spadafora, confirms the antipathy of the antichurch to anything that even approaches *true* Catholic integralism and strict adherence to the deposit of Faith. He also reveals the intended future path of the antichurch and its dealings with Muslims, conservatives, and world leaders. The address condemns the actions of Novus Ordo "ultra-conservatives" who have ranged themselves with Protestant Evangelicals. These Novus Ordo conservatives have allied themselves with Fundamentalists in order to stem the alarming tide of liberal ideas and policies that threaten to collapse the rule of law in this country. They believe they are working to ensure the exercise of true religious freedoms, promote the reversal of Roe v. Wade and defunding of Planned Parenthood, oppose same-sex marriage and transgender concessions, and generally to combat all proposals made in opposition to the natural law and the teaching of the Church as they understand it. And it seems they are not concerned with what Francis thinks.

Catholic obligation to defend faith and morals

Before attempting to point out the relevance of Spadafora's treatise to the premise of this work, a few distinctions need to be made. First of all, it is no sin in itself for Catholics to unite with Protestants of like mind regarding social issues to work for the common good and to combat prevailing evils. Pope Pius XII wrote in 1945:

> When it is a question of the fundamental morals of the family and the state, of the rights of God, and of the Church, all men and women, of whatever class and station

are strictly obliged to make use of their political rights in the service of a good cause. [3]

It was when World War II first began that Pope Pius XII encouraged all men of good will who love Christ, even those outside the Church, to combat the evils then afflicting the world. In one of his first addresses as pope, commemorating the 150th anniversary of the establishment of the hierarchy in the U.S., he wrote:

> [In America], power must not be dissipated through disunion but rather strengthened through harmony. To this salutary union of thought and policy, whence flow mighty deeds, in all charity We invite them too whom Mother Church laments as separated brethren... May the attempts with which the enemies secretly banded together seek to pull down the scepter of Christ be a spur to us to work in union for the establishment and advancement of His reign.[4]

And in *Summi Pontificatus*, Pius XII asks "all believers in God and Christ [who] share the consciousness of a common threat from a common danger" to join their prayers to his intentions. He calls the joint efforts of Catholics and non-Catholics in battling the evils of materialism, rationalism. and various social ills "a spiritual crusade...to lead peoples back from the muddy gulf of material and selfish interest to the living fountain of Divine law." [5] So how is it that this new type of crusade, launched specifically by these ultraconservatives to prevent the erosion of religious values and freedoms in this country, be contrary to Catholic principles as they were understood prior to Vatican 2?

The Right Reverend John Ryan also comments on the duties of those Catholics who participate in the electoral process:

> According to his abilities and opportunities, every Catholic must promote the welfare of the Church as a society in all its relations... The Catholic citizen is morally bound to make use of the electoral franchise... Legal justice obliges the voter to exercise the franchise always for the common good, not for private advantage... Every citizen has both the right and the duty to bring about the repeal of unjust

legislation. A Catholic citizen would have the right and the duty to oppose any unjust laws aimed at the rights of the Church or individual Catholics. Catholic citizens may properly appeal to legislators and to candidates for office, may threaten to vote against and actually vote against candidates who support legislation of this kind; but they do not need to organize themselves into a Catholic political party. Neither the Church as such nor the Catholic body as such should identify itself with any partisan political organization of a political character. This kind of political action the Holy Father has forbidden to Catholic Action. Nor should local Catholic bodies...commit themselves to the general support of one political party rather than another. [6]

This statement only reflects the position of the Roman Pontiffs themselves, who are committed to remaining neutral regarding matters which are strictly political. From the above it seems that while joint action with non-Catholics is not forbidden, neither is it to be partisan. But in Pope Pius XII's time, the majority of Democrats were not the rabid liberals they are today, either. The battle lines were drawn long ago with the advent of the Novus Ordo church and the resultant universal moral decay experienced under the rule of successive false popes. If it appears that the entire world is headed for destruction perhaps Rome should look to the real cause of this calamity — the lack of a canonically elected pope and the subsequent abrogation of the Latin Mass.

Reverend Martin Cochem, writing in the late 1800s, explained the consequences of the prophesied loss of the Continual Sacrifice. He answers the question "What restrains God from withdrawing His presence and delivering the world to Satan?" as follows:

Most decidedly it is the Holy Sacrifice of the Mass which averts this calamity. For although the divine majesty is continually blasphemed by ungodly men, on the other hand it is continually honored by priests in thousands of Masses, worthily blessed by Christ Himself. This tribute of praise far outweighs the blasphemies of the reprobate, and makes amends to God for the indignities shown to Him. We have indeed reason enough, and it is our bounden duty to give heartfelt thanks to Christ for having, of His pure mercy, instituted the Sacrifice of the Mass whereby the world, despite its iniquities is preserved from destruction. [7]

St. John Chrysostom aptly predicted: "If Christians were to abolish the Holy Sacrifice of the Mass…God would no longer be worshipped upon earth." [8] Cochem further relates that it is now only the intercession of Our Lady which protects the world from destruction. [9] As noted in Chapter II of this work, it is the unanimous opinion of the early Fathers, hence a rule of Faith, that the Continual Sacrifice as expressed in Holy Scripture will indeed cease at the command of Antichrist. (See also Chapter XIII.) The chaos we see in every corner of the world and every walk of life today can be directly attributed to this loss. The false church precipitated it, and now its members such as Spadafora must join the one-worlders in condemning all attempts to restore order to cover Rome's tracks, no matter how awkward or futile conservative efforts may be. But while Francis's junkyard dog's bark may sound alarming, it will soon be discovered the canine has no teeth.

Specious arguments

While the absolute "good" and "evil" Spadafora describes in his article on evangelical fundamentalism may be a reaction to the ultra-Liberals operating in the Democrat party, his comments miss their mark. In this article, Spadafora accuses the Novus Ordo conservatives of their own brand of ecumenism and denounces them for appearing to support such distinct Protestant "dogmas" as "dominionism" (a modern form of Manifest Destiny), positivism, the "theology of prosperity" and ironically, a false idea of religious liberty. While all these dangers of cooperation in the propagation of dogmas contrary to faith must be totally avoided, it is ludicrous for the leaders of the antichurch to even mention a false religious liberty when they were the authors of it so long ago, since any falsity or confusion can be traced back to them. And although it is not Catholic to even appear to align with a Protestant group supporting a specific party or agenda, one can certainly understand the desperation of those in the Novus Ordo, who feel so abandoned by their own church they have no choice but to seek the company of like-minded Protestants. By invoking Francis' false authority to chastise conservatives, however, Spadafora becomes trapped in his own quagmire.

First, he begins to speak of the idea of absolute good and absolute evil as an entirely Manichaean notion, effectively separating it from the idea of right and wrong. After all, St. Augustine, then, would have been guilty of the same, since he wrote the *City of God* and pitched it solely against the city of the devil. Secondly, he condemns the adherence of conservatives to the evangelical right which first became popular at the turn of the last century. Well how are conservatives to know they err, when the Novus Ordo church embraced with opens arms the charismatic movement, just as Protestant and just as "radicalized" today, which became popular in exactly the same time frame? At least the conservatives are not drunk with "holy laughter" and rolling around on the floor of the Oval Office, as surely some erstwhile Trump staffer would have already leaked this to the press. Rome can adopt one Protestant sect like the Charismatics that is censured even by non-Catholics as a publicity-whoring, money-grubbing, cult-like movement without any qualms. But it absolutely cannot countenance any right-leaning group that openly denounces "modernism…communism, [hedonism], feminism" and social abuses, errors condemned by several *true* popes.

Spadafora characterizes conservatives as favoring an apocalyptic scenario that would invite Armageddon and fulfill the evangelical perceptions of America as a "nation blessed by God" and the "promised land." He accuses them of fomenting an apocalypse and describes them as xenophobic and Islamophobic. Spadafora obviously forgets what the great Catholic author Hilaire Belloc pointed out decades ago: "I cannot but believe that a main unexpected thing of the future is the return of Islam." [10] In Belloc's opinion, Islam was still very much a threat in his day, needing only a charismatic leader to relaunch its efforts to conquer the world, and certainly that is well within the realm of possibility. And he did not believe any resultant assault would be a peaceful conquest, but a violent one. Commenting on Belloc's Islamic views, author Diane Moczar tends to agree, noting: "This analysis hardly seems dated by 70 years; it might have been written yesterday.... Saints and popes like Pius II never ceased to hope the threat could be neutralized. Dialogue and groveling won't do and it seems we have little else to offer." [11] This of course runs contrary to Francis' and his predecessors' perpetual mantra of love, peace, endless dialogue and non-violence in the face of repeated atrocities by ISIS, an attitude perfectly crystallized by columnist Maureen Mullarkey:

> If ever there was a time to call down judgment on acolytes of annihilation, this is it. Refusal to name the motive for slaughter comes unnervingly close to the old legal maxim: "silence equals consent." Francis...does not sanction violence. [He] assents to the multicultural dogma of religious equivalency — the Same God myth — and the lethal fairy tale that Islam is not violent.... This pope's inclination to advocate an ideological stance over rational judgment does not bode well for Catholicism or the future of the West. Willful blindness endangers both. [12]

Spadafora decries partisanship but the precious language of the left — peace, love, not violence or war — is Francis's credo, and that's as partisan as it gets. In the 1960s the "peace" cross favored by antiwar protestors, with its down-swept arms, was said to have a hidden significance. Some maintain it symbolizes the upside-down crucifixion of St. Peter and with him the papacy, renouncing any claim to the temporal order. No wonder it is once again so wildly popular these days. Spadafora assures us that Francis is very much opposed to any one religion or ethnic group lording it over another. As if darkness could be said to comingle with light. But even before Francis, Karol Wojtyla was condemning *all* religious fundamentalism as "a threat to world peace." In an address on World Peace Day 1990, Wojtyla announced people "must not attempt to impose their own 'truth' on others," toeing the same line as Luce and Murray decades before. [13]

As for the xenophobia Spadafora mentions, it is an intense or irrational dislike or fear of people from other countries or people who are in some way different. Note the key word here, "irrational." Those who fear individuals with felony criminal histories who illegally enter this country are far from irrational, given the frequency of criminal activity by these individuals. Those who fear individuals claiming a "sexual orientation" diametrically opposed to Christian moral standards do so because they are afraid sin and error will spread; their fear, based on their religious experience and education, is scarcely irrational.

And the accusations do not stop there. Spadafora identifies the geographic origin of the thinking he projects onto conservatives as the Deep South, a tactic also used by the liberal press and left-wing politicians to evoke vivid images of racism and the "hick" mentality. Integralism is reduced by Spadafora to a product of the fundamentalist mindset, and its traditional meaning is never explained. While it is true that in the time of Pope St. Pius X integralism became associated with some unfortunate political views, these views were later condemned by Benedict XV. They mainly involved the tendency to censure fellow Catholics for expressing their own opinions regarding matters not yet decided by the Holy See, as explained above in Chapter II. But this is not the type of false integralism Spadafora condemns. Instead he cites as something outdated and even predominantly Protestant the integralist teachings shared by both Catholics and Fundamentalists concerning Modernism, Communism, et al. He certainly fails to note, as Monsignor Fenton explains, that:

> Integralism...is essentially the teaching or the attitude of those who worked for the presentation of an integral Catholicism, of *Catholic dogma set forth accurately and in its entirety.* Understood in this fashion, *integralism was nothing else than the contradiction of heretical modernism. It was thus basically only the exposition of Catholic truth.*[14]

Spadafora takes his cues from the popular Vatican 2 figure Yves Congar, whose views Fenton examines as follows:

[Congar] describes integralists as those who 'proceed from an attitude of the right,' which stresses 'the determination of things by way of authority…. It is instinctively for what is done and defined, and what has only to be imposed and received.' [Fenton comments:] *The religious proposition of the integralists is also represented as characterized by a rigidity of doctrine. All that this expression would seem to mean is a resistance to any teaching which the integralist regards as involving a change in Catholic doctrine.* Certainly there can be little to stigmatize in this attitude. And just as certainly the designation of the activity of the integralists under these terms makes it difficult to see how Fr. Congar can believe that theirs is not a primarily doctrinal position. [15]

Everything that issues from the right, from what went before, is anathema to Spadafora, even those things that Protestants and Catholics both are obligated to oppose. It appears his real fear is that Novus Ordo conservatives will succeed in their venture, precipitate Armageddon, and usher in an era of peace. This he calls the result of misinterpretation of the Apocalypse by Protestants and the anticipation of an earthly millennium by NO conservatives, censured by Pope Pius XII. While Catholics are forbidden to believe in a literal 1,000-year reign of Christ on earth with his saints and a period of earthly plenty, they are not directly forbidden to entertain the idea of a spiritual revival and the restoration of the Church by the soldiers of Christ within Her ranks. But this is certainly not something Spadafora wishes to promote, for it is antithetical to everything Rome has stood for since the death of Pope Pius XII.

But there is another side of the story that needs to be told here, as outlined in Chapter VI. If conservatives and fundamentalists can be compared to Jihadists by Spadafora, then there is another very apt comparison that can be made regarding Francis as well. As explained above, few are aware of the astonishing inroads made into this country and Canada by Tantric Buddhist cults, or the growing number of devotees who follow this lama-worship cult today. Tantric Buddhist centers dot the North American landscape from coast to coast — hundreds of them. According to Wikipedia, between 1990 and 2008, 1.2 million became Buddhist followers, a 170 percent increase. Forty percent of these live in Southern California. A comparison of views expressed by the Dalai Lama and Francis on one Buddhist website shows little difference in their beliefs. [16]

Tantric Buddhists have no real sense of right or wrong, good and evil; they don't believe in "judging." They call proven facts strong enough to stand up in a court of law an "illusion." Rather than making firm decisions and following a set course of action, they insist on dialogue and consensus rule. They are anti-gun and anti-violence, although their history reveals they have been guilty of unspeakable acts of cruelty to the Tibetan peasants for centuries. Super ecumenists and unabashed globalists, they have penetrated academia and the psychological profession especially over the past 25 years. Many of their members are Hollywood types. These lamas secretly keep harems and several of their high gurus have been charged with pedophilia and sexual assault. They hate American capitalism and the rule of law in this country but hide this from their American followers; one is to support and obey only the guru. Curiously, they too believe, along with the Marxists, that they will rule the world for 1,000 years following a purge of the heretics (Christians and Jews) and a rain of fire. [17] But Francis of course would rather send someone after the conservatives and fundamentalists. Maybe he should focus on the sexual perversion so rampant in the ranks of his pseudo-clergy.

In fulfilling His will on earth, God often uses unforeseen events and unlikely characters to execute His Providence. It is Francis' intention to continue his quest for a New World Order; already he is calling for a new global political authority. In continuing Antichrist's earthly system, he cannot afford to allow members of his own church to interfere with something already so close to realization. This also accounts for the cacophony issuing from the far left: just short of fulfilling their goals, they are fighting with all their might the resurgence of any toleration of right-wing ideology and practice that would delay their arrival at the stated goal: a socialized existence for all, bringing with it the very chaos Spadafora lays at the feet of conservatives. America is experiencing the same process of dissolution applied to the Church over 75 years ago. She has had her doubtfully American president in Barack Obama, whose citizenship and right to rule the country was challenged by ultra-conservatives, just as the Church has had her false popes. She experienced a heightened agenda of socialization during his administration. Now we see the many successful attempts to destroy America's culture, with President Trump being styled as a Nazi in the same way the left attempted to smear Pope Pius XII. Traditions are being destroyed right and left, monuments razed, and conservative religious expression forbidden. The thesis and anti-thesis are locked in a life and death struggle to arrive at a synthesis — the hoped-for New World Order.

Not content with usurping the papacy, the agents in Rome are yet working to perpetuate Antichrist's system by destroying Christian civilization itself, the gift of the Church to a then pagan world. In his book, *The World's Debt to the Catholic Church*, Doctor James J. Walsh explains that civilization is an intellectual affair, one that is opposed to today's fascination and obsession with the body and worldly pleasures. He describes civilization as "The process by which man's sense of beauty is aroused and trained and satisfied." He explains that the Catholic Church has diverted man's focus from the body to "cultivation of his mind and the recognition of the beauties of the world around him and the creation of beautiful things... The Christian Church...has constantly and consistently lifted man up to what is highest and best in him." [18] The vulgar and disgusting trends in music, art, sculpture and architecture that have emerged in the past century are proof of the descent to the ugly and barbaric; in short, to the pagan. Science has been enthroned as the new god and its determinations advanced as formal certitude. Ethics and philosophy have been obliterated. Education at all levels is now so predominantly liberal it reduces to indoctrination in socialist propaganda.

Not content with destroying the intellectual content of civilization, the very symbols that represent it must be destroyed as well, particularly anything with even a hint of religious significance. Finely crafted statues of war heroes and historic figures, simple crosses, sculptures of the 10 Commandments, Nativity scenes, religious landmarks — all must go in order to make way for representations such as the one in Oklahoma of the pagan god Baal, or twisted sculptures and art forms said to represent one thing, but which are suggestive of sexual deviance, torment and chaos. Even in the so-called center of "Catholicism," Rome, we find the church dedicated to Padre Pio with its pyramidic altar and grotesque cross, a church said by some to actually be a monument to Freemasonry. [19] Then there is the Paul 6 audience hall called the Aula *Nervi*, mentioned above; fashioned after a serpent and filled with satanic sculpture. [20] The signs of the Antichrist have never been clearer, and how NO followers fail to see these alarming signs and not make the connection is incomprehensible.

But in reality, the reign of Antichrist's system is nearing its end; and they know it. For Holy Scripture assures the faithful that the system of Antichrist on earth *will* end, even though those who still believe themselves to be Catholic cannot know exactly when or how. Spadafora's instruction only served to increase the clamor for Francis's resignation or removal. In pursuing this course of action, Novus Ordo conservatives hopefully will begin to realize how deep the corruption in Rome truly is, and the desperate need to drain their own reeking swamp. The first step in accomplishing this is to unmask the shadow church ruling from Rome today; to make others aware it was built on a lie, was installed by secret societies working in concert with the American government and is currently run by individuals who are not Catholic and could never possess offices in the true Church established by Christ. This lie was forcefully imposed on Catholics in a psychological manner that they were not able to resist, and they are free today to reject it and return to the Church of their ancestors.

If those committed to faithfully maintaining the constant teachings and traditions of the one true Church on earth wish to turn back the clock and reset it, all they need to do is invoke the last valid papal election law, *Vacantis Apostolicae Sedis,* written in 1945 by Pope Pius XII. Ignored by Traditionalists and abrogated by the false popes of the antichurch, this clearly infallible constitution (as well as Pope Paul IV's *Cum ex Apostolatus Officio*) nullifies everything that happened during John 23's "election" and subsequent reign. It provides those of good will with a clean slate to restore the Church according to Her own laws and integral teachings, even though the election of a true pope is not possible at this time. The contention by the Spadaforas of the world that those aspiring to be true Catholics could not possibly do so without participating in their own brand of ecumenism and laicism is not only erroneous, but absurd. Repairing the critical core damage done to the Church by infiltrators decades ago of its very nature requires that all those desiring to be genuinely Catholic learn of the horrific attack on their faith and the Church itself in order to make truly educated decisions regarding their future as true Catholics.

Contrary to claims made by Traditionalist gurus and the antichurch, the Catholic laity was commissioned by Pope Pius XII to act in the stead of the hierarchy whenever the hierarchy cannot be consulted or have been imprisoned, exiled, or put to death.[21] Moreover, there is the general call to Catholic Action by all the popes, beginning with the Vatican Council; a call never answered by the laity in large part. In addition, Canon Law itself, as demonstrated by the commentators, allows Catholics to privately interpret the law if no authentic interpretation is available. This does *not* refer to the revised 1983 code issued by the antichurch, for that is null and void. Only the 1917 Code of Canon law promulgated by Pope Benedict XV is referenced in this work. Those who truly love the Church and call themselves Catholics could work more efficiently together to once again become a force for good in the world. But only accepting the whole truth and nothing but the truth will set them free to accomplish this.

As outlined in the section on Catholic Action, there are a host of things they could do even without the hierarchy. Using models for Catholic Action and other religious organizations in existence long before the destruction of the Church, a pro-active organization could be constructed that would satisfy the longing of many for a grassroots think-tank type group that would provide support for struggling families, education in the faith, guidelines on how to proceed regarding training for those wishing to instruct the faithful, etc. As victims of this egregious assault on their religious liberty and the enslavement of their intellectual processes, Catholics deserve fair and just compensation from the American government. At the very least, they should insist on standing firm in their conviction the church in Rome does not teach the Catholic faith and is not Catholic without fear of persecution or retribution from either Rome or the American government; and they should not hesitate to demand public recognition of the damages done to the true Church and the individual spiritual lives of faithful Catholics. U.S. government intelligence agencies should be forced to prove their willingness to reform by providing the best possible recompense for Catholics and the promise of true and unqualified religious liberty, free of any covert or other attenuation, in the future. The 20 Principles of Religious Liberty signed recently by U.S. Attorney General Jeff Sessions provides a starting point. The purpose of such a mission on the part of those of any religion, not just Catholics, would be to henceforth guarantee *true* religious freedom for all. And whatever might be the outcome for the Church — be it a glorious restoration or further sorrows — Catholics, however small they might be in numbers, would at least be vindicated and known as Christ's true Mystical Body on earth.

Conclusion Endnotes

[1] T. Lincoln Bouscaren, S.J., S.T.D., LL.B., *Canon Law Digest*, Vol. 3, "Freedom of Conscience," Canon 2314, AAS 38-391; 1956
[2] Henry Denzinger, *The Sources of Catholic Dogma*, 30th Edition, Marian House, Powers Lake, N.D., 1957, DZ 1967, 1968

[3] The Political Duties of Women, August and October, 1945, Ralph L. Woods, editor, *A Treasury of Catholic Thinking*, Thomas Y. Crowell and Co., New York, N.Y., 1953, 270

[4] *Sertum Laetitiae*, paras. 43 and 44, Nov. 1, 1939

[5] *Summi Pontificatus*, paras. 87 and 88, 1939; Christmas address, 1939

[6] Ralph L. Woods, editor, *A Treasury of Catholic Thinking*, Thomas Y. Crowell and Co., New York, N.Y., 1953; Rt. Rev. John Ryan, *Duties of the Catholic Citizen*, 1941, 273-274

[7] Rev. Martin von Cochem, *Explanation of the Mass*, Benziger Bros., New York, N.Y., et al., 1896, 168-169

[8] Ibid., 23

[9] Ibid., 227

[10] Hilaire Belloc, *The Great Heresies*, first published in 1938; reprinted by TAN Books, Rockford Ill., 1991, 77

[11] Diane Moczar, *Islam at the Gates*, Sophia Institute Press, Manchester, New Hampshire, 2008, 224, 226

[12] www.thefederalist.org Maureen Mullarkey, May 30, 2017

[13] *The Kansas City Star*, Dec. 19, 1990; reprint of an article from the *Los Angeles Times*

[14] Rev. Joseph C. Fenton, "Two Currents in Contemporary Catholic Thought, *The American Ecclesiastical Review,* Catholic University of America Press, Washington, D.C., reprinted by The Catholic Archives

[15] Msgr. Joseph C. Fenton, "Integralism and Reform," *The American Ecclesiastical Review*, Catholic University of America Press, Washington, D.C., February 1952

[16] https://www.elephantjournal.com/2013/10/pope-francis-i-the-catholic-dalai-lama/

[17] Christine A. Chandler, *Enthralled: The Guru Cult of Tibetan Buddhism*, Amazon, 2017

[18] Dr. James J. Walsh, M.D., PhD., ScD., *The World's Debt to the Catholic Church,* Stratford Co. Publishers, Boston, Mass., 1924, 1-2

[19] Doctor Eng. Franco Adessa, *A New Church Dedicated to St. Padre Pio, — Masonic Temple?*, February 20, 2006 Chiesa Viva, special edition

[20] https://www.quora.com/Why-does-the-Paul-VI-Audience-Hall-in-Rome-Vatican-City-look-like-a-serpent-And-what-does-this-say-about-the-intentions-of-the-Catholic-Church

INDEX

ABBREVIATIONS

AAS — Acta Apostolica Sedis, officials acts of the Holy Father

ASS — Acta Sancta Sedis, official acts of the Holy Father prior to the establishment of the AAS by Pope St. Pius X

Bl. — Blessed

C.I.A. — Central Intelligence Agency, intelligence gathering arm of the U.S. Government

CUA — Catholic University of America

CSsR — Congregation of the Most Holy Redeemer (Redemptorists)

D.C.L. — Doctor of Canon Law

D.D. — Doctor of Divinity

DZ — Henry Denzinger's Enchiridion Symbolorum, or Sources of Catholic Dogma

J.B.S. — John Birch Society, an ultra right-wing anti-communist group

K of M — Knights of Malta

NO — Novus Ordo or new order church

NOM — Novus Ordo Missae, or new order of the mass

O.S.S. — Office of Strategic Services in Great Britain

OTO — Order of Oriental Templars, a Masonic group practicing "sex magic"

Sen. — U.S. senator

S.J. — Society of Jesus (Jesuits)

SSPX — Society of St. Pius X, founded by rebel Archbishop Marcel Lefebvre

S.T.D. — Doctor of Sacred Theology

Trads — Traditionalists, or those who claim to represent the true Catholic Church today but are instead a schismatic sect

Vatican 2 — The false Vatican II council convened by the usurper John 23 in 1962.

VAS — *Vacantis Apostolicae Sedis*, Pope Pius XII's 1945 papal election law

Ven. — Venerable

GLOSSARY OF TERMS

Americanism — The teaching that it is necessary to adapt the Church to the exigencies of modern civilization, the relaxation of former Church teaching and discipline to accommodate democracy, greater latitude for individual freedom of thought and action, less reliance on prayer and contemplation and greater dependence on individual action. Pope Leo XIII condemned these errors in his encyclical *Testem Benevolentiae* in 1889.

Antiquarianism — Antiquarianism originated at the Jansenistic Council of Pistoia in the 1700s and was condemned by Pope Pius VI in *Auctorem Fidei*, (DZ 1533). It resurfaced again in the late 1800s. Pope Pius XII officially condemned this resurgent heresy in *Mediator Dei* (1947), after the liberals once again began promoting it in the name of liturgical renewal. In Pius XII's own words: "No Catholic in his right senses [can] repudiate existing legislation of the Church to revert to prescriptions based on the earliest sources of canon law. Just as obviously unwise and mistaken is the zeal of one who in matters liturgical would go back to the rites and usage of antiquity…by recalling a usage which prevailed in ages past. Yet everyone sees that all ecclesiastical discipline is overthrown if it is in any way lawful for one to restore arrangements which are no longer valid because the supreme authority of the Church long ago decreed otherwise."

Apostasy — The act by which a baptized person, after possessing the true Christian faith, totally rejects it by joining a non-Christian religion (Judaism, Buddhism, Islam) or embraces unbelief, atheism, materialism, agnosticism, rationalism, indifferentism or free-thought.

Apostolicity — The fourth mark of the Catholic Church, the backbone of its constitution, the guarantee of its continuity, and the condition of its fruitfulness. Apostolicity implies a *legitimate* continuity of succession to the chair occupied by Peter and the apostolic "college," with the keeping of the same doctrine, the same sacraments, and the same authority.

Apostolic succession — The uninterrupted relay of the popes as successors of St. Peter and of the bishops, the successors of the

Apostles, transmitting each to the next one throughout the ages, the same Deposit of Faith, the same blood of Christ and the same mantle of authority transmitted by Christ to Peter and through Peter to the Apostles.

Attributes — The three attributes of the Church as defined by Reverend Thomas Kinkead are authority, infallibility, indefectibility. Without the existence of the attributes, Reverend Kinkead teaches in his no. 3 Baltimore Catechism, the four marks cannot exist. Other theologians include additional properties in this list of attributes.

Canon Law — The body of laws formulated by the Church and promulgated by Pope Benedict XV in 1918 for the discipline of her members, obligatory on all baptized Catholics of the Latin rite over the age of seven. These laws derive mainly from papal documents and the ecumenical councils, especially the Council of Trent. In his infallible encyclical *Mystici Corporis*, Pope Pius XII's definition of the Mystical Body on earth includes as a necessary article of membership obedience to Canon Law.

"Catacomb" Catholics — Catholics who believe that they cannot attend the "masses" or receive the "sacraments" of those calling themselves priests or bishops who operate outside the Catholic Church without being in communion with a true pope. This group rejects the past six men professing to be popes as usurpers, believe the Church is experiencing an extended interregnum and say their Mass prayers, their Rosary, and Perfect Acts of Contrition/Spiritual Communions at home. They also are referred to derisively as "homealoners" by Traditionalist sects or by others as "stay-at-home Catholics.

Certitude — A state in which the mind firmly adheres to some truth without fear of error. This word encompasses varying degrees, culminating in that of formal certitude which must be irrevocably accorded to Divine Revelation and infallible decrees.

Charismatics — A Protestant evangelical sect which sprang up simultaneously in various states in the early 1900s. Members of the sect believe that they can possess the gifts or charisms of the Holy Ghost, which the Catholic Church has taught from her inception were available only to the Apostles, by being "baptized in the Holy Spirit," with or without the laying on of hands. These gifts include prophecy, healing, discerning spirits, discerning foreign tongues, speaking in tongues and other charismata. Since 1967, there have been "practicing" Charismatics within the Novus Ordo church, despite its previous designation as a non-Catholic sect.

Communicatio in sacris — Taking part in a non-Catholic cult with the intention of worshipping God in the manner of non-Catholics, *more acatholicorum*, judged in Canon Law as a denial of the Catholic faith. For a serious reason, a Catholic may attend non-Catholic services, but only provided no active part be taken in them. Canon 1258 declares illicit not only the communication in rites which are of their nature non-Catholic, but also in rites which are Catholic in nature but exercised under the direction of a non-Catholic sect. Those who frequent such rites are condemned under Canon 2314 §3 as guilty of heresy.

Conclavists — Those lay people and/or Traditional priests described as Sedevacantist who have "elected" their own "popes," mistakenly believing the laity have a right and even an obligation to elect in the present emergency. The Catholic Church forbids any lay participation in papal elections (DZ 960, 967; Canon 109).

Ecumenism — The free affiliation, formerly forbidden by the popes, with all kinds of associations and the ability to enter into discussions between groups and individuals of any religion and of no religion at all. The word is presently applied to what the continual magisterium previously defined as acts of religious indifferentism and *communicatio in sacris*.

Eirenism — Attempts to effect unity within the Catholic Church by distorting or clouding Catholic doctrine. It is related to ecumenism and the minimalizing of doctrine inherent in Americanism and other errors.

Existentialism — An error regarding the development of the human personality that endorses the solution of man's true purpose on earth aside from any consideration of his obligations to God and the salvation of his own soul.

Feeneyism — The belief that no one can be considered as attaining eternal salvation unless he receives Baptism by water. The teaching of this sect denies the ages-old doctrine of salvation by blood and desire which was confirmed by the Holy Office, under the direction of Pope Pius XII, in 1953. Feeney's excommunication is entered in the AAS.

Fideism — The doctrine that faith, not certitude, is the foundation of philosophy. Fideists, the first "traditionalists," hold that human reason is wholly incapable of attaining any truth whatsoever apart from revelation.

Gallicanism — The denial of the pope's jurisdiction over matters temporal and his power to depose his subjects. This heresy placed ecumenical councils as superior to the pope, declared the teachings of the pope must be subject to the consent of the Church and generally held that the pope was subject to the wishes and direction of the faithful, including the bishops and cardinals. It was condemned once and for all at the Vatican Council.

Gnosticism — A group of heretical systems which flourished in the first three centuries of Christianity. It taught salvation comes by knowledge and can be attained only by the few. Pre-Christian in origin, its members indulged in magic and corrupted Christian terminology and many dogmas.

Gradualism — The socialist technique of introducing change quietly and incrementally, without notice, in order to covertly effect the desired social change.

Heresy — The formal denial or doubt, by a baptized person who has professed the faith, of any article of the Catholic Faith proposed for belief by the Catholic Church. Those guilty of the crime of heresy incur excommunication *ipso facto*, reserved to the pope.

Humanism — Devotion to human interests without reference to God or divine things; the belief man is self-sufficient with no need for God and can proceed on strictly human values. In its secular form, it is the blasphemous belief man can become God's equal, and that God Himself teaches this.

Impediment — An obstacle in marriage and ordination which either prevents these two sacraments from taking place entirely or from which a dispensation must be sought before the sacrament can be received.

Indefectibility — One of the three attributes necessary to the existence of the four marks. If infallibility, another one of the attributes, is necessary that all four marks exist, then this gives the lie to those maintaining that the Church can exist and function with bishops and priests alone. The Church is indefectible only when the hierarchy is in communion with the Supreme Pontiff, and without this communion unity or oneness cannot exist. Only the Roman Pontiff was granted the gift or charism of infallibility. If it is lacking because a pope is lacking then the three attributes cannot exist and the four marks cannot exist. The Church will last unto the consummation, however, because Christ is head of His Mystical Body and there will exist faithful who profess the true faith unto the very end.

Indifferentism — The belief that God can be worshipped in any religious denomination whatsoever and those so doing can still have good expectation of eternal salvation.

Infamy — A stigma attached in canon law to the character of a person. Juridical infamy or infamy of law is a special punitive penance or vindicative penalty attached to certain grave offenses. It includes repulsion from any ministry in sacred functions and disqualification for legitimate ecclesiastical acts by clergy or laity.

Integralism — As referred to in this work, integralism is essentially the teaching or the attitude of those who worked for the presentation of an integral Catholicism, of Catholic dogma set forth accurately and in its entirety. It is basically the exposition of Catholic truth and the contradiction of heretical Modernism.

Interregnum — The period of time between the death of a true pope and the election of his legitimate successor. There has been no time limit placed on this period, but in the past the see was seldom vacant for more than a few years at a time.

Invalidity — An act that is invalid has no effect, no validity; it is considered to have never been performed. It has no force of law.

Ipso facto — By the very fact or automatically; without sentence of law.

Irregularity — A permanent canonical impediment rendering the exercise of Holy Orders illicit but not invalid. They are either criminal or arise from defects which are not crimes.

Jurisdiction — Jurisdiction is of divine institution and is exercised only by clerics. It is either attached to an office or is delegated to others by the officeholder and is intended for either the internal or external forum or both. Both Orders *and* jurisdiction are required before a validly and licitly ordained bishop or priest may administer the Sacraments and perform ecclesiastical acts. Apostolicity cannot exist, Reverends Devivier and Sasia teach, unless both are present. Ordinary jurisdiction is received by bishops from the pope when appointed by him to their diocese. Delegated jurisdiction is received by priests from the bishop to function as pastors or in other offices.

Kabbalah — A book containing what is purported to be the ancient religious Traditions of the Jews. There are different versions of the Kabbalah but the Church accepts only one version as possibly genuine. The Jews maintain that during the Renaissance period non-Jews issued Kabbalahs that introduced occult elements and perverted the work's intended meaning.

Latae sententiae — An ecclesiastical penalty is a deprivation of some temporal or spiritual benefit inflicted by the legitimate authority on the delinquent for his correction and in punishment of an offense (Canon 2215). A penalty is called *latae sententiae* if a specific penalty is attached to a law or a precept in such a manner that it is incurred *ipso facto* by the commission of the offense; *ferendae sententiae* attached to a law means the penalty must be inflicted by a judge (Canon 2217, no. 2).

Liberalism — The belief that an individual can choose to reject the authority of God, that society can decide for itself what is best for the people without regard for morals or religion, that the popular will must always prevail based on majority vote, that there must be absolute freedom of thought and worship and unrestrained freedom of the press. "In the doctrinal order it is heresy, and consequently a sin against faith" (Rev. Felix Sarda Salvany).

Liciety — Also known as licitness or licitity. Many Catholics confuse this term with validity. Liciety means lawfulness, and if an action by a cleric merely lacks liciety, it is assumed the action was valid. In the case of the Sacraments, for example, a lack of liciety means the intended fruits are not transmitted because the cleric conferring them is lacking the Church's permission to do so. Invalidity means the actual Sacraments are never received because the person transmitting them has not received the necessary powers from Holy Orders and/or been granted the jurisdiction necessary to confect the Sacraments.

Marxism — The teachings of the Communist Karl Marx, who believed that the struggle between the classes is a major force in history and that there should be no classes. Marxian Communism envisioned a theoretical, perfect, classless society where the economic means of production were commonly owned.

Modernism — A group of heresies which sprang up in the Church Herself as a result of the influence of modern philosophy and criticism. It hid under the guise of saving the Christian religion and Catholic Church by means of a radical renovation. It demeaned papal authority and the scholastic method of philosophy and reduced the sacraments to mere symbols that met a corresponding need among the faithful. It was condemned as "the synthesis of all heresies" by Pope Pius St. X in 1907.

Millenarianism — A theory of Jewish origin which preached a kingdom of the Messias as a golden age rich in glory and happiness, emphasizing the material nature of these delights. In its Catholic form, it taught that Christ, before the final judgement, would reign visibly on earth with His saints. This was condemned by the Holy Office in 1944. The condemnation does not, however, seem to forbid belief in the brief peace promised by Our Lady of Fatima, characterized by the Reign of Christ the King spiritually on earth.

Minimalism — The watering down of Catholic doctrine in order to make the faith more attractive to others wishing to convert. It was especially a component of the Americanist heresy.

Perpetuity — Lasting or destined to last forever; after an interruption, to go on with (Cassell's Latin Dictionary)

Phenomenalism — The theory that knowledge is limited to phenomena including (a) physical phenomena or the totality of objects of actual and possible perception and (b) mental phenomena, the totality of objects of introspection. In other words, it is any system of thought that has to do with appearances only and not an article's true substance.

Polygenism — The theory that the human race descended from a pool of an undetermined number of early human couples, of which Adam and Eve are only the symbol. It was condemned as part of the error of evolution and as a Modernist heresy.

Probabilism — A system of moral theology that allows one to follow an opinion favoring liberty provided it be truly and solidly probable, even though the opinion favoring the law is more probable. This applies however only to the lawfulness of an act and not its validity. It cannot be cited in favor of seeking the Sacraments from Traditionalists whose orders are not certainly valid or who cannot prove they possess the jurisdiction necessary for valid absolution. (See Ch. XII.)

Psychopolitics — Planned operations to convey selected information and indicators to foreign audiences to influence their emotions, motives, objective reasoning, and ultimately [their] behavior. The purpose of psychological operations is to induce behavior favorable to the originator's objectives.

Sacrilege — The irreverent treatment of sacred things, persons or places. Those attending services of questionably valid or illicit priests commit this sin by placing their perceived wants and needs over the sacredness of the Mass and Sacraments. If committed knowingly and despite advisement that such acts are forbidden by the Church, it is a mortal sin.

Schism — The crime of one who separates himself from the Catholic Church to form another sect under the pretext that the Catholic Church errs or approves disorders and abuses. It eventually denies the authority and infallibility of the Church.

Scholasticism — A system whereby an endeavor is made (by the Fathers of the Church and their successors) to bring into harmony faith and reason. It was developed by St. Thomas Aquinas and its founding principles were derived from the philosopher Aristotle.

Sedevacantism — Those who believe that the See of Peter is currently vacant, but that during that vacancy they are perfectly justified to attend Mass and receive the sacraments from priests who have no real claim to jurisdiction and bishops who are operating without a papal mandate. While rightly recognizing that the last (five or) six men claiming to be pope are actually usurpers, they disobey the teachings of Pope Pius XII by violating papal laws and usurping papal jurisdiction during an interregnum, forbidden in Pius XII's still valid papal election law, *Vacante Apostolicae Sedis*.

Socialism — A politic economic system which teaches that when the ownership of income-bearing wealth has been invested in civil society, this gives society exclusive control over production and distribution. It discourages the ownership of private property and tends to class warfare, since it is basically the prelude to the system of Communism. The Church has condemned both of these systems as heretical.

St. John's Mass — The prayers from the Canon of the Mass including the preamble to the Consecration, the consecration of the bread and wine and the *Ecce Agnus Dei*. The thanksgiving following what would be Holy Communion may also be included.

Tolerati — Those who have committed some delict worthy of censure but whose offense is known only to their confessor and one or two others.

Tonsure — A complete shaving of part of the head as required by canon law in order to designate one in an outward and visible manner as a cleric and entitle the one tonsured to all ecclesiastical privileges. Tonsure is not itself an order but is rather described by canonists as an act of jurisdiction. It is administered by a bishop or other delegated prelate.

Vitandus — Those whose offenses are grave and notorious and who have been personally named by the Holy See as *vitandus*. Earlier laws did not require the offender to be named personally by the Holy Father.

Xenophobia — Fear and hatred of strangers and foreigners or of anything foreign or unknown.

BIBILIOGRAPHY

Primary Reference Sources

- Attwater, Donald, *A Catholic Dictionary*, McMillan Company, New York, N.Y., 1941
- Ayrinhac, Very Rev. H. A., S.S, D.D., D.C.L., *Penal Legislation in the New Code of Canon Law*, Benziger Bros., New York, N.Y., 1920
- Bouscaren, Rev. T. Lincoln, S. J., LL.B S.T.D., and. O'Connor, Rev. James I, S.J., A.M., S.T.L., J.C.D, *Canon Law Digest*, Vols. I-V, Bruce Publishing Co., Milwaukee, Wis., 1954
- Cicognani, Rev. Amleto, *Canon Law*, Dolphin Press, Philadelphia, Penn., 1935
- *The Catholic Encyclopedia*, 1911 Edition, by several editors in several volumes and online
- Denzinger, Henry, *The Sources of Catholic Dogma*, 30th Edition, Marian House, Powers Lake, N.D., 1957
- Douay-Rheims version of Holy Scripture, 1899 edition issued by the John Murphy Co., Baltimore, Md., reprinted by TAN Books and Publishers, Rockford Illinois
- Fenton, Msgr. Joseph C, *The Concept of Sacred Theology,* Bruce Publishing Co., Milwaukee, Wis., 1941
- McHugh, Rev. John A and Callan, Rev. Charles J., *Moral Theology, A Complete Course*, Joseph Wagner, New York, N. Y., 1930
- Miaskiewicz, Rev. Francis J.C.L., *Supplied Jurisdiction According to Canon 209*, Catholic University of America, Washington, D.C., 1940
- Tanquerey, Rev. Adolphe, *Manual of Dogmatic Theology*, translated by Rt. Rev. Msgr. John J. Byrne, Desclee Co., New York, Tournai, Paris, Rome, 1959
- Woywod, Stanislaus and Smith, Callistus, *A Practical Commentary on the Code of Canon Law*, Joseph F. Wagner, Inc., New York and London, 1957
- Wuellner, Rev. Bernard, *Principles of Scholastic Theology*, Loyola University Press, Chicago, 1956

Secondary Sources

- *A Cabinet of Catholic Information*, various editors, Duggan Publishing, Buffalo, N.Y., 1903
- Anson, Peter Faber, *Bishops at Large*, October House, Inc., New York, N.Y., 1964

- Arminjon, Rev. Charles-Marie-Antoine, (translation from the 1881 French edition by Peter McEnerny), *The End of the Present World and Mysteries of the Future Life*, Briton's Catholic Library, 1985
- Armstrong, Herbert W., *The United States and Britain in Prophecy*, Worldwide Church of God, 1980
- Arriaga, Father Joaquin Saenz y, *The New Montinian Church*, translated by Edgar A. Lucidi M.D. from the Spanish, La Habra, Calif., 1985
- Barrett, William, *Shepherd of Mankind*, Doubleday and Company, Inc., Garden City, N.Y., 1964
- Baigent, Michael, Leigh, Richard and Lincoln, Henry, *The Messianic Legacy*, Dell Publishing, New York, N.Y., 1989
- Bellegrandi, Franco, *Nikita Roncalli*, 1995, (translated and made available in PDF format by Australian Traditionalist Hutton Gibson)
- Belloc, Hilaire, *The Great Heresies,* first published in 1938; reprinted by TAN Books and Publishers, Rockford Ill. in 1991
- Bergin, Robert, *Prophecy for Today*, Fatima International, 1970
- sacris, E. Sylvester, *The Church of Christ: An Apologetic and Dogmatic Treatise,* B. Herder Book Co., St. Louis Mo., 1927
- Berry, E. Sylvester, *The Apocalypse of St. John*, John W. Winterich, Columbus, Ohio, 1921
- Bottum, Joseph and Dalin, David, editors, *The Pius War: Responses to the Critics of Pius XII*, Lexington Books, Boulder, Colo., New York N.Y., Toronto, Canada, 2004
- Bouscaren, T. Lincoln, S.J. and Ellis, Adam, S.J., *Canon Law, A Text and Commentary*, The Bruce Publishing Co., Milwaukee, Wis., 1946
- Bradford, Ernle, *The Knights of the Order: St. John Jerusalem, Rhodes, Malta*, Dorset Press, New York, N. Y., 1991
- Bradley, Michael, *Secrets of Freemasons*, Metro Books, New York, N.Y., 2006
- Brennan, Richard, *Life of Pope Pius IX*, Benziger Bros., New York, N.Y., 1878
- Burton, Katherine, *The Great Mantle*, Longmans, Green and Co., New York, N.Y., 1950
- Capel, Rt. Rev. T.J., compiled by Rev. Berington, *The Faith of Catholics*, Fr. Pustet and Co., N.Y., N.Y. and Cincinnati, Ohio, 1885
- Carboni, Romolo, *An Apostolic Delegate Speaks*, St. Anthony's Guild, Paterson N.J., 1961

- Carey, Patrick, *Biographical Dictionary of Christian Theologians*, Westport, CT: Greenwood Press, 2000
- Casini, Tito, *The Torn Tunic*, Christian Book Club of America, Hawthorne, Calif., 1967
- Chandler, Christine, *Enthralled: The Guru Cult of Tibetan Buddhism*, Amazon Books, 2017
- Church, J.R., *Guardians of the Grail*, Prophecy Publications, Oklahoma City, Okla., 1989
- von Cochem, Rev. Martin, *Explanation of the Mass*, Benziger Bros., New York, N.Y., et al., 1896
- Compton, Piers, *The Broken Cross: The Hidden Hand in the Vatican*, Veritas Publishing Co., Party LTD, Australia, 1984
- Connor, Edward *Prophecy for Today*, Academy Library Guild, 1956; reprinted by TAN Books and Publishers, Rockford, Ill.,
- Conway, Rev. William, *Problems in Canon Law*, Brown and Nolan, LTD, Richview Press, Dublin, 1956
- Cotter, Rev. A.C., *ABC of Scholastic Philosophy*, Weston College Press, Weston, Mass.
- Cox, Rev. Thomas, *Pillar and Ground of Truth*, 1900 (available through Amazon)
- Cristiani, Msgr. L., *Satanism in the Modern World*, Barrie and Rockliff, London, 1959
- Cross, Robert, *The Emergence of Liberal Catholicism in America*, Swarthmore College Press, 1957
- Culleton, Rev. R. Gerald, *The Reign of Antichrist*, TAN Books and Publishers, Rockford, Ill., 1974
- Dagobert Runes, *Dictionary of Philosophy*, Littlefield, Adams and Co., N.Y, N.Y., 1942
- Davis, Melton, *All Rome Trembled*, G. Putnam's Sons, New York, N.Y., 1957
- de la Sainte Trinite, Frere Michel of the Little Brothers of the Sacred Heart, *The Whole Truth About Fatima, Vol. 3, The Third Secret,* Immaculate Heart Publications, Buffalo, New York, N.Y., 1986
- De La Taille, Rev. Maurice, *The Mystery of Faith*, Bk. 1, Sheed and Ward, New York, N.Y. and London, 1940
- de Poncins, Vicomte Leon, *Freemasonry and the Vatican*, Omni Publications, Palmdale, Calif., 1968
- DeTucci, William J., *Rome Has Spoken,* 2012

- Devivier, Rev. W., S.J., Rev. Joseph C. Sasia, S.J., *Christian Apologetics,* Vol. II, Joseph Wagner, Inc., New York, N.Y., and London, 1924
- Dillon, Msgr. George, *Grand Orient Freemasonry Unmasked,* (first printed in 1950, reprinted by Christian Book Club, Palmdale Calif., in 1999)
- Disandro, Dr. Carlos, *Paulo IV and Benedicto XV, Precisiones Doctrinales,* Instituto De Cultura Classica "San Antanasio," Cordoba, Argentina, 1979
- di Marchi, Rev. John, *Mother of Christ Crusade,* 1947
- Doheny, Msgr. William J., C.S.C, J.U.D and Kelly, Rev. Joseph P., S.T.D, editors; 1954, *Papal Documents on Mary,* Bruce Publishing Co., Milwaukee, Wis., 1954
- Donavan, Rev. J., Professor, Royal College, Maynooth, *The Catechism of the Council of Trent,* translated, 1829; Catholic Book Publishing Co., New York
- Dulac, Fr. R., *Episcopal Collegiality of The Second Vatican Council,* (French publ.)
- Elliot, Lawrence, *I Will be Called John,* Readers Digest Press, E. P. Dutton and Co., N.Y, N.Y., 1973
- Faber, Fr. Frederick William, D.D., *The Precious Blood,* 22nd American Edition, John Murphy Company, Baltimore Md. and New York, N.Y., 1860
- Fabert, Andre, *Pope Paul VI,* Monarch Books, Inc., Derby, Conn., 1963
- Fahey, Rev. Denis, *The Kingship of Christ According to the Principles of St. Thomas Aquinas,* reprinted by Christian Book Club of America, Palmdale Calif., (first printed in 1931)
- Fahey, Rev. Denis, *The Kingship of Christ and the Conversion of the Jewish Nation,* Christian Book Club of America, Hawthorne, Calif., reprinted 1987
- Finlay, Rev. Peter, S. J. *Divine Faith,* Longmans, Green and Co., New York, 1917, Lecture I
- Fitzsimons, John and McGuire, Paul, *Restoring All Things in Christ: A Guide to Catholic Action,* Sheed and Ward, New York, N.Y., and London, 1938
- Frazer, Sir James, *The Golden Bough,* McMillan Co., New York, N.Y., 1951
- Freemantle, Anne, *The Church and the Reconstruction of the Modern World, The Social Encyclicals of Pius XI,* Image Books, Doubleday and Co., Garden City N.Y., 1957

- Fouard, Abbe Constant, *St. John and the Close of the Apostolic Age*, Longmans. Green and Co., 1905
- Gallahue, John, *The Jesuit*, Stein and Day Publishers, New York, N.Y., 1973
- Garrigou-Lagrange, R., O.P., *The Theological Virtues*, Vol. I, *On Faith*, B. Herder Book Co., 1965
- Gasparri, Peter Cardinal, *Codex Iuris Canonici*, Newman Press, Westminster, Md.,1957
- Gueranger, Dom Prosper, *The Liturgical Year*, Britons Catholic Library edition, 1983, in several volumes
- Goode, Stephen, *The CIA*, Franklin Watts, New York, N. Y., 1982
- Gouin, Fr. Paul, *Sister Mary of the Cross, Shepherdess of La Salette*, 101 Publications, Asbury N.J., 1981
- Grant, Ryan, *Antichrist*, partial translation of St. Robert Bellarmine's *de Romano Pontifice*, (1590), Mediatrix Press, 2015
- Gury, Pierre, S. J., *Compendium of Moral Theology*, (condensed and adapted for use in American Seminaries by Aloysius Sabetti, S. J. and harmonized with the new Code of Canon Law by Timothy Barrett, S. J.; translated by Paul H. Hallett, St. Thomas Seminary, Denver, Colo.) no date given
- Guyot C. M., Rev. G. H., S.T.L., S.S., *Scriptural References for the Baltimore Catechism*, Joseph Wagner Inc., N.Y., 1946
- Haffert, John, *The Sign of Her Heart*, Ave Maria Institute, Washington, N.J., 1971
- Harrington, Rev. Wilfred O. P., *Understanding the Apocalypse*, Corpus Books, Washington, D.C., Cleveland, Ohio, 1969
- Hatch, Alden and Walshe, Seamus, *Crown of Glory*, Hawthorne Books, New York, N.Y., 1957
- Hatch, Alden, *A Man Named John: The Life of Pope John XXIII*, Hawthorne Books Inc., New York, N.Y., 1954
- Haydock, Rev. George Leo, Comprehensive Catholic Commentary on Douay-Rheims edition of Holy Scripture, original printed in 1859, reprinted in 1991 by Catholic Treasures, Monrovia, Calif.
- Heidt, Rev. William G., O.S.B. *The Book of the Apocalypse*, Liturgical Press, Collegeville, Minn., 1962
- Heimbichner, Craig, *Blood on the Altar*, Independent History and Research, 2005
- Huchede, Rev. P., *History of Antichrist*, first printed in 1884 and republished by TAN Books 1968

- Hughes, Philip, *The Church in Crisis: A History of the General Councils*, Hanover House, Garden City, N. Y., 1960
- Johnson, Kevin Orlin, Ph.D., *What's a Cult?*, Capital Booklets, Dallas, Texas, 1994
- Johnson, Paul, *Pope John XXIII*, Little, Brown and Co., New York, N.Y., 1974
- Jouin, Msgr. Ernest, Dec. 8, 1930, reprinted under the title *Papacy and Freemasonry* by the Christian Book Club of America, Palmdale, Calif.
- Kinkead, Rev. Thomas, Baltimore Catechism #3, Benziger Bros., 1885; reprinted by TAN Books, Rockford, Illinois, 1974
- Kittler, *The Papal Princes*, Dell Publishing Co., New York, N.Y., 1961
- *The Vatican Council and Its Definitions: A Pastoral Letter to the Clergy*, D. and J. Sadlier New York, N.Y., 1887
- Kramer, Herman Bernard, *The Book of Destiny,* Apostolate of Christian Action, Fresno, Calif., 1972
- LeFrois, Rev. Bernard, S.V.D, *The Woman Clothed With the Sun*, a commentary on Apocalypse XII, Orbis Catholicus, Rome, Italy, 1954
- Lemius, Rev. J. B., O.M.I, *A Catechism of Modernism* (St. Pius X's *Pascendi Dominici Gregis* in question form, originally published in 1908), reprinted by TAN Books, Rockford Ill., 1981
- Leroux, C., *The Son of Perdition*, Calais, France, 1982, translated by Dolores Rose Morris
- Leroux, Penny, *The People of God,* Penguin Books, New York, N. Y., 1989
- Lincoln, Henry, Baigent, Michael, Leigh, Richard, *The Messianic Legacy*, Dell Publishing, New York, N.Y., 1989
- Luddy, Rev. Albert, *The Life and Teaching of St. Bernard*, M.H. Gill and Son, Dublin, Ireland, 1950
- Macoy, Robert, 33rd Degree Mason, *Illustrated History and Cyclopedia of Freemasonry*, Macoy Publishing and Supply, New York, N.Y., 1908
- Madgett, Rev. Patrick, *Christian Origins*, Vol. II, Xavier University, 1943
- Mahony S. J., Rev. Michael, *Essentials of Formal Logic*, Frank Meany Co., New York, N.Y., 1918
- McFadden, Charles J., O.S.A., Ph.D. *The Philosophy of Communism,* Benziger Brothers, 1939
- McVey, Rev. John Joseph, *Manual of Christian Doctrine*, Philadelphia, Penn., 1926
- Manning, Henry Cardinal *The Present Crisis of the Holy See Tested by Prophecy*, Burns and Lambert, London, 1861

- Manning, Henry Cardinal, *The Vatican Council and Its Definitions: A Pastoral Letter to the Clergy*, D.   and J. Sadlier New York, N.Y., 1887
- Manning, Henry Cardinal, *The Vatican Decrees in Their Bearing on Civil Allegiance*, The Catholic Publication Society, New York, N.Y., 1875
- Manning, Henry Cardinal, *Temporal Power of the Vicar of Jesus Christ*, Burns and Lambert, 1862, London, reprinted by Refuge of Sinners Publishing, Inc., Pekin, In.
- Meagher, Rev. James, *How Christ Said the First Mass*, Christian Press Association Publishing Co., New York, N.Y., 1906
- Melton S. Davis, *All Rome Trembled*, G. Putnam's Sons, New York, N.Y., 1957
- Metz, Rene, *What is Canon Law?*, Hawthorn Publishers, New York, N.Y., 1960
- Mock, Rev. Timothy, *Disqualification of Electors in Ecclesiastical Elections*, (Canon Law dissertation) Catholic University of America Press, Washington D.C., 1958
- Moczar, Diane, *Islam at the Gates*, Sophia Institute Press, Manchester, New Hampshire, 2008
- Monks of Solesmes, *Papal Teachings: The Church,* translated by Mother E. O'Gorman, St. Paul Editions, 1962
- Montini, Giovanni BattistaMontini, Giovanni Battista (Paul 6) "Cardinal," *The Church*, Helicon, Baltimore, Md. and Dublin, Ireland, 1964
- Montini, Giovanni Battista,
- Morlion, Felix, *The Apostolate of Public Opinion*, Fides Publishing, Montreal, Canada, 1944
- Muggeridge, Anne Roch, *The Desolate City*, Harper and Rowe, San Francisco, Calif., 1986
- Muller, Rev. Michael, C.S.S.R., *The Catholic Dogma: Extra Ecclesiam Nullus Omnino Salvatur*, Benziger Brothers, New York, N.Y., (Printers to the Holy Apostolic See), 1888
- Muller, Rev. Michael, *God, the Teacher of Mankind*, Benziger Bros., 1880
- Murphy, Paul I. and Arlington, R. Rene, *La Popessa*, Warner Books, New York, N.Y., 1983
- Nelson, Rt. Rev. Msgr. Joseph, editor, *Roman Breviary in English*, (Autumn); Benziger Bros., New York, N.Y. et al, 1950
- Naughton, Rev. James, S. J., *Pius XII on World Problems*, The America Press, New York, N.Y., 1943

- Omlor, Patrick Henry, *The Robber Church*, The Collected Writings, 1968-1997
- Orchard, Dom Bernard, *A Catholic Commentary on Holy Scripture,* S. Bullough, O.P., Zach. 13:7, Thomas Nelson and Sons, New York, N.Y., 1953
- O'Reilly, Rev. Edmund James, S.J., *The Relations of the Church to Society — Theological Essays,* John Hodges, London, 1892
- Panakal, Francis, *The Antichrist* (date unknown; probably the 1970s) — self-published
- Pietro Parente, Antonio Piolanti, Salvatore Garofalo, *The Dictionary of Dogmatic Theology,* Bruce Publishing Company, Milwaukee, Wis., 1951
- Parsons, Rev. Anscar, O.F.M., Cap., J.C.L., *Canonical Elections: An Historic Synopsis and Commentary,* Catholic University of America Press, Washington D.C., 1939
- Passelecq, George and Suchesky, Bernard, *The Hidden Encyclical of Pope Pius XI,* Harcourt Brace & Co., New York, N.Y., San Diego, Calif, London, UK, 1997
- Pegues, R. P., O.P., *Catechism of the "Summa Theologica" of Saint Thomas Aquinas For the Use of the Faithful*, printed originally in 1922 and reprinted by Roman Catholic Books, Harrison New York, N.Y
- Pellegrino, (Gaudentius Rossi), *The Christian Trumpet*, Thomas A. Noonan and Co., Boston, Mass., 1878
- Peters, Walter H., *The Life of Pope Benedict XV*, Bruce Publishing Co., Milwaukee, Wis., 1959
- Pike, Albert, *Morals and Dogma*, printed at the behest of the Ancient and Accepted Scottish Rite Southern Jurisdiction, Charleston, W. H. Jenkins, Richmond, Va., 1923
- Pinay, Maurice, *The Plot Against the Church,* 1962; St. Anthony Press, Calif., 1967
- Pope, Rev. Hugh, O. P, S.T.M, D.S.S.cr , *The Catholic Student's Aids to the Bible*. Vol. V, Burns, Oates and Washbourne, 1926
- Prummer, Rev. Dominic, *Handbook of Moral Theology,* P.J. Kenedy and Sons, New York, N.Y., 1957
- Roch, Anne, Muggeridge, *The Desolate City*, Harper and Rowe, San Francisco, Calif., 1986
- Ryder, Rev. Henry, *The Catholic Controversy*, Burnes and Oates, Catholic Publication Society, N.Y, N.Y., 1886
- Saenz y Arriaga, Fr. Joaquin, *The New Montinian Church,* translated by Edgar A. Lucidi M.D. from the Spanish, La Habra, Calif., 1985

- Senan, Fr., O.F.M., Cap., *Angelic Shepherd*, Capuchin Annual Office, 1950
- Sertillanges, Rev. A. D., O.P., *The Intellectual Life*, Newman Press, Westminster, Md.,1956
- Sheen, Bp. Fulton J., *Communism and the Conscience of the West*, Bobbs-Merrill Company, Indianapolis, 1948
- Strojie, William F., *The Last Days of the Catholic Church*, self-published, 1978
- Szal, Rev. Ignatius J., A.B., J.C.L., *The Communication of Catholics with Schismatics*, (A Canon Law dissertation); The Catholic University of America, Washington, D.C., 1948
- Trevor, Meriol, *Pope John*, Doubleday and Co., Inc., New York, N.Y., 1967
- Vaughn, Rev. Kenelm, *The Divine Armory*, B. Herder Book Co., London, 1939
- Ventresca, Robert A., *Soldier of Christ: The Life of Pope Pius XII,* The Belknap Press of Harvard University Press, Cambridge, Mass., and London, 2013
- Vogl, Rev. Carl, *Begone Satan,* first published in the early 1900s by the Rev. Celestine Kapsner, O.S.B.; reprinted by TAN Books, 2010
- Walsh, Rev. Joseph, S. J., *Logic*, Fordham University Press, New York, N.Y., 1940
- Watt, J.A., translator (and author of introduction), John of Paris, *On Royal and Papal Power,* The Pontifical Institute of Medieval Studies, Toronto, Canada, 1971
- Webster, Nesta H., *Secret Societies*, Christian Book Club of America, 1924, Hawthorne, Calif.
- Wemhoff, David, Esq., *John Courtney Murray, Time/Life, and the American Proposition: How the C.I.A.'s Doctrinal Warfare Program Changed the Catholic Church*; South Bend: Fidelity Press, 2015
- Whalen, William J., *Christianity and American Freemasonry*, Bruce Publishing Co., Milwaukee, Wis., 1958
- Wilmers, Rev. W., S. J., *Handbook of the Christian Religion*, Benziger Bros., N.Y., Cincinnati, Chicago, 1891
- Woods, Ralph, editor, *A Treasury of Catholic Thinking,* Thomas Y. Crowell and Co,, New York, N.Y., 1953

Works by Saints

- St. Augustine of Hippo, *City of God*, Image Books, Doubleday and Co., Garden City N.Y., 1958

- St. Alphonsus Liguori, *The Holy Eucharist*, Edited by Rev. Eugene Grimm, Redemptorist Fathers, St. Louis, Mo., Brooklyn, N.Y., Toronto, Canada, 1934

- St. Francis de Sales, *The Catholic Controversy*, Burnes and Oates, Catholic Publication Society, N.Y, N.Y., 1886

- St. Robert Bellarmine, *de Concilio, 2,19; de Romano Pontifice*, Liber III, de Contoversiis Fidei Christianae and de Controversiis Christianae Fidei Adversus Huius Temporis Haereticos, 1590, Sartorius Publishers, Ingostadt.

- St. Thomas Aquinas, *Summa Contra Gentilis*, Vol. IV, Salvation, Image Books, a division of Doubleday and Co., Garden City, New York, 1957

- St. Thomas Aquinas, *Summa I*, Q. 114, Art. 4, Pt.1, Benziger Brothers Inc., New York, N.Y., 1947

- St. Vincent Lerins, *Commonitorium*, Tradibooks edition

Periodicals

- Doctor Eng. Franco Adessa, *A New Church Dedicated to St. Padre Pio, — Masonic Temple?*, February 20, 2006 Chiesa Viva, special edition
- Andrade, Dr. Cyril., J.C.L., *Was Pope John XXIII Really a Pope?* 1976, India
- *Briton's Catholic Library Letters*, Vol. 3, Letter no. 4, July 1985
- *Catholic Family News*, March 2004
- *Christian Order* magazine, November 2000

- Fenton, Msgr. Joseph C., *The American Ecclesiastical Review*, "The Necessity for the Definition of Papal Infallibility..." The Catholic University of America Press, December 1946
- Fenton, Msgr. Joseph C., *American Ecclesiastical Review*, "Infallibility in the Encyclicals," March, 1953
- Fenton, Rev. Joseph C., *The American Ecclesiastical Review*, "Two Currents in Contemporary Catholic Thought," (reprinted by The Catholic Archives)
- Fenton, Rev. Joseph C., *The American Ecclesiastical Review*, "Integralism and Reform," February 1952
The Pope Speaks Magazine, Joseph Sprug editor, Washington, D.C., 1956-1958
- Fenton, Rev. Joseph C., *The American Ecclesiastical Review*, "The Teaching of the Theological Manuals," April 1963
- Fenton, Msgr. Joseph C., "Sacrorum Antistitum and the Background of the Oath Against Modernism," *The American Ecclesiastical Review*, The Catholic University of America Press, October 1960
- Fenton, Msgr. Joseph C., Diaries from 1948-1966, published by the Catholic University of America
- *Homiletic and Pastoral Review*, Vol. 50, No. 1, Oct. 1949
- "How the Jews Changed Catholic Thinking," *Look* magazine, Jan. 25, 1966
- Kellner, Hugo Maria, *The Final Unmasking of "Archbishop" Lefebvre's Satan Inspired "Traditionalist" Imposture by the Detection of the Invalidity of His Own Orders*, 1976-77
- Lejeune, Mary, *Sword of Truth*, Sept.-Oct., 1976; May-June 1977
- *Mother Jones*, "Their Will be Done," July 1983
- *Paul VI — Beatified*? "Chiesa viva," September 2011
- Peters, Helen M., *One World*, Michigan, circa 1982
- Strojie, William, *Letters*, Letter no. 37, Feb. 14, 1979; Letter 84, April 15, 1986; Letter no. 72, Dec. 1986
- "The Censuring of John Courtney Murray," Part II, *Catholic World*, March/April 2008
- "The Pope of the Council," Part 19, *Sodalitum*, October-November 1996
- *Time* magazine October 20, 1958, "The Succession"

- Turner, Rev. William, Catholic University of America, *Ecclesiastical Review*, Vol. XI. 1909, Dolphin Press

Booklets
- *Our Parish Prays and Sings,* Order of St. Benedict, Collegeville, Minn., first edition printed January 1959
- *The People's Mass*, Paulist Press, January 1959
- *Rubrics, Inter oecumenici*, 1964, Chapter II, Mystery of the Eucharist, *I. ORDO MISSAE* (SC art. 50); (j)

Papal Documents
Pope Paul IV
Cum ex Apostolatus Officio,
1559

Cum Secundum Apostolum,
1559

Pope St. Pius V
Inter Multiplices

Quo Primum

Pope Pius VI
Auctorem Fidei

Charitas

Clement XII
In Eminenti

Clement XIII
Summa Quae

Pope Benedict XIV
Providas

Gregory XVI
Mirari Vos Arbitramur

Quo Graviora

Pope Pius IX
Etsi Multa

Graves Ac Diurturnae

Nostis et Nobiscum

Quartus Supra

Quae in Patriarchatu

Qui Pluribus

Si Diligus

Syllabus of Errors

Tuas Libentur

Pope Leo XIII
Aeterni Patris

Depuis Le Jour

Humanum Genus

Immortale Dei

Praedecessores Nostri

Providentissimus Deus

Sapientiae Christianae

Satis Cognitum
Pope St. Pius X
Acerbo Nimis

De Sede Apostolica Vacante.

E Supremi Apostolatus

Lamentabili sane

Notre Charge Apostolique

Oath Against Modernism

Pascendi Dominici Gregis

Promulgandi

Pope Benedict XV
Ad Beatissimi Apostolorum

Motu Proprio, *Bonum Sane*

Pope Pius XI
Ad Catholici Sacerdoti

Divini Redemptoris

Miserentissumus Redemptor

Mortalium Animos

Quadregessimo Anno

Studiorem Ducem

Summi Pontificatus

Pope Pius XII
Ad Apostolorum Principis

Ad Sinarum Gentum

Humani Generis

Mediator Dei

Munificentissumus Deus

Mystici Corporis Christi, 1943

"Preaching the Word of God," address given during the Sixth National Week on New Pastoral Methods, Sept. 14, 1956

Sedes Sapientiae

Six an se sont

"The Contradiction of Our Age," Dec. 23, 1956

"The Mission of the Catholic Woman," Sept. 29, 1957

Vacantis Apostolicae Sedis

ABOUT THE BACK COVER...

One of several from a collection of stained-glass panels entitled the Legend of Antichrist, this stained-glass window from St. Mary's Church in Frankfurt (Oder, East Germany), featured on the back cover, sat for centuries in the apex window of the church's chancel, right-hand side. An unknown artist crafted the windows around the year 1367.

The church was bombed during World War II and the windows were looted, eventually making their way to the Hermitage Museum in St. Petersburg, Russia. They were returned to church authorities in Germany in June 2002. According to reports from 2004, the windows were being restored and returned to their original setting. The chancery also was in the process of being re-vaulted after the Church was left in ruins for decades. The windows are said to be some of the only known stained glass examples from the medieval period treating the subject of Antichrist. To view the restoration of the windows, visit http://www.zentrum-ffo.de/pdf/faltblatt_marienkirche_eng.pdf, also https://www.flickr.com/photos/mathieustruck/6043508528/

CPSIA information can be obtained
at www.ICGtesting.com
Printed in the USA
BVHW071719300120
570849BV00001B/12